To Nation by Revolution
Indonesia in the 20th Century

To Nation by Revolution
Indonesia in the 20th Century

Anthony Reid

NUS PRESS
SINGAPORE

© 2011 Anthony Reid

Published by:

NUS Press
National University of Singapore
AS3-01-02, 3 Arts Link
Singapore 117569

Fax: (65) 6774-0652
E-mail: nusbooks@nus.edu.sg
Website: http://www.nus.edu.sg/nuspress

ISBN 978-9971-69-535-4 (Paper)

All rights reserved. This book, or parts thereof, may not be reproduced in any form or by any means, electronic or mechanical, including photocopying, recording or any information storage and retrieval system now known or to be invented, without written permission from the Publisher.

National Library Board, Singapore Cataloguing-in-Publication Data

Reid, Anthony, 1939–
 To nation by revolution : Indonesia in the 20th century / Anthony Reid. – Singapore : NUS Press, c2010.
 p. cm.
 Includes bibliographical references and index.
 ISBN-13 : 978-9971-69-535-4 (pbk.)

 1. Indonesia – History – 20th century. 2. Indonesia – Politics and government – 20th century. 3. Indonesia – Social conditions – 20th century. I. Title.

DS644
959.803 — dc22   OCN657576879

Cover image: Republican rally in Jogjakarta, 1947, being addressed by the then Defence Minister Amir Sjarifuddin (Courtesy of IPPHOS/KITLV)

Typeset by: Scientifik Graphics
Printed by : Mainland Press Pte Ltd

Contents

List of Illustrations		vi
Preface		viii
Acknowledgements		x
Chapter 1	Indonesia: Revolution without Socialism	1
Chapter 2	The Late Death of Slavery	45
Chapter 3	From Betel to Tobacco: The Modern Transformation	63
Chapter 4	Chains of Silver, Chains of Steel: Forcing Politics on Geography	84
Chapter 5	*Merdeka*: The Indonesian Key to Freedom	105
Chapter 6	The Quest for an Indonesian Past	123
Chapter 7	The Japanese Impact: From Briefcase to Samurai Sword	151
Chapter 8	The Revolution in Regional Perspective	169
Chapter 9	*Gestapu*: A Hesitant Assessment, 1967	184
Chapter 10	"Asian Tradition" and Indonesian Politics: The One and the Many	193
Chapter 11	Why not Federalism?	208
Chapter 12	Chinese and the State: The Jewish Analogy	229
Notes		265
Glossary		311
Bibliography		315
Index		342

List of Illustrations

Chapter 1

Map 1.1	Ethno-religious Indonesia, before the modern migrations.	3
Plate 1.1	Teachers, teacher-trainees and students in a government "native" school at Buitenzorg (Bogor), 1920. (Courtesy of KITLV)	12
Plate 1.2	Leadership of the first "Indonesian" organisation, Perhimpunan Indonesia, in the Netherlands, 1923.	20
Plate 1.3	Allied patrols in Jakarta, 1945. (Courtesy of the Imperial War Museum)	31
Plate 1.4	General Sudirman being sworn in as Army Commander by Sukarno, with Premier Sjahrir watching.	39
Plate 1.5	Amir Sjarifuddin, as Defence Minister, addressing a meeting of the provisional parliament (KNIP) at Malang, with Prime Minister Sjahrir seated beside him. (Courtesy of IPPHOS/KITLV)	40
Plate 1.6	Communist leaders in 1948, including Musso (left) and Amir Sjarifuddin (4th left). (Courtesy of KITLV)	41

Chapter 2

Plate 2.1	A woman of East Sumba still regarded as a slave at the time of this 1932 photograph. (Courtesy of KITLV)	46

Chapter 7

Plate 7.1	Japanese troops coming ashore in Rembang, Java, 1942. (Courtesy of KITLV)	153

Map 7.1   Indonesia under the Japanese.   168

Chapter 8
Plate 8.1   Republican poster, 1945: "We don't like the Dutch!"   175

Preface

Political histories have already been written of Indonesia's turbulent 20th century of national creation. This book is not a rival of such studies, and does not aim for comprehensiveness, although the first chapter provides an overview of the political process. Rather, it is a collection of studies of particular themes that have been critical for shaping identity and changing lives. These studies were originally written over several decades, and have been only slightly modified to recognise the new democratic conditions since 1998. Only Chapter 9 has been carefully left unchanged, as a part of the controversy that swirled around the appalling violence of 1965–1966 in Indonesia. For the most part, because each highlights a major issue Indonesia faced in that century, they have not been substantially outdated by the passage of time. Most of the chapters were placed in scattered collections that would escape the attention of Indonesianists (not to mention Indonesians), so that bringing them together appears justified.

A central thread running through many of the chapters is the importance of the <u>manner</u> in which Indonesia entered the modern community of nation-states, through political revolution. That revolution has often been denied or downplayed as failure because it did not have a communist outcome like those of China and Vietnam. The correct analogy is the French revolution rather than the Russian — a profound breaking with the *ancien régime* <u>without</u> the guiding hand of a disciplined party intent on power. Like all those revolutions, it demanded a huge price in violence, human suffering, and the loss of cultural traditions; like them too, it delivered a glittering prize. The prize turned out (as with all the revolutions in question) to be not the freedom and equality of which the revolutionaries dreamed, but a new unity under the umbrella of a state of a new kind, unimaginable under the former conditions. The Faustian bargain of this transaction is at the root of most of the chapters.

Included too, however, are two papers which are not directly political, regarding the demise of two important Southeast Asian institutions at the hands of 20th-century modernity. First, slavery, or more broadly the strong vertical bonds between a man and his master, stood in the way of the state absolutism that marks modernity. Second, the end of the habit of betel-chewing, which marked every social occasion and ritual in the old order of things, marked the arrival of a global pattern of fashion and consumption, including narcotics.

I have accumulated two further debts in the process of turning this set of papers into a book. First, my wife Helen, who began the process of scanning and editing the old papers; and second, Joyce Zaidi of the Asia Research Institute in Singapore, who brought this process to a conclusion. I am immensely grateful to both of them for this painstaking labour.

Anthony Reid
Canberra, Australia
November 2010

Acknowledgements

I must also acknowledge here the following publishers and institutions for permission to reprint updated versions of the chapters in question:

Chapter 1
Palgrave Macmillan for permission to reprint "Indonesia — Revolution without Socialism", in *Asia — The Winning of independence*, ed. Robin Jeffrey (1981).

Chapter 2
The University of Wisconsin Press for permission to reprint "The Decline of Slavery in Nineteenth Century Indonesia", in *Breaking the Chains: Slavery, Bondage and Emancipation in Modern Africa and Asia*, ed. Martin Klein (1993).

Chapter 3
The Association for Asian Studies for permission to reprint "From Betel Chewing to Tobacco Smoking in Indonesia", *Journal of Asian Studies* 44, iii (1985).

Chapter 4
The Royal Netherlands Academy of Arts and Sciences for permission to reprint "Chains of Steel; Chains of Silver: Forcing Politics on Geography, 1865–1965", in *Historical Foundations of a National Economy in Indonesia, 1890s–1990s*, ed. Thomas Lindblad (1996).

Chapter 5
Cambridge University Press for permission to reprint "*Merdeka*: The Concept of Freedom in Indonesia", in *Asian Freedoms: The Idea of Freedom in East and Southeast Asia*, eds. David Kelly and Anthony Reid (1998).

Chapters 6 and 10

The Asian Studies Association of Australia for permission to reprint "The Nationalist Quest for an Indonesian Past", in *Perceptions of the Past in Southeast Asia*, eds. Anthony Reid and David Marr (Heinemann Asia, 1979); and "Political 'Tradition' in Indonesia: The One and the Many", *Asian Studies Review* 22, 1 (February 1998).

Chapter 6 (latter part)

The Institute of Southeast Asian Studies, Singapore, for permission to reprint "Writing the History of Independent Indonesia", in *Nation-Building: Five Southeast Asian Histories*, ed. Wang Gungwu (2005).

Chapter 7

The Center for Southeast Asian Studies of Yale University for permission to reprint "Indonesia: From Briefcase to Samurai Sword", in *Southeast Asia under Japanese Occupation*, ed. A.W. McCoy (1979).

Chapter 8

Utrecht University, for permission to reprint "The Revolution in Regional Perspective", in *The Indonesian Revolution*, ed. J. van Goor (Utrechtse Historische Cahiers, 1986).

Chapter 9

The University of Malaya Historical Society, which published a useful *Journal* in the heady 1960s, of which this paper appeared in Vol. VI (1968).

Chapter 11

Edward Elgar for permission to reprint "Indonesia's Post-Revolutionary Aversion to Federalism", in *Federalism in Asia*, eds. Baogang He, Brian Galligan and Takashi Inoguchi (2007).

Chapter 12

The University of Washington Press for permission to reprint "Entrepreneurial Minorities, Nationalism and the State", in *Essential Outsiders: Chinese and Jews in the Modern Transformation of Southeast Asia and Central Europe*, eds. Daniel Chirot and Anthony Reid (1997).

CHAPTER 1

Indonesia: Revolution without Socialism

Proclaiming Independence

> *We the people of Indonesia hereby declare Indonesia's independence. Matters concerning the transfer of power and other matters will be executed in an orderly manner and in the shortest possible time.*

These simple words were read by Sukarno to a few hundred people gathered outside his house in Jakarta on the morning of 17 August 1945. They have been celebrated every year since by a grateful people.

Two days earlier, the proclamation had been the subject of an angry exchange between two generations of nationalists. The Japanese had surrendered to the Allies on 14 August, just too soon to allow the implementation of their last-minute preparations to grant "independence" to Indonesia. Sukarno and his then colleague Hatta were anxiously seeking a way to proceed on the agreed path to independence in a manner which would not provoke the intervention of the still-powerful Japanese occupying army. A delegation of young revolutionaries, including the future communist leader D.N. Aidit, came to Sukarno's house to deliver an ultimatum. Sukarno must, they insisted, "for the last time, proclaim independence at once and break all ties and connections with the promise of 'a gift of independence' from the Japanese." They demanded a revolutionary proclamation by Sukarno in the name of the people. The older leaders, knowing they could not fight the Japanese, replied that this was impossible "until we hear what the attitude of the Gunseikan and the Somubucho [the senior military administration officials] is to the independence which has been promised." The young men taunted Sukarno with cowardice, and threatened that they would not be answerable for the violence if independence was not proclaimed that very night. Sukarno leapt out of his chair in a fury, shouting, "Here is my neck ... go on, cut my head off ... Don't wait until tomorrow." Aidit replied bitterly, "You have crushed the hopes of our generation," and the youths had to return empty-handed, "overwhelmed with mixed feelings of anger and dejection."[1]

The proclamation of 17 August represented a characteristic compromise between the two positions, though not before the angry youth leaders had kidnapped Sukarno and Hatta to try to force them into a bolder stance. The conflict between a romantic vision of revolutionary struggle and the desire to obtain the maximum pragmatic advantage from the objective situation was at the heart of Indonesian nationalism throughout the century. The difference between the two parties was one of age and of closeness to power. They shared the same revolutionary rhetoric and the same goals. They could and did frequently change sides.

The Peoples of Indonesia

"Indonesia" is a new word for a nation which took clear shape only in the 20th century. Coined by European ethnologists in the late 19th century, the word was adopted by nationalism in the 1920s in an extraordinarily rapid discovery of national unity. It was scarcely two decades earlier that Dutch conquest or control had forced into a centralised polity the varied array of peoples and cultures that made up the archipelago.

The enormous linguistic and cultural complexity of Indonesia can be crudely categorised into three broad types of historical experience, each of which had its own relationship with Dutch colonialism and with independent Indonesia. In addition to the immigrant Chinese and European cultures, these were the Javanese, the coastal-Islamic, and the non-Islamic (see Map 1.1, p. 3).

The Javanese are by far the largest single ethno-linguistic group, comprising over 40 per cent of the Indonesian population. Inhabiting the most densely-cultivated eastern two-thirds of the island of Java, the Javanese had supported for more than a millennium a succession of diverse kingdoms, whose 20th-century relics remained in baroque but ineffective splendour at the four courts of Surakarta and Yogyakarta. Despite poverty and the low literacy level of the Javanese as a whole, the non-Javanese were ready to concede that they possessed an exceptionally high culture

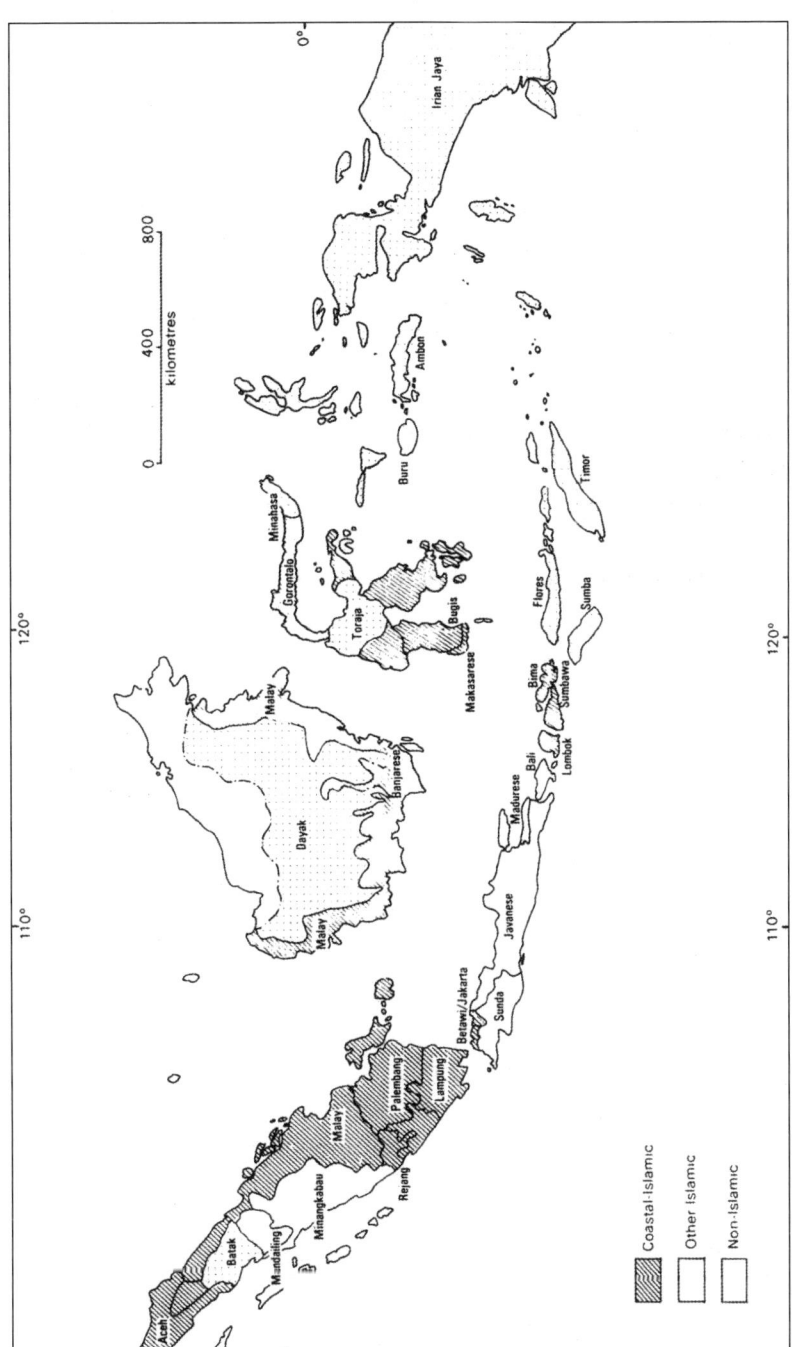

Map 1.1 Ethno-religious Indonesia, before the modern migrations.

based on dance, the gamelan orchestra, theatre and especially the *wayang kulit* shadow puppets which carried the ideology of the courts into the lowliest villages. Java had accepted Islam in the 16th century, but without surrendering the Hindu epics or the cultivation of inner spiritual strength which had marked its pre-Islamic religious system.

The gradual adaptation of the Javanese ruling class to the realities of Dutch power over three centuries had strengthened the passive, hierarchic elements in the value system of the *priyayi* aristocracy at the expense of an earlier warrior ethos. 20th-century formulations emphasised the mystical unity of the ruler and the ruled in an ordered and mutually dependent harmony. The various levels of *priyayi* rank were reinforced by speech levels, prescribed patterns of batik dress, and by an exquisite degree of deferential politeness which was of course taken advantage of by non-Indonesians. Dr Wahidin, a lower *priyayi* who founded the earliest nationalist organisation, Budi Utomo, in 1908, saw no contradiction between his progressive goals and refusing a preferred seat higher than his lowly origins merited, or prostrating himself before the desk of a Dutch official he wished to win to his cause.[2]

The coastal-Islamic peoples, less numerous than the Javanese, were also diverse and geographically scattered. Their cultures had for the most part been defined in one of the Islamic harbour-principalities of the 16th and 17th centuries, such as Aceh, Palembang, Riau-Johor, Makassar, Ternate or Banjarmasin. They had in common not only Islam but a commercial orientation, and Malay as the language of literature, trade and religion. Long before Indonesian nationalism, these coastal peoples had been conscious of Islam as a basis of unity against the Dutch infidels.

The third group, still more heterogeneous, comprise those communities which came abruptly into contact with Dutch colonialism without prior incorporation into Muslim polities of any kind. The Toba Bataks of North Sumatra underwent a rapid Christianisation from the late 19th century, while some Ambonese and Menadonese had already allied with the Portuguese and Christendom in the 16th century. The people of Bali, on the other hand, clung to the Hindu-animist culture they had once shared with pre-Islamic Java, even when faced with a brutal Dutch conquest in 1908. Throughout the outer islands of Indonesia, there were slash-and-burn or swidden cultivators little affected by the outside world even in the 20th century, though their isolation prevented them from playing any substantial role in the struggle against Dutch imperialism.

This tripartite division is of course too neat, and some important ethnic groups sit firmly astride the dividing lines. The Sundanese and Madurese absorbed a large degree of *priyayi* culture from their Javanese neighbours, although both are more Islamic in orientation than the great majority of Javanese. Similarly, the largest single ethnic group outside Java, the Minangkabau of Central Sumatra, has features of both the second and third categories. The Minangkabau are firmly within the Islamic camp, yet they share with many of the more isolated peoples a strong kinship system and a very weak tradition of kingship.

Economic Changes

The genius of Dutch colonialism was always its indirectness, making use of traditional authorities wherever these would serve the economic monopoly the Dutch had at heart. The more commercially-oriented peoples and leaders had the worst of a frequently violent competition with the Dutch, whereas the more hierarchic and agrarian were able to flourish in a complementary relationship with European and Chinese business. Although profound changes occurred during the three centuries the Dutch were in the archipelago, they were in the direction of isolating Indonesia's people from the more important effects of capitalism. The "ethical policy" inaugurated by a consciously Christian Dutch Government in 1900 was meant to change this. Indonesia would be repaid for decades of alternate oppression and neglect by an interventionist colonial policy directed towards native welfare, education and advancement. This policy shift came at a time of great European self-confidence, when the machine gun and the steamship provided a decisive military superiority over any indigenous opponent, and capitalism demanded the right to transform the whole world in its image. The first two decades of this century therefore marked a period of astonishing change for Indonesia, and especially for the islands outside Java.

In these Outer Islands, as we shall see, the building of roads and the more active penetration of the money economy had very mixed effects, bringing wealth to some, resentment to others, and social upheaval to most areas. In rural Java, on the other hand, the Ethical Policy had little chance of fundamentally changing the increasingly sombre economic pattern. Already in 1905, Java supported almost 30 million people in one of the densest agricultural settlement patterns in the world. Buoyant sugar prices and the increased productivity which European capital made possible kept Java's sugar exports growing until 1928, creating a superficial impression of prosperity. The profits of the sugar industry had only been possible, however, because of the extraordinarily low level of wages, and especially in this overcrowded island. Sugar had been grown in alternation with peasant rice, by leasing irrigated rice land on a rotation basis, and the collapse of the industry in the 1930s was a source of relief to the Javanese peasantry. "The Garden of the East", as Java had been known in the 19th century, was having increasing difficulty in feeding itself, let alone producing anything for export. In the 1930s, the rice production available per head of population in Java was about 82 kg a year[3] or 220 grams a day, less than half the normal requirement. Rice imports had made up the balance in the more affluent years before the First World War, but these declined again after 1913.[4] The Javanese could only live by increasing their production of less preferred subsidiary crops like cassava and maize — eaten only by the poor. Looked at in global figures, it is difficult to escape the conclusion that despite a possible small improvement in the first decade of the century, the welfare of the Javanese continued to decline thereafter.

Java no longer had a functioning middle class independent of government. Centuries of interdependence between Dutch and Chinese commerce on the one hand, and the Javanese aristocracy on the other, had seen to that. By 1865, near the end of the system of forced cultivation of export crops through the agency of the *bupati* (regents, or highest *priyayi*), a Dutch report had judged that "the *bupati* are the only group left in Javanese society with a high income, and it is wise of the Dutch to keep it so".[5] A thorough survey of the Javanese economy in 1904–1905 concluded: "A true Javanese trading class virtually does not exist, not even in the trading cities".[6] One prominent nationalist remembered of his youth at the beginning of the century that "the average person thought only about the glory connected with becoming a member of the priyayi", so that to aspire to being even a doctor or teacher seemed a revolutionary act.[7] Colonial Java's elite was based not on property, but on the extraordinary power and rewards of official position.

At the apex of the pyramid (outside the royal courts of South-Central Java) were the 66 *bupati*, with about half a million subjects each, salaries of 1,000 guilders a month, palaces at the very fulcrum of the district capital and enormous powers of patronage throughout the subordinate Javanese officialdom. Nevertheless, life was not easy for the *bupati*, caught between the traditional loyalty the Dutch wished to see him inspire and demand,

and the contempt with which both the Dutch and modern-minded Indonesians increasingly regarded him for doing so. At the base of the pyramid, the *lurah* (village head) had fewer real challenges to his authority. Instead of salary, village officials in Java received (and still receive) an allocation of communal village land. For the *lurah* himself, always among the wealthiest village landowners in his own right, this was likely to mean an additional 20 hectares in a village in which the average holding was less than half a hectare. The *lurah* also controlled the allocation of water, the distribution of collective village land, the leasing of land to the sugar estates and the imposition of tax and various "welfare" measures by the government. A large proportion of villagers were frequently in his debt, so that he gained half the product of their land as well as his own.

At the bottom of the scale was an ever greater proportion of Java's peasants who either had no land or not enough to support themselves. In some areas, more than half the villagers appear to have been already in this position in 1903. Buchler calculates that by 1932, 62.5 per cent of peasants in the Cirebon regency had no rice land, while others must have lost control of their land through indebtedness.[8] There is some truth in the picture of "shared poverty" to describe the Javanese village: private landlordism was not marked, the product of a given piece of land might be divided to feed a variety of people with different claims upon it, and an ethos of mutual obligation was maintained through village ceremonies and feasts. Yet the nature of these relationships was one which reinforced the authority of the *lurah*, and through him the whole bureaucratic structure, over Javanese life. Unlike the position in other parts of Asia, and indeed Indonesia, there appears to have been no tendency for capitalism to erode this authority, perhaps in part because the *lurah* had to remain in and of the village to exercise it.

The position was entirely different in the so-called "Outer Islands" which had a population density of only 11 per square kilometre in 1930 in contrast to Java's enormous 316. There, the bureaucratic control the Dutch sought to impose, in the first decade of the century, something quite new, and this came at the same time as remarkable changes in the economic sphere. The vigorous Dutch policy in the Outer Islands was attributable to three men who had made their reputations by apparently putting a forceful end to the last and costliest of Holland's colonial wars in Aceh at the turn of the century. They were General van Heutsz, who became Governor-General (1904–1909), the later arch-conservative Prime Minister Hendrik Colijn, who became his chief adviser for policy in the

Outer Islands, and the great Islamicist C. Snouck Hurgronje. Their energetic policy for the first time subjected the whole archipelago to effective control from Batavia, imposing direct taxes and corvée labour for massive road-building projects on societies which had never known such things.

Dutch power became universally felt, and almost as universally resented. Many societies, such as Aceh, South Bali, Lombok and some Bugis-Makassar states of South Sulawesi, had to cope with the physical and psychological burden of ruinous military defeat. In others, which included Tapanuli, Jambi, Minangkabau and parts of South Sulawesi and Lombok, there were vigorous "anti-tax" revolts which reached their peak with a widespread imposition of new direct taxes in 1908. In this first stage, it was typically the traditional chiefs who led resistance. Later, these were effectively made dependent on the colonial system — leaving to the *ulama*, or religious teachers, the role of potentially rebellious counter-elite. Resentment against taxation and corvée was manifested anew with each political movement to sweep the country, and it was still a factor in the welcome given the Japanese in 1942.

The Outer Islands were also the scene of most of the colony's economic expansion in the period 1905–1930. Oil was discovered in North and South Sumatra and in eastern Borneo, while the jungle was felled to provide the expanding needs of European and American industry for rubber, palm oil, copra and other tropical crops. By the 1930s, "the Netherlands Indies could well claim to represent the apogee of tropical export agriculture".[9] It then supplied the bulk of the world's needs for pepper, kapok and cinchona, about a third of its rubber and copra, a fifth of its palm oil and tea and about five per cent of its sugar and coffee. Rubber and oil, both Outer Island products, had replaced Javanese sugar as the colony's biggest export earners.

Indonesian "smallholders" outside Java grew a major share of some of these export crops — 43 per cent of the rubber, 30 per cent of the coffee, 90 per cent of the copra and 65 per cent of the pepper in 1940. The rapid expansion in the export of these crops and others brought a large number of small farmers into the modern world economy. There were estimated to be 800,000 such farmers growing rubber in 1930, a figure which would have to be doubled if we add the coffee growers of Central Sumatra, the pepper growers of Lampung, and the copra growers in the coastal districts of every island, but especially Sulawesi.

These cash-croppers typically retained some stake in the more labour-intensive rice economy, as a security against fluctuations in the price of export crops. Indeed, the major reason for the smallholder's better performance than the estate in the 1920s and 1930s was that he could cut costs to virtually nil in times of low rubber prices, leaving the trees untapped while he concentrated on his rice fields. Nevertheless, there was a substantial influx of money into Indonesian hands, which reached its peak during the 1920s. In 1921, the export value of Indonesian-grown crops amounted to 7.26 guilders per head of the Indonesian population in the Outer Islands, though only 1.88 guilders in Java (a discrepancy which continued to widen). In the income tax assessments for 1929, there were 239,000 Indonesian households in Java, or 2.9 per cent of the total, earning over 300 guilders a year, whereas in the whole Outer Islands, the figure was 698,000 households or 19 per cent. In West Sumatra, an area of relatively high adaptation to the cash economy, the proportion was about 28 per cent.[10]

The permanent effect of this wealth in consolidating a functioning middle class was perhaps less clear than might have been expected. Much of it undoubtedly went to Chinese and European dealers, in exchange for bicycles, sewing machines, radios and other consumer durables. Much certainly went on taking 400,000 Indonesian pilgrims to Mecca in the period 1911–1931. During these boom years, Indonesians especially from Sumatra, Borneo and West Java, were disproportionately represented in Mecca, providing half the total number of pilgrims in some years. Although not directly productive, the pilgrimage did in another sense contribute towards the creation of a middle class, for the returning *haji* (pilgrim) tended to be set apart from the community as a whole, not only by his presumed piety, but by his social and economic status. A degree of entrepreneurial skill and miserliness was almost expected of him.

The wealth of the smallholder export boom did make it possible for a number of Indonesians, particularly Muslims in Sumatra, to move into bulk trade, transportation, shopkeeping and even finance and manufacturing. In 1941, there were 2,800 buses and 8,000 taxis owned by Indonesians, frequently on a cooperative basis.[11] A handful of small banks had been formed to promote the business activity of a particular ethnic group or interest. A few rubber traders of Palembang and Padang in Sumatra became large enough during the prosperous 1920s to diversify their activities in the more difficult years that were to follow. Some moved into textile manufacture during the Great Depression when Indonesia's exports dropped to a third of their 1924 value. Only this crisis, at its worst in 1933–1934, forced the Netherlands Indies government to create the opportunity for an indigenous textile industry to again arise, and even then chiefly in the hope that excluding Japanese and British cloth would help the ailing industry in Holland. The indigenous industry responded by growing with enormous speed, especially in the Bandung plateau of West Java. Most Indonesian entrepreneurs operated by "putting-out" the yarn to five or ten home weavers, but there were also 77 factories with more than 50 looms in Indonesia by 1937, where there had been none in 1930.[12]

The economic opportunities of the 1920s contributed to the atmosphere of hope and progress which took hold of much of Outer Indonesia. They also provided the basis for a great deal of social conflict. New wealth put strains on the older status system and on the collective manner in which many communities had allocated land. The position of many Dutch-backed chiefly families was politicised by the way they used official position to enrich themselves, while at the same time, the rivals of these officials found new sources of strength in commerce, religious organisation, the press and eventually the nationalist movement itself. In some areas of Aceh, West Sumatra and East Sumatra's Karoland, there was by 1940 a polarisation of society between the Dutch-backed aristocratic hierarchy and its opponents that could almost be labelled a class conflict. The opponents were too heterogeneous to be seen as a real middle class, but they were beginning to forge some of the weapons which would make them independent of government. Insofar as there was comparable conflict in Java, it tended to be created by Dutch education and the challenge which the "new *priyayi*" of educated professionals offered to the established hierarchies of race and official rank.

The collapse in the price of all export commodities in 1929 threw much of this economic advance into reverse. Cash-cropping had to be neglected in favour of a return to subsistence farming, and the need to meet the continued high levels of taxation left little if by any margin. The depression of the 1930s can be seen as the beginning of a period lasting until 1950 in which export opportunities were minimal and the return on any capital investment highly uncertain. The return to their home villages of thousands of refugees from the devastated cash economy of city and plantation restored some power to the village heads and the aristocracy. At the same time, the Dutch continued to experiment with further ways of reinvigorating threatened traditional rulers, including the restoration of rajas in Bali and in Goa (South Sulawesi). These changes tended to accentuate the social conflicts described above rather than to ease them. In the long run, however, the economic setbacks of the 1930s and 1940s undoubtedly weakened cash-cropping as the basis for a strong Outer Islands middle class. Entrepreneurial elements remained very significant in many societies, but they had not captured the high points of the economy before their energies had to be diverted into the more complicated game of economic and political survival in an unstable post-colonial Indonesia.

From Darkness to Light[13]

For the cultural leaders of every part of Indonesia, the discovery of Dutch domination around the turn of the century had been both painful and bewildering. At one extreme, the ruling elite in Bali could only respond to their crushing military defeats in 1894 (Lombok) and 1908 (Badung and Klungkung) by a ritual suicide or *puputan*. Whole ruling families were wiped out, thereby seeming to release their subjects to find their own way in a new era. Muslim Acehnese or Bugis, in the same dilemma, could only explain the victory of the unbelievers as a product of Muslim sinfulness, perhaps as a sign of the approaching end of the world. Even the Javanese courts, whose humiliation had been gradual and disguised by every aristocratic artifice, sensed a crisis in the late 19th century. Before his death in 1873, the last court poet of Surakarta saw that "there is no example left ... everything is darkened; the world immersed in misery".[14] No successor could be found to celebrate the grandeur of the royal dynasty. Only another generation of Indonesians, armed with the new weapon of education, could find a way through this sense of gloom.

Only with the Ethical Policy did the Dutch accept any serious responsibility to educate the people of the Indies. In 1901, a small handful of Indonesians — 1,600 at primary level and fewer than 50 at secondary — had struggled among a sea of white faces. Four years later, the Indonesian numbers had tripled, and by 1930, there were 60,000 pupils in Dutch-medium government-supported primary schools. The pioneers at the beginning of the century had been marginal men, alienated from both Indonesian and Dutch societies. Parents were inclined to believe that they would never see their children again, that pupils would be Christianised or at least that they would suffer terrible punishments in the next life for sitting at the feet of the infidels. By the second decade

Plate 1.1 Teachers, teacher-trainees and students in a government "native" school at Buitenzorg (Bogor), 1920.

of the century, however, there were already enough Indonesians at secondary schools to create a constituency for new ideas, and by the third decade, a Dutch education began to seem the new talisman, the magical key to status, to progress, and eventually, to power. Indonesians demanded much more than the colonial authorities were prepared to give. A private Indonesian school system grew up to meet this thirst for a Dutch-style education, and by 1940, it catered for more than twice as many pupils as the government system.[15] Netherlands India continued to lag behind most of its neighbours in literacy — 6.44 per cent of all Indonesians in 1930, though more for Sumatra (13 per cent) than for Java (5.5 per cent), and for men (10.8 per cent) than for women (2.2 per cent). Those literate in Dutch were less than one in 300. Nevertheless, Dutch education was rigorous and a startling departure from traditional Indonesian ways, and there is no denying its impact on the new elite who experienced it (Plate 1.1).

This change from reluctance to enthusiasm for a Western type of education was part of a fundamental adjustment from the pessimism of defeat to a new faith in progress and modernisation. The transition was easiest in the colonial cities, whose cosmopolitanism formed the nucleus around which a new urban Indonesian superculture would form. It was based on Malay/Indonesian as a language medium, on economic rather than personal relationships, and on an assumption of ethnic competition between Indonesians, Chinese and the dominant Dutch. By 1930, 1.87 million Indonesians inhabited centres which could be considered fully urban, and they changed in step with the cities themselves. For most Indonesians, however, it was by no means obvious how one could become "modern" while still remaining Javanese on the one hand, or Islamic on the other.

Among the first Western-education generation in Java were some who insisted that no one could be considered Javanese who abandoned his uncut hair wrapped inside his traditional headcloth. Long hair was nevertheless the first thing to go in a wholesale shift towards Western dress during the second decade. If for some this was betrayal, for most it represented liberation. "It is always surprising to see a slavish attitude and manners, yes even opinions, change into ways which are unforced, free, but still polite in the Oriental fashion, through the change of clothes," remarked Ki Hadjar Dewantara.[16] Radicals like Tjipto Mangoenkoesoemo demanded the abandonment of Javanese culture altogether, including even its language — "a language of slaves", with its hierarchic speech-levels — as the price of progress.[17]

The first organisation to mobilise a substantial section of the new Javanese elite, Budi Utomo, was born out of this struggle for a new definition of identity. The student activist who initiated it in 1908, Dr Soetomo, suggests that what inspired him in his older mentor, Dr Wahidin, was a new way of being Javanese: "His tranquil features, his wise manner and tone ... his conviction ... his melodious serene voice ... brought me new ideals and a new world that could, it seemed, console my wounded heart."[18]

One of the most radical young nationalists of this first generation, Ki Hadjar Dewantara, later gave birth to a still more influential syncretism in his Taman Siswa school system, founded in Yogyakarta in 1922. "Government Western education," he argued, "provides an abundance [of knowledge] but not the capacity to bring it to a synthesis. It enables youth to take note of everything, but gives them no centre, no cultural basis of their own. They thereby neither remain Javanese nor become Western, they break into pieces".[19] His *Panca Darma* (Five Duties), foreshadowing the nationalist *Panca Sila* of 1945, were freedom, natural harmony, culture, nationality and humaneness. In practice, this meant a relaxed, family atmosphere in the classroom, development of the whole person, and "socialism without class conflict" in which fees and teachers' salaries would be adjusted to need rather than rank. As the movement spread outside Java in the 1930s, it developed a pattern of integrating other cultures as well as the Javanese into its national-progressive format. Although the number of students in its school system never rose above 25,000, Taman Siswa provided remarkable leadership in developing a new and secure identity which belonged to the modern world. It also reinforced the point that once a *modern* identity had been defined for the Javanese, as for Muslims, the step to a *national* identity was a relatively short one.

Muslims had a less complicated path to follow, since religion itself was the guarantee that they had not sold their birthright to the West. Some of the most profoundly individualistic and iconoclastic Indonesians of the century were strict Muslims. The modernists of Egypt in the late 19th century had already provided the argument that Islamic societies were in decline because they had not been truly Muslim, failing to learn from the world around them. Islamic reformism made its earliest Indonesian impact in West Sumatra, but the appearance of a Dutch-educated generation gave it new impetus everywhere. In 1912, Indonesia's most successful religious organisation, Muhammadiah, was founded in Yogyakarta precisely to cater for disoriented Muslims in Dutch schools. Gradually, it developed its own modern school system, and by the 1930s, it had almost 1,000 branches throughout the archipelago, each supporting one or more schools as well as women's, youth and scouting organisations. In Yogyakarta itself, and in West Sumatra from the 1920s, it developed strong populist roots. Elsewhere, it had a predominantly urban and Western-educated membership. Even as an irritant to the more traditional rural *ulama*, it was important, however, because these in turn eventually formed their own movements which imitated Muhammadiah's organisation even while opposing its theology. Such traditionally-oriented organisations as Nahdatul Ulama in East Java (1926), Perti in West Sumatra, Al Jamiatul Wasliyah in North Sumatra (1930) and PUSA in

Aceh (1939) did have an enormous potential rural constituency. Gradually, the distance between these organisations and Muhammadiah narrowed, and their common ground against the alien government became more marked. In 1937, the major Islamic organisations joined in a federative council called MIAI, which in turn joined forces with the secular nationalists in a number of political campaigns in 1939–1941. Under the Japanese, the same organisations were again united on a Java-wide basis into MASJUMI, which provided the name and much of the leadership for independent Indonesia's biggest political party in the period 1945–1953. By independence, in other words, the Indonesian Islamic community was represented by modern organisations quite different from, and frequently hostile towards, the rajas, chiefs and *bupatis* who had official control of the Muslim juridical apparatus under the Dutch. Their basis was not the *kadi*, the religious judge, but the Islamic school — whether of traditional or modern type. It could form a powerful ally of the secular nationalists against the Dutch and Japanese, but its fundamental goal could only be an Islamic State based on religious law. It was therefore also a rival of secular nationalism, and the relative strength of the two forces remained uncertain until 1955, when Islamic parties took 45 per cent of the vote in Indonesia's first election. In the second period of democratic elections, after 1998, it would be much less.

The Politics of Anti-colonialism

As we have seen, ideas of progress, solidarity and party formation had begun to be important in Indonesia at least from the time of the first political organisations — Budi Utomo (1908), the Indische Partij and Sarekat Islam (both 1912). These parties, like all those that followed, were led by Dutch-educated intellectuals sensitive to Dutch power and arrogance on one hand, and anachronistic aristocratic pretension on the other. It was a small group of privileged urban people. Even in 1940, when the numbers of the Dutch-educated had expanded many times, only about 50,000 Indonesians were associated with nationalist parties. Aided by the Japanese occupation, this small group would succeed in 1945 in making itself both spokesman and leader of the Indonesian people. At no point, however, did it mobilise mass support in really effective political organisations at the grassroots level.

The very weak position of an indigenous middle class of financiers and traders limited the opportunities for building organisations which could reach the rural masses. The most important linkages between city and country remaining in indigenous hands were the bureaucratic hierarchy and the *ulama*. The first was effectively controlled by the Dutch, who quickly dismissed any official who joined a political party. The second, in conjunction with the embryonic middle-class elements described above, became the basis for Indonesia's first experiment with mass politics in 1912–1926.

Sarekat Islam (SI), which pioneered this experiment, was not initially inspired by the Dutch-educated element at all. It sprang from the resentment of Javanese *batik* makers in Surakarta at Chinese economic pressure, and thus it had a populist anti-Chinese base from the start. Its founder saw the need for educated *priyayi* leadership, however, and he turned to H.O.S. Tjokroaminoto to organise an association for mutual self-help among Muslims — which in 1912, was still the most common term by which Indonesians designated themselves in contrast to Europeans and Chinese. Within two years, the organisation had received membership fees from 366,000 people, almost all in Java. This astonishing growth owed something to the desire of Western-educated lower *priyayi*, *ulama* and small traders for a vehicle for their interests in a time of rapid change, but more to the messianic longings of a downtrodden people whose traditional leaders had long since ceased to be a source of hope. Tjokroaminoto was widely identified with the *Heru Tjokro* or *Ratu Adil*, the messianic deliverer of Javanese prophecy, and secret oaths and rituals underlined the supernatural power the organisation was thought to possess.[20]

After 1914, this popular following declined in Java as more cautious leaders discouraged the messianic elements. The loss was for a time made good by the Outer Islands, where there were already 83,000 members by 1916. Here, where the Dutch conquest was still a recent memory, SI was embraced as a new and more promising way to continue the struggle. As a propagandist in Aceh put it: "Formerly we became *Muslimin* [Muslim fighters] by carrying a gun, but now that is no longer necessary, now unity [through SI] is enough. If we have unity we are already numerous and we will achieve whatever we want."[21] Violent incidents began to frighten the Dutch and even the urban leadership of SI in the period 1918–1920. Numerous rural activists were arrested, and the movement lost its enthusiasm for rapid expansion of membership.

At its height, however, Sarekat Islam had become the voice of the national awakening, and any who wished to participate in that awakening had to join it. Among them were a handful of able Indonesian Marxists in the Semarang stronghold of the Indies Socialist Party. The pioneers of Marxist activism in the Indies had been Dutch, but the exile of the European leaders in 1918 only made it easier for their young Indonesian protégées, Semaun and Darsono, to argue that imperialism and capitalism were the same enemy. The same men led the militant Semarang branch of Sarekat Islam, the radicalism of which was a constant challenge to the original SI leadership. In its anxiety to preserve its role as the united voice for all oppressed Indonesians, Sarekat Islam was forced by Semarang to condemn "sinful" capitalism in October 1917 — a compromise which retained for a time the indispensable support of the small Muslim entrepreneurial group. The conflict between the left and right wings could not be papered over for long, however, especially when the former became increasingly influenced by the Comintern and the latter by pan-Islam. In 1920, Semaun and Darsono formed the Partai Komunis di Hindia (from 1924, Partai Komunis Indonesia, or PKI), though they remained in the executive of SI. There were stormy scenes at each subsequent SI Congress, until the PKI members walked out for the last time in February 1923.

The SI henceforth became an urban party catering for Islamic nationalists. Many of its wealthier supporters transferred their energies to Muhammadiah, concluding that the quality of religious practice had to be improved before entering the political arena. It was left to the PKI to pursue the dangerous course of mass mobilisation, between the twin perils of government repression and popular expectations of the millennium. It was no use for some Dutch Marxists to argue that Indonesian capitalism had to grow stronger before there was any chance for the proletariat. The demand from politicised rural Indonesians, whether Sumatran coffee and rubber growers, Javanese sugar and railway workers, or village schoolteachers, was for an end to taxes, forced labour and domination by foreigners. Marxism was irresistible as long as it not only gave a modern name to the enemy, "capitalism", but promised rapid success against it. As one left-wing newspaper ended its explanation:

> Communism knows that as long as this world is ruled by capitalism, there must be misery and general difficulty. So in short "communism" is anti "Capitalism", or better "Communism" is the science [*ilmu*] of

people who are at present squeezed, milked, oppressed, etc. Now do you understand and agree with the existence of communism? "Oh sure — really great if that's what it is. When is the hour of this 'Communism' coming?" Wait on, in a little while it must rule the world, for its turn has nearly come.[22]

In its attempt to avoid these dangerous pressures, the PKI dissolved its peasant branches in 1924, complaining about their "petty bourgeois" values and tendency "to give up in despair or go over into terrorism".[23] The tightrope act nevertheless soon broke down and a suicidal revolt was planned on grounds that it was "better to die fighting than let oneself be killed".[24] Scheduled for 12 November 1926, the revolt was very poorly coordinated, largely as a result of pre-emptive Dutch action. The disturbances which took place in West Java in November 1926, and in West Sumatra in early 1927, gained strongest support from the despised rural branches but were suppressed within a few days. They provided the pretext for the Dutch to arrest 13,000 people associated with the PKI, and to intern 1,308 of them in the swamps of Boven Digul, New Guinea. From having been the strongest communist party in Asia, the PKI was now entirely removed from the public arena. Even had it sought a Maoist retreat to a rural stronghold, there was nowhere it could have gone and no hope of help from abroad. Marxist ideas remained influential and the PKI's reputation as arch-revolutionary was unchallengeable, but when the party reappeared two decades later, it was extremely weak in organisation.

The revolt marked the end of mass mobilisation as a feasible tactic. Government bureaucratic control was sufficient to ensure that no later party could penetrate the rural areas, had any sought to do so. Except in cities and some Christian areas of whose loyalty the Dutch were very sure, there were no popular elections before independence. Indonesian members of the *Volksraad*, established in 1918 but never developed beyond its weak co-legislative functions, were either appointed or elected by minute electoral colleges of elite Indonesians.

Nevertheless, the national ideal continued to develop rapidly among the nearly two million urban or educated Indonesians. Taking from Marxism the opposition to capitalism, from Sarekat Islam the solidarity of "us" against "them", and from European scholarship the name "Indonesia" and the rediscovery of a glorious pre-European past, secular nationalism became the dominant political force after 1926. The first organisation to use the term "Indonesia" in 1917 had been a non-political association of students in the Netherlands. Becoming steadily more radical, this adopted in 1925 the name "Perhimpunan Indonesia" and issued a militant journal called *Indonesia Merdeka (Free Indonesia)*. Dominated in the period 1924–1931 by a thoughtful Minangkabau economist, Mohammad Hatta, this association developed many of the ideas and symbols which would inspire the struggle of the 1930s. As we have seen, the PKI incorporated "Indonesia" into its title in 1924, Sarekat Islam followed suit in 1929 and even Budi Utomo, originally restricted to Java, fused into the Indonesian nationalist PARINDRA in 1935. Student activists in Indonesia were especially quick to respond to the new national symbols. At a national Youth Congress in 1928, a pledge was made by all delegates — "We the youth of Indonesia have only one fatherland, Indonesia. We have only one nation, Indonesia. We have only one language, the Indonesian language." The same Congress first heard the composition "Indonesia Raya", which quickly gained the status of the anthem of nationalism.

The most popular spokesman for the nationalist position soon became a young architecture graduate in Bandung named Sukarno. As a student, Sukarno had lived with Tjokroaminoto and taken his landlord's daughter as his first wife. He shared the older man's concern for unity as well as his faith in charismatic oratory rather than careful organisation. In July 1927, he founded the PNI (Indonesian Nationalist Party) on a platform of complete non-cooperation in government-sponsored councils such as the *Volksraad*, drawing into the party a number of returned members of the Perhimpunan Indonesia in Holland. Only five months later, he had succeeded in forming the first federation of nationalist political parties, the PPPKI. Sukarno wrote and spoke tirelessly on the theme that Muslims, Marxists and nationalists all had the same central aim, to rid Indonesia of imperialism, but could never achieve it unless united (Plate 1.2). At his urging, the PPPKI adopted the "Indonesian way" of reaching decisions by consultation (*musyawarah*) and consensus (*mufakat*). The major policies of Sukarno as future president were already clearly delineated before he was 30.

The superficial unity he had built up did not outlast his first imprisonment (December 1929–January 1932). Another young Minangkabau intellectual, Sutan Sjahrir, established a "New PNI" dedicated to the education of party cadres rather than the cultivation of "sacred unity"

Plate 1.2 Leadership of the first "Indonesian" organisation, Perhimpunan Indonesia, in the Netherlands, 1923. Hatta standing left, Iwa Kusuma Sumantri centre as President.

at all costs. Hatta joined this new party on his return in 1932, whereas Sukarno after his release joined PARTINDO, the successor to the first PNI. Both rival leaderships were put out of circulation altogether by the reactionary Governor-General de Jonge by early 1934. Hatta and Sjahrir were exiled to Boven Digul, while Sukarno had a more comfortable exile in Flores, perhaps as a reward for the abject letters he wrote to the Dutch after his second arrest. The tactics of Sukarno and Hatta were in striking contrast, though neither had been a great success. Hatta's party structure barely survived on a harried semi-legal basis until 1942, while Sukarno had to hope that he lived on in the memory of his people.

Since 1920, Dutch colonial policy had grown steadily more conservative. To understand the intransigence of Holland, one must recall the importance in popular consciousness of its oversized colony. This alone gave Holland the status of a major power. By 1930, US$2,000 million had been invested in Netherlands India, and 73 per cent of it was Dutch. It was estimated that between one in five and one in ten of the Dutch population depended directly on the Indies for their livelihood.[25] Many took it as axiomatic that "if the bonds which attach the Netherlands to the Indies are severed there will be a permanent reduction in the national income of the Netherlands which will lead to the country's pauperisation"[26] — though the reverse proved the case after 1950. The two men who dominated colonial policy in the 1930s, Hendrik Colijn (Prime Minister, 1933–1937) and B.C. de Jonge (Governor-General, 1931–1936), were both former Directors of Royal Dutch Shell — the largest single economic interest in the Indies. The challenge of Indonesian nationalism led such men to adopt a rigid position excluding even the discussion of movement towards independence. De Jonge inaugurated his term of office by announcing that Holland had been in the Indies for 300 years and would be there for another 300. Under his regime and that of his successor, the police silenced nationalist speakers or broke up their meetings if the word "independence" was uttered, or even if it was implied that the economic difficulties of Indonesians were related to imperialism.

Such repression created a superficial calm, but the alienation of urban Indonesians from the colonial system steadily deepened. The small but vigorous Indonesian press (with a total, overlapping, circulation of about 500,000), the Islamic movement, Taman Siswa and the other private schools, the moderate Indonesian spokesmen in the *Volksraad*, all came to share with the nationalists a sense of identity as Indonesians and a conviction that Dutch intransigence was the principal barrier to progress. Dutch commitment to the *Pangreh Praja* corps (no longer a traditional aristocracy but not yet a professional bureaucracy) as the legitimate leaders of Indonesia, placed both in an awkward straitjacket. As Heather Sutherland puts it: "The theoretically apolitical *Beamtenstaat* [bureaucratic state] became a protective scaffolding supporting indigenous authority. Paradoxically, this imprisoned the *Pangreh Praja*, inhibited its responses and so further weakened a corps already suffering from the contempt of many of its defenders as well as the challenges of new elites. Ultimately, maintenance of the status quo necessitated the development of a police regime".[27]

Only cooperative, pragmatic political parties were permitted to operate in the late 1930s. PARINDRA, which incorporated Budi Utomo in 1935, attracted many professionals and retired officials with a practical programme of social reforms. GERINDO was born two years later as a vehicle for former members of Sukarno's parties and a number of covert communists, on the basis of the Moscow-approved "common front against fascism". The key figure in the latter group was a Surabaya lawyer named Amir Sjarifuddin, an attractive and persuasive Sumatran who had converted to Christianity as a student and was later drawn into the "underground PKI" through GERINDO.

Unlike their predecessors, these parties did not frighten cautious or pious Indonesians. In a quieter way than Sukarno's, a more effective political front gradually emerged to link the political parties, the Islamic organisations (beginning to lose their fear of politics), and even the union representing much of the more educated *Pangreh Praja*. These elements joined to promote such modest aims as the Soetardjo petition (1936) for a Dutch-Indonesian constitutional conference, the call for an Indonesian parliament in 1939–1940, and the wider use of the title "Indonesia" and the Indonesian language. Dutch rejection of all these requests pushed moderate Indonesians into the arms of the nationalists. Despite the outward calm, alienation from the colonial regime was universal by 1942, and the Japanese were welcomed as liberators. One left-wing nationalist intellectually committed to opposing the Japanese had to concede: "For the average Indonesian the war ... was simply a struggle in which the Dutch colonial rulers would finally be punished by providence for the evil, the arrogance, and the oppression they had brought to Indonesia."[28]

The Japanese Occupation, 1942–1945

Even the Japanese were astonished at the ease of their victory in the East Indies. In some areas, the speed of the Dutch capitulation owed as much to fear of the Indonesian population as to the Japanese advance. By 8 March 1942, only three months after Pearl Harbour and three weeks after the fall of Singapore, the Dutch colonial regime was at an end. Despite the intensity of colonial penetration of Indonesia, with its 300,000 European residents, 100,000 students in Dutch-medium schools and the high degree of Westernisation in the clothes, manners and lifestyle of millions of Indonesians, it had gone for good. The Dutch language was effectively forbidden from the public arena by the Japanese, giving to Indonesians a primacy which would never again be challenged. The Japanese did not succeed in Japanising Indonesian culture in any significant respect, but they made possible the consolidation of a very strong sense of the meaning of being Indonesian.

The Japanese were welcomed in part because they were assumed to represent change. The contradictions kept under the carpet by Dutch police measures now had an opportunity to emerge. In Sumatra, there were demonstrations against the rajas and demands for their abolition. A number of village and district heads were killed or injured by their angry subjects. Local peacekeeping committees which oversaw the transfer of power usually represented the political activists hoping for an end to the rule of the *Pangreh Praja*. In Jakarta, the Japanese were presented with a list of nationalist politicians to form a Cabinet for the new Indonesia. Javanese *priyayi* and Sumatran rajas were denounced as pro-Dutch collaborators, though they in turn were not slow to point out the dangers their opponents would present to the Japanese. The Japanese, in other words, were "overwhelmed with willing, yet warring, collaborators".[29] Indonesian society had never seemed so divided. Sukarno was not far from the truth in labelling the enmity between the national movement and the *Pangreh Praja* "the most rotten wound caused by the Dutch policy of *divide et impera*".[30]

The Japanese did bring change, but not of the sort expected. Their primary aim in the Pacific War was to obtain access to the raw materials of the archipelago for industries at home. Independence, even in name, had already been ruled out before the war began for all the islands except Java, the status of which remained for a time uncertain. In terms of administration, the policy laid down in Tokyo had been that "existing government organizations shall be utilized as much as possible, with due respect for past organization structure and native practice".[31] The *Pangreh Praja* continued to be used as the backbone of administration. The hereditary element the Dutch had continued to value was removed, and the service moved closer to a true bureaucracy subject to frequent transfer and intervention from above. On the other hand, the disappearance of local councils and of the ever-watchful Dutch *controleur*, together with Japanese unfamiliarity with conditions, gave Indonesian administrators more real authority than ever.

Unlike the Dutch, the Japanese also had places for Islamic and political "counter-elites" even if not the ones they had sought. Indeed, few avenues were open to politicians and journalists except on the government payroll in organisations directly answerable to the Japanese. Political parties were banned, independent newspapers were closed, and the opportunities for pursuing a private career in law, engineering or business were sharply curtailed. In this sense, the Japanese period drastically eroded the fragile autonomy which Indonesian organisations had prided themselves on in relation to the Dutch. On the other hand, a significant role was provided for politicians and journalists in city administration, in the one official newspaper the Japanese permitted in each major city and in the organisations set up for propaganda and popular mobilisation.

Surprisingly, few politicians declined these opportunities. The only significant nationalist group to attempt anti-Japanese activity was the "Illegal PKI" re-established by Musso during a brief clandestine visit to Surabaya in 1935, though more effective under the GERINDO umbrella of 1937–1941. The Dutch, apparently unaware of his communist connection, gave Amir Sjarifuddin 25,000 guilders to finance an anti-Japanese underground. This made it easy for the Japanese to trace the PKI leaders, executing many of them although Amir himself was spared through Sukarno's intervention.[32] Sutan Sjahrir also stood aloof from Japanese-orchestrated activity in order to act as a link between anti-Japanese elements and the cooperating politicians, notably Sukarno and Hatta.

The overwhelming majority had no objection to working with the Japanese, some politicians seeing it as "a magnificent opportunity to educate and ready our people".[33] Despite greater restraints than ever on freedom to speak and organise, there were some precious, if unintended, advantages. Favoured leaders were not only allowed but required to stump the country addressing huge rallies, their audiences often trucked in from the surrounding villages. In their determination to mobilise greater sacrifices for the war effort, the Japanese gave Indonesians their first experience of real political theatre. Secondly, a unitary leadership was forced upon the politicians of each area. The quarrelling factions which had greeted the Japanese in 1942 were obliged to join single propaganda bodies in each area, responsible to clearly identified leaders. Muslim modernists and traditionalists, and Christians whether Protestant or Catholic, were obliged to merge into single representative bodies. The different elites, secular nationalist, religious and *Pangreh Praja*, were in turn fused at the top of the pyramid in local advisory councils and "loyalty" organisations in which the leading local politician usually enjoyed the position of chairman. Although the tensions of 1942 were by no means eliminated, all these rival elites found themselves in a very similar predicament. All now enjoyed official status, a relatively high income in a time of general hardship and privileged access to travel, information and scarce resources. In return, they shared a vulnerable role as mediators between the unpredictable, demanding Japanese and an increasingly desperate population.

The leaders who rose to the top under the Japanese proved durable both at the local and national levels. The overtly pro-Japanese figures without popular support were tried and found wanting during 1942, and the Japanese turned to those who seemed likely to be most effective in the task of wartime mobilisation. Those selected for highest office were seldom challenged either before or after the Japanese surrender, because their colleagues in the wartime elite groups were aware of the dangers such prominence brought with it. Moreover, the power of the official media ensured that only the officially designated leaders were known and recognised at the grassroots level, making them indispensable in the struggle that would follow.

In the Outer Islands, this process of developing an Indonesian leadership did not go beyond the Residency level (close to the Provinces of the Suharto era). Sumatra, seen as strategically vital by the Japanese, had been united with Malaya in 1942 under the command of the 25th Army. Even when its links with Malaya were broken the following year, the 25th Army insisted that Sumatra was not ready for independence and defended its territory from the more liberal ideas emanating from Java. The eastern islands had been entrusted to the Japanese Navy as "sparsely populated primitive areas, which shall be retained in future for the benefit of the [Japanese] Empire".[34] Java, on the other hand, had no special strategic value to Japan, and was fortunate that General Imamura Hitoshi established what was known to the Japanese as a "soft" policy there. In particular, Imamura developed a good relationship with Sukarno, the most obvious potential leader since the deaths of the two major PARINDRA figures shortly before the war. At a meeting in July 1942, Imamura promised Sukarno "greater political participation by the people and greater welfare than in the Dutch period",[35] though he was replaced before he could persuade Tokyo to sanction any significant concession. The Indonesian politicians were allowed only to establish a Java-wide propaganda body named PUTERA (March 1943–February 1944) and a completely powerless Java advisory council in October 1943. Later, even PUTERA was abolished in favour of the broader Djawa Hokokai, in which the influence of the nationalists was effectively diluted by the *Pangreh Praja* and other groups. Until September 1944, when independence for "the

Indies" was at last promised by a Japan which knew it was losing the war, Sukarno had no substantial concessions whatsoever to show for his bargaining with the Japanese. Mohammad Hatta, who had decided that cooperation was the only realistic option despite his obvious distaste for Japanese methods, was very lucky to escape a Kenpeitai plan to eliminate him in a traffic "accident" during 1943.[36] Nevertheless, Sukarno and Hatta, who remained loyal to each other despite profound differences during this difficult period, were unchallenged as Indonesian spokesmen throughout Java. Since so little had been achieved beyond the local level in the other islands, there would be no alternative in 1945 than for the Java leadership to become the Indonesian leadership. Java's more advanced political climate has to be seen against its appalling shortages of food and other vital supplies. The policy of local self-sufficiency and the collapse of export earnings brought shortages of cloth and other imported articles everywhere. Food production became inadequate even in rice-surplus areas because the increasingly arbitrary Japanese policy of forcible requisitions reduced any incentive to produce. Java, already unable to feed its 50 million people before the war, was in a critical situation by 1944–1945. Possibilities of import had disappeared, the Japanese were preparing large stockpiles for a last-ditch defence of the island, and 40,000 tons were even ordered to be sent to Singapore. In their determination to keep themselves, the cities and workers in strategic industries well fed, the Japanese imposed requisitions on rural areas which rose as high as 50 per cent of the crop in 1944. Lucas has calculated that the rice remaining for the Indonesian population in Pekalongan Residency may have fallen as low as 63 grams per head per day — less than one-seventh of a healthy ration. The effects of starvation could be seen throughout Java. The promised time of deliverance had become a time of despair.

All over Java and Sumatra, there were incidents of rural rebellion, sometimes directed against the Japanese themselves but more often against the local officials through whom Japanese demands for rice and forced labour were imposed on the people. A number of village and district heads were killed in these spontaneous outbursts of anger, and many more would be punished in the "social revolutions" which followed the departure of the Japanese. Had there been a more effective underground guerrilla movement, it could have capitalised on this popular bitterness, at its peak in 1945. But the political elite seemed now to be a captive of the Japanese, clinging to the hope that the increasingly frenzied preparations for the final military struggle would at last bring real independence to Indonesia.

If the Japanese distanced the pre-war elites in this way from the masses in whose name they professed to speak, they also created a wholly new class without parallel in the Dutch time. They made a complete break with the Dutch educational system, which they considered elitist, academic and impractical. Japanese training would emphasise physical fitness, discipline, toughness, and above all, a spirit of sacrificial patriotism. Indonesians who were taught by young, idealistic Japanese teachers testify to their closeness to their students and to the self-confident spirit they produced in young Indonesians. Beyond the relatively small number of Japanese schools, a wide sector of Indonesian youth experienced at least some form of military drilling and patriotic rhetoric. About half a million youths in Java were trained in the urban *Seinendan* (Youth Corps) and over a million in the rural *Keibodan* (Vigilance Corps). At the end of the occupation, some radical nationalists were encouraged to set up further paramilitary groups of this type, the Sukarnoist *Barisan Pelopor* in Java being the biggest, on grounds that these would have the strongest motivation to fight against the returning Allies. The numerous young people who were radicalised in an inchoate way by this training at a time of general crisis would become the *pemuda* (youth) of the revolution, ready for action, though uncertain what its object would be.

The elect of this Japanese-influenced generation were the young men selected for officer training in the embryo Indonesian army. Known as PETA in Java and as *Giyugun* in Sumatra and Bali, this force amounted to about 60,000 men by the surrender. The officer training was the same as that provided for junior Japanese officers, emphasising group solidarity, discipline, physical toughness and a spirit of heroic patriotism. This intensive training was designed to equip educated youths of 18–25 to become company and platoon commanders. Although there was probably no conscious bias on the part of the Japanese, most of those selected appear to have been from well-placed *priyayi* families and their Sumatran equivalent. In Java alone, older men thought to have some popular influence, typically as religious leaders, were given a shorter training to become battalion commanders. Although this gave a superficial Islamic cast to the PETA army, these men were intended as political advisers rather than professional soldiers and most of them did not remain in the army after independence. The PETA/*Giyugun* represented potentially the most effective legacy of the Japanese period in both organisational and ideological terms, but its leadership in 1945 was still very young and extremely decentralised.

The Revolutionary Republic

Preparation for independence was going on at two levels during the middle of 1945. Politicised youth leaders and the shadowy left-wing underground were banking on a Japanese defeat followed by some kind of revolution for which they were hopelessly unprepared. Meanwhile, the political leadership which had emerged under the Japanese umbrella was, when it seemed almost too late, being given the opportunity it had sought since 1942. Although "independence" had been promised in September 1944, little was done to implement it except at the symbolic level of flag and anthem until May 1945 — and then only in Java. On 28 May, a 62-man assembly met in Jakarta to debate the shape of a future state. Some potential for disagreement was removed by the underrepresentation of the Outer Islands, Muslims and liberal constitutionalists. The delegates voted convincingly for a unitary Republic under a strong president. The most divisive issue was the religious one, and instead of polarising the country through a vote, a compromise was arranged whereby a prologue to the draft constitution pronounced "the obligation for those who profess the Islamic faith to abide by Islamic laws". Although the "1945 Constitution", as it later became known, was authoritarian and integralist in tone, it was a remarkable achievement to have reached agreement in less than a month on a document which served for 40 years (after Sukarno returned to it in 1959) as the constitutional basis for the world's fifth most populous state.

The further collapse of Japanese defences in July caused a rapid acceleration of preparations for recognition of independence, now scheduled for 7 September. In Java, capable *Pangreh Praja* had already been appointed substantive or deputy Residents in late 1944, while each department of the Military Administration received an Indonesian adviser as a shadow minister. Now in Sumatra and the Navy area similar moves were belatedly made, usually appointing the leading local politician as deputy Resident and capable aristocrats at the lower levels. For the first time, the Japanese brought together a committee representing all three military administrations, scheduled to begin the final preparations for independence on 16 August. The 22 delegates, including three flown in from Sumatra, two from Sulawesi and one from Bali, were therefore on hand to witness the dramatic events surrounding the proclamation of Indonesian independence on 17 August. When they finally did meet the following day, Sukarno and Hatta were able to tell the Japanese that they were simply following the plans laid down under previous Japanese authority, while attempting to explain to suspicious youth leaders that this was at the same time a revolutionary national committee.

Despite some initial misgivings from the Outer Islands delegates, this committee unanimously elected Sukarno to fill the all-powerful role of president under the "1945 Constitution" which it adopted. Hatta would be vice-president. These two men continued to have the major responsibility for delicate diplomacy with the Japanese commanders to prevent their moving against the new republic at least until its authority was firmly established. To this end, they sought to give the appearance of adhering as closely as possible to the Japanese-sponsored preparations. Sukarno's first Cabinet (4 September–11 November 1945) was made up almost entirely of ministers already acting as "advisers" to their respective departments under the Japanese. *Pangreh Praja* members were appointed to the positions of Resident (in Java) or Assistant Resident (in Sumatra) for which they had been prepared. Similarly, the Preparatory Committee which dispersed on 22 August had made few changes to the agreed Constitution. The concessions to an Islamic state were dropped in the hope of improving the Republic's appeal to potentially pro-Dutch Christians in the East, and a high degree of autonomy in practice, if not in constitutional guarantees, was given to the Provincial Governments established in Sumatra, Borneo, Sulawesi, the Lesser Sundas and Maluku. Provision was made for a single state party, though this quickly became a dead letter, and for national committees at national, province and residency levels. The delicate question of an armed force was left unresolved by defining a People's Security Body but appointing no one to head it.

These measures were successful in avoiding the kind of provocation which might have obliged the Japanese to intervene. Real change was very gradual for the first month after the proclamation, as Indonesians gradually gained more courage in disregarding their now dispirited Japanese superiors and acting in the name of the Republic. There was an explicit "gentlemen's agreement" at the national level, replicated locally, that Indonesians could proceed along the promised path to independence provided they did not make the position of the Japanese impossible by violence against Japanese or overt rejection of nominal Allied authority. The *Pangreh Praja* to whom power was meant to devolve at most levels, however, were not the men to take risks on behalf of a revolutionary Republic. They were typically wary of their position with the victorious Allies, some of them going so far as to remove Republican flags and insignia from public places. A positive force for change had to be mobilised before the Republic could acquire real substance. The *diplomasi* of the older elite had to be complemented by the *perjuangan* (struggle) of revolutionary youth.

It would be fair to say that most Indonesians were initially bewildered by news of the Japanese surrender, and found it hard to know whether the noises of independence coming from Jakarta were the last act of the Japanese play or something entirely new. Only two groups had prepared themselves for this moment — older left-wingers who had been anti-Japanese all along, and angry youth leaders whom the Japanese had mobilised but failed to control. The revolutionary youth movement started most quickly in towns where these two elements were able to find each other. They began by putting up red-and-white insignia and revolutionary posters, and proceeded to call the bluff of Japanese guards by replacing the Japanese flag with the Republican flag on public buildings. During the months of September in Java, and October in Sumatra, they organised mass rallies to show their strength. Where necessary, they forced reluctant officials to take a tougher line with the Japanese. By the time the first Allied forces arrived, at the end of September in Jakarta and the middle of October in Sumatra, they had ensured that the Japanese had withdrawn to their barracks and power was in Indonesian hands — however ill-coordinated.

The officers of the *PETA/Giyugun* army were initially at a greater disadvantage than semi-militarised urban youth, since their Japanese commanders had disarmed and dispersed them before the surrender was generally known. In September and October, however, they began to reform as the Republican Army, officially designated as such on 5 October. They took an increasingly large part in the struggle which now turned on the control of Japanese arms. A pattern quickly emerged to be replicated in one centre after another, where crowds of militant youth armed only with sharpened bamboos, knives and a few pistols would descend on a Japanese post and demand weapons. The Japanese always agreed to

Plate 1.3 Allied patrols in Jakarta, 1945.

negotiate, and some or all of their arms would then be transferred, as if under compulsion, to some Republican authority. In Central and East Java alone, it appeared that 26,000 rifles and over 1,300 machine guns and mortars passed into Indonesian hands.[37] Most went to the official army whose officer corps was overwhelmingly Japanese-trained, but much also fell to politically-oriented youth groups bold enough to seize them. The ease of these victories must have appeared to validate the lesson of Japanese training that spirit was the key to military success.

The eventual arrival of British Indian troops, representing the Allied military administration whose task was to preserve law and order until the Dutch administration could resume, interrupted these relatively bloodless exchanges (Plate 1.3). In Jakarta, *diplomasi* with the Republican leaders prevented any serious violence, and the city slipped gradually out of Republican control. In Bandung, British pressure induced the Japanese to retake the city from Republican forces on 10 October. In Semarang the following week, a small war developed between Japanese and Indonesians before British troops took over. The climax to this phase came in Surabaya, where uniquely well-armed Indonesian forces had been aggravated by the fact that the first Allied representatives were all Dutch. When the first British brigade arrived on 25 October, the militant youth were in the mood to resist, and wholesale fighting broke out on 28 October. The intervention of Sukarno, Hatta and Amir Sjarifuddin established a tense ceasefire, but the ground was cut from under their feet when an undisciplined sniper killed the British commander, General Mallaby. On 10 November, the outraged British launched a massive air, sea and ground operation against the city, whose leaders announced that they would resist to the last. In the "Battle of Surabaya" which ensued, the Republic received its baptism of fire. Less startling to the British than the tanks and field artillery which opposed them, were the hordes of villagers armed only with bamboo stakes and knives, throwing themselves before British guns in a frenzy of religious fervour. About 15,000 Indonesians probably died in the fighting.[38] Despite the enormous sacrifice of lives and armament, Indonesians had convinced the British and themselves that their country was not to be reconquered by force alone. Since then, 10 November has been celebrated as "Heroes' Day" — a holiday second only in importance to 17 August.

Even though the leaders of *diplomasi* had had to oppose the *perjuangan* of Surabaya, they knew that without it, their bargaining position with the British would have been very weak. The same could not be said when revolutionary zeal was turned against its internal enemies. As we have seen, there was widespread revulsion among villagers against the power-holders who had enforced Japanese demands for rice and labour. Once it was clear there was no longer any power structure behind these men, there was spontaneous action in village after village to dismiss the village headman, sometimes with violence. In one seemingly typical district of Central Java, we know that 80 village heads were overthrown within a few months, out of a total of 180.[39] In most areas, a change of office-holder was all that was achieved — the system through which the headman was able to dominate the village was shaken but not fundamentally altered. Where a more ambitious radical leadership existed, however, the revolutionary impetus could be carried to higher levels of government. In the strongly Islamic northern coast of Java, from the Sunda Strait in the west to Semarang in the east, a series of such actions in the last three months of 1945 eliminated most of the *Pangreh Praja* even though they were now designated Republican officials. In December, the ruling class of Aceh was permanently removed from power; in March 1946, the same thing happened to the Malay sultans of East Sumatra; and in April–June, it was the turn of the rulers of Surakarta. Except in Surakarta and East Sumatra, these were rural phenomena in which the Japanese-trained *pemuda* whom we have met in the towns played a relatively small role. Three types of leadership were involved, frequently in combination — semi-bandit figures, Islamic teachers and communist veterans of 1926 or the anti-Japanese underground. The first category, very prominent to the west of Jakarta and in Tegal (Central Java), often went in for social banditry claiming to help the small man, but they were better equipped for tearing down than for building up. The more politicised Islamic leaders were involved everywhere, playing their time-honoured role as spokesmen for discontent. Only in Aceh were they united and strong enough not only to oust the secular elite, but to replace them effectively in control of the local Republican government. In this sense, Aceh's was the only "social revolution" to succeed. It did put a new class into power, but one which in the long run proved too difficult for the central Republican government to handle, resulting in the Aceh rebellion of 1953.

The communist element in these revolutionary actions is the least understood, partly because the people concerned were not supported by the Party. It had been so difficult for any party structures to survive the decades of Dutch and Japanese repression that individuals and small cells appeared everywhere in 1945, believing that they acted in the interests of communism. In the western part of Pekalongan Residency (Central Java), such a group had continued the tradition of the "Illegal PKI" to the best of its ability, carrying out some sabotage against the Japanese and preparing for their defeat. Though only a handful of men, they steered the action committee which coordinated the ousting of the *Pangreh Praja* and eventually took over the Residency capital itself for a few days in December. In a similar way, a small group of communist veterans in North Sumatra were able to guide the chaotic youth bands around Medan for a time in a social revolutionary direction, and even to exercise a guiding hand on the Islamic revolutionaries of Aceh. These few individuals had such disproportionate influence because they offered legitimation and further direction to the angry popular mood. However, in none of these revolutionary outbursts did the Left stay in power for more than a few weeks. The reasons were that their enemies — the Republican army apparatus, sometimes assisted by modernist Muslim forces — were too strong, that their presumed friends in the central Government failed to support them, and that they lacked any organised popular base.

The urban intellectuals who were the national-level leaders of the Left were at best embarrassed by these "social revolutions". Amir Sjarifuddin, who was appointed from a Japanese prison to Sukarno's first cabinet and became the strong man of the succeeding four cabinets (November 1945–January 1948), washed his hands of the "Illegal PKI" radicals of Pekalongan who looked to him as their leader. In East Sumatra, he campaigned vigorously and with some success against the "social revolution", arguing that "as a Marxist ... I want an egalitarian society with fair distribution. But every theoretician of revolution must accept that that aspiration must be attained in stages".[40] The reason for this stance was less that he and the other Marxist intellectuals were remote from popular aspirations (although they may have been) than that they were playing the same game as the local social revolutionaries for higher national stakes. That game was not the forming of an organised mass base, for which the communists were badly placed in 1945, but the direct capturing of the revolution from within by making use of their revolutionary credentials at an extraordinarily favourable moment. For Amir, this meant *diplomasi* with the Allies to prevent any external attack on the Republic, while doing his utmost to strengthen his position in the government and especially in the Army where control of the revolution would finally be decided.

The strength of the revolutionary process is that it produces such bewildering change that leadership can be assumed by wholly unrepresentative radical intellectuals who had been outsiders until the day before. Such men were the Marxists who had opposed the Japanese or held aloof from them. Because of this, they became in the first months of independence the heroes of the young activists who wanted a complete break with the Japanese. With the arrival of Allied forces, even their rivals who had cooperated with the Japanese could see that men with "anti-fascist" records were indispensable. Sjahrir and Amir Sjarifuddin were given a free hand in October 1945 to "democratise" government by making the Central National Committee (KNIP) a provisional legislature, whose functions between sessions would be exercised by a working committee chosen by themselves. On 14 November, they formed a cabinet responsible not to the president (as provided in the Constitution) but to the KNIP, themselves holding the key portfolios of foreign affairs, interior and defence. The initiative in the capital was so much in the hands of these two men that they might have chosen to dispense with Sukarno as president; but two young Sumatran intellectuals could not afford to do without the massive popularity of Sukarno in Central and East Java. The only serious challenger as president was another Sumatran, Tan Malaka, a veteran "national communist" whose writings of the 1920s had given him a wide following, and who reappeared in Jakarta in August 1945 after decades of shadowy underground existence. However, after meeting him, Sjahrir came to distrust Tan Malaka as irresponsibly leftist, while Amir opposed him as an alleged "Trotskyist" who had broken with Moscow. An alliance was therefore struck with Sukarno. Initially, he was a passive "parliamentary" president suffering from his pro-Japanese image, but during each subsequent crisis of the Sjahrir-Amir government, he became more powerful as a bridge to mass support.

In the jockeying for power at the national level in the Republic, the conflict between *perjuangan* (struggle) ideals and *diplomasi* reality was the most powerful weapon. As we have seen, none of the national-level leaders, including Tan Malaka, gave any support to *perjuangan* in practice when it meant social dislocation within the Republic. All (with the possible exception of Tan Malaka, who was never put to the test) accepted when in government the need for negotiating with the Allies. But the euphoria marking the early months of total independence, improvised government and spontaneous revolution was such that every subsequent compromise was highly unpopular with the armed youth who provided the muscle of the revolution. Sjahrir and Amir had profited from the desire for *perjuangan* against the Japanese. Now it was Tan Malaka who became the spokesman for *perjuangan* against the compromises Sjahrir and Amir had to make with the Dutch. Tan Malaka was arrested in March 1946 and many of his political allies were arrested on 3 July. The cabinet was steadily enlarged in an attempt to increase its support, seducing some modernising intellectuals of the Muslim and nationalist parties (MASJUMI and PNI) away from the opposition. Sjahrir himself, as the man most closely identified with *diplomasi*, was eventually sacrificed in June 1947. Amir Sjarifuddin now carried on the same policies with an even broader cabinet. However, it was Sukarno, who had successfully identified himself in the public eye with *perjuangan* while backing the *diplomasi* government at each crisis, who was now in the most strategic position. When Amir in turn was forced to resign in January 1948 because of the unpopularity of his diplomatic concessions, Sukarno was able to appoint a presidential cabinet with Hatta as Prime Minister. Amir's controversial tenure of the defence portfolio, where he had striven since 1945 to make the army more responsive to left-wing control, was ended. In disgust, the communist parties went for the first time into opposition. The policy of capturing the revolution from within appeared to have failed.

Whether it could have succeeded will long be debated by revolutionary theorists. As in 1965, the strategy appeared extraordinarily close to fulfilment. Subsequent PKI analysis attacked Amir for his "very important error ... that the cabinet resigned voluntarily, without offering any resistance whatever".[41] What is certain is that the alternative policy of attempting to acquire a mass base with which to attack the "bourgeois" leadership was a far more complete and disastrous failure. Once again, as in 1926, the PKI found itself pushed by its own rhetoric and by pressures from below into an armed struggle for which it was not ready. Also, as in 1926, Moscow probably opposed the communist rising, although the Soviet contribution to the Cold War — the "two-camp" doctrine which had replaced the conciliatory "common front against fascism" by early 1948 — helped to polarise Indonesian politics to a point where a clash was inevitable.

In his time as Defence Minister, Amir Sjarifuddin had built some support among regular Army units, as well as a loyal leftist force in the PESINDO youth movement. This was not enough to balance the hostility the majority of Japanese-trained officers felt towards him for his "antifascist" stand and his attempt to politicise the Army. When PESINDO began the communist revolt in Madiun on 15 September 1948 and the leading communists felt obliged to join it, the government of Sukarno and Hatta threw against them all the forces it could muster. By the end of November, the last communist forces had been hunted down. Most significant PKI leaders including Amir were executed the following month. Their belated attempt to mobilise the peasants of Java had been no more successful. The short period of communist control of some rural areas appeared to be remembered as a time of confusion and bloodshed rather than of developing reliable rural cadres. In any case, the defeat of the communist forces which had been a mainstay of government for the first two years of the revolution made it unlikely that any fundamental restructuring of Indonesian society would take place.

The Victory of the Republic

The Dutch response to the revolutionary Republic was a policy of federalism emphasising minority interests. The Republic had been able to form effective governments only in Java and Sumatra. The "national" politics described above took place in Java, where the Republic had moved its capital to Yogyakarta in January 1946 as the Allies became too strong in Jakarta. The autonomous revolutions which had taken place in each Residency of Sumatra gradually began to be coordinated with Yogyakarta during 1946. In Borneo and the East, the Allies, represented by Australian troops, had arrived before any Republican authority could be established, and they proceeded to pass authority to the Dutch according to plan. Since the British were unwilling and the Dutch militarily were unable to move beyond their seven urban enclaves in Java and Sumatra, there was no alternative for the Dutch than to use the Outer Islands as a base to surround the Republican stronghold. Once they had accepted the painful reality that some form of independence would have to be conceded, the Dutch therefore aimed at a federal "United States of Indonesia", the diversity of which would provide a continuing role for a Dutch "referee". A host of semi-autonomous federal bodies were developed in the very fragmented area under Dutch control, but they failed to conceal the strong arm of the Dutch holding the whole structure together. The culmination of this policy was the State of East Indonesia (NIT), established in December 1946 to embrace all the communities of eastern Indonesia except New Guinea.

Meanwhile, under strong British and American pressure, the Dutch negotiated the Linggajati Agreement (12 November 1946) with the Republic, whereby the two sides would work together to create a United States of Indonesia whose three constituents would be the Republic (Java and Sumatra), Borneo, and the East. Neither side was happy with this compromise, and the Dutch were particularly frustrated to be making no progress politically at a time when their military forces grew stronger. On 20 July 1947, the Dutch launched swift military action to occupy the wealthiest parts of Java and Sumatra, which were also the homes of potentially anti-Javanese ethnic groups — notably the Sundanese, the Madurese and the Malays of East Sumatra. Republican forces retreated, and the Dutch set about extending the federal idea by the erection of further states there. The most important was Pasundan, occupying the Sundanese-speaking area of West Java. Instead of the federal model appealing to Republicans, however, pro-Republican sentiment gradually took over the federal states, which knew that Dutch concessions to them had been won by the struggle of the Republic. As a concept, federalism made a great deal of sense for a country as large and diverse as Indonesia, but the fact that the Dutch had backed it, and backed it unsuccessfully, made it a dirty word for independent Indonesia (see Chapter 11).

Frustrated by the steady erosion of their position even in Dutch-occupied areas, the Dutch launched a second attack on 19 December 1948. This time, the objective was to eliminate the Republic by a direct attack on Yogyakarta and all other significant cities, hoping desperately that this *fait accompli* would vitiate the United Nations' attempts to pursue a negotiated solution. It was a suicidal move, which was to ensure the final frustration of Dutch plans. Despite the military success of taking all the cities of Java within a week, no Republican leaders went over to the Dutch side. Instead, anti-Dutch guerrilla activity commenced on a considerable scale, while the governments of NIT and Pasundan resigned in sympathy with the Republic. Holland was eventually forced by the pressure of the United Nations, in particular the United States, to reopen negotiations with the Republican leaders they had captured, and eventually to restore them to power in Yogyakarta on 6 July 1949. With this, the moral victory of the Republic seemed complete. Although a Federal Indonesian Republic (RIS) was duly formed under United Nations auspices in December 1949, its federal components were all dissolved into the unitary Republic within eight months. With appropriate symbolism, the date chosen for the final destruction of federalism was 17 August 1950, while the date on which sovereignty was formally transferred from the Dutch to the RIS was almost forgotten.

The period when the Dutch controlled all the Republican cities (December 1948–July 1949) is known in Indonesia as the "guerrilla period". The civilian leaders of the Republic had allowed themselves (or so it seemed to the military) to be captured by Dutch paratroops despite Sukarno's constant promises to fight to the bitter end. Leadership of the guerrilla struggle was therefore contested between the three elements which had most effectively organised armed support — the Army, the Muslims and the communists. Since the orthodox communists were still reeling from their defeat at Madiun, Tan Malaka renewed his bid for ideological leadership of the revolution, but he was killed on military orders in February 1949. A separate Islamic army known as Darul Islam also clashed frequently with other units in West Java, and remained a thorn in the side of the Republic for years after the Dutch had departed. Yet it

Indonesia: Revolution without Socialism

Plate 1.4 General Sudirman being sworn in as Army Commander by Sukarno, with Premier Sjahrir watching.

was the official Republican Army who pre-eminently "felt themselves to be boss" during the guerrilla period.[42]

Because the Japanese-trained officers were all so young and inexperienced in higher staff functions, the Army had faced leadership difficulties ever since 1945. In attempting to set up a general staff in October 1945, the Republican leaders had turned to a small group of officers trained in the pre-war Dutch colonial army (KNIL). Urip Sumohardjo, who had been a KNIL major, was made General and Chief-of-Staff, while a number of younger and better-educated officers like A.H. Nasution filled the major staff positions. Meanwhile, the Japanese-trained officers, who had not been taught to accept orders from civilian politicians, were sorting out their own leadership. Their choice for Commander fell in November on a former PETA battalion commander and Muhammadiah teacher, Sudirman, aged only 30. It was not until six weeks later that Amir as Defence Minister and Sudirman as Commander accepted the legitimacy of each other's positions, with obvious reluctance on both sides (see Plate 1.4). Sudirman did, however, establish a good working

Plate 1.5 Amir Sjarifuddin, as Defence Minister, addressing a meeting of the provsional parliament (KNIP) at Malang, with Prime Minister Sjahrir seated beside him.

relationship with Urip, 25 years his senior, and deferred to him on technical questions of supply and organisation.

Sudirman and his ex-PETA colleagues were among the more consistent supporters of *perjuangan*, and bitterly distrustful of the compromises Dutch-educated civilians kept making with the Dutch. The "guerrilla period" confirmed that suspicion, while underlining the army's image of itself as the true saviour of the Republic working in harmony with the rural masses. When the Republic was restored to Yogyakarta, Sudirman made no secret of his great reluctance to leave his guerrilla headquarters and embrace Sukarno again as President.

There seems little doubt that if Sudirman had lived, he would have presented an immediate threat to civilian control of the independent Republic. However, he was mortally ill in 1949 and his colleague Urip was already dead, the Commander attributing both ailments to grief caused by the inconstancy of the civilian leadership. At the level of the Residency, the military continued to wield enormous power which civilians could do nothing to override. At the centre, however, there was a long breathing

Plate 1.6 Communist leaders in 1948, including Musso (left) and Amir Sjarifuddin (4th left).

space for civilian leadership while the young officers gained experience and developed some unity of action among themselves.

The Revolutionary Path to Independence

The major achievement of the Indonesian revolution was the creation of a united nation with an assured sense of its own identity and significance. The national idea had by 1950 become an irresistible myth, sanctified by the blood sacrificed for it. Subsequent challenges would be made only in the context of a sovereign, united Indonesia, by dissidents with their own distinct sense of the goal for which the revolutionary struggle had been fought. Nationalism acquired a moral urgency which would create problems both for Indonesians who sought a pragmatic process of nation-building, and for some of the country's neighbours.

The revolution had begun as a series of autonomous but parallel uprisings in a dozen parts of the archipelago. These sought to find each other, and succeeded in eliminating most of the barriers that impeded a fuller union — federal state structures, traditional rajas and even separate ethnic nationalisms. What bound the country together positively, however, were ideas and sentiment rather than political institutions. Because the contest between *diplomasi* and *perjuangan* had ended in a draw through United Nations intervention, none of the various elements which made up the revolutionary struggle had succeeded in making it fully their own. On the surface, it appeared as though the Dutch-educated nationalist politicians had emerged victorious. They dominated the politics of the 1950s, occupied cabinet posts and distributed government positions to their colleagues through the patronage system. Yet the basis for their power was far from strong. The weakness of an indigenous middle class, accentuated by the instability of the 1940s, made the politicians heavily dependent on the state they had themselves created. Their political parties had not been required to mobilise for elections; they possessed few economic resources except the patronage which power alone conveyed; they tended to flourish by identifying with a particular cultural stream rather than by mobilising reliable cadres. Despite its decimation in 1948, the PKI quickly proved itself again the strongest party in organisational terms, although — as was demonstrated again in 1965 — its supporters too were less than reliable in a contest against the apparatus and ideology of the state.

Nor was the Indonesian bureaucracy the integrated professional force it was in some former British colonies. Having had such an ambiguous role under the Dutch, it was much attacked in the 1940s for the "feudal" attributes which lingered around it. In principle, its scope was enormously expanded by the victory of the revolution. A uniform bureaucratic structure now covered the whole country. Because government position was now seen as the reward for an earlier anti-government stance, bureaucratic numbers swelled enormously — about 2.8 million were estimated to be employed by the Central Government in 1953. The system of patronage brought the morale of the administrative corps to a low ebb. Towards the people they governed, the administrators preserved much of the extraordinary power they had held in the past, but they seemed powerless to protect themselves against constant intervention from political and military power-holders. It was the Army which was institutionally strongest by the end of the revolution, though as we have seen, it was not until 1966 that the Army became unified enough to take and keep power at the national level.

There remains Islam — a permanent source of ideas and leadership outside the government's power to control. Since independence, as for centuries before, it has acted as a vital focus of opposition rather than as a basis for state power. In the 1950s, it appeared as if there was a natural alliance of interests between Islam and the embryonic middle class whose major sources of strength were the Outer Islands. In the first great crisis of the post-revolutionary Republic, however, the alliance of the Army, PKI and Sukarno — all predominantly based in Java — proved too strong for that fragile alliance. The crushing of the Outer Island rebellions of 1953–1958, the banning of the MASJUMI party, the transition to Guided Democracy in 1959, and the gradual unification of the Army on a more Javanese base than previously, were all part of a process which moved Indonesia still further away from a path which might have led to the strengthening of these middle-class elements.[43]

The result was neither socialism nor capitalism but a system in which the state itself dominated the formation of capital and the crucial relationships with foreign economic enterprise (especially in oil). The revolutionary experience had weakened or broken most of the political, administrative or economic institutions of pre-war Indonesia. The legal system became a less reliable safeguard for investment than political patronage. In seeking to characterise this new type of state, political analysts used such terms as "bureaucratic polity", "neo-traditional" and "neo-patrimonial" — the last referring to Max Weber's "patrimonialism" where the ruling power is exercised personally and intense competition occurs between court factions for access to the spoils of office.[44] While none of these labels was entirely satisfactory, each sought to explain the enormous economic predominance of the nation's capital and (in 1959–1998) the presidency, and the rivalry of military/political or military/bureaucratic factions for access to the wealth derived from foreign, Chinese or government investment. The pursuit of the heirs of colonial power in Indonesia did not, in other words, lead to a single dominant "class" in the Marxist sense. It did lead to a remarkably cohesive, expanding, urban elite which was firmly Indonesian in identity even while drawn from more than 20 diverse ethnic backgrounds. Some of the values of this elite derived from the colonial and pre-colonial past, but its confidence and cohesiveness were the fruit of its successful anti-colonial revolution. It believed in Indonesia, distrusted the machinations of outside powers, yet was essentially cosmopolitan in its love for the verbal play of different languages and cultures. If it did not bring the golden age of prosperity and justice of which Sukarno dreamt, it undoubtedly wrought a nation with a profound sense of unity and purpose out of the world's largest and most diverse archipelago.

CHAPTER 2

The Late Death of Slavery[1]

Slavery in Southeast Asia is not a remote historical phenomenon. Laws certainly have prohibited private ownership of persons for a century or more, yet in more remote hills and islands of the region, one still encounters people who admit to being slaves or the children of slaves. Much more widespread are people who work without payment for a patron to whom they feel bound — by tradition, by monetary debt, in return for past favours or protection. The centrality of such relations of obligation in Southeast Asian social structure lends importance to any investigation of slavery but also renders it sensitive and problematic. The pejorative connotations given to the term "slavery" by liberal and Marxist discourse remain, even though the clear-eyed recent literature[2] has made abundantly clear that the conjunction between slavery and periods of economic and intellectual progress in most cultures was not accidental. It is difficult to use the term without appearing to denigrate Southeast Asian cultural traditions which still have force and value.

Some Southeast Asian scholars[3] have opted to avoid using such a powerful comparative concept at least until the indigenous social realities are better understood. There are a number of problems with this position. First, slavery was one of the most important means of interaction between ethno-linguistic groups. A Visayan woman of the 18th century, for example, might have been taken captive by a Samal raider from Balangingi, sold by him to a Tausug dealer in Sulu, and resold to a Bugis trader who took her to the great emporium of Batavia, where she was sold to a Dutch or Chinese merchant who may have had children by her and eventually freed her. Less dramatically, stronger lowland communities everywhere incorporated men and women from divided hill tribes through capture and temporary slavery. One group's perception of these

Plate 2.1 A woman of East Sumba still regarded as a slave at the time of this 1932 photograph.

transactions may have differed from another's, but the historian has need of terminology which is outside any particular culture.

Second, a refusal to use a broadly comparative term is often based on an association-laden stereotype rather than a clear definition. Recent work by Finley, Davis, and Patterson has certainly reemphasised the extraordinary diversity of the social forms of slavery, including the exceptional power exerted by some eunuchs and other royal slaves. The slave always represents a paradox: he is a commodity and yet human, exploited and yet loyal, inferior and yet intimate. That paradox is nowhere clearer than in Southeast Asia, and we learn more from confronting it than from trying to explain it away. Finally, the growing literature on slavery and on Southeast Asia have need of each other. To the great pioneer of the cross-cultural study of slavery, H.J. Nieboer, and to some of his precursors such as Montesquieu, La Loubère, and Marini,[4] it was apparent that Southeast Asian societies offered important evidence on the origins and variations of slavery, particularly in a "mild", domestic form. Since Nieboer, none of the great theorists of slavery have had access to the early Dutch ethnographic literature on Indonesia, and Southeast Asian specialists have been reluctant to help them by synthesising the rich source material on this subject. In consequence, Southeast Asia remains the weakest area in a survey as comprehensive as Patterson's remarkable book *Slavery and Social Death*.

In a recent study of the subject,[5] I therefore opted to retain the word "slave" for a saleable person regarded as the property of another, of explicitly lower social status, and performing compulsory labour. At the same time, it is necessary to have a broader term, for which I use "bondage" to cover the related but more extensive system of obligation to labour for a patron without direct recompense. A number of features of Southeast Asia in general, and of Indonesia in particular, determined the character of bondage at least during the four centuries before 1900.

First, a relatively low population density made control of population always more important than control of land. Second, vertical bonding was the crucial system of social organisation. Its centrality was emphasised, for example, by the necessity of using pronouns expressing superiority or inferiority in order to establish a comfortable and intimate pattern of speech. In the languages of the region, the most common first-person pronoun is frequently the word for slave: *saya* in Malay or *kawula* in Javanese.

Third, debt was important as a source of bondage, including forms which should be considered slavery. Indonesian texts often describe the routes which led to slavery: inheritance, incapacity to pay one's debts, capture in war, or condemnation by a court. Except for capture in war, all could be interpreted as a form of debt, since most crimes were punished by fines and the non-payment of these fines led to enslavement. While some societies distinguished between debt bondsmen and captured slaves, most did not. Europeans emphasised this distinction in a quest to identify an "acceptable" form of bondage.

Fourth, a concept of wage labour was absent until quite recent times. Of seven examples of "wage rates" paid by Europeans in the great cities of Southeast Asia in the 16th and 17th centuries, six of them varied between 11 and 600 times the value of a daily rice ration. The seventh was only twice this basic subsistence rate, but it was a food allowance paid by the Portuguese to their own slaves.[6] The other cases appear all to have been very high rates paid to masters for the privilege of hiring their bondsmen. A Persian traveller pointed to a common feature of Muslim Aceh, in northern Sumatra, and Buddhist Siam: "It is their custom to rent slaves. They pay the slave a sum of money, which he gives to his master, and then they use the slave that day for whatever work they wish".[7] The only sources of free wage labour for several centuries were Chinese settlers or Indian sailors. Indigenous Indonesians, at least in the towns, identified manual labour with servility and were very reluctant to perform it for anyone not regarded as their legitimate lord.[8] "Free" wage labour became important in Java in the 19th century, in step with overpopulation and landlessness,[9] but elsewhere not until the 20th.

Finally, the "mild" character of Southeast Asian "slavery" was often remarked by early European sources. Since a slave could be beaten, sold, or sacrificed for a ritual need — at least in Borneo, Sulawesi, and Nias — the word "mild" hardly seems appropriate. More to the point was the lack of strict legal definition of slave status (except under exceptionally strong Indian, Islamic, or European influence) or of a strong state anxious to enforce it. The Indonesian words used (*hamba, kawula, ata, hulun*) could be variously defined as "slave", "subject", or "retainer", because the imperative question was whose bondsman one was rather than the precise legal quality of that bondage. Consequently, the slaves most fully assimilated into a household were free to seek their own livelihood, to marry, and to possess their own houses, property, and other slaves.

Even European slave owners in Indonesia gradually adapted themselves to a type of slavery more flexible than their own. Two very practical considerations motivated them to do so: Indonesian slaves had a reputation for revenging themselves violently against masters who humiliated them, and before the rise of the modern state, it was relatively easy to flee from an oppressive master. Pierre-Yves Manguin cited the complaint of one of the first European masters of Southeast Asian slaves, a Portuguese captain of Malacca: "Malacca is a place like no other ... One has to take care of everything: of the slave, to rear his son; to provide him with clothes for his wife and for himself; one has to pamper him so that he does not run away".[10]

Examples could be found in the literature of the 17th and 18th centuries of people described as slaves filling almost every conceivable function. They included agriculturalists, miners, traders large and small, textile workers, domestics, concubines, prostitutes, construction workers, dock labourers, soldiers, surgeons, and entertainers. There are many instances of captured or bought slaves being put to work on the land: bought eastern Indonesians worked the pepper estates of southern Borneo, bought Indians cultivated rice in Aceh, and captured Filipinos produced the food crops of Sulu. In the absence of centrally managed latifundia, however, the slave character of these agriculturalists quickly dissolved with the second generation into a kind of serfdom or sharecropping.[11] In the affluent trading cities of the 16th century, bondage retained its servile and saleable character longer, with most if not all urban labour bonded either to a powerful individual or to the king.

The most characteristic role of the slave in Southeast Asia was as a retainer of an urban aristocrat. Numerous sources of the 16th and 17th centuries attest the importance for those of high status to be surrounded whenever they went out by a retinue of umbrella carriers, betel carriers, guards, and other followers. The upper class invested in slaves predominantly for status, but also for protection — slaves were armed — and to assist their productive enterprises in trade, textile manufacture, and agriculture. Able slaves were trusted with great responsibilities, and some rose to become ministers or local governors.

The Dutch East India Company, which by the second half of the 17th century dominated the long-distance trade of the archipelago, introduced a new rigidity into the concept of slavery. The Dutch brought with them a legally enforced concept of the slave as servile outsider which was only partially modified by the more flexible pattern of bondage prevailing in the archipelago. Slaves, mostly of Balinese, Bugis, and other eastern Indonesian origin, became the indispensable labour source of all the Dutch enclave cities, with 25,000 or more in Batavia alone over most of the period 1680–1770.[12] The only true latifundia in the region were introduced by the Dutch Company in the tiny Banda Islands, which produced all the world's nutmeg until the monopoly was broken in the mid-18th century. Of the 3,842 inhabitants of the islands in 1638, 2,190 were slaves (835 men, 881 women, and 474 children), and the nutmeg was grown and harvested entirely with their labour.[13]

Before turning to the decline of slavery, it will be useful to give some indications of the dimensions of its most visible and measurable aspect: the movement of slaves between regions or across ethno-linguistic boundaries. The largest such movements are probably the hardest on which to find concrete data: those whereby stateless hill peoples such as the Orang Asli of Malaya,[14] the Batak of Sumatra,[15] the Toraja of Sulawesi, and various Dayak groups of Borneo lost population through capture or sale to the more powerful Islamic coastal peoples adjacent to them. It is probable that the majority of the urban population of such flourishing commercial centres as Malacca, Aceh, Banten, Patani, and Makasar in the 16th and 17th centuries were unfree people brought there as captives, in the retinue of the powerful men who settled there, or as cargo in commercial voyages. This was certainly the case with the Dutch enclaves of Batavia, Malacca (after 1641) and Makasar (after 1669).[16]

H.G. Schulte Nordholt[17] estimated that Bali exported 100,000 of its people, primarily to Dutch Batavia, in the period 1620–1830. Bugis and Makasar slaves from southern Sulawesi were being taken to Batavia at the rate of about 200 a year in the late 17th century and about 3,000 a year in the middle of the 18th. In the whole period of this trade, 1660 to 1810, southern Sulawesi must have lost over 100,000 of its people. The small island of Nias was even more profligate with its people, losing about 0.5 per cent each year as slaves, or 20 per cent in total for the period 1790–1830.[18] In the few decades before 1905, when the slave trade was making heavy inroads on the Sa'dan Toraja population of Sulawesi, the region may have lost 10–15 per cent of its population.[19]

The Decline of Slavery

The more we know about 19th-century slavery, especially in Southeast Asia, the less appropriate it seems to refer to its "abolition" by enlightened legislation. Certainly that legislation under pressure from European reformers ended overt slaveholding in the towns, removed legal sanctions, and discouraged the trade. But slavery had already become much less important long before it was legally abolished, and it survived long after the legislation. More important factors in the decline of slavery were profound but gradual changes in the nature of Indonesian society.

Impoverishment was undoubtedly one of these factors. Acquiring and maintaining slaves was expensive. It is no accident that slavery was most central an institution in societies at the peak of their urban florescence: classical Greece, imperial Rome, the Abbasid caliphate, the Italian city-states of the 14th and 15th centuries. In Southeast Asia too, slavery was most marked a feature of the social and economic system during the 16th and 17th centuries, when indigenous maritime cities were at their commercial peak. These cities were all in decline or total eclipse by the end of the 17th century. Dutch Batavia, which replaced them in many respects, including in the large-scale importation of slaves, was itself in decline a century later. Slaves ceased to be captured or bought on the same scale, and patrons encouraged their dependents to find their own livelihoods when they could no longer afford to maintain them. The growth of an impoverished population provided cheaper ways to acquire labour, particularly in Java. Crawfurd commented that "the numbers and servility of the population in Java have, among them, rendered slaves of little value".[20] Even Europeans, as soon as they gained a working relationship with the Indonesians around them, found they could acquire bonded labour more cheaply through debt bondage or corvée. A German in Semarang in 1772 was delighted to find he could buy a debt slave for only 25 rijksdaalders, whereas a "true" (i.e., exportable) slave would have cost him 150.[21]

The advance of two universalist religious systems, Islam and Christianity, also tended to restrict the scope of slavery. Both religions brought clearer legal concepts of the category of slave and opposed the sale of slaves to those of a different religion. When Malay legal codes incorporated from Islamic law different punishments for crimes involving slaves or free men, they tended to use the Arabic-derived term *abdi*, which implied a more precise slave category than the Malay *hamba*. Islam, even more explicitly than Christianity, forbade the enslavement of coreligionists. When in the 17th century, Islam spread to southern Sulawesi, where slavery was a central institution, this doctrine became a major point of conflict. The initial compromise, as recorded in a Bugis chronicle, was that "God would reward those who freed their [fellow Muslim] slaves" but that debt bondsmen should be defined as outside even this mild provision. When one zealous ruler of Bone tried to release all slaves in the name of Islam in the 1640s, he was overpowered by his neighbours.[22] Slavery remained a factor here as in other Muslim states, but the growing pressure of orthodoxy tended to redefine "true slaves" (*abdi*) as those taken from non-Islamic societies in the hills or in islands such as Nias, Bali, Sumba, and Flores. As such slaves became converted and assimilated, the quality of their bondage softened.

Dutch and English Christians had a narrower and more negative concept of slavery. They preferred not to Christianise their slaves, except in the case of favoured concubines, because this allowed them to retain the social distance they felt appropriate on grounds of both race and status. Moreover, there was always pressure to free Christian slaves, and in 1770, this became a legal requirement for the Dutch in the East Indies. In practice, the majority of slaves of the Dutch and the English eventually assimilated to Islam rather than to Christianity.

Finally, the most fundamental reason for the decline of slavery was the rise in power of the absolutist state. Divided or stateless regions readily exported labour, but the strongest states never did so. Southern Sulawesi, for example, was one of the region's greatest providers of slaves in the 16th century and again in the 18th, when it was divided into numerous competitive states. But between 1610–1669, when the Sultans of Makasar succeeded in unifying the Makasar and Bugis states under their control, they forbade the sale of their subjects to outsiders. In general, it has been shown for Southeast Asia as for Europe that an increase in the power of the king in relation to the nobility brought about a decline of private slavery in favour of direct obligations to the Crown. Akin Rabibhadana[23] has shown this for Siam, as Lieberman[24] has for Burma. It is equally true for Aceh. In the 19th century, the relentless growth in power of the colonial state was undoubtedly the most important reason for the retreat of the institution of slavery.

The United Kingdom banned the traffic in slaves in 1807 and imposed a similar ban at the Congress of Vienna in 1815. In consequence, the restored kingdom of the Netherlands also prohibited the slave trade throughout its colonies in 1818. Nevertheless, the purchase of slaves from Bali, Nias, the Batak area of Sumatra, Flores, Timor, and the slave-raiding centre of Sulu continued. In fact, the impossibility of buying slaves from older established areas now under colonial control increased the traffic in many of these still independent corners of Indonesia. The slave exports of Nias peaked after the ban of 1807, supplying the Dutch ports of Padang and Priaman, British Bengkulen and Penang, and Aceh with labourers and the Chinese population of the colonial cities with wives.[25] Batak slaves from the east coast of Sumatra, as well as Balinese, Bugis, and east Indonesians, were also exported in large numbers to supply Penang and Singapore, especially the overwhelmingly male Chinese population.[26]

The Dutch justified their continuing purchase of Nias slaves up to the 1840s by claiming them to be *pandelingen* (debt bondsmen).

> The Dutch gravely talk of "debtors", of "sending to Nias for debtors". But here [Nias] things go by their right names. It is selling slaves. They are brought down to the beach corded, and while the trade is going on, are bound to a post and on board are fettered, and carried to a foreign land. I have never yet met with any one who has seen these people return to their native land, or who has known them to be liberated.[27]

The British turned a blind eye to the importation of the predominantly female slaves, since it

> was of immense advantage in procuring a female population for Penang ... the condition of the slaves who were brought to the British Settlements was materially improved, and ... they contributed so much to the happiness of the male population and the general prosperity of the settlement.[28]

Most of this traffic was conducted in small Chinese or Indonesian craft. The only large-scale shippers of Indonesian slaves after 1820 were French and other vessels supplying the sugar planters of Mauritius and Reunion. Deprived of older sources of supply in India and Africa, these islands took over the role of Batavia as principal destinations for slaves from Bali and Nias between 1815 and 1830. In the latter year, the French began seriously to discourage the importation, which had taken place clandestinely through their colony of Reunion. Only when slavery itself was finally abolished in Mauritius in 1835 and Reunion in 1848 did the flow of Indonesian slaves cease entirely.[29]

In the second half of the 19th century, therefore, the slave trade was continued only in small Indonesian *prahu*, which might carry a handful of Florenese or Sumbanese to Lombok or Bima, of Batak or Nias to the Straits Settlements or Aceh, of Balinese to the neighbouring islands or to Singapore. Local Dutch authorities often used the official rhetoric of horror at this small-scale trade as the justification for a forward step against those Indonesian rulers who remained independent. Though they were less purist once they were in control, the trade retreated steadily as Dutch power advanced.

Colonial Labour Needs

The Dutch East India Company had been the largest slave owner in the archipelago in the 17th and 18th centuries. Its successor in the 19th century, the government of Netherlands India, had far more extensive needs for labour. Having denied itself the option of continuing to buy slaves, it nevertheless continued for some time to recruit its labour in ways which differed only in details from the old ones. We have seen how Nias slaves were redefined as debtors but bought through exactly the same channels as before, for use in mining, port labour, and domestic service on Sumatra's west coast. In the same way, the Dutch government in Java returned to traditional sources of Balinese slaves in 1826 when it needed manpower to help fight the Javanese rebel Diponegoro. An agreement was made to pay the raja of Badung, in southern Bali, five Spanish dollars for every "recruit" delivered to the Dutch through traditional slave dealers. About 400 such involuntary recruits were delivered to Dutch ships at Kuta each year between 1827 and the end of the Java War in 1830. The force required to take these men away from their homes was most graphically illustrated in 1828, when 85 Balinese "recruits" rebelled on board the Dutch warship *Anna Palowna*, leading to the deaths of 72 of them as well as of two Dutch soldiers.[30]

The primary source of unpaid labour for the colonial government in the 19th century, however, was corvée. In the period 1830–1860, when the system was at its peak, the Dutch required the Javanese to labour for up to two-fifths of their time on export crops of Dutch choosing. This was the *cultuurstelsel* (cultivation system), probably the most systematic exploitation of labour as tribute ever imposed by a colonial power. Several million Javanese each year were mobilised through their chiefs to cultivate coffee, sugar, indigo, and other crops, delivered to Dutch overseers at such negligible costs that the sugar could compete with slave-produced sugar from the West Indies.[31]

Whereas the East India Company had been a private slave-owning corporation in a pluralistic archipelago, Netherlands India after 1830 was a state which claimed as a sovereign right the labour of its subjects. Having made the *cultuurstelsel* work so profitably for export crops, the colonial government found the use of corvée irresistible for all other public works.

> Government corvée (*herendiensten*), usually unpaid, was demanded for the construction and maintenance of roads, bridges, irrigation ditches, dams, weirs, canals, fortifications; for the building of houses for European and native officials, *pasangrahans* [rest houses for travelling officials], and post houses; for delivering mail and parcels in the interior; the transport of convicts; the guarding of public buildings and the houses of officials; the cutting of grass for the government post-horses; and the provision and maintenance of so-called freemen's horses, which spared the government the required expenditure for the post-horses; for the carriage of government travellers and goods; for the transport of the considerable quantity of copper coins which were received from the

land tax and the provision of the carts and draft animals. Corvée was, in a word, required to provide for all possible needs of the government and its servants. Indeed, it was often promoted to satisfy the whims, the vanity, the desires, and the ambition of officials.³²

Contemporary critics estimated that the effect of the *cultuurstelsel* was to increase the burden of corvée between ten and a hundredfold over the indigenous Javanese system and that about a quarter of total working time of all Javanese was occupied with it.³³

As opposition mounted to the *cultuurstelsel* from both idealistic reformers and private Dutch entrepreneurs who wanted a share of the action, the system was gradually dismantled, beginning in the 1860s. Forced labour was abandoned first for the crops for which it proved least profitable. For coffee, the most profitable, it was not finally terminated until 1919.³⁴ The first use of wage labour for public works occurred in the cities of Java in the liberal "spring" after 1848. From 1857, official policy provided that wage labour should be used for all public works, but this was not effective in rural areas for another half century.³⁵

As corvée was being abolished in Java, where desperate landless peasants first became available as cheap wage labour, the system was making its greatest gains in the outer islands of Sumatra, Borneo, Sulawesi, and the Lesser Sundas. In most of these areas, Dutch intervention had been minimal before 1870, but thereafter the rapid expansion of the infrastructure of a modern state required the building of roads, prisons, and public buildings all over the archipelago. Between 1870 and 1910, onerous labour obligations were imposed on diverse peoples, many of whom had never known anything of the kind, and resistance to these demands was responsible for many of the outbreaks of rebellion in this period. The epic poem *Hikayat Perang Sabil*, a clarion call to holy war against the Dutch in Aceh (northern Sumatra), complained bitterly that one day in seven had to be worked for the requirements of the hated Kompeni (the Dutch government). "Such are the laws they make up: women and men, chiefs and people, old and young, even small children and the sick — as soon as they are strong enough, make them come out".³⁶ Although these demands were modified in the 1920s, notably by allowing people to commute their labour obligation into a money tax, in the outer islands of Indonesia the Dutch could never do without corvée altogether.

Subjects obligated to labour for their colonial government were far cheaper and more abundant than the slaves of the former East India Company. Their only disadvantage was that they could not be sent far from home to open up the frontiers of the colony. For this purpose, the Netherlands Indian Government made use of convicts.

The Napoleonic ruler of Java, Daendels, ended mutilation such as the chopping off of a hand or a foot as a penal measure in the Dutch possessions. The English, who defeated Daendels in 1811, in turn repudiated the more Southeast Asian practice of condemning criminals to slavery. After the Dutch restoration, forced labour (*dwangarbeid*) became overwhelmingly dominant as a form of punishment for every type of crime. An 1828 decree regulating punishments in Netherlands India put into practice "the express will of the king, that forced labour should as far as possible replace all other punishments, so that the state could make use of the labour of the criminals".[37] Offenders in Java were sentenced to varying terms in one of four categories, in descending order of severity: a chain gang at a specified place outside Java; a chain gang somewhere in Java; labour without chains, either with or without payment, at a specified place outside Java; labour without chains in Java. A fifth category for prominent aristocratic rebels was simple banishment from Java.

The number of labourers made available by this system rose far beyond the 18th-century slaveholdings of the East India Company. In the 1850s, about 2,000 Indonesians in Java were sentenced to forced labour each year, for terms which averaged three to four years.[38] The numbers increased steadily, passing 4,000 in 1862 and 6,000 in 1865. At the beginning of 1866, there were 9,335 convict labourers in Netherlands India, of whom 3,692 were in chains (2,346 of them outside Java). Of the total, 622 died in captivity during the year, while about half were released and replaced by newly sentenced convicts.[39] In the period 1880–1900, the number of convict labourers appears to have reached its peak, averaging about 26,000 at any one time, of whom between a third and a half were available to be sent anywhere.[40]

The convicts sentenced to labour outside Java were particularly valuable to the colonial government for heavy work in dangerously disease-affected areas. The coal mines opened up in the 19th century relied heavily on convict labour. More than 400 convicts were working at the southern Borneo coal mines in the 1860s.[41] The much bigger mines at Ombilin in western Sumatra began to be exploited in 1892, and between

2,000–3,000 convicts were required for the mine and the railway which served it. Their health was appalling. In 1898, the Ombilin mines had an average work force of 2,453 convicts, of whom about 500 were always hospitalised with fevers or chest and eye problems, while 1,748 had to be evacuated because they were too ill to work.[42] In the 20th century, an increasing proportion of the Ombilin workforce comprised selected former convicts who had behaved well and were offered contracts as "free" labourers once their penal terms expired. Yet in 1922, there were still 4,822 convicts, now paid a small allowance, alongside 4,574 contract labourers at Ombilin.[43]

The other major employers of convicts sentenced to be sent away were the Dutch expeditionary forces. For the whole period 1873–1903, Dutch military resources were overextended in the attempt to conquer or contain Aceh, and the army constantly asked for more convict labour to build fortifications and railways and to carry supplies. Between 500 and 1,000 men were sent to Aceh in most of these years, and again they suffered heavily from illness. As against 625 convicts sent to Aceh in 1887, 57 died there, and 435 had to be evacuated because of illness.[44] There was a big build-up in 1898 for Van Heutsz's strategy to bring the war to an end. Almost 3,800 men were sent to Aceh in that year, consuming all the available convict labour and depleting the labour force in Ombilin.[45] After the submission of the major Acehnese resistance leaders in 1903, however, the supply of convict labour for the army there returned to about 700 per year for the remainder of the colonial period.[46]

These convicts far from home were the closest in function to earlier East India Company slaves, but they were by no means the most numerous source of unpaid labour. A far larger number of Indonesians, close to 100,000 per year in the second half of the 19th century, was sentenced at the lowest-level police courts (*politierol*), where the local Dutch official advised by Javanese subordinates gave quick, rough justice on the veranda of his residence at a twice-weekly sitting. Dutch officials in the field valued the system precisely because of its lack of formal safeguards. "Its defenders argued that the public exercise of arbitrary authority was important to the protection of Dutch interests and to the maintenance of a strong presence".[47] Anything could be construed as an offence against public order or the interests of Dutch and Javanese officials. Although the great majority of convictions were simply listed as "other offenses", those recorded included such items as "selling charms, 'insanity', sleeping under the trees, seduction, overtaking the Resident's carriage, and wizardry".[48] After 1866, when whipping was in principle (though not always in practice) abolished, forced labour for up to three months was the routine punishment for all *politierol* offenses. At any one time, almost as many of these short-term minor offenders were at work on local projects (around 15,000 on average in the 1880s) as there were long-term convicts condemned by higher courts.

The economic value of the convict labourers was the principal reason that the Indies government resisted attempts in The Hague to reform the system. In 1880, Batavia could still protest that it was unwise to carry out the reforms ordered 13 years earlier because of the need for labour on public works.[49] Even the long-debated new penal code which became effective in 1918 continued forced labour as the cornerstone of the penal system, though now with payment of a small allowance.[50]

The determination of liberal reformers in the years after 1860 to end the system of unpaid forced labour for the government had something to do with humanitarian ideals, but much also to do with the rising influence of private capital in Holland and its need for a different kind of labour system. Free wage labour was the goal of liberal rhetoric, but while wages were paid by private estates, a free labour market remained elusive. In Java, private European planters continued to use local headmen, as the government had, to force villagers to surrender their land and their labour to the sugar and coffee estates.[51] Outside Java, the new plantations opened up after 1870, notably in East Sumatra, and found it impossible to recruit local labour at the rates they were prepared to pay. A system of contracts quickly developed on the model of British indenture — the "new system of slavery"[52] — which took millions of Indians to labour on estates in the British colonies. Until 1900, the largest number of "contract coolies" came from China; thereafter the recruits from Java were far more numerous. By 1916, 150,000 Javanese were already at work on the tobacco and rubber estates of East Sumatra under three-year contracts.[53] In the pioneering phase of transforming the jungle into a vast tropical estate, these coolies suffered many of the horrors that had marked slavery in its cruelest form: transportation far from home, miserable health, unremitting toil, the constant threat of violence, the disruption of families, obligatory prostitution or concubinage for women, and no possibility of escape or redress from the actions of cruel overseers.[54] Of course, contract labour differed from slavery in that it was voluntary and temporary. Migrant workers were recruited in Java with substantial advances, which were often used to repay pressing debts or obligations there. Ideally, they had worked off this debt in time to be repatriated after three years, though a high percentage never succeeded in doing so. In one respect, however, the system was harsher than most Southeast Asian forms of slavery: there was no physical means of escape. The planters were supported by a strong, centralised colonial government which fined or imprisoned any coolie who attempted to flee. The whole plantation region resembled an outdoor prison, as its critics alleged. Although the welfare of coolies was far better protected by the 1920s, it was only in 1929, when the United States Congress voted to ban imports of tobacco produced under duress, that the penal sanction attached to labour contracts was abolished.

The Abolition of Slavery

Although the Netherlands banned the slave trade in 1818, it did not prohibit the ownership of slaves until 1860, long after Britain and France did so. Even then, the prohibition was interpreted as applying only to slaves owned by Europeans and Chinese in the areas under direct Dutch control. Despite the efforts of reformers in Holland, the 1860s were still marked by great hesitation regarding Indonesian-owned slaves in the outer islands. Not until 1874 did Batavia require that regional officials propose measures for liberating all the slaves under the direct authority of the colonial government and report the situation of slaves in indirectly ruled areas.

The governor of Sumatra's West Coast reported that it would cost 1.8 million guilders to buy the freedom of all those servants (presumably about 20,000) "who before 1860 would have been called slaves". Batavia characteristically refused to pay such a sum, but the local officials had nevertheless to persuade the Minangkabau elite that all their *kemanakan dibawah lutut* (literally "nephews below the knees") were now of free status as *kemanakan kandong*.[55] At the end of 1876, the Resident of the Minangkabau area reported optimistically that these former slaves were now admitted to village rituals and allowed to marry as free people, even though "the majority of them have continued to live with their former owners".[56] Elsewhere, Dutch officials held elaborate festivities to announce the liberation of slaves, whose owners were compensated at about 50 guilders per slave. At Jembrana (northern Bali) in 1877 and in Ternate (northern Moluccas) in 1879, for example, there were speeches, the reading of a proclamation, a ball at the palace, and entertainment for the people.[57]

Without such public fanfare, the officials undoubtedly feared that the "liberation" would be unnoticed by the population. In the northern Moluccas, after all, the Dutch had ruled for more than two centuries, and both sides had long accustomed themselves to circumventing official disapproval of slavery. In 1877, a new and zealous Resident reported that the Sultan of Tidore still expected an annual tribute of slaves from New Guinea, while the Sultan of Ternate sent his theoretically free subjects to serve as guarantees for his debts to the merchants of the town. These people worked for the merchants as virtual slaves.[58] Undoubtedly, it took more than proclamations to change the way people perceived these obligations, but some steps were at last being taken in the 1870s.

Where Dutch authority was less well established, the local officials did not even pretend to carry out the anti-slavery policy. The Assistant Resident of Sintang (West Borneo) pointed out that "according to the contracts the Dayaks are free, but the chiefs who signed these contracts have never understood these noble aims, or they would never have signed the contracts". Unless colonial authority was vastly strengthened, it would take more than a century of persuasion for the Dayak chiefs to accept the loss of their slaves. Moreover, most of the slaves "have no desire for their freedom", even if some of them were sacrificed at the burials of their chiefs.[59] In independent southern Bali, the Resident reported that even the most enlightened chiefs refused to consider giving up their slaves, no matter how gradually. The hundreds of slaves in their palaces were considered crucial to both their status and their wealth.[60] The government therefore accepted that nothing effective would be done. Similarly for the rajas of Sumba and Flores, "the possession of slaves is a question of 'to be or not to be', and their strength is in the number of their slaves". The Resident based in Kupang had given up his earlier attempts to buy the liberty of the slaves he encountered on tour, since new slaves could easily be created to replace them, and moreover, the slaves themselves tended to fear "that in buying them the 'Company' [the Dutch] will use them for still harder labour than they now suffer from".[61]

The slaves probably had good reason for this attitude. Corvée had for many Southeast Asians been more demanding than private slavery, particularly so when exacted by a government with the unprecedented power of that of Netherlands India. Reports on the situation of slaves continued to reach Batavia into the 20th century, and they made clear that slavery could only be ended as the whole social structure changed. Some of the reports pointed to the heart of the problem, like this one from northern Sulawesi in 1896:

> The slaves and debt slaves were not always attracted to their so-called freedom. They enjoyed certain rights: they performed no corvée and paid no tax — and this for the simple reason that they were considered not free to dispose of either their labour or their property. It has often happened that slaves refused to be made free [mardika]; that debt bondsmen, immediately after having been redeemed, again borrowed money from someone else and place themselves in debt bondage to him.[62]

When in eastern Lombok in 1902, the government took steps to buy out the last registered slaves, it found that the masters so identified with their slaves that they preferred to liberate them than to "sell them to the government" for a sum of money. The officials congratulated themselves on having saved the money, even though they appear to have realised that without it, a kind of bondage would continue:

> The bond between many masters and former slaves is undoubtedly not wholly broken after their freeing; they will in many cases continue to help each other when this is necessary and help is asked for, but when this occurs by free will on both sides no objection can be made to it.[63]

It was possible to abolish slavery only in the sense of denying it any legal validity in the eyes of the state. In reality, the bonds of obligation from one individual to another in Southeast Asia were slowly loosened over a period of more than a century. Three related processes were at work, in addition to formal legislation. First, the absolutist state became ever stronger and ever more intolerant that any agency but itself should demand from its subjects their money in taxes, their labour in corvée, or their service on the battlefield. Second, the spread of money, the growth of a national market, and above all the growing numbers of landless poor made wage labour cheaply and widely available. Finally, and most gradually, the spirit of individual liberty gained ground in people's minds.

These processes were still at work when the Dutch empire collapsed in 1942. Though greatly stimulated by Indonesian independence, they are not in sole command of the field today. The sense of obligation to serve a patron or a creditor, which was at the heart of the pre-colonial bondage system, still leaves its mark in many of the cultures which make up contemporary Indonesia.

CHAPTER 3

From Betel to Tobacco: The Modern Transformation

Southeast Asians appear to have been extensive users of mild narcotics throughout their recorded history. For all but the past century of this history, the betel quid, composed of areca nut, betel leaves, and lime, was the characteristic relaxant central to the agreeable social interaction that Southeast Asians valued. For thousands of years, the peoples of Southern Asia and Melanesia were inveterate chewers of betel, giving rise to the claim that it was the most widely used narcotic in human history.[1] In this region, most other narcotics began to be used as a part of the betel chew.

Cigarette smoking has almost completely replaced the chewing of betel among male Indonesians during the past century. According to a 1980 survey,[2] 85 per cent of adult Indonesian men smoked when they could afford it, although less than 1.5 per cent of Indonesian women did so. Women have abandoned the chewing of betel more slowly, presumably because cigarette-smoking was not deemed an appropriate substitute for their use. This article will examine the massive shift in Indonesian consumption as the major case study of tropical Asia in general. The implications of such a large-scale change for Indonesian health, expenditure patterns, and social and ritual interaction are of major importance.

Betel in Indonesian History

The three essential ingredients of the betel quid are all naturally available in Indonesia. Lime is readily obtained from crushed shells. The two plant elements are the seed or "nut" of the areca palm (*areca catechu*) and the fresh leaf of the betel vine (*piper betle*), which forms the wrapper for the quid. In eastern Indonesia and New Guinea, the fruit or pod of the *siriboa* variant of the betel vine is preferred to the leaf, and has the same chemical effect.[3] Areca and betel both appear to be native to the Indonesian Archipelago; this is indicated by the diversity of indigenous terms that are applied to them.

English	Malay	Aceh	Toba Batak	Low Javanese	Bali	Makasar	Bugis	Ternate
areca	pinang	pineung		jambe	banda	rappo	alossi	hena
betel	sirih	ranub	napuran	Suroh	chanang	leko'	ota	bido marau

The same diversity is to be found in the Philippines — Tagalog *bunga/ikmo*, Pampangan *luyos/sumat*; Visayan *bunga/mamon*. By contrast, the languages of India tend to use cognates of the words *supari* and *pan*,[4] suggesting a more recent introduction of the plants. Indian sources began to refer to betel-chewing only during the first four centuries of the Christian era, and therefore it is assumed that the precious plants were introduced from Southeast Asia during that period.[5]

In Southeast Asia, there is no indigenous evidence from such early periods, though Chinese references go as far back as a second-century BC description of betel-chewing in Vietnam.[6] By the Tang period, we have numerous Chinese references to the use and export of areca from the Indonesian area.[7] Chau Ju-kua noted that in 12th-century Po-ni (Brunei?), betel was prominent in both marriage ritual and court ceremonial,[8] while Ma Huan reported of Java in the early 15th century:

> Men and women take areca-nut and betel-leaf, and mix them with lime, made from clam-shells; their mouths are never without this mixture ... When they receive passing guests, they entertain them, not with tea, but only with areca-nut.[9]

The fact that the Chinese term for areca since at least Tang times, *pin-lang*, derives from Malay *pinang* suggests that the area then dominated by Malay-speaking Sriwijaya (Sumatra, Malayan Peninsula, western Borneo) was the major source of this commodity. On the other hand, the more isolated upland peoples of the Peninsula (as distinct from coastal Malays) until recently used betel sparingly if at all, whereas the Negritos of northern Luzon in the 16th century were even more addicted to it than were lowlanders.[10] This tends to confirm the linguistic evidence that it is to the islands rather than the mainland of Southeast Asia that we should look for the sources from which areca and betel spread.

By the 16th and 17th centuries, when we have much fuller descriptions, the chewing of betel was established virtually everywhere in tropical Asia as the indispensable politeness to be offered a guest in court or village, as a central ritual symbol, as digestive, dentifrice, and mouth freshener, and as the relaxant that made life more bearable — especially when travelling, warring, or otherwise short of food.

The earliest European visitors to Asia were much struck by this phenomenon. Antonio Pigafetta, whose voyage with the Magellan expedition took him to the Central Philippines, Brunei, the Moluccas, and the lesser Sundas in 1521, explained:

> Those people are constantly chewing a fruit which they call *areca*, and which resembles a pear. They wrap it in the leaves of their tree which they call *betre* ... they mix it with a little lime, and when they have chewed it thoroughly they spit it out ... All the people in those parts of the world use it, for it is very cooling to the heart, and if they ceased to use it they would die.[11]

Two decades later, Galvão observed that of all herbs the Moluccans made greatest use of the betel, "They use it so continuously that they never take it from their mouths".[12]

The habit was equally universal when the first Dutch fleet reached Banten (West Java) in 1598:

> One seldom sees the Javanese when they are not constantly chewing Betel and Areca mixed with lime, from which their whole mouth becomes red ... and if they wish to speak with the King ... also in visiting one another, the betel set will immediately be placed in the centre.[13]

From the earliest descriptions until well into the 19th century we learn that no important person left his house without a retainer or slave to carry his betel equipment, a bronze tray with containers for each of the ingredients. The king of Ternate had female dwarfs, reputedly deliberately crippled in childhood, to carry his set.[14] Betel sets were among the few metal utensils in most Indonesian households and their manufacture was one of the major sources of employment for such renowned copper- and brass-working centres as Negara (South Borneo), Grisek (East Java), Sungei Puar (West Sumatra), and Trengganu (Malayan Peninsula).

A betel set was as essential for entertaining guests as a tea set is in China or in modern Britain.

Chewing betel, in short, was not a matter of personal preference, still less of indulgence. It was a social necessity for every adult in society. To refuse to offer betel, or to refuse to take it when proffered, was esteemed a deadly insult.

The centrality of betel-chewing in Indonesian life reaches a deeper level, however, when we consider its role in almost every type of ritual. Areca and betel frequently accompanied the dead during funerals,[15] and in 16th-century Luzon, betel juice was used to embalm the dead.[16] Betel-chewing and its ingredients were featured widely in healing rituals and practices,[17] in offerings to the ubiquitous spirits of the dead, and in every social and ritual function. In many societies, particularly in East Indonesia, young people began to chew betel after the teeth-filing ritual that marked their passage to adulthood; betel-chewing became a mark of full membership of the ritual community.[18]

The most characteristic roles of betel in the Indonesian world (and well beyond it), however, were in the rituals of courtship and marriage. The offering and acceptance of betel were so much identified with courtship and betrothal that compounds of the Malay word for areca, *pinang*, have passed into the modern vocabulary on this subject. *Meminang* is "to ask in marriage" or "to court"; *pinangan* is "betrothal"; *pinang muda* became a euphemism for a go-between of lovers because of the image of the ideal young areca with two perfectly matching halves.[19] In other languages, the betel leaves, rather than the areca, became the primary symbol for betrothal. Acehnese *ba ranub* (to bring betel) is to offer a love gift; Makassarese *leko' passiko'* (a bundle of betel leaves) is the offer of marriage, while *leko'-lompo* (great leaves) represents the formal bride-price.

At the marriage ceremony itself, the betel ingredients are usually present as part of the bride-price. A Javanese bride and groom throw betel leaves at each other. At Malay and Sumatran weddings in the 19th century, an ornate "betel tree" (Malay *pokok sirih*; Acehnese *ranub dong*) comprising betel leaves was carried in procession.[20] Acehnese men divorced their women, on the other hand, by giving them three pieces of areca.[21] Today, among people who have abandoned the use of betel, a bronze betel set is often displayed among the ritual apparatus at the wedding, and it is handed down as an heirloom for this purpose.

There appear to be a number of reasons for the close association of betel-chewing with marital or sexual union. Presumably, the most important is that it is the promoter of all social intercourse, including the bond between man and woman. Beyond that, the union of its two major elements, areca and betel, undoubtedly represents complementarity and balance, particularly as areca is seen as "hot" in the universal humoral classification of Southeast Asia, and betel leaves are seen as "cool". In eastern Indonesia, where the long pod of the betel vine is a more appropriate male symbol than the leaves used elsewhere to match the feminine roundness of the areca, an explicit sexual symbolism is understood.[22] Forman argues for his Timor evidence that the chewing of betel is seen as a prerequisite for real or symbolic birth, the red spittle symbolising the blood that is believed to be the female contribution to an embryo.[23] Among the Makassae of Timor, the groom's mother ritually chews betel in the house with the bridal couple on their first night together; after childbirth, the new mother and her mother-in-law ritually chew betel together. Similar ideas may underlie the use of betel leaves or juice throughout the Archipelago for pregnancy and post-pregnancy disorders,[24] or the spitting of pieces of areca nut into the mother's vagina in the case of a difficult childbirth in Malaya.[25] Equally, however, we may here be dealing primarily with the need to "heat" during pregnancy and "cool" after it.[26]

The three key ingredients of the betel quid were widely available in the Archipelago, and consequently, it is almost impossible to establish the extent of its consumption by using trade figures. Around 1830, James Low[27] calculated the annual consumption of betel leaves by the inhabitants of Penang and Province Wellesley as 6,211,440 bundles of 100 leaves, which would represent a consumption of 20 leaves per day by every man, woman, and child in the settlement. The leaves were so cheap that the total expenditure for them would have been only 50 cents per person per year. Gambir became, as we shall see, an increasingly popular additive to the betel quid, especially in Java, which had to import almost all of its needs from Riau and Sumatra. If Raffles was correct in estimating that most of Riau's annual production of 20,000–30,000 *pikul* of gambir went in 1815 to Javanese betel-chewers,[28] this would have supplied 120 million *biji* (small cubes weighing approximately 10 g) to a Java whose population in 1815 was less than six million. My contemporary informants reckon one *biji* would last a regular chewer 15 days; hence, this would have been enough to keep every man, woman, and child chewing constantly. Since the cost of a *biji* of gambir was less than a guilder cent, however, this must have made little impact on the expenditure of the average consumer.

Betel, Tobacco, and the Brain

The similarity of function of betel-chewing and cigarette-smoking seems obvious to modern Indonesians. "Men are expected to smoke if they do not chew betelnut".[29] The two drugs are felt to have the same calming effect on tension, pain, and hunger while stimulating the appropriate mood for agreeable social intercourse. This similarity of effect was brought to the attention of the scientific world as early as the 18th century by Kaempfer.[30] In the 1930s, it was shown that arecoline, one of the major alkaloids in the areca nut, had an effect similar to that of nicotine in stimulating the central nervous system, increasing breathing and perspiration while keeping the heart rate steady.[31] For reasons of this sort, most of the general literature still classifies the betel quid as a mild stimulant.[32]

The situation is more complicated, however. As Emboden puts it, tobacco can act variously as "a stimulant, a depressant, a tranquilliser or a hallucinogen",[33] and recent research has revealed a similar mixture of seemingly contradictory properties in the betel quid. It has been shown that arecoline hydrolyses when chewed with lime into arecadaine, which along with another areca constituent, guvacine, is an amino acid that enhances the sedative effect of GABA (Gamma Aminobutyric Acid) in the brain. Experimentally, these amino acids have been shown to have a sedative effect on mice, reducing their spontaneous activity and curbing artificially induced epilepsy.[34] The only controlled experiment with human subjects of which I am aware[35] showed that betel-chewing markedly slowed reaction time among a group of Micronesian students. The major psychic effect of betel-chewing, as of smoking, appears therefore to be a sedative or relaxant one, even though certain other metabolic and nervous functions are stimulated by it.

The extraordinary place that betel-chewing assumed in the ritual and social lives of Southeast Asians has to be attributed primarily to its relaxant properties, which are readily acknowledged in the literature. In the *Sejarah Melayu*, Javanese women sick with love for Hang Tuah were offered betel "to allay the pangs of love".[36] In the 18th-century Acehnese epic, *Hikayat Pocut Mohammad*, tired and frightened warriors calmed and revived themselves by chewing betel, even swallowing the spittle for maximum effect.[37] The chewing of betel before social or diplomatic encounters must have made it easier for Indonesians to bear the demands made on men of higher social levels, in particular, for self-restraint and calmness.

Medicinal Effects of Betel-Chewing

The use of betel, like the use of tobacco and opium, was justified by its apologists in terms of the manifold medical benefits thought to flow from it. Some of these claims were real, some were imagined, and many have not yet been adequately tested. There seems to be little doubt, however, that the balance of positive and negative effects on health is much more favourable in the case of betel than in the case of either of its two modern rivals. The most universal claims for betel-chewing have been that it prevents dental decay and toothaches and sweetens the breath. The 16th-century tribute of Tomé Pires may be taken as representative:

> It greatly helps digestion, comforts the brain, strengthens the teeth, so that men here who eat it usually have all their teeth, without any missing, even at eighty years of age. Those who eat it have good breath, and if they do not eat it one day their breath is unbearable.[38]

Indonesian informants in modern times continue to stress the care of the teeth as the primary medical advantage of chewing betel. On the other hand, Bontius[39] was the first of a number of Western observers who took the contrary view that in prolonged betel-chewing, the lime caused decay, giving as evidence that many betel-chewers became toothless in old age, and most had their teeth stained — in reality, the stain was a deliberate attempt to achieve the black teeth then admired by Southeast Asians. On balance, Western scientific opinion has been in favour of betel for the teeth, however, attributing negative effects to the lack of proper cleaning. Many Europeans adopted the chewing of betel for this reason, and powdered areca nut was sold in England as a dentifrice as late as the 1930s.[40]

Only recently have these rival claims been subjected to controlled analysis. Surveys of patients in New Guinea[41] and in East Java[42] have shown conclusively that dental caries are markedly less frequent among betel-chewers, although the reasons for this are not entirely clear.

Unfortunately for English areca users, it appears probable that it is the fluoride content and antibacterial effect of the betel leaves which produce the positive effect.[43] On the other hand, it has also become clear that betel-chewers are relatively prone to periodontal disease and breakdown. Bachand reported of his betel-chewing patients in Vietnam that far more of them lost teeth through periodontal causes than through tooth decay. In attributing this to the irritational effect of the lime, he to some extent confirmed the views of Bontius three centuries earlier.[44]

That betel-chewing sweetens the breath may be accepted fairly readily: this is attested with confidence by all the early European observers (whose own breath must have been appalling). Numerous writers assert that Asian women would not think of making love without first sweetening their breath with betel, and we know that Portuguese and Dutch women in Southeast Asia quickly adopted the same precaution.[45]

The next most frequently attested virtue of betel-chewing among early writers is that it aided digestion. In the 12th century, Chau Ju-kua noted that betel-chewing prevented Southeast Asians from belching after meals.[46] Subsequent visitors such as Pires, Garcia da Orta, the writer of the Boxer Codex, Pyrard, Dampier and Bowrey all insisted that betel-chewing settled the stomach and prevented intestinal and digestive disorders. Early in this century, Louis Lewin provided a plausible explanation of this observation in relation to the nitrogen-deficient diet of tropical Asians:

> An excess of acid decomposition products of this overuniform food is very liable to formation in the stomach. The alkaline juice of the betel morsel neutralizes this acidity and acts as an astringent, hardening the mucous membranes of the stomach.[47]

For similar reasons, French military doctors in Vietnam in the 1890s prescribed the betel ingredients as part of military rations for all soldiers.[48]

Among the other claims made in the literature for betel-chewing, the most common were that it prevented diarrhoea and dysentery,[49] as well as scurvy;[50] that it combated parasitic worms,[51] aided menstruation,[52] and prevented hunger pains, enabling people to journey for several days without food.[53] Numerous writers also claimed areca was an aphrodisiac,[54] but we may ascribe this with reasonable confidence to the symbolic and stimulating qualities described above, and to the classification of areca as "heating" in the humoral system.

From this list, which could be lengthened, the only claim that appears to have been adequately tested by modern methods is that betel-chewing is effective against parasites — notably roundworms and tapeworms.[55]

Although less prominent in Western historical literature, the role of betel leaves as an antiseptic, antibacterial agent is particularly striking in the contemporary pharmacopoeia of Indian and Southeast Asian practice. The juice of betel leaves has long been used against eye infections.[56] Betel leaves were also placed over wounds and sores to prevent infection.[57] The effectiveness of such remedies appears to be the only way to account for the striking absence of infections noted by numerous early observers of Southeast Asia, even in cases of the most appalling wounds.[58] The juice of the betel leaf is also believed to be effective against swelling, morning sickness, headaches, drunkenness, and fever[59] — perhaps partly because of its humoral reputation as "cooling".

Recent research in Vietnam has isolated the following bacteria against which an extract of betel leaves has been found to be effective: bacterium pyocyaneum, candida albicans, diplococcus pneumoniae, salmonella para typhi B, shigella flexneri, shigella largei sachsii, staphylococcus aureus, and streptococcus haemolyticus.[60] These are responsible for various types of dysentery and typhoid. Scientific work on the beneficial effects of betel-chewing is still in its infancy, even by contrast with the efforts that have gone into studying the higher incidence of oral cancer among betel chewers, particularly those who mix tobacco with their chew.[61] The beneficial properties already demonstrated, however, seem to justify the claim that the constant chewing of the betel mixture by pre-modern Indonesians (and others) had extensive medical implications, not only in preventing dental decay and promoting digestion but also in protecting users against some of the more serious hazards of their environment, including intestinal parasites and water-borne diseases.

The betel-chewing habit seems likely to have been one factor that may explain the surprise of early European visitors to Southeast Asia at the seeming good health of the people they encountered, in contrast not only to the enormous mortality of Europeans in the East in the 16th to 18th centuries, but also to conditions in Europe itself. Miguel de Loarca noted of Visayans in the 1560s, "Among them are found no crippled, maimed, deaf or dumb persons ... They reach an advanced age in perfect health".[62] Similar comments are made of the Javanese in the 1650s by Rijklof van Goens;[63] of the Acehnese in the 1680s by ibn Muhammad

Ibrahim, a Persian,[64] of West Sumatrans in the 1770s by William Marsden,[65] and as late as the early 1800s of Vietnamese by de la Bissachère;[66] and of Siamese by Brugière.[67]

Tobacco as a Supplement to Betel

Despite John Crawfurd's argument in favour of the Portuguese, it appears to have been the Spanish who introduced tobacco to Asia; they brought the plant from Mexico to the Philippines in 1575. When the first Dutch expedition reached Banten (Java) in 1596, there was no sign of tobacco, whereas Scott[68] noted only a decade later how fond the Bantenese were of it. The Kartasura chronicle dates the arrival of tobacco in Central Java much more exactly, in the Saka year 1523 (March 1601–February 1602):

> In the same year [as King Senopati's death] was the first tobacco; when it had appeared was the beginning of people smoking, and "two fires fell upon the earth" [chronogram for 1523].[69]

The chronicle no doubt refers to the practice of the Mataram court, which appears to have been introduced to tobacco in the way it was then smoked by fashionable Europeans, using a long reed pipe. Among the 30 young women who accompanied Amangkurat I (1646–1677) whenever he went outside the palace, there was one to carry his pipe and tobacco and another to carry the fire to light it. Yet another carried his betel set.[70] Guests at royal banquets appeared to have been offered the choice of smoking or chewing betel after the meal.[71]

The growing of tobacco spread quickly in Java, as it did in the Philippines and most other parts of Southeast Asia. Java tobacco acquired a special reputation and was exported to other parts of the Archipelago, and by the late 19th century,

> there [was] virtually no inhabited area of the Netherlands Indies, whether in the lowlands or in highlands up to about 1500 m, where more or less tobacco is not cultivated by the native population for their own use or for the native market.[72]

Gradually, therefore, the use of tobacco came within the reach of almost everyone.

Stavorinus noted in the 1760s that the Javanese still used the pipe to some extent.[73] As early as 1658, however, an indigenous form of cigarette appeared; it was known as *bungkus* (lit. bundle) and composed of shredded

"Java tobacco" wrapped in a dried leaf of maize or banana.[74] This must have been a cheaper, easier, and therefore more popular way of smoking the new drug, although the pipe retained a certain *deftig* (genteel) status among the elite of Batavia and the Javanese aristocracy who intermingled with them. It was not until the end of the 18th century that the pipe began to lose its fashionable associations in Europe, and eventually also in Asia.[75]

The *bungkus* appears to have come along the same route as the original pipe tobacco, initially spreading from the Philippines to the Moluccas, where native cultivation of tobacco for use in the *bungkus* was noted by Rumphius in the 1660s.[76] "Ternatan bungkus" were especially popular in Java in the 18th century.[77] The *bungkus* appears to have preceded and probably influenced the Indian and Burmese cheroot (from Tamil *shuruttu*), of which the earliest recorded citations are in the 18th century. Lockyer (1711) implies that the common term for such homemade cigarettes, even in India at that time, was the Malay word *bungkus* (*bunco, buncus*[78]). In Sumatra and Malaya, on the other hand, a similar form of homemade cigarette, frequently wrapped in a *nipah* palm leaf, was referred to by the 18th century as *roko* or *rokok* (the modern Malaysian and Indonesian word for "smoke" or "cigarette"), probably because the usage was first spread by Dutch seamen and traders (Dutch *roken*, to smoke).[79]

In various forms, then, the smoking of tobacco established itself throughout Indonesia — indeed, throughout the world — during the 17th and 18th centuries. However, none of these forms were ever as popular among ordinary Indonesians as the habit of adding tobacco to the chew of betel became by the end of the 18th century.

As we have seen, the earliest European accounts of betel-chewing in Indonesia mentioned only the three key ingredients — areca, betel and lime. Nevertheless, the habit of adding spices, aromatics and other precious commodities to the betel quid was of long standing, particularly as a luxury among the rich. Some of the Sanskrit literature of the first Christian millennium refers to the "five fruits" that flavour betel, although there is no fixed list of what these were. The most frequently mentioned additives in this Indian literature are camphor (the most prized aromatic of the time), cloves, nutmeg, ambergris, cardamom and musk. A single clove has remained in India as a fastener for the elegant betel quid of polite society, the same role it plays in Sumatra and Malaya.[80] Cloves and cardamom were among the additives that the Javanese and Sumatran aristocracy kept in their betel sets.[81] Opium was also added to the quid by those requiring a stronger relaxant.[82]

By the end of the 18th century, however, throughout Indonesia gambier and tobacco had become the two standard additions to the three ancient elements. Whether or not as a reflection of the Sanskrit convention of "five fruits", Indonesian bronze and silver betel sets in the 19th century had to have five containers for these five conventional elements.

Gambier, an extract of the climbing shrub *uncuria gambir*, was the earlier of the two new ingredients to take its place. The Dutch encountered gambier for sale in the Banten market in 1596, as a medicine rather than in that part of the market where betel ingredients were sold.[83] About this time, however, the Indian habit of adding cutch, the astringent extract of the acacia *catechu*, to the betel quid was beginning to spread to Southeast Asian ports. During the 17th century, gambier was recognised as a better and cheaper locally available substitute for cutch. Rumphius described it as being chewed with betel in the Moluccas in the late 17th century.[84]

Gambier (Malay *gambir*) appears to be native to the Sumatra/Malaya area, and its leaves were probably used medicinally (as they are today, notably against dysentery[85]) for centuries before the imitation of cutch began. To achieve the effect of cutch, the juice of the leaves was boiled down until it reached a rubbery consistency; it was then cut into the characteristic one-inch cubes (*biji*) in which it was sold throughout the Archipelago. During the 17th century, a trade in gambier developed from Palembang to all points of the Archipelago; in the 1740s, the Bugis, followed by the Chinese, made Riau the primary export base.[86] Chinese, followed by Europeans, eventually discovered in gambier the best natural source of tannin, so that a major international trade was added in the 19th century to the longer-standing interisland trade.

Although gambier was valued for its medicinal effects against dysentery and diarrhoea, the main reason for its prominence in the betel chew was presumably its taste, "affecting the tongue at first with a mixed sensation of bitterness and astringency ... and leaving a lasting and not disagreeable sweetness".[87] Having come to appreciate this astringency from the areca nut, betel users must have found gambier a durable and transportable substitute when fresh areca was not available. In Central Java, gambier had almost completely replaced areca in this role by the 1980s.

When and how the chewing of tobacco with betel became common is far from clear. Van Lookeren Campagne speculates that Indonesians may have learnt the habit of chewing tobacco from Portuguese and Dutch sailors, who were forbidden to smoke onboard ships because of the risk of fire.[88] Given the precedent of chewing so many other things in the betel quid, however, as well as the difficulty of procuring fire when travelling, such an example was probably not necessary. I have not been able to find definite references to the addition of tobacco to the betel quid before the second half of the 18th century.[89] If the practice really began as late as this, its progress was extremely rapid. By the time of the British interregnum in the Indies (1811–1816), the primary use of tobacco in the Archipelago was undoubtedly as a wad to cram between lip and gum after the initial salivation produced by the betel chew:

> The practice of *smoking* tobacco, first tried, has been generally discontinued, and the Indian islanders now use it in a peculiar manner. The tobacco is finely shred, and a portion of it, in this form, is pretty constantly held between the lips and teeth, and, when the person wishes to speak, thrust between the latter and the gums, adding, in either case, greatly, in the opinion of a stranger, to the disgusting effects of the betel and areca preparation.[90]

The *bungkus* never died out entirely; it made its greatest comeback in the form of *kretek* in the 20th century. However, most 19th-century Indonesians absorbed their nicotine directly through the sensitive tissues of the gums. As a narcotic, this must have had a stronger effect than the areca nut. I interviewed betel-chewing women in Central Java and the Sa'dan Toraja area in the 1980s, who conceded that they got their "kick" primarily from the tobacco. With gambier to provide the astringency, it is therefore understandable that the areca nut, the original source of the appeal of betel-chewing, should have largely dropped out of use in Java.

Tobacco as a Substitute for Betel

Europeans never took the step of adding a wad of tobacco to the betel chew. Dutch men in Batavia abandoned the habit of betel-chewing during the middle years of the 18th century, although their womenfolk continued it well into the 19th century.[91] In its new, unsightly form, with the tobacco wad held in the mouth, the betel-chewing habit began to seem repulsive to Europeans who encountered it.

For European men in the East, it was the Manila cigar that assumed the role in the first half of the 19th century which betel-chewing and pipe-smoking had once occupied. About 230 million Manila cigars were imported to Java in the period 1856–1864, at a cost of over eight million guilders, for wealthy Europeans and Chinese and for aristocratic Javanese. From imported cigars, the transition was not a large one to imported cigarettes. These first made their appearance in Batavia in 1845, substantially earlier than they did in England (1854), and following the latest mode in France and Italy.[92] Once European males, the highest social caste of colonial society, became firmly committed to the smoking of cigars or cigarettes, it was only a matter of time before most other men adopted the habit.

As the 19th century wore on, the cultural gulf between the European (by 1900, typically a Dutch-born *totok*) and the Indonesian became ever wider. To the European, nothing seemed more emotive a demonstration of the inferiority of the Indonesian than his habit of chewing betel, spitting the saliva on the roadside or even in the house, and stuffing a wad of tobacco in his mouth. No doubt the development of bacteriological theory at the end of the 19th century added to the righteous indignation with which Europeans from then onward viewed the habit of spitting in a public place. One Dutch traveller described the Raja of Goa (Makasar), whom he met in the 1880s, as "a dirty old fellow who chewed betel and looked more like a monkey than a man".[93] Little wonder that the successor of this ruler chose to impress Dutch visitors by handing round cigars.

The transition in South Sulawesi from betel-chewing to cigarette-smoking must have been one of the more spectacular in its speed. Eerdmans pointed out that no Makassarese in the 1890s smoked cigarettes or cigars except those few princes most anxious to impress Europeans: the bulk of the population "chew *sirih* the whole day and often night, as long as they are awake".[94] Yet in the market of Makasar (Ujung Pandang) in 1980, there were only two Torajan women selling the betel ingredients (one of whom was not herself a user), and the buyers were exclusively elderly Torajans. When Makassarese or Bugis bought betel at all, it was purely for the ritual requirements of marriage. The transition among Bugis and Makassarese seemed to have been completed in a half-century. Virtually everybody chewed betel in 1900, and virtually nobody did so in 1950.

In Java, Bali, and Sumatra, the impact of "modernisation", like that of colonialism, was rather more gradual. Already in 1903, hardly any Javanese regents chewed betel, even though the betel set was ritually carried on all formal occasions. By the second half of the 19th century, the elite of Java were already smoking, and the habit gradually spread downwards.[95]

> Around 1900 in West Sumatra, where once the Padris campaigned in vain against the use of *sirih* ... the young men in particular begin to adopt the chic which is associated with a new type of civilization (also evident in the clothing which more and more diverges from that of the *adat*), leaving the use of betel to older people. To far in the interior one now finds "modern" young men ... They leave the *sirih*-tray for the oldies, just as we in our youth left the snuffbox. A very educated native teacher confirmed to me ... that formerly everyone chewed betel the whole day. "But now only the old people are fond of it, and the young chew it only when courting ... or during feasts and rituals."[96]

The spread of Western-style education appears to have been closely correlated with the abandonment of chewing betel. In areas such as Tana Toraja, where betel-chewing among both sexes is still common, the first generation to have been exposed to education was also the first to abandon betel. The whole image of "modernity" that education conveys to a young person is contradictory to the chewing of betel. Their association with education, and subsequent employment in the modern sector of the economy, is no doubt part of the reason why men generally abandoned betel-chewing a generation or so ahead of women. It is by no means the whole reason, however, for men without any education had abandoned betel for cigarettes in most of Java and the towns of outer Indonesia by 1950. The second factor is that the fashion, which steadily descended through colonial society from the dominant Dutch down, was exclusively a *male* image of cigarette-smoking. For women, there was nothing to fill the enormous social and relaxant role of betel.

During the 19th century, those who wished to follow the "modern" style had to purchase imported cigars or cigarettes, since homemade *bungkus*, now known as *strootjes* (Dutch) or *kelobot* (Javanese), had an image almost as rustic as betel itself. Local manufacture of international-style "white" cigarettes was begun by British American Tobacco (BAT), with a factory in Cirebon in 1924 and a subsequent one in Semarang.

BAT's "white" cigarettes led the expansion of the industry consistently until the 1970s. In the long run, however, the new dominant fashion did make it possible for the indigenous style of cigarette to make a comeback on a large scale.

The *bungkus* or *kelobot* had always resembled betel in the propensity of Indonesians to add aromatic spices to it. Among the additives for roll-your-own cigarettes sold in the tobacco section of the Yogyakarta market in 1982 were ground cloves, *menyan madu* (gum of the Styrax Benzoin), *kelembak* (root of the Rheum officinale), and *woor* (an alternative to cloves). Local manufacturers found that a mixture of cloves, tobacco, and a little sweetening *saus* (flavour) proved to be the most popular. The manufacture of such cigarettes on hand-operated rollers began in Kudus in the 1880s, initially with traditional maize leaves as wrappers. After the First World War, production in Kudus expanded to the point that it catered to a substantial proportion of the Java market. Such clove cigarettes became known as *kretek*, evidently an onomatopoeic reflection of the tendency of the cloves to crackle and explode as they burned. To judge by the level of import of Zanzibar cloves for this expanding industry, its output grew roughly tenfold during the 1920s. The depression curbed its expansion, largely because BAT lowered the cost of its "white" cigarettes to compete directly with the Javanese *kretek*.[97] Nevertheless, *kretek* production reached a pre-war peak in 1939 with an annual output that has been variously calculated (depending on the formula used) at between five and 16 billion cigarettes.[98] The labour-intensive industry of rolling *kretek* cigarettes became one of the great success stories of indigenous enterprise, employing 80,000 people in 1934. Most of them were women in the two Javanese manufacturing centres of Kudus and Blitar.[99]

Table 1. Indonesian Clove Consumption in Metric Tons

	Domestic Production	Imported	Total
1920	—	185	185
1930	—	3,039	3,039
1940	—	7,060	7,060
1956	4,000	12,700	16,700
1974	15,000	4,900	19,900
1978	21,100	9,800	30,900

Sources: Segers 1982: Bijl 5; Biro Pusat Statistik, *Statistical Pocketbook*, relevant years.

By the time of independence in 1945, cigarettes had usurped the role of betel for most Indonesian men, as a relaxant as well as a polite prelude to social intercourse. In areas where traditional rites of passage were still celebrated, tobacco was even taking over some ritual functions. As early as the 19th century, some brides and grooms among the Sarawak Dayaks exchanged cigars as well as betel at marriages.[100] In Kelantan of the 1930s, betel was still essential in all social and ritual occasions, but Rosemary Firth was told that she might use cigarettes if she was unable to obtain in England the betel which had to be offered to spirits at every birth.[101] The Berawan of Borneo in the 1970s used cigarettes to substitute for betel in accompanying the dead on their last journey.[102] At the great death feasts of the Sa'dan Toraja, hosts and guests now reciprocally offer cigarettes rather than betel.

Tobacco in Contemporary Indonesia

Like betel-chewing before it, cigarette-smoking for males became more than a personal indulgence. It was a social necessity in many circumstances. Unlike opium, which was always condemned by a large section of Islamic and other leaders and did not therefore become socially central, cigarettes had few critics in 20th-century Indonesia. The social and ritual gap left by the passing of betel was filled, if at all, by cigarettes. No doubt there was also a physiological gap for a people whose culture required them to endure poverty and injustice with calm and elegant civility. In this respect, opium became a more potent resource than betel for a minority in the 19th century, but its even more sudden passing left tobacco without major competitors.

The extent of Indonesians smoking since the Second World War is not fully revealed in the official statistics derived from excise duties paid. An indication of the speed of the increase in *kretek* production is given by the rapid escalation in clove consumption in Indonesia during the period 1920–1978. While we may reasonably posit a tenfold increase in the smoking of *kretek* cigarettes between 1930 and 1978 on the basis of the figures in Table 1, it is difficult to translate this into numbers of cigarettes smoked because of the large proportion of homemade cigarettes outside any government control. Official figures for the large-scale industrial production of cigarettes subject to excise nevertheless indicate the continuing increase in consumption (see Table 2). Indonesian men consume much more than most of their Southeast Asian neighbours. The WHO estimated that while the proportion of Indonesian women who smoked were among the world's lowest at 1.3%, the proportion of adult males who smoked was among the world's highest at 62.2% in 2001, down from 63.4% in 1995.[103] While per capita consumption has long been above most Asian and African countries, but still below the levels of affluent European countries and North America, which have seen major decline since the 1970s but still consume around 1,500 cigarettes per adult per year. Indonesian figures for consumption peaked in 2000, both in absolute and per capita terms. Subsequently, the consumption of white cigarettes declined sharply, while *kretek*, comprising over 90% of the market, declined slowly.[104] Given the understatement caused by homemade cigarettes in Indonesia, the much more intensive use of each cigarette than in affluent countries, and the content of Indonesian cigarettes, there is no cause for complacency concerning the impact of smoking on the health of Indonesian males.

Table 2. Annual Production of Cigarettes in Indonesia

	Production in billions			Consumption per head of adult population*
	Kretek	"White"	Total	
1972	20.1	21.6	41.6	613
1976	37.9	30.0	67.9	883
1980	51.0	29.1	80.1	924
2000	207	25.8	233	1,129
2005	203	16.9	220	1,006

Source: Biro Pusat Statistik, *Statistik Industri*, relevant years to 1980, at <http://www.indonesiamatters.com/1021/cigarette-production-consumption> [accessed October 2009].

* To 1980 the figures are for production per adult, which should be increased slightly to account for the small and declining excess of imports of "white" cigarettes over exports of *kretek*. (The excess of imports measured in weight was 1,300 tonnes in 1976 and 477 tonnes in 1980.)

The increasing share of the market occupied by *kretek* cigarettes, whose popularity spread from Java throughout the Archipelago in the 1970s, multiplies the effect of a single cigarette on health. One 1980 Australian analysis of four *kretek* brands in comparison with the international standard brands smoked in Australia yielded the results that are shown in Table 3. Smoke analyses such as these were designed especially to test the nicotine content of the tobacco smoked, which appears to be five times as high in *kretek* as in international brands. The effect of smoking the cloves and other additives in the *kretek* remains unknown, although it may be expected that the eugenol of the cloves when burned would produce vanillin, which has soothing anaesthetic properties.[105] Lung cancer is still not listed among the ten major causes of death in Indonesia, though the WHO *Tobacco Atlas* estimated over 15% of adult males died of tobacco-related causes. Since the *kretek* industry continues to be one of the most remarkable successes of the Indonesian manufacturing sector, there is little official encouragement for research into its effects on health.

Table 3. Smoke Analysis of Four Kretek Brands and Australian Brands of Cigarettes

Brand of *kretek*	Puff count	Moisture	Dry particulate matter	Nicotine	Carbon Monoxide
Djarum	17.1	2.4 mg	51.3 mg	5.07 mg	19.5 mg
Djarum	16.7	2.56	51.6	5.02	18.9
Dji Sam Soe	23.2	2.09	38.6	5.31	23.0
Gudang Garam	16.8	2.26	49.7	5.28	18.2
Gudang Garam	15.0	2.83	44.5	5.37	14.9
Wismilak	16.4	3.01	45.3	5.1	19.7
Wismilak	17.0	2.77	46.5	5.02	21.3
Australian brands (average)	8.0	2.0	15.0	1.1	14.0

Source: Australian Government Analyst Laboratory analysis for Dr Robert MacLennan, April 1980 (made available by Dr MacLennan).

The shift from betel to tobacco has important social implications too. Whereas betel-chewing pre-eminently symbolised the union of male and female, cigarette-smoking has become one of the most important symbols of the expanding modern sector of the economy which is dominated by men, in contrast to an older agricultural market economy in which women were prominent. Smoking is almost entirely restricted to men, and is seen as a luxury item men pay for outside the household budget that is controlled by women. Smoking therefore celebrates both modernity and maleness. It also celebrates the increasing role of wealth in the new status system. Betel was economically within the reach of all, and its ritual functions served chiefly to underline status based on age or birth. The great variation in price range of cigarettes, from the cheapest homemade *kelobot* to the most expensive Bentul Biru, serves as a precise marker of the achieved status of the host who dispenses this new narcotic.

Betel and Tobacco in Indonesian Expenditure

Betel was always regarded as an important item of expenditure. The pocket money received by Dutch-owned slaves in the 18th century was known as *siriegeld* ("betel money"),[106] just as similar pocket money today is known as *uang rokok* (cigarette money). A time-honoured Indonesian saying to express the deepest poverty was *kepeng pembeli sirih tidak ada lagi* ("he hasn't even the money to buy betel").[107] However, the expenditure required for a chew of betel was very modest, and it remains so. For those who bought all the ingredients in the market (many would have grown at least the betel leaf themselves), the cost of a chew in markets in Java and Sulawesi in 1982 was, on average:

betel leaves (*sirih*)	1 rupiah
areca (114 nut)	1
lime (tiny amount)	0.4
gambier (fragment)	0.6
	3 rupiah (then equivalent to 0.4 US cents)

A quid of tobacco to add to the betel chew cost, by contrast, almost 100 rupiah, though many chewers reused the tobacco for the three to six betel-chews they had in a single day. A packet of cigarettes in Indonesia cost from 200 rupiah (30 US cents) upwards.

A detailed survey of expenditure by Javanese workers in 1938–1939 showed that the richest categories of skilled workers and supervisors spent no more than 0.22 guilders per family per month on betel, whereas the expenditure on tobacco was between 0.24 guilders and 1.17 guilders. Every group of workers spent three or more times as much on tobacco as on betel, the two items together amounting to about 5 per cent of total expenditure for ordinary farmers, and up to 8–9 per cent for estate workers.[108]

The most recent measure of Indonesian expenditure is the increasingly sophisticated National Socio-Economic Survey (SUSENAS), which breaks expenditure patterns of a large sample of urban and rural households into 11 income categories. Biennial surveys have given the average proportion of expenditure for "tobacco and betel nut" over all Indonesian households as 5.37 per cent of the total expenditure in 1976, 4.95 per cent in 1978, and 5.7 per cent in 1980. Indonesian households in 1980 spent more on tobacco than they did on clothing and footwear, on meat, or on medical and educational needs combined, and twice as much as they spent on festivals. The poorest households spent more on tobacco than they did on fish, meat, and eggs combined.

The breakdown of the "betel and tobacco" category shows that expenditure on betel is now low enough to be taken as insignificant. The poorest households spend mainly on shredded tobacco, not on cigarettes, revealing the inadequacy of the cigarette production figures as a measure of total consumption. The higher the income category, the more cigarettes dominate in expenditure. Overall, almost twice as much is spent on *kretek* cigarettes as on "white" brands.[109]

Conclusion

The large role once played by betel in Indonesian life has been partly filled by cigarette-smoking. Today, men enjoy relaxant, analgesic, and social advantages from cigarettes similar to those they once derived from betel; women appear increasingly to be able to get through the day without any such support. The passing of betel-chewing has meant the loss of certain antibacterial safeguards, which are still imperfectly understood. The large and rising consumption of cigarettes, on the other hand, brings with it a very certain negative effect on Indonesian health. Indonesian medical statistics, unaided by autopsies, are not sufficiently accurate to distinguish tobacco-related deaths among the large proportion of respiratory, pulmonary, and cardiovascular disorders recorded. From research elsewhere, however, we know that Indonesian lives are being shortened by the smoking habit, almost certainly on an increasing scale.

CHAPTER 4

Chains of Silver, Chains of Steel: Forcing Politics on Geography

Batavia rose to prominence in the archipelago in the period 1650–1750 in the same way as earlier centres since Sriwijaya — with symbolic political primacy *following* commercial dominance. Since 1800, however, Batavia/Jakarta has had to fight an uphill battle *against* market economic forces in order to counter the influence of Singapore and Penang. The Netherlands Indies government gradually achieved economic control in Sumatra, Kalimantan and East Indonesia by a mixture of brute force, strategic concessions to Straits-based trade and foreign investment, and support for national institutions such as the KPM shipping line. The institutional basis of this forcing of trade to fit political boundaries largely collapsed in the 1940s and the Republic has subsequently had a sequence of uphill battles to reconstruct a similar policy.

Introduction

Although Sukarno claimed that "a child" could see the natural unity of Indonesia by looking at a map; the construction of its boundaries has cost a great deal of blood over the past two centuries. The Malacca Straits are the greatest artery of commerce passing through Southeast Asia, but also a highway linking the Malay-speaking peoples around it. Its best natural ports are situated on the Malaysian side. Constructing two mutually exclusive political units, one including all of Sumatra and Java and the other the ports of Malaya, was bound to be a task akin to pushing rocks uphill.

In our own time, the map-fixed frontiers of late colonialism are at last becoming less oppressive. The aspiration towards two growth triangles centring on Singapore and Penang respectively, and attempting to transcend national boundaries in the context of both ASEAN solidarity and economic globalisation,[1] is a sign that the problems created in 1824 are being resolved at last.

Background: Political Status Follows Trade

The nexus between economic and political power was close to the surface in the Indonesian archipelago. The emperors of China, Delhi or Byzantium might have spurned commerce as unworthy of the attention of rulers, but not so the rajas below the winds. As Wolters puts it: "The conviction everywhere in this cultural zone was that busy harbours brought power and brilliance to the local ruler", so that this was the first priority of the ambitious.[2] Milner examines 19th-century Malay texts for his conclusion that the Malay elite "sought wealth not for its own sake but as a means of gaining political influence in the form of a sizeable personal following".[3] Some recent writing may have suggested that in Bali, central Java and Luwu (Sulawesi) rulers sought more theatrical means to establish their power. But such constructions should be read into an earlier past only with caution. Viewing Java from the outside (admittedly at an unusually turbulent period), one of the first and most acute European observers, Tome Pires, noted in 1515 that the coastal kings, at least, "were not Javanese of long standing", but foreign merchants who had prospered in Java, "made themselves masters of the sea coast and took over trade and power in Java".[4]

Military and cultural prowess was not unimportant. Wars were constantly fought for control of people, regalia, strategic sites and trade routes. But these were usually between rival centres of commerce and power, not between a hinterland and a metropolis. Between minor ports and major ones, upstream populations and the downstream port-capital, stateless and migratory peoples and an urban trade centre, there was more often acceptance of a necessary symbiotic relation. Some form of tribute to such centres was part of the process of communicating with the outside world. Vital necessities such as salt, dried fish, iron weapons and tools, bronze artefacts, Chinese ceramics and Indian cloth entered through these centres. Hinterland populations brought their forest, marine and agricultural produce to exchange in them against the imported and manufactured goods, and accepted that part of that transaction was to render some of their trade goods to the king and his officials as tribute: the price of trading in their port. In turn, the port-ruler was almost invariably involved in a similar relationship with a bigger commercial centre elsewhere, in Sriwijaya, Majapahit, Melaka, Aceh, Makasar or Siam, and ultimately in China.

Most of the major Southeast Asian trade centres were close enough to the Straits of Malacca and Sunda to act as entrepôts in the busy trade between the Indian Ocean and the South China Sea. They necessarily maintained relations with China, the most important trade partner of the Malay World for most of the period 1200–1840, gathering exotic tropical products of Southeast Asia to be sent to the Middle Kingdom in tribute missions. Majapahit moved the centre of the Malay World briefly further east in the 14th century, mainly by exploiting the spice route to Maluku on the one hand and the abundance of its own food exports on the other.

Into this world, the VOC often had to fight its way. Not only the Portuguese and Spanish, but Aceh, Banten, Makasar and Johor, were rivals of the ambition of Batavia to become the single commercial focus of the archipelago. With the military victories of the period 1641–1682 (from Melaka through Ambon, Palembang and Makasar to Banten), however, Batavia achieved a decisive primacy. For the century between about 1660 and 1760, it was the unquestioned trade centre of the Malay world, the heir to Sriwijaya, Majapahit and Melaka before it. Chinese shipping focussed on Batavia in the period 1682–1740, when the 18 junks a year which on average visited Batavia constituted a large majority of those trading to the Malay World and about a third of those sailing to Southeast Asia as a whole.[5] The volume of shipping in Batavia overall must have exceeded that of its nearest archipelago rival, Aceh, by a huge margin. In fact, Batavia had no rival in this period. The manufactured goods of China, India and Europe reached most of the peoples of the archipelago through its mediation. Its economic domination of the region was probably greater than that of any major entrepôt before it.

With this commercial domination, Batavia assumed the status which had been the lot of Sriwijaya and other ports before it. After the conquest of Banten in 1682, the VOC had no major wars to fight against maritime rivals; it began to direct its military efforts to costly campaigns in the interior of Java. (The Mongol rulers of China had made the same mistake centuries earlier, profoundly misreading the role of a Southeast Asian economic-and-status centre).[6]

Political primacy, not necessarily authority, control or a modern understanding of sovereignty, followed naturally from commercial supremacy. Sultan Mahmud of Palembang put the situation nicely around 1740: "I cannot understand why kings who are allies of the Company quarrel with it, while experience shows us that they always succumb and the Company triumphs. I war with the Company, but in quite a different manner. I fire pepper and tin at the Company, and it bombards me with good Spanish rials".[7]

An eastern Javanese *babad* of 1774 describes Batavia much as earlier texts had referred to the wonders of the great Southeast Asian capitals of the past, from which power and wealth flowed effortlessly:

> The world of the prince [*i.e.* Governor-General] is the city of Batavia, which is indeed the Company's fort. It is as if heaven descended. The fort of Batavia has a wall of white ceramic; if I were to tell you about it for a whole day I could not come to the end.[8]

Batavia lost this commercial supremacy progressively after 1760. Els Jacobs has demonstrated how the intra-Asian trade which had sustained the Company for a century declined in value from 37.5 million guilders in 1751–1752 to 21.5 million guilders in 1771–1772 (excluding specie).[9] The import of Indian cloth by the VOC through Batavia for the supply of Indonesia declined rapidly from 272,000 pieces (worth 1.5 million guilders) a year around 1758, to 82,000 pieces (worth 535,000 guilders) in 1780–1781.[10] Chinese junks visited Batavia in the 1760s and 1770s in less than half the numbers they had before 1740, whereas the overall junk trade began to flourish in a diversity of ports such as Riau, Brunei, Banjarmasin and Sambas.[11] As the VOC indices declined, those of the English, American and Chinese vessels trading to independent ports in Southeast Asia accelerated.

Batavia was never able to regain the commercial primacy it had held before 1760. The Napoleonic wars and the British occupation encouraged its rival ports; the stagnation of Dutch commerce and economic life generally between 1700 and 1850[12] made it impossible for a purely Dutch port again to dominate the region. But it was the foundation of Singapore in 1819 which set the seal on the displacement of Batavia. Singapore was better placed to take advantage of the trade between the Indian Ocean and the South China Sea. It was the port of preference for the British trade then beginning to bestride the world. And above all, it was a free port, offering the dynamic Chinese and archipelago traders for the first time a base where they could exchange their goods for those of the world without being squeezed or mistreated by rulers. From its foundation, Singapore attracted most of the British and Chinese trade on the archipelago. Because Batavia could only keep some of the imports into Java itself in Dutch hands by imposing tariffs as discriminatory as the 1824 treaty would allow, British and Chinese manufactures (and Bengal opium) were available more cheaply in Singapore than in any Dutch port. Hence, any ports and traders who were free to do so would choose to frequent Singapore (or its northern equivalent, Penang) rather than Batavia.

Coping with Singapore

In the first three decades of its existence, about 35 per cent of Singapore's total trade was with the Malay Archipelago.[13] In the 1820s, Singapore's imports from these regions appeared to have exceeded Java's[14] and they remained very high throughout the 19th century. The two most important areas wholly independent of the Dutch — northern Sumatra and Bali-Lombok — gained particularly from this link to Singapore and Penang. The trade of Bali and Lombok on Singapore expanded from 106,000 Spanish dollars in 1830–1831 to 572,500 Spanish dollars in 1843–1844. The two regions exported rice to Singapore and Australia, and imported firearms and other manufactures.[15] Aceh sent its pepper and betel nut chiefly to Penang, to a value of a million Spanish dollars in 1828–1829 and three million 30 years later.[16]

Fortunately for Dutch colonialism, Britain after the Napoleonic wars had a strong interest in upholding a strong Netherlands as a bulwark against French or German influence. For all Raffles' scheming to prevent it, London was therefore determined to maintain and even extend Dutch power in the archipelago. The 1824 treaty was intended to ensure this result — an Anglo-Dutch alliance to divide the Malay world between them, Holland taking the lion's share, and to keep other powers out. British commercial interests ensured however that the Netherlands Indies administration could not exclude them, as the VOC had done, from any of the rich markets of the archipelago. The 1824 treaty prevented either party from levying more than twice the duty on the ships and goods of the other party than it did on its own. A determination to be master of its own house frequently led Batavia to bend or ignore this treaty, notably during the Cultivation System of 1830–1870, when Dutch authorities pretended to charge a tariff on Netherlands goods at 50 per cent of the high rate it charged British goods, but secretly repaid this amount as a subsidy to the state trading company NHM.[17] Nevertheless, the British alliance was far too important to the Netherlands for The Hague permanently to withstand the bitter complaints of British and Straits traders, and the 1871 Sumatra Treaty allowed for free British commerce there (see below).

In consequence of these factors, the Dutch could not pursue the exclusionary or discriminatory trade policies by which the French and Spanish tried to maintain a monopoly of economic as well as political power in their colonial possessions. The Netherlands Indies became an exceptionally open colony, with a high proportion of its trade, shipping and investment in non-Dutch hands. For most of the years 1879–1904, imports from Singapore alone were higher than those from the Netherlands. After 1910, Singapore's grip was loosened by the measures described below, but the Dutch share of the colony's exports dropped steadily from 29 per cent to below 20 per cent, and of its imports from 33 per cent to around 20 per cent.[18] This is a striking contrast with Indochina, where France reacted to similar competition from Singapore, Hong Kong and Japan with an extreme protectionist policy. About 50 per cent of Indochina's imports came from France throughout the whole of the period 1897–1939 except during the First World War. While the Netherlands gradually bowed to economic and geographic realities, the trend in Indochina was the other way around, with France accounting for about 60 per cent of Indochina imports and 50 per cent of exports in the 1930s.[19]

This economic openness and multi-polarity in turn gave the Netherlands Indies a different type of authority from that of the VOC, which had owed whatever political eminence it had in the Outer Islands to its commercial primacy. The Netherlands Indies government had to impose its authority by force of arms, especially in Sumatra, Bali-Lombok and Borneo, because it lacked the hegemony (and even the knowledge) which emanates from commercial dominance. Dutch dealings with these states in the 19th century showed great anxiety about symbolic Dutch primacy, leading to a number of ill-considered wars, but not much concern with internal or economic issues. For their part, Acehnese and Balinese were well aware that Holland was a small country, and that there were alternative sources of technology and capital in the Straits Settlements, Europe, and America. Even after the bloody conquest of these regions was completed in the first decade of this century, Batavia's authority was never unquestioned in them.

A Difficult Pacification: The Aceh Problem

A prelude to the problem of Aceh (one of many in Sumatra) was enacted on the east coast of Sumatra in the 1860s. All the small states between Langkat and Asahan conducted most of their trade through Penang and Singapore. Elias Netscher, Resident of Riau, began the Dutch advance into this area in 1862, and was skillful in exploiting the many divisions between the various river-ports. The strongest resistance predictably came from Asahan, which had flourished in the preceding two decades by entrusting most of its trade to the Penang merchant Boon Teng, and his influential British associate Lawrence Nairne. They were in a position to arouse noisy British opposition to Dutch control. The senior official in Penang, Major Man, was sent with a gunboat to follow Netscher's visit, and predictably declared that:

> The traditional policy of the Dutch has inspired our European merchants with such a deep rooted distrust of their commercial system, and the Natives with such an utter hatred of their rule, that any extension of their authority creates universal alarm.[20]

The policy of the Straits merchants and their official supporters was to keep all the tiny ports open, to encourage competition among the sellers of their produce and develop Penang and Singapore as their natural commercial centre. Thus, when the Sultan of Aceh complained to the British that Netscher had violated his sovereignty on the coast, no support was given because this "would tend only to interfere with the freedom of trade in the several ports and rivers along the coast of Sumatra".[21]

Netscher had his way in 1865 with a sizeable military expedition to cow the rulers of all the small states, or in the case of Asahan to drive them into the hills. Dutch rule was established and tobacco soon made it a huge success (except among the embittered Karo-Batak). But in a sense, the Straits merchants also had their way. In order to pacify British objections to their forceful occupation of this Penang hinterland, the

Dutch government agreed to keep virtually all the tiny ports open and to impose minimal restrictions on British trade. The plantations of East Sumatra were supplied with labour and material from the Straits Settlements, the Straits dollar was its effective currency, and the "British" character of the settlement became a matter of pride.

Much of Holland's generosity in this regard had an eye to the much bigger problem of Aceh. This was the most substantial independent state in the archipelago. Its independence had moreover been guaranteed in an exchange of notes with the 1824 Anglo-Dutch treaty, the Dutch side undertaking "that that state, without losing anything of its independence, may offer that constant security which can only be established by the moderate exercise of European influence".[22] Aceh had a proud history and a variety of connections with Turkey, Italy, the United States and France, any of which might provide difficulties for the Anglo-Dutch compact. Some in Aceh and the Straits Settlements believed that its 1819 treaty of mutual defence with Britain was still valid. In 1872, the young sultan was attempting to purchase a steamer in Singapore. A modernising entrepreneurial group of *uleëbalang* centred around the Raja of Simpang Ulim in northeast Aceh had especially close links with Penang, where the Raja, Teuku Muda Nyak Malim, owned a prominent city building known as *Gedung Aceh* and valued at 40,000 Spanish dollars. Teuku Muda employed at least two Europeans in commercial and military roles, and overall there may have been as many as 18 Europeans, mostly married to locals and converted to Islam, living in Aceh. Teuku Muda's right hand man, the wealthy pepper-grower and dealer Teuku Paya, owned a well-armed new Western-style schooner, the "Gypsy", which took part in local military operations as well as the pepper trade to Penang. The total tonnage of schooners and other European-style vessels under Acehnese colours visiting Penang rose from 786 tons in 1868 to 5,100 tons in 1872. There were about 300 Acehnese at any one time in Penang. A large proportion of the political elite had visited the British port for business or pleasure. It was not only Aceh's market but its window on the world, through which most of its diplomacy was conducted. Moreover, the town as a whole was strongly committed to the Acehnese side in its conflict with the Dutch, including the few journalists who wrote stories there for local or foreign papers.[23]

Singapore was not much better in Dutch eyes. As the Minister of Colonial Affairs, Fransen van de Putte, had complained in 1864:

> Singapore is the gathering place not only for the many pilgrims who yearly go to Mecca from our possessions, but also for many malcontents, adventurers, etc., who, as has frequently been shown, readily choose this place as the base for undertakings detrimental to Netherlands interests in the Indian archipelago.[24]

In Whitehall, the British connections with Aceh and the other states in Sumatra were pragmatically seen as bargaining chips, to be exchanged for more open access for British trade to an expanded Netherlands India. As the leading Foreign Office strategist, Sir Percy Anderson argued in 1868,

> the British could not prevent the Dutch from having Acheen some day or other ... it never will be of any use to anyone as long as it belongs to the Sultan ... We can never have it, and therefore why not the Dutch, except on some dog-in-the-manger principle?[25]

This strategy led to the Sumatra treaty of 1871, which withdrew British objections to incorporation of Aceh into Netherlands India in return for a Dutch undertaking that the trade of British subjects would enjoy all the same rights and privileges as that of Dutch subjects in the whole of what became the East Coast of Sumatra Residency and Aceh. The outcome was of course much worse than anything either British or Dutch negotiators had been able to foresee, having failed to pay much attention to the Achenese. Not only did the treaty lead directly to the most ruinous of Dutch colonial wars, it also played a role in the simultaneous Ashanti War in the Gold Coast (Ghana), since gains in Sumatra were identified as compensation for Dutch losses in the Gold Coast, where Elmina was transferred to the British.

Aceh has a long coast, and Dutch naval power would normally have been its strongest weapon in bringing the whole country to heel. But there was great caution in using it, both because of the formal obligations to Britain under the treaty of 1871 and because blockades further enraged the Straits traders who had such influence over Holland's most important ally. Dutch policy alternated alarmingly between imposing harsher blockades to stop the flow of money and arms to the Acehnese resistance, and raising them again to mollify Britain, which was frequently on the point of embarrassing the Dutch by a public offer of mediation or intervention. In April 1874, for example, the Governor of the Straits Settlements sought British mediation, claiming that "I might make peace in five minutes", so insistent were the Acehnese on having Britain as party to any settlement. This prompted the Dutch colonial minister to an angry minute, declaring the British "are very badly suited now to want to act as angels of peace".[26]

One of the reasons the Dutch declared peace in 1881 and installed a civil government in Aceh was to defuse another mounting British protest against blockades, strongly supported by another Governor of the Straits Settlements, Frederick Weld. British outrage was diverted into the appointment of a British Consul in Uleëleue, the port of Kutaraja (Banda Aceh). In reality, Penang and Singapore were then the major international ports for Sumatra, but it was decided that the Consul had to be near the seat of the Dutch Government of Aceh because it was against that government that all the complaints of the Straits merchants were directed. The Consulate was a fiasco, with its occupant in a state of virtual war against the Dutch Civil Resident, Sol. Consul Kennedy was withdrawn after less than three years of struggle, and decades would pass before a replacement British Consul for Sumatra was appointed, this time more sensibly in Medan.

Having abandoned a military solution to their Aceh problem, Dutch strategists on the ground were more than ever convinced that they could influence the Acehnese "dependencies" only by systematically restricting trade to five Dutch-ruled ports, and there controlling the trade income of all Acehnese *uleëbalang*. This would have meant defying British protests and ignoring past undertakings given, and hence the earliest schemes to implement such a *scheepvaartregeling* (shipping regulation) were vetoed in Batavia and The Hague. As the Dutch position in Aceh grew more desperate, however, without public opinion in the Netherlands being prepared to sacrifice further lives and money in the war, the opinion gathered strength that a strict control of trade was the only way the Dutch could appear to be strong enough to disguise a retreat they had determined to take within a "concentrated line" around Kutaraja.

All these issues reached a crisis in the "Nisero affair". The British steamer "Nisero" ran aground near Teunom, north of Meulaboh on the west coast, on 8 November 1883, and its 29 (mainly British) crew were taken into custody by the Raja (*uleëbalang*) of Teunom, Teuku Imam. Probably under advice from some of his trading partners, Teuku Imam conceived the brilliant stroke of demanding in return for their release a British guarantee that his ports would remain permanently free from

Dutch interference or restrictions. Matters quickly escalated as spokesmen in the Straits Settlements, the British House of Commons and Whitehall insisted that British intervention, supported by the claimant to the Acehnese throne, was the only means to end not only the captivity of the Britons but the whole wretched war. For The Hague, this was the ultimate anathema. Minister of Colonial Affairs, Sprenger van Eyk, conceived an ingenious means to solve all his problems at once. The whole coast would be closed to all shipping, ostensibly as punishment for seizing the hostages but really to cover the retreat in Aceh. It would be declared that all ports would be open when the hostages were released and when attacks on the Dutch ceased in Aceh Besar, which they inevitably would because there would be nothing left to attack. "The inevitable concentration will have taken place without allowing any weakness on our side to be suspected, and without disadvantage to our prestige".[27]

The hostages were finally released on 10 September 1884 to a joint Anglo-Dutch military mission in return for both money and the opening of Teunom's ports. The worst Dutch fears of a separate British intervention were not realised. But although Dutch face was saved in the short run, the Acehnese had had a splendid victory. Not only did Dutch control contract to a small triangle of less than 60 square kilometres around Kutaraja; all attempts to control trade were also abandoned, chiefly in deference to the promises made to Britain during the "Nisero" affair. It would be almost another decade before Holland found the will to try again to conquer Aceh.[28]

Before Straits influence in Sumatra could be eliminated, it was helpful for Sumatra's role in the Straits to decline. When the Penang merchants had protested in the 1870s, they were defending the most important branch of their trade. But British influence had subsequently expanded greatly in Perak and Kedah, and the booming tin industry there and in south Thailand provided opportunities free of difficulties with Dutch administrators. While Penang's trade with Sumatra was virtually stagnant between 1883 and 1905, that with the Malayan Peninsula increased eightfold, to become the lifeline of the colony. The contracts to supply the Dutch army in Aceh, which had been in the hands of Penang merchants (partly in an attempt to mollify them), went to a Dutch firm in 1884. Shipping was still all Straits-based though flying Dutch flags, divided between the British-owned Nederlandsch-Indische Stoomvaart Maatschappij (NISM), which had the mail contract, and the

Penang Chinese magnate Chang Chen-hsun (Thio Tiauw Siat), who had opium and spirit farms and the navy contract in Aceh as well as East Sumatra and Malaya. These two firms were in no position to fight Dutch policy publicly, and the majority of Penang business was looking elsewhere by the 1890s. Another factor which shifted Straits sympathies was the series of bloody attacks by Acehnese on the remaining steamers plying the pepper-routes — almost all of them belonging to Chang Chen-hsun. Whether or not these Acehnese were inspired by the success of Teuku Imam with his "Nisero" captives, the effects on British and Straits opinion were the exact reverse when Acehnese killed three Europeans on the "Hok Canton" in 1886 (this the work of the later Acehnese hero Teuku Umar), 24 passengers on the "Rajah Kongsee Atjeh" in 1893, and eight on the "Pegu" in 1897.[29]

Until 1890, virtually all shipping to northern and eastern Sumatra, as well as most of that from Borneo and Celebes, was centred on Penang and Singapore, where goods were exchanged by the major British lines to Europe, India, China and Australia. The big Dutch lines like the Rotterdamsche Lloyd were not even able to take much of the traffic between Holland and the Indies, because the NISM fed into its own group (British India Association) and Alfred Holt's steamers. Muslim pilgrims to Mecca, as well as Dutch officials on leave, transshipped in Singapore or Penang where their contacts were not necessarily to the liking of Batavia. A rising tide of nationalist sentiment, business interest, and hard-headed calculation in the late 1880s obliged the Netherlands Indies Government to give the monopoly on mail services in the Indies to a truly Dutch firm, the Koninklijke Paketvaart Maatschappij (KPM), when the contract of the NISM expired in 1890. Set up essentially by the two big Dutch international lines, the KPM aimed explicitly to focus Netherlands Indian trade on Netherlands Indian ports, especially Tanjung Priuk, and to ensure that people and goods were transshipped there, and not in Singapore and Penang. Nationalist objectives took precedence over longstanding liberal principle, giving the KPM a monopoly of government and much non-government business.[30]

In Aceh, the efforts of the KPM to cut the links to the Straits were firmly seconded by Snouck Hurgronje, the great strategist of the successful prosecution of the war after 1892. As he saw it:

> For the Acehnese Penang is truly the gateway to the world; yes the world itself ... The Acehnese, who frequently go to Penang, fall under

influences there which bring them anything but closer to the *Gompeuni* (that is, Netherlands Indies government). They are also led to compare Penang with the abnormal condition of their own country, or with that of the neighbouring Netherlands possessions, and these comparisons are very detrimental to our Government. Exclusively on the experience of the Acehnese in Penang rests the *general* conviction that the rule of the English would be infinitely preferable to ours ... In view of all this ... no difficulty or sacrifice can be too great for us to give the Acehnese in their own country what Penang is for them now, and at the same time to open a direct route to Europe for their products.[31]

Within three years, the KPM had driven all opposition from the field in Aceh, by a mixture of price war, government pressure and buyout. Snouck's next objective, to replace Penang with an Acehnese entrepôt linked to Europe, was harder to achieve. Sabang, a fine natural harbour on an island just off Uleëlheue, was developed into a free port and coaling station from 1893, and in 1903, was made a port of call for the European service of the Stoomvaart Maatschappij "Nederland". But the KPM found it could not bypass Singapore and Penang entirely on its routes. Instead, it adopted a strategy of linking some of its routes to Singapore but trying to make agreements with competitors on these routes to push up freight rates, thus striving to diminish the price advantage that Singapore always enjoyed.[32]

The Aceh War was won (or for Acehnese, the Dutch war was lost), after a fashion, by the ruthless policy of search and destroy initiated by Snouck Hurgronje and van Heutsz in 1898 and continued until the last active resistance was defeated around 1913. As always, this policy had to overcome resistance about the attitude of the British. The Dutch policy of indirect rule had long been based on a pattern of elaborate treaties with local rulers, invariably accepting Dutch sovereignty, excluding any relations with non-Dutch foreigners, promoting the suppression of slavery and piracy, and providing for Dutch advice in various matters. Aceh had been treated as a collection of scores of small "native states", largely because of the early mistake of accepting claims of autonomy by the most pro-Dutch and anti-sultan *uleëbalang*. The contracts with each of these *uleëbalang*, like those with small river-princes of eastern Sumatra, were communicated to the British under the terms of the 1824 treaty. At least by those who favoured this kind of indirect rule, it was assumed that promises to the British about commercial access to the native states of

Sumatra applied to these *uleëbalangschap*, and they could not simply be incorporated into directly ruled Dutch territory. Snouck Hurgronje and Van Heutsz, then "Native Advisor" and Governor of Aceh respectively, insisted that all such contacts should be replaced by a simple "Short Declaration" (*Korte Verklaring*) by local rulers to the effect that their territory was part of Netherlands India and that they would accept all instructions from its Government. As Snouck pointed out, the Acehnese never had much interest in the content of the long contracts, but accepted Dutch rule only insofar as they were forced to do so. The new forceful policy won the day, and British protests were not forthcoming. The Straits merchants had by then lost all interest in Aceh, which was no longer a major producer of pepper or anything else.[33] Aceh was conquered, but only by the constant application of force. Dutch authority there was shortlived and never accepted as legitimate.

In Aceh, the stakes had been particularly high, but a similar story was played out throughout the Outer Islands. The successful partnership of Van Heutsz and Snouck Hurgronje was continued at a higher level when the General became Governor-General in 1904. The *Korte Verklaring*, the relentless pursuit of resisters, and the acceptance that Dutch officials would *rule*, not simply advise, laid the foundation for a unified state. At sea, the KPM won its own war against Singapore-based shipping. The European shipping lines quickly made deals with the KPM or sold out to it. Straits-based Chinese shippers were much tougher competitors. They had lower costs, engaged in a variety of commercial operations (including smuggling of opium) which the KPM could not match, and attracted trade and passengers to the British-dominated international lines. There were 33 Chinese steamers running archipelago routes in 1891, mostly Singapore-based, as against only 12 KPM steamers. The KPM began by a policy of trying to run them out of business, but had little success. After 1900, it adopted a more subtle policy of encouraging small Chinese firms to service particular niches in cooperation with its own routes. "By supporting the cooperative Chinese in many respects, the KPM transformed its former adversaries into vassals. In 1911, the maritime pacification was almost complete".[34] In 1913, the KPM had 85 steamers in the archipelago, more than twice the number of Chinese steamers. The latter, moreover, were now primarily based in Dutch ports, and serving the overall unifying purposes of the KPM.

Beginning Again, 1942–1949

The period of undisputed Dutch control over the Outer Islands of Indonesia was hardly more than three decades. In corners such as Aceh, Tanah Karo, South Sulawesi and Lombok, there remained a sullen acceptance rather than an active participation in the modernising project which colonialism at its best aspired to. Although the problem of Singapore as a rival pole of attraction was largely contained in the period 1910–1940, publications, ideas and people still circulated from there with the heavy flow of traffic across the Straits. Despite close cooperation with its British counterpart (generally more concerned with Chinese radicals than Islamic or Indonesian ones), Dutch intelligence had to operate its own agents in Singapore to keep an eye on revolutionaries. Here and there, and particularly in East Sumatra with its close ties with the Straits, there were private schools which made a point of teaching in English so their graduates could go on to study in Singapore or elsewhere.

British policy, despite all the problems chronicled above, was fundamentally pro-Dutch and appreciative of the style of Dutch colonial administration. How different things could be with a hostile power across the Straits became clear on 19 December 1941, when Penang fell to the Japanese forces advancing rapidly down the Peninsula. There was a rush from Sumatra to contact these potential liberators. A number of Sumatrans were already in Malaya, the most notable being Samin Taib, the Medan Sarekat Islam leader of the 1918–1920 period, who was soon broadcasting to Sumatra over Japanese-controlled Penang radio, and the religious teacher of the Acehnese community in Yen (Kedah), Said Abubakar. Within a month, Abubakar and a dozen others had offered their services to the Japanese to become a fifth column in Sumatra. They were sent across the Straits in small boats to spread pro-Japanese propaganda and protect bridges and supplies from any scorched-earth tactics of the Dutch defenders. Meanwhile, in February, several boats reached Malaya from Aceh's east coast carrying nationalist and Islamic envoys from both Aceh and East Sumatra.

Although the most the Japanese had in mind was to use this support as a helpful fifth column during their invasion scheduled for March, the Acehnese were quickly stirred up to a national revolt by the returning envoys. Two Dutch officials were killed in a premature outburst in Seulimeum on 23 February. The coordinated rebellion which began on

7 March, five days before the Japanese landings, made the Dutch position in Aceh untenable, and their forces withdrew even before the Japanese landings.[35] There was no such unity of purpose elsewhere in Sumatra, but plenty of aroused expectations, particularly among the Karo of East Sumatra.

For three and a half years, the Japanese ruled both sides of the Malacca Straits, and were in a position to redraw boundaries. Their decision was to make *Shonan* (Singapore) the capital of a new unit comprising Sumatra and Malaya, under the authority of the 25th Army and separate from both Java under the 16th Army and the rest of the archipelago administered by the Navy. Sumatra-Malaya was "the nuclear zone of the Empire's plans for the Southern Area", because of its command of strategic arteries and its resources of oil, rubber and tin. Communication everywhere was difficult under the Japanese, but during their first year, there were a few initiatives for common projects, both economic and educational. In May 1943, the experiment was abandoned, however. The 25th Army moved its headquarters to Bukittinggi, and Sumatra was administratively separated from Malaya. Japanese communications by sea and air were already becoming vulnerable and chaotic, and economic self-sufficiency was increasingly imposed on each island, and indeed each district. Of previously Dutch territory, only the Riau Archipelago (including Batam and Bintan) remained under *Shonan* authority.

Indonesian nationalism was not a major factor in this move, though the Japanese must have discovered that the similar institutions developed by the Dutch in Java and Sumatra made some consultation between their commanders appropriate. Indonesians themselves were unable to travel between Java and Sumatra for the duration of the war. Prominent Sumatrans who left the island were taken to Singapore or Tokyo, never Jakarta, until the final desperate days of August 1945. The 30 years of centralised Dutch rule, school systems and newspapers had nevertheless succeeded brilliantly in creating an Indonesian "imagined community". The elites of Sumatra and Java did not doubt that they were Indonesian in 1945, despite the lack of direct contact for three years.

As Twang Peck Yang has shown, a whole new set of commercial relationships began to form during the Japanese occupation which continued and blossomed after the surrender.[36] Because legal trade became very difficult, much of the movement of foodstuffs and other goods across the Straits was in the form of risky smuggling for high profits, often with the connivance of bribable Japanese officers. With the surrender of Japan, the Indonesian declaration of independence, and the arrival of Allied forces of reoccupation in 1945, "normality" in the form of the pre-war KPM-dominated shipping network was very slow to return. Dutch authority was never re-established in Aceh, and not until mid-1947 in ports such as Tanjung Balei and Labuhan Bilik in East Sumatra. A lively, uncontrolled trade therefore began between these ports and Singapore and Penang.

This trade was generally regarded as "barter trade" by the British but as "smuggling" by the Dutch. The struggling Republican politicians, military and *lasykar* (partisan) units were desperate for money, arms and supplies, and trade across the Straits was the obvious means to acquire them. Thanks to Dutch intelligence in Singapore, we are well informed about some of these shipments. In June 1946, for example, Chinese traders in Tanjung Balei managed to bring in 20 boatloads (each of 20–30 tons) of arms, motorcycles and other military equipment for the Republicans, in exchange for rubber and other plantation produce. After a military setback in March 1947, the scale of the trade increased enormously as all Republican authorities devoted themselves to improving their material. Mahruzar, the brother of Indonesia's first Prime Minister Sutan Sjahrir, set up a trading company working with Chinese merchants in Penang, while a couple of enterprising Mandailings set up an analogous "Nusantara Agency" in Singapore, both devoted to developing the barter trade to east Sumatra.[37] Much of the stock of rubber, palm oil, tea, and pepper built up during the war was shipped out in this way, for prices which were often well below their real value. *Lasykar* units occupied many of the estates, and generated a large private income by shipping to Malaya the export produce and even some of the processing machinery of the estates.

While the trade in plantation produce from East Sumatra tended to accentuate the ethnic and political conflicts between competing Republican groups there, in Palembang it better served the interests of the official Republic. Dr A.K. Gani, first Republican Resident of Palembang, in October 1946 became Minister of "Prosperity" in the Republican Cabinet on the strength of his success in siphoning off some of the fruits of the barter trade for official Republican purposes.[38] The Palembang-Singapore nexus was perhaps the most important for both sides of the Straits, and a number of key Singapore capitalists of the post-war era obtained their start as Palembang "smugglers".[39] Gani also represented within Republican counsels a sympathetic view towards Chinese business, in contrast to Hatta and other representatives of pribumi business who saw their role as competitive with Indonesians.[40] In reality, the Republic could not have survived without this new group of Chinese who were taking risks on its behalf, and thereby getting their own start in commerce. As the Jakarta Chinese newspaper *Sheng Hua Pao* noted on 4 December 1946:

> The trade between Sumatra and Malaya has created not a few newly prosperous Chinese merchants who began their enterprises during the Japanese occupation. Unlike the pre-war Chinese capitalists who are night and day expecting the return of the Dutch government, these newly prosperous merchants are hoping for complete independence for the Indonesians.[41]

These new men were largely China-born *totok* Chinese, Hokchia in Java but Hokkien in Sumatra, who were willing to take bigger risks both in smuggling and in cutting deals with Republican power-holders. In the second half of 1948, Dutch authorities reported capturing more than 100 smuggling vessels in the Malacca Straits. But as they controlled more territory and put pressure for cooperation on the British authorities, smuggling activity was forced further north, using Aceh as the only outlet whose ports were not controlled by the Dutch, and eventually evading even British controls by selling the rubber in South Thailand.[42] It is not easy to trace the scale of the barter trade, because much of it was determined to avoid official detection at either end. In the years 1946–1948, British statistics showed vastly more imports to Singapore from Indonesia than did Dutch statistics, but the millions of dollars involved for example in the smuggling of pre-war stocks of opium from Java to Singapore in exchange for military equipment for the Republic, certainly escaped any statistics.[43] Singapore's declared imports of rubber from Indonesia reached over 200,000 tons in 1947 and 1948 — more than double the pre-war level.[44] Singapore records show total imports from Indonesia worth 222 million Malayan dollars in 1947 and 291 million Malayan dollars in 1948 — 22 per cent of Singapore's total imports. In an attempt to obtain British support to control the barter trade, the Netherlands signed an agreement with Britain in March 1948 to implement "a system of controlled barter trading", but by no means all of the trade across the Straits was brought within the purview of this arrangement.[45]

Indonesian Attempts to Regain Control

With its independence accepted in 1950, Indonesia did not have Holland's need to placate powerful British commercial interests, but in other respects was very weakly placed to regain control. The Dutch-owned KPM had only partially re-established its archipelago network by 1957, and at that point, all its vessels left Indonesia to escape nationalisation. The gap was largely filled by smaller Chinese-owned shipping firms which had started as risk-taking "smugglers" in Palembang and other Indonesian ports but eventually achieved respectability as Singapore-registered firms. By 1949, more than 20 such firms were registered in Singapore for trade with the archipelago, where there had been virtually none before the war. Among them were Swan Liong (key owner Ban Hin Liong from West Java), which operated seven ships by 1951, Ho Chiang (Koh Teck Kin from Palembang, later President of the Singapore Chinese Chamber of Commerce), which operated four already in 1947, and Kie Hock (the Tay brothers from Palembang), which operated 60 at its peak in 1958.[46] Far from the "curtains for the Singapore connection" suggested in Yong Mun Cheong's account,[47] Indonesian independence introduced another period of extreme difficulty for Indonesia-based shipping, ensuring that Singapore would enter another phase of domination. Whereas in 1938, only 20 per cent of Indonesian exports went through Singapore and Malaya, the official figure was 23 per cent in 1956 and 32 per cent in 1958 (after the loss of the KPM), without counting the substantial amount of unrecorded smuggling.[48] Smuggling and barter trade to Singapore and other Peninsula ports remained at their maximum in the late 1950s and 1960s, when these were the essential lifelines for an economy broken by economic nationalism and overregulation. The stabler and stronger governments that followed brought Singapore's share of Indonesia's recorded exports down to a healthier 8.2% in 1995 and 7.8% in 2005.[49]

Under Sukarno's "Guided Democracy" period of turbulence (1958–1965), Indonesian efforts to reconstitute a unified economy were largely counterproductive. The bonds of silver again attracted the Archipelago's goods to Singapore, and the military bonds of steel (and one must add, of ideology and sentiment) had to be employed to bring much of Sumatra and Sulawesi into subjection. Though Sukarno railed against the dominance of Singapore and Penang over the Indonesian economy, and finally banned all trade with them in September 1963, it was chiefly the chaotic conditions within Indonesia that forced shipping companies to make their base across the Straits, and smugglers again to do what legitimate trade could not.

Only the relative stability and growth-oriented policies from the 1970s began to provide the infrastructure and economic wherewithal to make the highly centralising policies of General Suharto's government (1966–1998) effective. During this era, power clearly emanated as never before from Jakarta, and the lines of communication multiplied between the capital and its provinces. Even so, informal trade, regarded in Indonesia as smuggling or corruption and in Singapore as an informal system of "barter trade", has continued to be as important as official trade. In 2003, Indonesia's Trade Minister brought this longstanding secret into the open by asking Singapore to explain why its figures for imports from and exports to Indonesia in 2002 (US$7.41 billion and 5.25 billion respectively) were almost double the Indonesian figures (4.61bn and 2.44bn).[50] Singapore responded that the Indonesian side had itself sought to keep this under wraps, implicitly because it was embarrassing but profitable to many power-holders.

The tin trade has provided probably the most important leakage in recent times for Jakarta's quest for control of exports. The resources of Bangka and Billiton islands to the south of Singapore make Indonesia the world's second largest tin producer after China, but the proximity and efficiency of the Singapore tin market has rendered Jakarta's control over these resources always problematic. The fall of Suharto in 1998 and the climate of democracy and regional autonomy which followed ended a period of attempted monopoly by the Suharto government over tin production and export, backed by periodic violent crackdowns. A proliferation of "informal" mining operations followed, encouraged by a newly assertive local Bangka government, with 4,671 such operations claimed by one report in 2001. Much of this informal tin, especially that in the form of tin sand, was smuggled to Singapore.[51]

In consequence, the remarkable role of Singapore as a tin exporter (despite zero production of tin) reached another peak in this reform period. The 2001 trade figures show that Singapore was the second biggest tin exporter in the world, exporting US$196 million worth of tin while importing only $22 million worth! By contrast, Indonesia was only recorded as exporting 190 million worth of tin.[52] The discrepancy came chiefly from the informal miners now able to exploit regional autonomy by sending their product directly to Singapore as "informal trade" rather than submit to the cumbrous official agencies, whose "price was low, their enterprise bureaucratic, and their smelting capacity low".[53]

From 2002, the Jakarta government sought various means to regain control, banning all exports of tin sand and progressively seeking to tighten regulations. In October 2006, 84 unlicenced mining firms and the three principal smelters in Bangka were closed, and six local tin industry leaders were arrested, leading to large-scale protests on the island.[54] In consequence, a higher percentage of tin again flowed through official channels, so that in 2008 Indonesia was again officially the world's largest tin exporter, followed by Singapore and China.

As in the past, a period of political transition and loosened central control such as that of 1998–2002 tended to recentre trading networks on Singapore. In the new climate of democracy and regional autonomy, Jakarta must use carrots as well as sticks in re-establishing its economic authority over regions which profit from the direct trade. An advantage, however, is that in the recent crisis, unlike the 1940s and the 1960s, Jakarta had solid cooperative arrangements with its neighbours. Within the context of the Association of Southeast Asian Nations (ASEAN, since 1967), regional cooperation has become normal, leading in 1989 to the first of the "Growth Triangles", SIJORI, facilitating trade and investment across the adjoining territories of Singapore, Johor (Malaysia) and Riau (Indonesia). These fruits of greater economic confidence are finally softening the tyranny of the imaginary lines on the maps of 1824.

CHAPTER 5

Merdeka: The Indonesian Key to Freedom[1]

> *Merdeka — melody to me that word ... On its account the red blood of courage was spilt brave and bold ... But in the end it evoked greater joy and pride and honour than was ever known before in South East Asia.*
>
> *Merdeka, in the language of Indonesia, means freedom. Nothing more. Historians may come in time to chronicle its evolution and interpret its development in textbook terms of political autonomy and nationhood. To me Merdeka is a native battle-cry beautifully sad, echoing far into the night across the island kampongs and fires.*[2]

Suharto's Indonesia was low on the league tables for the practice of political and civic freedoms, and its government did not put these high on its list of national priorities. Human rights did become an issue in the post-Suharto reform era from 1998, but it was conservatives who were more likely to cite Indonesian tradition, while human rights activists sought personal freedoms as an inherent aspect of that universal modernity towards which they strove. Freedom as a key concept is likely to be seen as Western or as modern, in other words, and seldom as inherently Indonesian.

The scholarship on slavery, on the other hand, has challenged the equation of liberty with progress and modernity. Slavery was once seen as the antithesis of both freedom and progress, its gradual elimination from the world as "proof of a transcendent purpose in history".[3] We now have to confront the paradox that freedom is most valued where it is most denied, so that we should look towards cultures in which slavery played a major part for potential seedbeds of the idea of liberty. Perry Anderson and Moses Finley each perceived that the conjunction in ancient Greece of an urban social system based on slavery and the birth of concepts of democracy and personal liberty was not coincidental.⁴ These two phenomena rose together, and they declined together. The similar symbiosis between slavery and liberty in the birth of American democracy was explored by E.S. Morgan.⁵

Orlando Patterson's *Freedom in the Making of Western Culture* made explicit and universal the connection between slavery and the idea of freedom. It was slaves, and those owning them, who conceived "the unusual idea that being free was not only a value to be cherished but the most important thing that someone could possess". Though one of his main objectives is "to show that freedom was a peculiarly Western value and ideal", Patterson devotes only one chapter to the question of why freedom failed in the non-Western world. He concedes that "some notion of freedom existed wherever slavery was found", and specifically that among the (Bare'e-speaking) Toraja of central Sulawesi, his only Asian example, "freedom did become something of an ideal ... it would certainly have been listed among the important things in life".⁶ He categorises this freedom, however, as only the most basic of his three elements — the one he calls sovereignal freedom, the ability to do as one likes with others. The Toraja scarcely ever freed their slaves. They needed neither to motivate the slaves with the hope of eventual freedom nor to placate non-slave-owning freedmen by giving them some rights in society. There was no progress, he argues, towards either of the other central elements in the Western triad: personal freedom and civic freedom.

In arguing that the centrality which freedom came to occupy in the value-systems of several European cultures grew out of particular social conjunctions rather than disembodied intellectual debates, Patterson has taken an important step forward. Nevertheless, this path invites a response from those in a position to study particular Asian social forms more carefully. In an earlier study of slavery, I had already called for comparative work on how far slave institutions in non-European societies generated values analogous to that which freedom represents in European languages.⁷ Here I wish to respond to the challenge in relation to the development of the concept of "merdeka" within Indonesian cultures.⁸ As one of the few Asian terms for political freedom which resonates positively with the ancient world's distinction from slavery, this is a particularly important case. The Torajas of central Sulawesi are only a small part of it, for other Indonesian societies proceeded much further, both in freeing slaves and in building civic traditions.

Origins of the Merdeka Idea

The word came to the Indonesian archipelago from the Sanskrit *maharddika*, meaning "eminent, wise, rich or illustrious". It appears in this form in a number of Javanese texts from the tenth to the 18th century.[9] In the seventh-century Telagu Batu inscription of southern Sumatra, on the other hand, it had already adopted a Malay form, *murdhaka*, with a meaning more like the leader of a group of subjects or bondsmen.[10] Since in some Borneo, Sulawesi and Philippine languages (for example, Sa'dan Toraja *ma'dika*; Tagalog *maharlika*), it refers to the intermediate group above slaves but below the ruler, we might guess that the term was first dispersed by Indian-influenced kingdoms in the Archipelago to mean a rank of official or headman, and later a superior social category.

In the first clearly dated dictionary to mention the word, the Malay wordlist collected by Frederick de Houtman in Aceh in 1600, it had already assumed its modern sense as the antonym of slavery: "*mardeka*: vryman/geen slaef zijn" (freeman, not being a slave).[11] At some point in the 16th century or before, this meaning had spread to all the Indonesian languages which were in contact with Malay-speaking urban life — at least Acehnese, Minangkabau, southern Sumatran languages, Javanese, Bugis and Makasarese, as well as the Malay lingua franca itself. In the cosmopolitan Malayo-Muslim world of the 16th- and 17th-century cities, slaves and slave-owners came from different cultural backgrounds, and clear legal notions were required to govern their status. It is in this context that *merdehika* (the classical Malay form of the word) became a term with defined legal status, the equivalent of Arabic *hurr* in Islamic law, in which criminals, victims and citizens were given different values according to whether they were slaves or free.

In the interior of Java, this meaning appears to have arrived fairly late, presumably because slaves never became an important or clearly defined legal category (despite a lively export of slaves from pre-Muslim areas in the 16th century). In 18th-century texts, the Sanskrit form *maharddhika*, or *amardika*, was still being used in the sense of an old or wise person, or perhaps someone freed from obligations by retirement.[12] Although by the late 19th century, Javanese had imported from Malay the opposition between merdeka and slavery, the older and deeper Javanese uses of the word had more to do with being pensioned or liberated from government service. The *pardikan desa* (freed villages) of Java were given a charter freeing them from any tax or service to the king.[13]

John Crawfurd developed a theory of slavery on the basis of his experience in Indonesia in the second decade of the 19th century: "wherever the manners of the lower orders are most intractable, there slavery most prevails, and where they are most docile, it is rarest. For the extremes of both, Celebes and Java may be quoted as examples".[14]

While the servility of 19th-century Javanese towards their superiors made slavery unnecessary, and therefore freedom ill-defined, Bugis and Makasarese slave-holders were the most passionate about their freedom. Because the slave/free dichotomy had only a small part in the way Javanese understood this concept, merdeka in modern times came to have "few resonances in Javanese" in contrast to its emotive power in Malay and Indonesian.[15] One of the pioneers of the teaching of Javanese to Dutch officials in the 1840s had insisted that the inherently hierarchic nature of Javanese speech made it indispensable for retaining control of the colony. Malay, he complained, encouraged a sense of equality and freedom, and if these ideas spread, "Java is lost to us".[16]

Following a dichotomy developed by James Watson, I have argued elsewhere that Southeast Asia had both "open" and "closed" slave systems.[17] In relatively self-contained "closed" systems such as those of the Batak, Niha, Ngaju Dayak and Toraja (including those discussed by Patterson), slavery was a means of retaining the labour of a valuable subordinate group, who were therefore ritually defined as distinct, subordinate pariahs with very little prospect of obtaining their freedom. But during the rapid commercialisation of the Archipelago in the 15th to 17th centuries, there was an immense trade in slaves and captives, and larger cities such as Banten, Aceh, Palembang and Makasar grew by incorporating slaves into the dominant society. In these "open" systems, freeing slaves was a well-established legal procedure, expressed in Malay, Javanese and Bugis legal codes.

Freedmen and freemen were both merdeka (correctly *merdehika*) in the Malay of the 16th and 17th centuries, and the verb for "manumission" was *merdehikakan* (to free). In the most important Malay legal text, the *Undang-undang Melaka*, often copied but thought to have been initially drawn up around 1500, both freemen and slaves have specified values and rights, including the right to defend their dignity if abused.[18] This would hardly be imaginable in the "closed" systems of outcast slaves.

This code also gives sufficient attention to issues of contested manumission to make clear that this was a frequent occurrence.

> If someone lays claim to an adult person, saying that he is his slave, but that person says, "I am a freeman (*merdehika*) from birth", the claimant should be asked to produce his witnesses, or his documents to support the claim. If neither party can produce a witness or a document to that effect, the case will be cancelled.
>
> If a man lays claim to another person, saying "you are my slave," but the one claimed replies, "It is true I was your slave, but you freed me," or "The person who sold me to you had already set me free," then he will be asked for witnesses that he was set live by his master.

In this latter case, the code specifies that if each side can produce contradictory witnesses, the person seeking his freedom will be given the benefit of the doubt, and will be free.[19]

Ethnographic evidence of the 19th and 20th centuries indicates that laws relating to freeing of slaves were present in many other societies. In the Makasar area, there were complex rules to govern the case of slaves whose testimony that they were promised manumission at the death of their owner was contested by the heirs.[20] There were various Makasarese methods of manumission (*pamaradeka*), including the making of a written declaration by the master, but most commonly, the slave passed coins obtained from the master to 30 different people, who then became the witnesses of his status.[21] Derek Freeman describes the ritual of "enfranchisement" (a term he prefers to "manumission" because he is arguing that slavery is anomalous among Ibans), by which Ibans freed enslaved captives and rendered them members of the dominant society.[22] Among the most successful trading states which incorporated large numbers of servile outsiders through capture or purchase, there is no doubt that similar patterns of incorporation obtained. Slavery was the major source of labour mobility, and each city or commercial frontier had its subclass of unfree labourers who could hope that they or their locally-born descendants would be able to rise to free status.[23]

The growing role of Europeans as slave-owners, and the increasing trend for Islamic societies to restrict enslavement to non-Muslims by preference, gave the boundary between slave and non-slave a sharper racial or cultural character in the 17th and 18th centuries. Slavery also declined as the wealth of the Indonesian indigenous cities decreased, and as long-established rural patterns of exploiting labour through corvée became more dominant (especially in Java). Nevertheless, the importance of non-slave status as an aspect of the good life was established by the

17th century, and gave the subsequent career of the concept of merdeka a positive start.

James Scott observes perceptively that the freedom of Southeast Asians at a practical level has generally depended, and still depends, on "the relative autonomy of the social units within which they live".[24] It is therefore important that some of these social units described their autonomy in terms of merdeka. The tax-free *pardikan desa* of Java, already referred to, are one such case. Another developed in the upper reaches of the Musi River in southern Sumatra, where a number of highland peoples considered themselves *orang mardeka* (free people) because they had no king themselves and explicitly declined to submit in even the most nominal way to the downstream ruler of Palembang. A Dutch official in 1870 recorded the origin story of the six self-governing clans of the Besemah (Pasumah) plateau, and the council known as "Four mats and two frees" (*Lampik empat merdike due*), which regulated their affairs in times of crisis. Local legend had it that when their founding ancestor had failed to make peace among the six Besemah clans; four of the clan leaders journeyed to Palembang where they each received a mat from the sultan as a token of pre-eminence, while the other two refused to go for fear of losing some of their treasured freedom, and hence became known as the "two frees".[25] The Besemah were reported by Dutch officials in the 19th century to constitute "a Republic in the most democratic sense. The people rules itself; for that purpose great public meetings would be convened in which all important matters would be discussed".[26] Another source noted, "The untamed, freedom-loving masses in Besemah are the tyrant of their own leaders; democracy prevails there to the point of anarchy".[27]

Freedom in State Institutions — The Bugis Case

The existence of a concept of free status as the antithesis of slavery is a necessary step, but only a first step, towards modern understandings of rights to personal freedom. In all parts of the world where slavery was important and recognised as a legal category there was such a concept, but most state ideologies developed without regard to it. The pre-colonial Indonesian states for which both slavery and freedom were most important were the pluralistic port-states of the period roughly 1450–1630, in which law codes such as the *Undang-undang Melaka* originated.

The merchant-aristocrats who dominated these states found ingenious ways of evading the absolutist ideology of kings, such as female and child rulers and dual monarchies, but for the most part, they failed to generate an alternative ideology which protected the rights of others against the king.[28] Pre-colonial states remained unstable, caught in the tensions among weak state institutions, strong local traditions, and royal claims to untrammelled authority.

This background makes the particular case of the Bugis, the dominant people of southern Sulawesi, important as the most advanced pre-colonial attempt to institutionalise freedom in the way states were run. The Bugis and Makasar peoples of the southwestern peninsula of Sulawesi developed their states relatively late and with little of the Indian-derived rhetoric of universal kingship which influenced Java and Sumatra. Each local community which acknowledged a political and military leader identified the legitimacy of that leader with the sacred regalia of the place, believed to be found by the heaven-descended founder of the local lineage. When these communities federated into larger states in the 15th and 16th centuries, they retained most of their autonomy, still magically sanctioned by the intrinsic power of the regalia (*arajang*).[29] Federations remained therefore contractual, and the terms on which they formed broader units were sanctioned by powerful supernatural forces.

Makasar, the most powerful state in the period 1550–1660 by dint of its dominant port and brilliant leadership, might have been expected to absorb the whole of southern Sulawesi into a new state in this period, as happened with sultanates in Java and Sumatra. But this contractual pattern stood in its way. Makasar's own strength was built on a central dualism between the two states of Gowa and Tallo', which in turn were federations of seven or nine lineages each with rights within the united kingdom. The Dutch admiral who conquered Makasar with Bugis help in 1667, astonished at the series of extremely complex rights, contracts and obligations to which he became heir, noted that "the kings of Gowa and Tallo' cannot make one false step once outside their own gates".[30]

Southern Sulawesi also had a distinctive form of slavery, where slaves were regarded with the sort of contempt which obtained in the closed systems like those of the Toraja, but where commercialisation and warfare produced all the movement of the "open" system, with thousands of Bugis slaves being exported every year in the 18th century. Although freemen used the term *ata* to refer not only to slaves but to themselves as loyal subjects of a ruler, they knew very well what slavery and non-slavery meant. As indicated above, they had elaborate procedures to publicise the emancipation of individual slaves, indicating that this was also common.

The autonomy of several of the Bugis kingdoms was severely threatened in the 17th century when Indonesian kings, like European ones, profited from new wealth, weapons and ideas to extend their power. Makasar twice conquered Bone, the largest Bugis state, and reduced it to the invidious status of slave (*ata*), without a ruler of its own. When Bone freed itself from this humiliating yoke by its alliance with the Dutch, it in turn subjected other states including Wajo' to the same unacceptable "slavery". When full independence and equality were again achieved, as in 1737 when Wajo' threw off Bone rule, liberation was naturally described with the term "merdeka".[31]

The Bugis state of Wajo', based around Lake Tempe and the Cenrana River to the north of Bone, was particularly attached to the contractual autonomies of its freemen, repeatedly expressed in the ideal of merdeka. Wajo' was also, from the late 17th century to the late 19th, the source of most of Sulawesi's seafaring entrepreneurs, the renowned Bugis mariners who traded throughout the Indonesian Archipelago and as far as Cambodia. There was clearly a connection between this individual entrepreneurship and the attachment to an ideology of freedom, both of which were well established in the 18th century. The Wajo' chronicles were rewritten after the "liberation" of 1737, and the resounding declarations then placed in the mouths of the state founders of two or three centuries earlier may reflect 18th-century values better than 15th-century ones.

These texts were clearly written with the intention of codifying what they call "the freedoms of Wajo" (*am-maradeka-ngenna to Wajo'*). Though chronicles and local traditions differ, the declaration that "the people of Wajo' are free" (*maradeka to Wajo'*) is common to all of them. In a more elaborate version put into the mouth of one of the founding fathers, "the people of Wajo' are free; free from birth. Only their land is subject, the owners of the land are all free. Their only master is the customary law which is agreed consensually".[32]

The major chronicle tradition of Wajo', the *Lontara Sukku'na Wajo'*, is largely an exemplary account of how the state was formed by agreement, how two of the earliest rulers transgressed the "freedoms" of the people and were duly killed, and how the people ensured through agreements solemnly witnessed by the (pre-Muslim) gods that their freedoms would thereafter be safeguarded. These freedoms are repeatedly enlarged on. At one point, the Wajo' people declare:

> To secure freedom, only three things are decisive: firstly not to interfere with people's wishes; secondly not to forbid the expression of opinions; thirdly not to prevent [people going] to the south, the north, the west, the east, upstream or downstream. These are the freedoms of the people of Wajo'.[33]

Elsewhere, more extensive lists of concerns are spelt out. The people of Wajo' must not be unjustly punished. Even if they are guilty, the punishment must be mild, no others should suffer for the crime of one, and death sentences should be commuted to fines or exile. Their family, their property and their slaves must not be taken from them. They must be free to come and go, with the doors of Wajo' always open to them.[34]

The rituals by which new Arung Matoa of Wajo', as well as heads of local communities, were installed, repeated for each generation the consensual ideals of the 18th-century chronicle writers. The new ruler protested his inadequacy: "I am not worthy to be appointed ruler of Wajo', for I am stupid, fearful, poor and weak", to which the people's representative replies, "Simply accept the decision of Wajo', for Wajo' is clever, Wajo' is brave, Wajo' is rich, and Wajo' is strong".[35] The head of each constituting lineage would then express his loyalty at the same time as his autonomy: "I will conduct my own affairs, I will preserve my manners, I will maintain my custom, only if I need it will I appeal to your advice". In return, the ruler declared to the assembly, "I will not oppose myself to your will; I will not contradict your words; I will not prevent you from leaving Wajo' or returning to it".[36]

At least one Indonesian people appear to have arrived quite independently at a well-defined idea of freedom by the 18th century. English liberals such as Thomas Forrest and James Brooke, children of a British Enlightenment not a great deal older than that of the Bugis, could discern in these attitudes and institutions a parallel to their own ideas. After visiting Wajo' in 1840, the future "white raja" of Sarawak declared that, "amid all the nations of the East, amid all the people professing the Mahometan religion from Turkey to China, the Bugis alone have arrived at the threshold of recognised rights, and have alone emancipated themselves from the fetters of despotism".[37]

Slavery and Freedom in the European Settlements

Of declining commercial importance in the late 19th century, the Bugis were not central to the development of modern Indonesian political culture, except insofar as they carried their intellectual traditions to the cities. It was in the European-ruled but multicultural cities of the Archipelago, including Singapore, that the Malay language (the basis for both Indonesian and Malaysian national languages) was adapted to cope with modern political ideas such as freedom and democracy. Since it was also in these cities that slavery was most sharply defined, it was not surprising that "merdeka" (non-slave) became the term to translate that freedom.

Europeans in the Archipelago themselves adopted the word "merdeka" (usually in the Dutch form, *Mardijker*) to refer to the earliest Asian slaves who were freed after becoming Christian. The Portuguese were more inclined than the Dutch to Christianise their slaves, but it appears to have been the Dutch who perceived the resulting Portuguese-speaking, Christian Asians as a distinct ethnic or social group whom they called Mardijkers — "freed people". The Dutch Company captured many on Portuguese ships or in Portuguese settlements such as Melaka and Pulicat and found them useful as a military force. They were gradually converted to Dutch Calvinism and became a vital source of relatively loyal support for the Dutch in Batavia. A 1673 enumeration of the Batavia population showed 5,362 Mardijkers, twice as numerous as Dutch and Eurasian groups combined. They formed the backbone of the local militia, and were responsible for Portuguese becoming the predominant language of Dutch Batavia.[38]

Far more numerous in the 1673 register were the slaves, at 13,278, about half the Batavian population within the walls. Indonesian slaves continued to be imported to Batavia at a rate of about 1,000 a year in the 17th century, and 3,000 a year for much of the 18th. After 1760, larger numbers were needed as replacements for the slaves, who were then dying at a rate in excess of 1,300 a year in Batavia's unhealthy conditions. The total slave population of Batavia from 1689 to 1770 remained between 20,000 and 30,000, but the numbers of freed slaves and their descendants gradually rose to become the dominant factor in Batavia's population by the time of the English interregnum in 1812–1816.[39] The slave trade was made illegal by Britain in 1807 and the Netherlands in 1818, but there were still about 3,350 slaves in the Batavia area when slave-holding was finally abolished in Dutch colonial territory in 1860.

The British settlements of Singapore and Pinang, which were among the most important points of interaction between Malay-speakers and the outside world in the 19th century, did not legally countenance slavery. Nevertheless, several hundred slaves each year from Bali, Sumbawa, Flores, southern Sulawesi, the Batak area and Nias were being shipped to these settlements in the first half of the century, where they were valued by some as "of immense advantage in procuring a female population".[40] Munshi Abdullah bin Abdul Kadir, Malay writer for the British founders of Singapore, gives a poignant description of one such cargo of about 300 slaves being sold at the Singapore dockside around 1820. When he reported it to Stamford Raffles, he received a predictable lecture on the evils of slavery, but the hope that "if we live a long time we may see all these slaves become free (*mardehika*) as we all are free".[41] Later, he describes how John Crawfurd, British Resident of Singapore, freed 27 girls, "young and beautiful to look at", who were slaves of the British protégé Sultan Husain Shah. Crawfurd explained to the fearful girls that they might go "wherever you wish, and nobody can order you about or do anything to you". Abdullah then described Crawfurd's meeting with the indignant sultan, when he firmly insisted that "instructions have come from the Governor-General in Bengal that in any English state no one whatsoever may keep slaves, but on the contrary everybody is free (*mardehika*)".[42] These events clearly made a great impression on Abdullah, and his subsequent influential writings dwelt on the contrast between the oppression exercised by the Malay sultans of the Peninsula and the freedom conveyed by the British rule of law. Anthony Milner has hailed Abdullah as the unrivalled "founder of Malay modernism" in the 19th century, not least in his insistence on the importance of personal freedom for the individual to develop his own intellect.[43]

It may have been the influence of Abdullah and Raffles, for both of whom freedom from slavery and civic freedom were undoubtedly linked, which led English dictionaries of Malay in the 19th century to see merdeka as the natural equivalent of the liberty of which Locke and Mill wrote. Although the more pedestrian word *bebas* was always available to indicate freedom of movement, the English dictionaries gave primacy to merdeka. The first post-Enlightenment effort to render liberty into Malay went as follows:

> Free (manumitted) *mardika*; (on an equality) *sama rata*; (unrestrained) *bibas* ...

Freedom *hal mardika* ...
Liberty (enfranchisement) *ka-mardika-an;* (permission) *mohon, bibas.*[44]

As the century progressed, English writers tended to broaden the reference of merdeka to cover all the political meanings of English "free". Crawfurd's 1852 dictionary translated it as "free, not enslaved; manumitted, emancipated",[45] while Wilkinson in 1903 broadened it right out, perhaps under the influence of Munshi Abdullah, whose use of the term he quotes: "Freedom, in contrast to servitude; free".[46]

The Dutch scholarly tradition differed significantly, accepting merdeka as the equivalent of the abstract "freedom" (*vrijheid*), but finding numerous other words for "free".[47] Ignorant or resentful of what the nationalist movement had done to build revolutionary implications into merdeka, the editors of the 1947 edition of Klinkert's much-used dictionary (significantly still called Malay, despite long-held nationalist insistence on "Indonesian") continued to define it with breathtaking Orientalist irrelevance.[48]

It would be wrong to suggest that in the rural heartlands of 19th-century Indonesia, merdeka was prominent as an ideal. The numerous rebellions and wars fought against the Dutch in the Archipelago in that period do not appear to have expressed themselves in terms of freedom so much as through holy wars, obligations on the Islamic faithful to fight against the unbeliever, or simply defence of territory or prerogatives.[49] It may have been only in southern Sulawesi and parts of southern Sumatra, where the slave/free dichotomy of the early modern period had been developed in interstate or intergroup relations, that 19th-century battles were fought in the name of freedom. Elsewhere, the older concept of freeman had faded before new concepts of a free man had begun to penetrate.

Freedom as a Modern Political Goal

Nevertheless, merdeka remained a positive and expansive term with "not a slave" connotations which could not be unhitched from personal freedom. As Dutch rule became vastly more pervasive around the turn of the 20th century, merdeka became again a central concept for those who resented taxes, corvée, registrations, vaccination campaigns and a host of other intrusions by the colonial state. One such manifestation, remarkable because it occurred far from the influence of Western ideas, was the Samin movement in rural areas around Blora, central Java, at the beginning of this century. Its members rejected paying taxes or having anything else to do with the government, considering themselves free (merdeka) and self-sufficient.[50]

But it was in the second decade of the century that the idea of freedom as both a personal and political goal moved to the centre of the agenda of young Indonesians. The first generation began to benefit from the expansion of Dutch schooling opportunities under the so-called "Ethical Policy" ("developmentalism" in today's terminology), which then began to absorb ideas of progress, education, science, freedom and democracy, and to form organisations to promote them. The large Dutch and Chinese communities also began to generate modern organisations to promote such ideas. Between 1908 and about 1922, there was an extraordinary hothouse of diverse ideas before the colonial authorities began to take fright and impose ever tighter controls.

In this atmosphere, the concept of "free" appears to have commended itself first as a description of the new kind of person being brought into being by these new conditions — free from traditional loyalties and able to make their own decisions about what to believe and what organisation to join. The first association set up by the pioneer Javanese journalist and activist Tirtoadisurjo, a commercial association to rival the Chinese Chamber of Commerce, proclaimed itself "an association of free people" in 1909, using the Malay *kaum mardika* to translate the Dutch *vrije burgers*.[51] The first women's organisation for Indonesians was called *Puteri Mardika* (free daughters), and aimed at encouraging not only female education but also a "merdeka attitude" among women.[52]

The newspapers which began to service the mushrooming organisations also sought to call themselves free. First into the field may have been the Dutch-language publication *Het Vrije Woord*, put out by the Dutch-led Indies Socialist Party from 1917. When the party produced a Malay-language newspaper two years later, it was called the same thing — *Soeara Merdika* (*Free Voice*, or equally *The Voice of Freedom*). In 1920, as the Indonesian wing of the Indies Social Democratic Association transformed itself into the Indonesian Communist Party, this became the "People's Voice" — *Soeara Ra'jat*. But meanwhile, a number of other newspapers had begun to trumpet the importance of freedom. *Benih Mardika* (*Seeds of Freedom*), a Medan (Sumatra) daily of the years

1916–1922, was the most important, but Tasikmalaya had its *Sora Merdika* (1920), Purwokerto its *Doenia Merdeka* (*Free World*, 1924), Padang Panjang its *Djago Djago* (*Soeara Mardeka*) (*Champion — Free Voice*, 1923–1924), while the Surakarta leftist publishing firm was simply called Mardika.

In the period before communism, radical Islam, democracy and nationalism had taken fixed positions against one another; this concern for freedom was especially found in the inchoate Islamic-communist radicalism associated with Sarekat Islam and Sarekat Rakyat. At the grassroots level, the Russian revolution itself was interpreted as having blazed the trail to merdeka: "The communists have seized freedom in Russia ... Now Russia is free. Everybody is equal there, free from all oppression".[53] One of the powerful expressions for this group was *rasa merdeka*, which could be translated as "the taste, sense or experience of freedom", but also "a free spirit". It resonated with the cultivation of the inner being (*batin*), for which Javanese are especially renowned. The early Javanese Communist Semaun defined it in terms of two other words often applied to the *batin*: *selamat* and *ayem* (literally "secure" and "contented", but with mystical overtones).[54] Even the Dutch-educated Communist Tan Malaka had *rasa merdeka* inscribed on the red scarves worn by the students at his revolutionary school, while the same phrase was used as the title of the propagandist novel of another leader of the then left wing of the Sarekat Islam.[55] This did not (yet) refer to national independence in the first instance; rather, it was a way of standing up against all kinds of authorities. Shiraishi has well described the magical effect of Haji Misbach's oratory in the rural areas of Java as he told ragged groups of oppressed and hungry farmers that they should stand up as free men. "The peasants experienced their taste of 'freedom' in the suppression of their shared fear of the state".[56]

One writer in central Java made the connection with Javanese tradition by explaining that there were two forms of freedom: *kemerdekaan lahir* ("outer", or "ordinary" freedom) and *kemerdekaan batin*, which he explained in religious terms as "the freedom of a person who has liberated himself from every worldly temptation". The ordinary or outer freedom was also distinguished in ways which seem to prefigure Patterson's "sovereignal freedom". There was the kind of freedom from restraints which stemmed from conquest and imperialism, but the freedom this writer sought to focus on was "a *kemerdekaan* based on humanity ... which seeks and values common goals". This freedom was a universal right, universally desired, but he was sure his readers would feel that they did not enjoy it.

> Merdeka is a right given by God to each one of us, that is a right which cannot be taken away or reduced by anyone at all ... The flood of desire to demand freedom cannot be dammed; it arises spontaneously in the thinking of each person, who until now still feels in a situation which is far from the name of merdeka. Every person feels it is essential to possess and use that right ... only with that freedom will people be able to overcome whatever is not pure.[57]

This enthusiasm for freedom brought about a reaction, and not only from the side of an increasingly reactionary colonial government. In October 1925, as pressure was building for an ultimately disastrous revolutionary outburst, an article appeared in the leading Surakarta left-Muslim newspaper:

> The word "free" [Merdeka] can be heard from every direction. Wherever people gather, there we hear people talking about freedom. We want to sit free, sleep free, eat free, work free, talk free, play free, have a good time ... is there anything that people do not want [to do] freely? In short, to be free is generally understood to mean "not to be interfered with," "not to be prohibited from," etc. Thus people who pursue freedom can fall into violent, brutish, and ill-considered ways, and sometimes thus become people who are indifferent, or senseless.
>
> If one seeks freedom, [one should] not simply dare to speak low Javanese [i.e., not using the polite high form to superiors], dare to quarrel, dare to go on strike, and dare to make a big hoo-hah in brothels and hotels, but first of all one must have seriousness to study the science of true freedom and to perform all the obligations thereby involved.[58]

The author, and both the communist and Islamic wings into which the Sarekat Islam had now split, were sure that the intoxication with freedom had gone too far. Discipline was called for to reach specific goals, and the Party would define what they were.

Nevertheless, the roots of this *rasa merdeka* ran deep. The most creative attempts to build a non-colonial, autonomous education system between the wars, those of Ki Hadjar Dewantoro and Tan Malaka, both put at the top of their agenda the development of a sense of personal freedom in their students. Tan Malaka's attempt was relatively shortlived, consumed in the communist rebellions of 1926–1927 and the subsequent government crackdown on radicalism of all sorts. But Ki Hadjar Dewantoro founded a national education system which still endures and was an important intellectual influence on the whole nationalist movement. The aim of his schools, as he explained in opening the first one in 1922, was "to develop our culture by planting the seeds of freedom in the hearts of the people, by using a system of education with a national character".[59] Building on the educational ideas of Montessori and Tagore, he sought schools that were totally independent of government control. *Kemerdekaan* ("freedom" or "independence") was the second of the five principles on which Taman Siswa based itself.[60] But like others on the more conservative side of the national movement, he increasingly stressed self-control and self-reliance as the true essence of liberty. In 1940, he defined merdeka a little differently: "It is not the absence of authority, it is knowing how to control oneself".[61]

If freedom began to be defined more cautiously after the upheavals of the mid-1920s, it was also increasingly harnessed to the purposes of nationalism. As controls tightened in the colony, it was to Indonesian students in Holland that radical nationalist leadership fell. In 1925, their organisation, the Perhimpunan Indonesia, launched a new journal, *Indonesia Merdeka*, and a new radical policy which declared the national liberation of Indonesia as the prime objective. Increasingly in the years that followed, nationalists linked the new word "Indonesia" to the old word "merdeka", defining the latter above all as independence. The politically repressive policies pursued by colonial governments after 1926 tended to confirm the idea that this was the one freedom which had to be won before anything else could change.

This shift was encouraged during the Japanese occupation of 1942–1945. Nationalists such as Soekarno cooperated with the Japanese in the hope of achieving Indonesia Merdeka, and were finally rewarded in the last year of the occupation. Facing one defeat after another in the Pacific, the Japanese promised independence in September 1944. The nationalists finally had something to show for the miseries of wartime life and seized the opportunity to build up expectations of independence. Other aspects of merdeka such as individual rights, however, were anathema to the Japanese military. Messianic expectations centred around the fact of independence itself, not its content. Ancient prophecies of King Joyoboyo were adapted to suggest that after ruling for three and a half years, the Japanese would go and Indonesia would be free.

It was during the Indonesian revolution of 1945–1949 that merdeka became a talisman, the keyword of an aroused people. It happened quickly and spontaneously during the almost delirious days of September and October 1945, when the youth of Java and Sumatra realised that Japanese power had collapsed without any other regime taking its place. Merdeka suddenly became not just a political programme but a felt reality. Crowds of people swarmed into the streets "in response to the magic summons of Merdeka",[62] and nobody stopped them. The youth who mobilised first to confront the Japanese and then to fight the Dutch found themselves virtual masters of the cities in which they had lived. The *rasa merdeka* was theirs.

During this period, merdeka became the battle cry with which the citizenry was summoned to support the cause, the salute with which revolutionaries would greet each other, the cry of solidarity at every mass rally, and the signature at the end of every Republican document. Newspapers, hotels, offices and city squares were renamed Merdeka.

In the fighting against the Dutch, radical youth groups were animated by the slogan "freedom or death" (*merdeka atau mati*). One Australian correspondent who travelled with Soekarno through East Java in December 1945 noted that his train pulled up "amidst a vast roar of 'Merdekas' [People thought it] a fine thing to have the privilege of shouting 'Merdeka' [and] speeches always ended with a triple 'Merdeka' salute, thunderously returned by the crowd".[63] Later in the difficult struggle for independence, it may have become as routine as "citoyen" did in the French Revolution, but during the first emotive years 1945–1946 when the world was overturned, it was almost supernaturally powerful.

What did it mean to the revolutionaries? Certainly different things to different people. It began by meaning national independence, and the defence of the declaration of independence of 17 August 1945. For the leaders of the Republic, this had to remain its primary reference, and all other freedoms should if necessary be sacrificed to that end. Yet, there is no doubt that the people, and especially the young people who spontaneously supported the revolution and gave it momentum, experienced it as a freedom far more immediate and personal. For some urban youth, the exhilaration of merdeka was felt when they discovered they could ride free on the trams and trains. For others, it meant the escape from family and institutional authority to the newfound solidarity of revolutionary youth (*pemuda*). In some areas of Java's north coast where the "social revolution" against local power-holders was particularly intense, the cry of "Merdeka" by one revolutionary would be answered by another shouting its twin: *bebas* ("free" in the sense of "unfettered"). As Anton Lucas described the memories of the hundreds of revolutionaries he interviewed, "nothing should be too organized; each person was seeking his own freedom in the exhilaration of looking for new personal liberty, which in turn formed a new consciousness".[64]

This freedom quickly got out of hand, and the more disciplined elements of what was slowly becoming a national army went to considerable lengths to suppress its more radical manifestations. The military ideologues of Soeharto's New Order government after 1966 sought to redefine the revolution as a struggle for independence, and the spontaneous social revolutions within it as outbreaks of counterproductive terror. Merdeka itself was increasingly defined in official texts and state rituals as simply independence — that which was proclaimed in August 1945 and ritually celebrated on every 17 August since. Yet its other connotations will not go away. The positive resonance of a merdeka that is opposed to slavery, oppression and control is rooted too deep in Indonesian history to ever be forgotten.

CHAPTER 6

The Quest for an Indonesian Past[1]

Perceptions of the future and the past tend to be interdependent; particularly for emergent nationalisms as they reassess their national destiny. Indonesian nationalism was however slower than most in developing this reassessment into a complete history. Not until the period of Japanese military rule did a substantial national history by an Indonesian appear, in the form of Sanusi Pane's *Sedjarah Indonesia*, reprinted many times since as a standard textbook. At least one brief history appeared earlier in Padang, *Ringkasan Sedjarah Indonesia*, produced in 1938 by two little-known young men. The hazards of the undertaking were well brought out by one nationalist reviewer who complained that a reader might reasonably ask whether it was written by a foreigner. Faithfully following the pattern established by the standard Dutch textbook, Eijkman and Stapel, the writers had clearly failed to develop a picture of the past to match Indonesia's growing faith in its national future.[2] A similar reception appears to have greeted the more scholarly *Riwajat Indonesia* of Poerbatjaraka in 1952.

Even Malaya, whose pre-war nationalism was but a small rivulet to the major current in Indonesia, had produced its first modern national history more than a decade earlier. The first volume of Abdul Hadi bin Haji Hasan's *Sejarah Alam Melayu* appeared in 1925, encouraged and authorised by conservative colonial officials.[3] Published under the auspices of the colonial Education Department, it offered a coherent, detailed picture of the Malay past drawing as much from the Malay chronicles and Munshi Abdullah as from Western scholars like Mills, Fruin-Mees and Winstedt. The national theme for Abdul Hadi was self-evident, requiring a relatively short leap from the traditional perspective of Malay writers. It was the story of the Malay people, their kingdoms, and their dealings with foreigners.

The task of the Indonesian historian was in every way more difficult. Pride in the separate pasts of various regions and peoples had to be reconciled with the theme of a new unity whose limits were a colonial boundary. An analogous problem might have been expected to face early Philippine nationalists, but the unifying work of the friars was there much older and deeper that that of Dutch officials, and it was not seriously contested by the cultural nationalisms of each people.

One of the few early Indonesian nationalists who could accept a Dutch-created historical unity with equanimity was E.F.E. Douwes Dekker — the intellectual founder of *Indisch* (Indies) nationalism, but significantly a Eurasian uncommitted to any specific Indonesian cultural tradition. He has a claim to be the first national historian of Indonesia, though his *Vluchtig Overzicht van de Geschiedenis van Indonesia*, apparently written in Dutch for the pupils of his Ksatrian Institute in the 1930s, was not published until an Indonesian translation appeared in 1942. Douwes Dekker ingenuously explained that the various islands

> as a result of various events gradually became one archipelago, and fell under one authority, the Dutch government. The laws are the same in all these islands. The social structure is the same. Because of this it can be said that these islands became one region.

He was candid enough to admit in addition that among the islands "The most important is Java ... our knowledge of this island far exceeds that of others; moreover this island has the highest civilization. For this reason what we will emphasise is the history of Java".[4]

Douwes Dekker's definition of national history was convincing only to those who shared his belief that the political power of a remote government in The Hague was the primary issue. Among the first generation of Indonesians graduating from high schools during the First World War, there were many who reacted against the Dutch in quite a different way. For them, the "Indisch nationalism" promoted by Douwes Dekker and Tjipto Mangoenkoesoemo was an aggressive form of that same Dutch cultural dominance they resented. They sought a revival and strengthening of their own heritage, not identification with an artificial new polity of Dutch making.

The origins of this controversy belong to the history of Indonesia's first modern political organisation Budi Utomo, in which Tjipto represented a tendency towards anti-Dutch politics, while Dr Radjiman led the dominant group which wanted to work primarily for the revival of Javanese culture. Although Tjipto lost this contest within the Budi Utomo leadership, his political radicalism was much more appealing to the younger element in the organisation.[5] The young intellectuals who promoted "Javanese nationalism" from about 1917 admired his courage and shared his anti-Dutch politics. They differed radically only over Tjipto's advocacy of Indisch nationalism:

> Our history will develop towards the unity of the Indisch people, but not towards an Indisch national unity. An Indisch nation — could this be attained — would again fly into fragments ... Anyone who is sympathetic to a natural, gradual development ... can not demand that the Javanese nation sacrifice itself to an Indisch nation ... The sacrifice is too great.[6]

The intellectual centre of this argument was the "Committee for Javanese nationalism" established in Batavia in 1917. Its leaders, Soerio Koesoemo, Abdoel Rachman, and Satiman, wrote in Dutch like the Indisch nationalists, but they did so apologetically, believing that their future, like their past, must be Javanese. They wished their colleagues in the outer islands well, but implicitly felt them to be so behind Java in every field that they could only be a millstone to the Javanese nation.

> So you stay in Sumatra, and you there in Ambon. Only in this way will our friendship be long preserved. If we live in the same house and conduct our housekeeping jointly, no good can be expected from that. Our tastes now differ; our culture is absolutely different. We also have our history; we have our own great men; we have our Pajajaran period and the ancient Majapahit — this last associated for you with disagreeable memories ... Our duty is now determined by our birth, our way by the past, and our ideal by the knowledge of KAWULO·GUSTI, of the fact that we are now ruled (Kawulo) but were once rulers (Gusti).[7]

These Java-nationalists were passionately concerned with the pattern of Java's past. They were perhaps the first group to use this past as the basis for a national identity in the modern sense. They held fast to the essential cultural unity of the whole island of Java (with Madura and Bali), embracing the Sundanese on grounds that the Javanese *babad* themselves traced the origin of the Majapahit tradition to Sunda (West Java). Soeriokoesoemo devoted a lengthy adulation to Sultan Agung, arguing that his mystical work *Sastro Gending* entitled him to a place among the great thinkers of the ages.[8]

Tjipto's response to this challenge was characteristically in terms of European rather than Indonesian history. The way in which the mediaeval principalities of Holland, Friesland, and Utrecht had given way to the modern Netherlands nation, the similar development of nations in Germany and Italy, showed the inevitable path of progress "India" must follow. The criteria of race or culture were less important for him than the material interests which bound the people of "India" together. "The Javanese will gradually be forced to abandon their *adatistiadat* (customs) and adopt habits which prevail among the Chinese, as among the Lapps, the Americans, or the Australians". This process was already well advanced and could not be resisted.[9]

Another of the principal Indisch nationalists, Suwardi Suryaningrat [Ki Hadjar Dewantara], spiritually closer to the Java nationalists, was able to respond more sensitively to their arguments. He readily granted that Indisch nationalism had no cultural basis, but grew out of the purely negative factor of Dutch domination. The cultural case for Javanese nationalism, on the other hand, he found irresistible. Java formed a relatively homogeneous cultural whole, in contrast with the diversity everywhere else in the archipelago.

> The presence of so many great *candi* monuments, of classical Javanese music which has reached a high development, of Javanese art in general, of literature, and of other remnants of civilisation which remind us of the glorious days of old, of the beautiful Javanese past, give us the right to speak of Javanese nationalism. They may be only remnants of an earlier civilisation, but precisely on that account the word is particularly appropriate. For whenever nationalism is an essential element in a popular movement that is always in a period of decline.[10]

This nationalism remained vague and uncertain for "the so-called better educated because Dutch schools have already turned us into little half-Dutchmen". In the *vorstenlanden* (principalities), where the aristocracy remained fully Javanese, it was however a full-blooded and living reality:

> What is our knowledge of Javanese history, who have learned so much in Dutch schools ... in comparison with the knowledge of the Javanese rulers and nobles. There in the *vorstenlanden* they know

what Java was, how Java was feared by foreigners, but also how Java has suffered. They know also what contempt the Dutch have for the Javanese rulers, whose power and influence they have steadily confined. Javanese nationalism — that means a restoration of independent Java and thus, destruction of foreign rule.

One has only to exchange a few words with a Jogjanese about Javanese history to know that there in the land which is still Javanese they continue to hope for the coming of Heru Cokro, the man who will free Java, named by King Joyoboyo in his book of prophecy.[11]

Suryaningrat sought to resolve this burgeoning contradiction between Javanese and Indisch nationalism by making a clear distinction between the cultural basis of the former and the political emphasis of the latter. Javanese nationalism was entitled to pursue its cultural objectives, but the political aspect of its goals were in reality an aspect of Indisch (i.e., anti-Dutch) nationalism, which required the greatest degree of common purpose to overcome Dutch divide-and-rule tactics.[12]

The arguments of these founding fathers of Indisch nationalism were in practice less damaging to the Java nationalist ideal than its own internal contradictions. In their enthusiasm to state the historical case for the unity of Java, Soeriokoesoemo and his friends proved much more offensive to Sundanese opinion than the pragmatic politicians of Budi Utomo and the other parties.

Sundanese and Javan — even if the two do not stand on the same cultural level — are nevertheless one and the same culture which governs the people of Java. It is the culture of Pajajaran, which later took a higher flight in the time of Majapahit, in which today the people of Java consciously or unconsciously live ...

The founders of our present culture were the Sundanese themselves in the time of Pajajaran. That there are now Sundanese who no longer recognize their own culture after this reached a higher development during the reign of Brawijaya, has its own explanation.[13]

Few Sundanese appear to have relished such an image as "incomplete Javanese". More in sorrow than in anger, a Sundanese correspondent asked how he could be expected to feel a pride in the Javanese heritage as it was presented by Soeriokoesoemo's *Wederopbouw*, and whether dwelling on the past was the right way to promote a sense of unity.[14] Tactfully, he refrained from instancing the "Bubat War" so prominent in Sundanese memory, in which the renowned Majapahit chancellor Gajah Mada first insulted and then annihilated a Sundanese royal delegation which had come to arrange a marriage.[15]

Religion provided another divisive element. As a Sumatran intellectual later pointed out, "the current of Javanism ... was in reality suffused with the spirit of *Hindu*-Javanism".[16] Again the historical enthusiasm of the young Java nationalists made explicit what remained an unspoken assumption for other Javanese aristocratic politicians. For Soeriokoesoemo, Arabian Islam was a form of imperialism no less pernicious than the Dutch. "The beginning of this [foreign economic] domination was only made possible by the confusion which Islam introduced into the original conception of life of the Javanese people"; Islam forced the Javanese to abandon their art, and with that went all their economic incentives. The domination of a foreign holy place, Mecca, must give way to "Java, the holy land of the Javanese".[17]

The desire of these Java nationalists to revive and identify with a historical tradition still alive around them was not unique. Most of the peoples of the outer islands had still more immediate recollections of past heroes and vanished greatness, of a developing tradition thrown off course by Dutch conquest or control. Through its numbers, its relative homogeneity and its educational development, Java alone was in a strong position to relate such a past to the needs of modern nationalism. Yet even for the Java nationalists, history proved as much a source of distrust as of unity. The successful youth organisation Jong Java did not attempt to pursue very far the intellectual currents set in motion by Wederopbouw.

Sumatran Nationalism

The example of Javanese nationalism, and the organisational successes of Jong Java in mobilising politically-inclined secondary and tertiary students, found a reaction among Sumatrans studying in Dutch schools in Java. In December 1917, a group of Sumatran (primarily Minangkabau) students at the STOVIA (Medical school) in Weltevreden established the Jong Sumatranen Bond (JSB), to unite all Sumatran students, promote Sumatran languages and culture, and "to pose the inescapable demand to every member, that he call himself a Sumatran".[18] It did not claim, like many Javanese nationalists, that Sumatra was already a nation or that its interests conflicted with Indisch nationalism. Its primary slogan was simply that unity is strength: "Only a united Sumatra can fulfil Sumatra's greatness".[19] Nevertheless, it shared with Javanese nationalism a concern with cultural identity as the essence of any nationalist movement. First among the activities listed in its constitution was "the study and exercise of the history, languages, culture and art of Sumatra".[20]

The task of establishing the historical identity of Sumatra was no easy one. Even if Minangkabaus were proportionally almost as dominant in JSB as were ethnic Javanese in Jong Java, they could not overlook the enormous differences in language, religion and *adat* within Sumatra. In enthusiasm and ingenuity, young Sumatrans like Mohammad Amir, Muhammad Yamin and Bahder Djohan yielded nothing to the Java nationalists, but their efforts necessarily had a more artificial and academic character.

The most ambitious work was that of Amir, the second JSB chairman, who brought his very impressive scholarship to bear on the former greatness and dynamic of the Sumatran people. He was not content to show that Minangkabau had once been a great empire,[21] but went on to describe the peculiar genius of Sumatrans in history as seafarers, merchants, colonists (in Madagascar as well as Malaya), and as villagers (quoting Marsden) who knew how to construct an orderly *adat* system which approached a constitutional system of government. "There we see a few glimpses from the economic past of the Sumatran people — examples of daring, vitality, and commercial spirit". Like the Germanic peoples whose decline was deplored by Tacitus, the Sumatrans had demonstrated their potential to rise again to great things.[22]

Bahder Djohan, the next JSB chairman, led the movement into greater concern with economics and politics, which was reflected in turn in his reading of Sumatran history. He extolled the Padri movement in Minangkabau as a revolutionary force which could not accept the static society and the political disunity of its time.[23] Finally, a precocious Muhammad Yamin was then throwing all his youthful enthusiasm behind the Malay language as the symbol and vehicle of Sumatran (and ultimately Indonesian) unity.

Towards an Indonesian Identity

The evolution of Sumatran and Javanese nationalism had been in a similar direction. Having rejected Indisch nationalism during the First World

War as alien and Dutch-inspired, each had sought a pattern of identity within more familiar limits. As denizens of ethnically-mixed schools and cities, each had, however, felt obliged to go beyond the particular ethno-linguistic group, the *suku*, to the apparently more rational boundaries of whole islands. Having made this leap, there was to be no turning back. The new attempts at cultural definition proved unconvincing, while the interests of younger thinkers in both Sumatran and Javanese movements turned to economic and political issues. This was the ground that united them. As attention shifted in the mid-20s to the movement to amalgamate the regional youth groups into one Indonesian federation, interest in the more divisive questions of historical identity tended to wane.

Even the pure Javanese nationalists of *Wederopbouw* were gradually seduced by their own historical concerns into a renewed interest in a wider Indonesian unity. In 1919, the first volume of Fruin-Mees' *Geschiedenis van Java* was published in Batavia,[24] to be translated before long into Malay. Designed for a wide Indonesian readership, it made available the results of scholarly research on pre-Muslim Java, in particular Brandes' editions of the *Pararaton* and the *Nagarakrtagama*. Its listing of the "conquests" of Majapahit according to the *Nagarakrtagama* and its explicit map of "the Majapahit empire" embracing all of contemporary Indonesia and Malaysia (a map incidentally copied by Yamin in his *Gadjah Mada*), made a deep impression.[25] The Javanese nationalists had talked of a lost greatness on the basis of the more recent *babad* and Dutch travel accounts, but never in such grandiose terms. Now Wederopbouw took a new line:

> The history of our country from prehistoric times to the time of the philosopher-king of Mataram teaches us with undeniable wisdom that in every period Java has been the centre, the axle of the turning wheel, the *cakra-penggilingan* of the past, the present, and necessarily of the future ...
>
> All these islands, the Indonesia of today, have always existed as an unshakable unity, of which Java serves as the threshold of the southern ocean. The thrust towards unity has always gone out from Java, the cradle of every dynamic force in this archipelago.[26]

Since Gajah Mada (not Douwes Dekker) was now seen as the great founder of the ideal of Indonesian unity, the erstwhile Javanese nationalists could not be left behind. Henceforth, their task would be to join with their brother Indonesians in "the fulfilment and ennobling of the unitary state, the empire of Gajah Mada, for our descendants".[27]

Such sentiments may have warmed few hearts outside Java, but they were of great importance in re-orienting the historical concerns of Javanese nationalists in a direction compatible with Indonesian unity. Such concerns were in any case giving way to more immediate economic and political ones. As Suryaningrat had predicted in 1918,[28] Dutch imperial intransigence had the effect of driving Javanese nationalism and non-Javanese movements together. The problem of imperialism itself became more interesting to most Indonesian intellectuals than a continuing search for historical identity. Jong Java and Jong Sumatra were talking almost the same language by the mid-1920s, and their fusion became only a matter of time. The celebrated *Sumpah Pemuda* (youth oath) of Indonesian unity in 1928 and the establishment of the Partai Nasional Indonesia a year earlier marked the end of the identity debate with a victory for colonial boundaries.

With this critical issue settled, there was a slackening of serious historical inquiry by nationalists. History had to become an armoury in the anti-colonial struggle, and certain stereotypes quickly developed as the most useful weapons. The "unitary state" of Majapahit was among them, along with the other kingdoms of Java now increasingly well delineated in the textbooks. Fortunately for the geographical balance of the picture, the Sumatra-based empire of Sriwijaya was gradually emerging from the work of scholars like Krom, Ferrand, and Coedès in the 1920s.[29] Destined eventually to be coupled with Majapahit as the other great demonstration of historic Indonesian unity, Sriwijaya was initially handicapped by the obscurity of the sources.

A number of Indonesians of scholarly talents continued their study of particular cultural traditions, among whom Hussein Djajadiningrat, Noto Soeroto, and Poerbatjaraka were perhaps the most important.[30] They wrote in Dutch, for a predominantly Dutch audience, and had little to do with the development of a coherent historical dimension for the new Indonesian-nationalist idea. The young nationalists, on the other hand, wrote increasingly in Indonesian for Indonesians, and it was they who would mould the framework within which regional experience could somehow be related to national needs.

Sukarno himself was intensely interested in aspects of Indonesian history and had a major role in fashioning the nationalist orthodoxy.

After graduating, he briefly taught national history at Douwes Dekker's Ksatrian Institute, where he confesses to having "never quite assimilated the theory that children must be instructed factually. My idea was to stir them passionately".[31] The clearest expression of the importance of history for the national struggle was his 1930 defence speech:

> First: we show the people that they have a past, a glorious past;
>
> Second: we increase the people's consciousness that they have a present, a dark present;
>
> Third: we show the people the rays of the future, shining and clear, and the means to bring about that future full of promise ...
>
> ... The PNI knows that it is only this triad which can make a flower bloom, which will bring back to life the withered nationalism of the people.
>
> We have a glorious past; we have a glittering future ... What Indonesian's national spirit will not live when hearing the greatness of the kingdoms of Melayu and Sriwijaya, the greatness of the first Mataram, the greatness of the time of Sindok and Erlangga and Kediri and Singasari and Majapahit and Pajajaran — the greatness too of Bintara, Banten, and Mataram under Sultan Agung! What Indonesian's heart will not sigh when he thinks of his flag which was once encountered and honoured as far as Madagascar, Persia, and China! But on the other hand, whose hope and faith will not live, that a people with *such* a great past, *must* have enough strength also to attain a glorious future.[32]

In the interests of Indonesian unity, it was appropriate to concentrate on the grandeur of these pre-colonial (and for the most part, pre-Islamic) kingdoms in a one-dimensional fashion, rather than to inquire further into their diverse social structures, belief systems, and economies. The question of national identity had in essence been resolved, as arising from common oppression by the Netherlands. Mohammad Ali has well described the needs which lay behind what he called "the classic theory of Indonesian history", developed during the anti-colonial struggle but "still regarded as legitimate and true until today". The theory had to:

> arouse the spirit of struggle and strengthen our self-respect as a people, and eventually to eliminate our inferiority complex towards the Dutch. Thus the primary function of Indonesian history has been to show that the Indonesian nation:

1. is a nation with the same standards and worth as any white nation;
2. is a nation with a history, which occupied a place of honour in our golden age;
3. that the summit of our greatness was equal to that of any nation;
4. that our fall and humiliation as a colonized nation was a *consequence* of the trickery, cunning, and deception of the Dutch and their divide and rule policy.[33]

One of the open questions within this nationalist format was the cause of the transition from glorious past to dark present. Dutch trickery was a constant factor, but something needed to be said about the fault to be put right and the grounds for hope in the future. The tendency of the Java nationalists to see in Islam a force which had eroded the pristine strength and harmony of Majapahit was barely disguised in the writing of some later intellectuals. In the 1930s, Hatta and Alisjahbana still found it necessary to condemn what they called the "cultural nationalists" who wanted to revive Majapahit.[34] For the Muslims, this would not do, nor indeed for the Marxists who saw in Islam a progressive "peoples' movement" against the tyranny of Brahmanic Majapahit.[35] Although the nationalists could not develop an orthodoxy on this difficult issue, Sukarno made a characteristic attempt at synthesis in what has been called his Marxist period. Indonesia lost its freedom in the 17th century, he argued, because it was in the midst of a transition from the "old feudalism" of Hinduism to a "new feudalism, Islamic feudalism, which was a little more democratic". The conflict between these two forces created a "fever" in Indonesian society which weakened it fatally against the foreign assault.[36]

A more persuasive argument at a popular level, particularly in the period before 1926, was that freedom had been lost through disunity, and would be regained by unity.[37] Here, the nationalists of the 1920s were continuing, in terms more attractive to the urban elite, the theme of unity which had been the great popular message of Sarekat Islam in its decade as a mass movement. Throughout Java, Sumatra, and Sulawesi, a new gospel had been preached that *sepakat* (accord), *sama rasa* (feeling-as-one, or brotherhood), and solidarity were the secret of strength. "If we are *sepakat* we are already numerous, and whatever we want to achieve will take place".[38] If unity for urban nationalists meant modern organisations and parties, to the rural mass, it had taken the form of oaths of mutual support and a flowering of semi-secret societies loosely linked to Sarekat Islam. Here is one possible point of contact between

134   *To Nation by Revolution*

urban elite (necessarily the subject of this chapter) and mass consciousness. A sense of rapid progress on the basis of unity appeared to take root widely in the decade before 1926.

The Hero Phenomenon

The forms taken by the new nationalist past cannot of course be understood in isolation from Dutch writing of the 1920s and 1930s to which nationalists were exposed. The earliest Dutch-educated Indonesians suffered in the ELS and HBS a syllabus designed purely for Dutch students; they learnt much about Dutch history and almost nothing about Indonesian. Attempts to alter this situation began during the First World War, and resulted in the introduction of the subject "Netherlands Indies History", and eventually the establishment in Surakarta in 1926 of the so-called "Oosters-letterkundig" high school, for an Indisch-centred study of the humanities. For Dutch policymakers, an incentive for this trend was the belief that "the best guarantee against revolutionary tendencies lies in ... individuals educated as harmoniously as possible, i.e. according to their own, national, character".[39] While a few nationalists, like Tjipto and Takdir Alisjahbana, confirmed this analysis by their preference for a thoroughly Western education, a growing majority echoed Dr Radjiman's demand in the Volksraad that Indisch history be taught to all students.[40]

The results of this growing focus on Netherlands Indian history for Indonesian students were the by now familiar textbook stereotypes. As G.J. Resink made clear,[41] the textbooks (first Fruin-Mees, then Eijkman and Stapel) and the more scholarly work which lay behind them (N.J. Krom, Stapel, Colenbrander) presented a Java-centred pre-European history focused on a mighty Majapahit, and an outrageously Dutch-centred modern history focused almost exclusively on the VOC and the Netherlands Indies state. The Indonesian student learnt virtually nothing of the history, or indeed the existence, of the independent political life of the archipelago after 1600, let alone of Indonesian social history. The first two elements of Sukarno's triad were confirmed in the Dutch textbooks. After the "glorious past" of Majapahit, there were for the Indonesian side of the story apparently 350 years of defeat and humiliation. Individual Indonesians fitted into this textbook stereotype as obstacles or antagonists to the steady rise of Dutch power. "Care is taken that they [Indonesian students] understand very well who and what Dipo Negoro,

Surapati, Trunojoyo, Sultan Agung of Mataram, Abdul Fatah of Bantam, Tuanku of Rentjeh, Teuku Umar ... were; for the child these personalities are nothing but the greatest villains, breakers of their word, rebels, traitors against the Company".[42]

For the nationalist stereotype, the positive interest in post-1600 Indonesian history became this roll-call of enemies of the Dutch as recorded in the colonial textbooks. They were not necessarily the folk heroes whose names remained vivid in the oral traditions and holy graves of various regions. Those who emerged first into the pantheon were invariably those who had excited enough interest on the part of Dutch writers to appear as real characters for their Dutch-educated Indonesian successors. Surapati and Dipanagara were already in this category before the First World War,[43] but by the 1930s, the established trinity had become Dipanagara, Tuanku Imam Bonjol, and Teuku Uma — representing the three great 19th-century wars the Dutch fought in the Archipelago.[44]

Fanon points out that in colonised Africa, too, the leaders of the earlier anti-colonial resistance "spring again to life with peculiar intensity in the period which comes directly before action".[45] In multi-ethnic Indonesia, however, the *pahlawan* (heroes) quickly assumed an additional role beyond that of inspiring sacrificial patriotism. Through the anti-Dutch struggle of the *pahlawan*, each people in the Archipelago found a formula to relate its own unique experience of the past with the new nationalist identity. Nationalist spokesmen increasingly selected their heroes with an eye to a broad geographical representation, a factor which appeared to become paramount when "Guided Democracy" later made the *pahlawan* status an official one.[46]

The relationship between popular memory at the local level and the new nationalist format can be seen in the case of Aceh, liberally endowed with *pahlawan* of the approved type but scarcely represented in the pre-war nationalist movement. In Dutch textbook treatments of their colonial wars, the interest focused on the "happy ending", when the problem was solved, resistance overcome, and the *pax Neerlandica* definitively established. The condensed "small Stapel", for example, mentions only the last of the great Padri leaders in West Sumatra, Tuanku Imam Bonjol. It cites only three Acehnese in its chapter on the Aceh War, the two (Sultan Daud and Panglima Polem) whose surrender in 1903 was declared by the Dutch to be the end of the war, and Teuku Uma, whose change of sides in 1896 provoked the Dutch into adopting their eventually successful aggressive policy.⁴⁷ Polem later became a pillar of the colonial regime in Aceh and his role as a resistance leader was therefore exaggerated by many Dutch writers. But it was Uma who gripped the attention of both Dutch and nationalist spokesmen, not only because of his motives in so frequently changing sides, and his violent death, but also the romantic interest provided by his Danish hostage Mrs Hansen (wife of the captain of a ship he had attacked in 1886), and his militant wife Cut Nyak Din (who attracted an article in *De Gids* in 1918 and a full romantic biography by Mevr. Szekely-Lulofs in 1948). Despite his great military services to the Dutch, and the lack of real popular interest in him in Aceh (except perhaps in his own west coast), Uma became accepted by the mid-1920s as the symbol of the Aceh War and one of the big three Indonesian *pahlawan*.

It was not until the late 1930s that Acehnese themselves were seriously affected by the new nationalist mythology. Some were grateful enough to see they had a place in it to accept the primacy of Teuku Uma. A Marxist journalist experienced in Aceh though not Acehnese, Xarim M.S., wrote a popular biography of Uma in 1939 which aroused much local interest. Almost immediately, however, the talented young Acehnese writer Teungku Ismail Jakub, educated in the Islamic rather than the Dutch tradition, began to explain in the Indonesian press that it was Teungku Cik di Tiro who was regarded by the majority of Acehnese as the great hero and inspiration for resistance.⁴⁸ Even Ismail Jakub was undoubtedly influenced by the respectability and the hard data given to the Cik di Tiro memory by the publication in 1938 of Zentgraaf's *Atjeh*, the first Dutch work to do partial justice to the great *ulama* and his sons. Yet Jakub correctly assessed both the relative importance of Tiro in the Acehnese war effort and the ability of his memory to continue to inspire Acehnese. The revolution which began in 1945 was declared by Acehnese *ulama* to be "a continuation of the former struggle in Aceh which was led by the late Teungku Cik di Tiro",⁴⁹ and an important "peoples' army" was named after him. When it became necessary to find uncontroversial names for Aceh's army division and university after 1950, however, more remote 17th-century heroes were selected in Sultan Iskandar Muda and the great Muslim mystic Abdul Rauf (popularly known as Syiah Kuala). Though scarcely part of the early nationalist pantheon at all, these were indeed the names universally revered in Acehnese society.

Nationalist Orthodoxy and Its Rivals

By the end of Dutch rule, the shape of the new nationalist past had been clearly drawn. Even leaving out of account the dominant colonial school, however, it still had to compete with a number of rival Indonesian perceptions. The Westernising intellectuals typified by Takdir Alisjahbana made no secret of their conviction that the spirit of the new Indonesia had absolutely nothing do with Sriwijaya and Majapahit, and not much with the later *pahlawan*.[50] The only schools of thought which began to offer coherent alternative perceptions to the nationalists, however, were the Islamic and the Marxist. Both were firmly internationalist, seeing the fate of Indonesia tied up in a much larger pattern; both were sceptical of the merits of the Hindu kingdoms; both were inspired by a sense of progress, the glorious fulfilment of which was nevertheless conditional on the application and rationality of the human actors.

Muslim spokesmen were preoccupied with the problem of why the whole Islamic world had fallen from greatness into defeat and humiliation at the hands of the infidel West. The answers provided for Egypt, the Arab world, and India were equally true for Indonesia — disunity, faithlessness, indolence, corruption, and a failure to use God-given intelligence. A new confidence in Islamic resurgence nevertheless aroused a passionate wave of hope throughout the Archipelago, perhaps earlier in Java (c. 1912–1920) than in Minangkabau (1920s) or Aceh (1930s).[51]

The great fascination of Marxist historiography for Indonesians, as for Vietnamese, was its coherent explanation of the reasons for the rise of European capitalism and imperialism, and its assurance that their fall was equally inevitable. Although Asian Marxists were not content to wait for the cataclysm to take place in Europe,[52] there was an inherent Eurocentrism in their analysis. Tan Malaka and Hatta in particular exhibited a lively interest in European history, and in common with most Marxist writers, took a relatively negative view of Indonesia's past. Tan Malaka's early writing insisted that Indonesia had never been free, having been enslaved by one group of foreign bandits after another. "The true Indonesian nation does not yet have a history of its own except one of slavery ... The history of the Indonesian nation will first begin when it is freed from imperialist oppression".[53]

The Hindu kingdoms became stereotyped as "feudal" regimes where all land was owned by a small ruling class which exploited a population of serfs for temple-building, warfare, and an agricultural surplus.[54] Hatta's opposite picture of a democratic, self-regulating traditional village, exemplified of course by Minangkabau,[55] aroused little interest among more doctrinaire Marxists. On the other hand, the elimination of an Indonesian bourgeoisie by 17th-century Dutch intervention was a point Marxist historians were the first to see.[56] Thereafter, the purely Indonesian side of the story held little interest. The struggles of the anti-Dutch *pahlawan* were sometimes dignified as "peasant revolts", though without appropriate class leadership and tactics they had been destined to fail.

Some aspects of this Marxist analysis quickly found their way into the nationalist format, including the universal identification of monarchy with "feudalism", and the economic motivation for imperialism. For the most part, however, it was the Muslims and Marxists who fell under the influence of the nationalists. For during the Japanese occupation of Indonesia, the nationalist perception was suddenly transformed from one of several struggling counter-myths (colonial historiography still having an overwhelmingly dominant position) into a new orthodoxy.

A new picture of the past was suddenly in great demand after 1942 to replace proscribed Dutch textbooks, myths, and heroes. The Marxists and Westernisers were temporarily barred from the contest by the Japanese, whereas nationalist politicians and journalists were concentrated by the Japanese in precisely the "consciousness-raising" areas of the media and the *sendenhan* (propaganda service). Muhammad Yamin rose quickly to become the senior Indonesian in the propaganda service in Java, the key position to promote and develop his view of Majapahit as the great unifier of Indonesia and of the anti-Dutch fighters as the bearers of national dignity. There was a spate of new writing; including Yamin's own work[57] and Sanusi Pane's standard national history. In each region, the local *sendenhan* devoted itself to popularising the anti-Dutch struggle through drama as well as speeches and pamphlets. In Aceh, it sponsored a competition for the best historical novel on an anti-Dutch theme.[58] As Dutch street names gave way to Indonesian ones, the pantheon of *pahlawan* for the first time received official sanction. Public speeches constantly drove home the myth of three and a half centuries of Dutch rule, often in order to draw the contrast with three and a half years of Japanese achievement.

Much of this writing was creative and perceptive. No one could doubt the value of its achievement, in conveying the importance and the content of the new national identity to a much wider spectrum of the population than ever before. Yet this newly dominant perception could not free itself from the inhibitions with which it had begun. Too close a concern with the remembered past of the various Indonesian peoples always threatened to endanger rather than confirm the newly defined unity. The historical orthodoxy therefore acquired a somewhat brittle quality which did not invite too rich an elaboration. Its central elements, to repeat, were great Hindu kingdoms bringing political unity to the archipelago, followed by 350 years of Dutch oppression dignified by the resistance at some time or another of each Indonesian region and people. The needs of this orthodoxy allowed little room for historical judgement or even causation, except when discussing the Dutch. Sanusi Pane managed to exonerate both Amangkurat I for massacring thousands of *ulama* and Sultan Iskandar Muda for murdering many including his own son.[59] Like Sriwijaya and Majapahit, these heroes "existed, and were great — that was enough".[60]

Long after independence was achieved, the same inhibitions appeared to restrict the range of historical writing in Indonesian. Mohammad Ali could still complain in 1963 that "the structure and contents of 1001 Indonesian history books are all drearily the same".[61] The iconoclasm of the Indonesian revolution brought only a shortlived rethinking of history. Mohammad Ali's own *Perdjuangan Feodal Indonesia* (written in 1948 though not published until 1952) was perhaps the most ambitious attempt of that revolutionary period to view the past in social rather than purely anti-colonial terms — condemning Sultan Agung, for example, for his destruction of the most progressive elements in Indonesian society. The 1960s brought a return to the sense of the 20s and 30s, that historical enquiry should remain within certain limits in the interests of national identity.

Reconciling the Local with the National

The determination of governments since the Guided Democracy period (1959–1965) to make historical consciousness serve the national idea further restricted the scope of history as taught in Indonesia's schools and universities. Since the most obvious common factor of Netherlands Indies history had been Dutch rule itself, an interchanging of heroes and villains could make resistance to Dutch rule the leitmotif of the new national history.

This theme created a point of contact between the separate histories of the Archipelago and the new national myth. Those who had fought most passionately against incorporation into the Netherlands Indian state, like the Acehnese resistance of 1873–1912, the Batak millenarian supporters of Sisingamangaraja XII, or the militant Wahabbi zealots in Minangkabau of the 1830s, were transformed into unwitting proto-nationalist heroes. A striking example of how this magic was effected (temporarily) was 23-year-old Hasan Muhammad Tiro, who in 1948 wrote what he claimed to be the first history of the Aceh war in "our language", Indonesian, to prove that the bitter Acehnese resistance was "one undivided part of Indonesian history".[62] This worked very well for the needs of the revolutionary struggle. As a permanent basis for understanding the diversities of Indonesian history, however, the formula was dangerously flawed.

For the majority of Indonesians whose rulers had made the necessary accommodations to Dutch commercial hegemony, this format either distorted or ignored their own history. Even the great liberator of the Bugis from their subjection to Makasar, Arung Palakka, had to be declared a villain or a non-entity because he allied with the Dutch. More sadly, whole peoples (like those of Flores or Nias, the Toraja, the Dayak) seemed to *have* no history unless or until they could find a rebel to fit the formula. Even Acehnese, who received far more than their demographic share of national heroes, increasingly failed to see the connection between what their ancestors fought for and the state that ruled them after 1950 (see below). On the other hand, the new Indonesian-educated generation who began writing dissertations in the 1980s increasingly lacked the language skills, the local knowledge or the motivation to explore local pasts.

The hero phenomenon described above became a key instrument in President Sukarno's remaking of Indonesian memory around the nationalist theme. In a set of decrees between 1957 and 1963, he laid down the procedure for declaring as national heroes people who had outstandingly resisted colonialism or served the cause of independence. Remuneration was arranged for the descendants of those so named (creating a small industry of lobbyists) and the manner of commemorating them through monuments, anniversaries, schools texts and street names was specified. Beginning in 1959, Sukarno proclaimed deceased members of the nationalist movement as national heroes, and gradually added to the list the earlier kings and warriors who had loomed as antagonists of the Dutch. 94 heroes (only nine women) were declared between 1959 and 1992, and the list continued to grow thereafter. Suharto's regime also removed from the list the two communists, Tan Malaka and Alimin, who had been included before 1965.[63]

Despite its anti-communist stance, the regime of General Suharto continued the theme of anti-Dutch struggle, but militarised it. If armed struggle was the leitmotif of national history, then the national army was its natural fulfilment. The six officers, whose murder in the coup attempt of 1965 had become the pretext for the wholesale massacre of communists, were quickly declared national heroes. Other generals followed — more than a third of the heroes added to the pantheon under Suharto's regime were military officers.

The key figure in the development of official history under Suharto was (Brigadier General) Dr Nugroho Notosusanto (1931–1985), a capable professional historian who was convinced that history was the way to build an integral state with the army as its backbone. General Nasution brought him into the military in 1964 to set up the History Centre of the Armed Forces (Pusat Sejarah ABRI). He was asked to counter then dominant left-wing interpretations of Indonesia's past, and ensure in particular that the Communist Party (PKI)'s "treacherous" role in 1948, as the army saw it, was not forgotten. Once the military-backed Suharto regime was in place, Nugroho directed the Centre to prepare "an integral history curriculum for the whole armed forces". He declared that "history is the most effective means to achieve the two [principal] goals, that is the goal of strengthening the spirit of integration in the Armed Forces, and the goal of perpetuating the precious values of the 1945 struggle".[64] Already then, in the late 1960s, he saw this project as a model for a true "history textbook that was systematic and integrated" for the whole national education system.[65] The latter task proved difficult, and Nugroho did not have things all his own way in the National History which was finally and controversially presented to schools in 1977.[66]

Nevertheless, his was by far the most influential voice in establishing an official view of history in the 1970s and 1980s. As Minister of Education from 1983, he was able to ensure not only that the obligatory history subject in all schools served his objective of national unity, but also that an additional compulsory subject, "History of National Struggle" was added in 1985 — though removed ten years later. Together, these two compulsory subjects represented a larger share of the primary and secondary curriculum than any other subject. As Jean Taylor put it, "The history classroom functioned to suppress knowledge of difference".[67] Dr Nugroho was also the prime mover in the design in the late 1960s of the National Monument Museum and the Armed Forces Museum of the struggle of Indonesia, both showing the nation's history and identity as essentially a military struggle against enemies within and without.[68]

As Niels Mulder has explained, the textbooks used in all Indonesian classrooms up to the end of the Suharto regime expressed the meaning of Indonesian history in terms that projected modern boundaries back as a kind of past "given", with local kings acting always in a benign way to develop the people, while the outsiders come to oppress. Dutch oppression was given purpose, however, by the canonical series of armed actions against the Dutch, led by the established heroes of different areas. The events of 1945–1950 and the abortive coup of 1965 were covered in exhaustive detail, both stressing communist "treachery" and the military's role as national saviour. Many other key events were ignored, notably including the massive killings of 1965–1966 and all other New Order violence. The two key values of Indonesian national identity were the *Pancasila* national philosophy and the 1945 Constitution, both imposed by Sukarno's Guided Democracy, and institutionalised into national consciousness under Suharto. Rebellions and conflicts were explained as deviations from these two principles, requiring the military to act.[69]

This heavy national imprint certainly did not encourage the flowering of local, social, or alternative history. Most of those who continued to write history did so within the national paradigm, finding anti-Dutch, revolutionary, and military themes also in their own locality. Many of those most strongly connected to local pasts as aristocrats or intellectuals had supported the wrong, federal/Dutch side in the war of 1945–1949, and therefore kept their silence if they remained in Indonesia after 1950. Partly because the case for continuity with a local past was so difficult to make within Indonesia in the 1950s and 1960s, the most passionate arguments for autonomous histories were made by exiles outside Indonesia, especially from supporters of a separate destiny for West Papua, South Maluku, and Aceh.

Acehnese understandably felt they had the strongest credentials in terms of anti-Dutch struggle, including choosing the right side, the Indonesian Republic, in 1945–1949. They were therefore not intimidated by the new order after 1950, and produced the most frequent celebrations of a particular past. The most extreme was Hasan Muhammad Tiro (1925–2010), a descendant through his mother of the famous Tiro *ulamas* who had led the last phase of resistance to the Dutch, and a passionate youth activist himself on the Republican side in 1945, distinguished by his great interest in history. Once outside Indonesia, as a student and part-time assistant of the Indonesian mission to the UN, he gradually parted company with official history. The first step was his support for Daud Beureu'eh's 1953 Aceh rebellion, which led to the immediate cancellation of his Indonesian passport, permanent domicile in the US (and later Sweden), and publication of a polemic for a less centralised and federal Indonesia.[70] By 1973, he had studied enough Acehnese history to celebrate publicly in New York the centenary of Aceh's defeat of the first Dutch expedition against it in 1873. Three years later, he returned to Aceh secretly and proclaimed its independence, in a declaration which set out his radically different ideas about the past:

> Our fatherland, Acheh,[71] Sumatra, had always been a free and sovereign state since the world begun [sic]. Holland was the first foreign power to attempt to colonise us when it declared war against the Sovereign State of Acheh on March 26, 1873, and on the same day invaded our territory, aided by Javanese mercenaries ...
>
> However, when, after World War II, the Dutch East Indies was supposed to have been liquidated ... our fatherland, Acheh, was not returned to us. Instead, our fatherland was turned over by the Dutch to the Javanese — their ex-mercenaries — by hasty fiat of colonial powers. The Javanese are alien and foreign people to us Achehnese Sumatrans. We have no historic, political, cultural, economic, or geographic relationship with them. When the fruits of Dutch conquest are preserved, intact, and then bequeathed, as it were, to the Javanese, the result is inevitable that a Javanese colonial empire would be established in place of that of the Dutch over our fatherland ...
>
> 'Indonesia' was a fraud: a cloak to cover up Javanese colonialism. Since the world begun, there never was a people, much less a nation, in our part of the world by that name ... 'Indonesia' is merely a new label, in a totally foreign nomenclature which has nothing to do with our own history, language, culture, or interests; it was a new label considered useful by the Dutch[72] to replace the despicable 'Dutch East Indies' in an attempt to unite the administration of their ill-gotten far-flung colonies ... If Dutch colonialism was wrong, then Javanese colonialism which was squarely based on it cannot be right.[73]

Needless to say, this radically regionalist construction of the past was never debated inside Indonesia, where even federalism was difficult to raise until the late 1990s. Arguably, however, teaching millions of diverse schoolchildren a monolithic national syllabus bearing "no direct relationship to the lived history of their parents and grandparents"[74] made such extreme appeals as Tiro's more credible.

Dealing with Democracy

The army strategists behind the official history of the New Order also consolidated Sukarno's negative view of the period of parliamentary democracy (1950–1958). The first of the textbooks produced by Pusat Sejarah ABRI declared that "As a result of the 'liberal' Western system which was applied in Indonesia, there was a rise of anarchy".[75] One analyst of Suharto-era ideology concluded that putting Dr Nugroho in charge of developing an integral master text of Indonesian history was a means to convince "the younger generation in particular that the only alternative to the present [Suharto] system of rule was anarchy".[76]

The school texts achieved this by portraying the 1945–1949 period as essentially a military struggle in which party politics were a dangerous distraction, and the skillful diplomatic negotiations of the civilian leadership were almost treasonous. The 1950s were then portrayed as dominated by regional rebellions. The junior high school text, for example, devoted 23 paragraphs to various regional rebellions suppressed by the military in the 1950s, and only two paragraphs to parliamentary politics.[77] Hatta's decree of 3 November 1945, which in reality saved the Republic by broadening its base beyond the Japanese-nurtured group who had set it up, was portrayed as a "dark day" when the Republic went down the ruinous road of party politics. The 1950 "liberal" constitution was portrayed as a fundamentally flawed document arising from the compromises of civilian politicians, and Sukarno's return to the authoritarian 1945 Constitution as a necessary step to restore an "Indonesian" spirit to the political system.[78]

In the battle over the authoritative resource book for teachers, the six-volume *Sejarah Nasional Indonesia*, the other authors had little choice but to concede to Nugroho the definition of what post-independence history was about.[79] Among the dissident voices that emerged in the 1990s, it was not historians but two lawyers who launched the most thorough critiques of New Order historiography. The pioneer of legal aid in Indonesia, Buyung Nasution, decided to write his dissertation in the Netherlands on the constituent assembly which Sukarno abolished by decree in 1959, revealing that it was the danger of its being close to success, rather than its failure, which had most troubled Sukarno and the Army.[80] Democracy activist Marsillam Simanjuntak went further in his critique of the role of quasi-fascist integralist thinking in the minds of those who drew up the 1945 Constitution, subsequently sanctified under the New Order.[81]

The 1965 Trauma

Democracy at least was constantly talked about through the Suharto years. The violent events that began the New Order regime were covered by a deeper silence. An ostensibly pro-Sukarno coup attempt against anti-communist generals in the small hours of 1 October 1965 had misfired, and seven generals were killed instead of captured. The murder of these generals was blamed on the PKI by the military, and used as a justification for the subsequent destruction of communism through killings and detentions, and for General Suharto's seizure of power. As Suharto gradually drew all effective power into his hands, the military rounded up many of the 300,000 cadres of the Communist Party and encouraged Muslim and other youth groups to kill local leftist leaders and sympathisers. The PKI was completely eliminated as a factor in Indonesian politics, despite its claimed three million members and over six million voters (in 1955). Although nobody knows the full toll, military spokesmen later conceded that around a half million people were probably murdered in the violence between November 1965 and February 1966, and other estimates have ranged much higher. Around a million more were detained for periods of up to 15 years, and permanently deprived of many of their rights as citizens.

These mass killings were much less documented and analyzed in the West than their importance justified, perhaps because they were not as explicitly state-directed as in Cambodia or Nazi Germany, perhaps because they made possible a change of direction very welcome to the cold war capitals of the West. Reportage was difficult, survivors were few and terrified. Moreover, the issue was immediately caught up in cold war polemics. One of the most careful studies of the 1 October coup attempt and the violence that followed, the famous "Cornell paper", was only published, its authors claimed, because anti-communist commentators were beginning to claim that it was being suppressed out of cold war motives.[82] Although the horrific events were known through newspaper and journal articles soon after the time, only in the 1990s did a few book-length studies begin to be published on them.[83]

Inside Indonesia, the silence was much graver. In an atmosphere of great fear, the penalties for condemning or publicising the killings seemed likely to be very heavy. Many of the elite who on other issues might be democratic and liberal believed that they would themselves have been killed if the communists had come out on top. Hostility between the two camps had become intense and bitter in the late Sukarno years. The now dominant Armed Forces put great emphasis on establishing their version of events in the public mind. The first step was to focus public attention on the killing of six generals (and one lieutenant) during the Untung coup attempt, and linking this with Madiun (1948) as evidence of the diabolical treachery of the PKI. 1 October became a national holiday as "Sanctifying Pancasila" (through the blood of these martyrs), and the site of the generals' death was built into a national shrine and museum of PKI treachery. An expensive feature film, *The Treachery of G-30-S*, was prepared under the direction of Nugroho and leading film director Arifin C. Noer, and shown on television on every anniversary of 1 October.[84] All of this heavy-handed consciousness-building was designed to leave no room for memory of the hundreds of thousands of dead communists.

The official history of the textbooks was also guided very firmly on these issues. Nugroho began work immediately after 1965 on chronicling the attempted coup from the army's point of view, as PKI treachery. After the "Cornell paper" was circulated abroad, he was tasked also to produce an English-language rebuttal, published in early 1968.[85] These studies naturally portrayed the whole affair not as a massacre, but as a restoration of order by the military. The history textbooks Nugroho inspired made no mention of the mass killings, while carefully setting out the way in which the Armed Forces had rescued the nation from the PKI. Even the more academic and substantial National History, in the final volume edited by Nugroho, makes no mention of mass killings that devastated Central and East Java and killed five per cent of the population of Bali.

Although the official myth of the Suharto era encouraged Indonesians to think that atrocities were committed only by colonialists and communists, in fact there was increasingly public debate about state violence in the 1990s, which became much more open after Suharto's fall. Islamic organisations tended to demand accountability for the bloody suppression of Muslim protestors in Tanjung Priuk and Lampung. Megawati's PDI-P party demanded accounting for the violent break up of its key meeting in 1996. Chinese Indonesians, and after 1998 church and women's groups and Chinese diaspora networks, demanded accounting for military-linked violence against the Chinese-Indonesian minority, of which the systematic rapes of 1998 were particularly emotive. Increasingly active, foreign-funded human rights groups drew attention to the much larger number of murders of alleged criminals, unionists, oppositionists, and others disapproved by the regime, including several thousand victims of "mysterious killings" (dubbed *petrus* for *pembunuhan misterius*) in the years from 1983. International pressure eventually led to Indonesian enquiries and trials of a few officers held responsible for atrocities in East Timor, and after 1998, also in Aceh and West Papua. Increasingly, in other words, there is public acceptance of the fact that the Indonesian military has used systematic terror against its opponents, and that its extra-judicial violence has been the chief obstacle to a rule of law in the country.

But few have spoken up for the victims of 1965. The destruction of the left was so total and so devastating that those survivors with a personal interest in rehabilitation have themselves scarcely dared to raise the issue, as other interested parties have done for less portentous crimes. Reducing the hold of government and army on power, moreover, leaves minorities prey to even more frightening intimidation. A brave little NGO was born in 2001, the Institute to Investigate the 1965–1966 Massacres, but when it planned a religious reburial of 26 victims in one Central Java hamlet, death threats from the local Islamic solidarity front obliged them to call it off.[86]

Post-Suharto Reconsiderations

The pattern strongly established under Nugroho's guidance appears to have been little changed in the textbooks published since the fall of Suharto's government in 1998. While we might have hoped for an outpouring of questions long suppressed, the truth may be that 30 years of suppressing curiosity about the past have taken too heavy a toll.

Textbooks on sale in 2003 appeared to differ in no basic way from the established format described above. Colonialism and the long-established "Process of Resistance in various regions to foreign domination" remained the sole ways to understand national history in the period before 1900.[87] The 2003 edition of the history textbook for senior high schools claimed to have incorporated "new nuances" in response to a 2002 decree by the Minister of National Education. "In some sections there are improvements, both editorially and in layout".[88] At least there was some revision of the uncomfortable inflation of Suharto's heroism in the revolution. The "six hours in Jogja" incident which became so prominent in the late Suharto period, because Suharto's role in it could be exaggerated to heroic proportions, was simply not mentioned in the 2003 edition. But it is fair to say that nothing was done to reconsider what national history should be about. More worrying is the continuing absence of any invitation to critical thinking in discussing national history. Despite the robust parliamentary democracy and free media at present, revisiting the past to assist these debates seems discouragingly difficult.

The process of changing the history syllabus in a profound enough way to make it relevant, interesting and helpful to Indonesian students will no doubt take another generation. A beginning has been made in the customary top-down way. In 2001, the Minister of Education entrusted a team of 80 historians with the task of rewriting in eight volumes the six-volume *Sejarah Nasional Indonesia* of 1977. The large team and greater length already suggests the expanding number of regional and sectional points of view that now have to be accommodated. Anhar Gonggong, a senior member of the team later appointed by President Yudhoyono as Director for History at the Department of National Education, defined some principal areas for revision, around the edges of the official format. The chief incidents Anhar listed in 2003 included three standard controversies between the official versions of the Sukarno and Suharto regimes.

1) 'Lahirnya Pancasila'. Nugroho Notosusanto had disputed Sukarno's claim to be the author of Pancasila, preferring to give the credit to Muhammad Yamin. Sukarno's claim may be reasserted.
2) 'Six hours in Jogja'. Suharto's youthful role in the 1949 attack on Jogjakarta will certainly be reduced.
3) 'Supersemar'. The Sukarno letter giving official authority to Suharto on 11 March 1966 has never been found, and the New Order's subsequent celebration of the decree as the basis for its constitutionality will be questioned.[89]

Two more fundamental issues were on Anhar's list, however. One was the responsibility for the Untung coup attempt of 1 October 1965, or the 30 September movement (G30S) as it is usually known in Indonesia. The new history promises to consider the line of argument long common outside Indonesia but banned under Suharto's rule, that the PKI was only marginally involved in what was essentially an internal army conflict, and that there is evidence that Suharto himself, the most senior general not targeted by the plotters, had prior knowledge that some kind of action was being planned. Anhar in this interview notably did not mention the much more difficult issue of the subsequent massacres.

The only regional issue mentioned by Anhar was the 1975 invasion and subsequent annexation of East Timor. The older version that had Indonesia selflessly bringing help to a grateful people certainly requires revision, if only for the sake of civil relations with a new neighbour. The term "annexation" will now be used.[90] Will the new treatment encourage discussion of other regional issues that trouble minorities, including different views on the incorporation of reluctant Papuans in the 1960s, or the reasons for Acehnese alienation since the 1950s? The new official history will at least need to allow for plural interpretations, and to acknowledge that Indonesians legitimately have different interests and aspirations, which need to be discussed and negotiated.

Younger historians, with no particular stake in the compromises of the Suharto period, are naturally more radical in their probing. Being now convinced that they were lied to about the events of the 1960s, before most of them were born, they want to know what really happened. The forbidden pre-1965 literature of the left is now being republished, and works by Pramoedya Ananta Toer, Tan Malaka, Njoto and Aidit, not to mention Marx, fill the university bookshops. The memoir of a doctor activist of the new left sold well under the title "I am proud to be a child of the PKI".[91]

Meanwhile, there has been debate in the press about how to reinterpret the past in an era of relative freedom, though it has to be said that the established historians have not been very prominent in it. Probably the most debated issue has been the 1965 coup attempt, and the way it was used to justify the military seizure of effective power (but not the massacres). The professional historian most inclined to raise these issues has been Asvi Warman Adam of LIPI, perhaps significantly French-trained and thereby outside the elite consensus. He has revisited the theories about Soeharto's and the army's responsibility for the coup attempt, and has demanded the demilitarisation of the history of the 1950s, where textbooks portrayed regional rebellion purely in terms of armed conflicts and the army's defense of the nation.[92] More strident was Slamet Soetrisno, a Gadjah Mada Philosophy graduate and independent writer, who in 1999–2000 raised not only the standard issues referred to by Anhar Gonggong, but also the uncritical silence about the military's attempted coup of 17 October 1952, and Sukarno's 1959 shift to authoritarianism through the 1945 Constitution. The blurb on the back of these collected articles reads: "History has been used as a tool of power to legitimate a dictatorship. As a result, society has experienced amnesia towards important and meaningful historical events. The reconstruction of history is essential to awake from that amnesia". Though Soetrisno is by no means part of the professional history establishment, one of the leading Gadjah Mada University historians did provide a preface welcoming the book.[93]

In a repeat of Suharto tactics of ending debate with the "right" answer, President Megawati in 2003 appointed a three-man commission to investigate the 1965 coup attempt. Asvi Warman was there, but balanced by the two most senior historians still active in A.B. Lapian and Taufik Abdullah. This had no discernable effect.

Of course, more profound critiques are to be found. At the Seventh National History Conference in October 2001, Rommel Cumaring noted at least two of the hundred papers, by younger European-trained professional historians, Mestika Zed and Bambang Purwanto, struck at the heart of the old nationalist format. Dismayed at the tendency to replace Suharto with some other hero figure in a basically unchanged format, they wanted to overthrow the "tyranny of national history" itself.[94]

The 1965–1966 killings, as the basis for the Suharto government's unprecedented control of the population through extra-judicial means, represent the hardest of the issues. If the newer national narratives condemn state violence and terror, they will need to find a deeper and richer framework for national identity itself. As the colossus of New Order history is gradually chipped away, it is unthinkable that any single format will arise to replace it. Indonesia's histories will be plural as its people are plural. A new generation will learn to cope with difference and conflict in the past as in the present, and to draw inspiration from the way these differences have invigorated the nation.

CHAPTER 7

The Japanese Impact: From Briefcase to Samurai Sword

The role of the Japanese in the creation of modern Indonesia long remained an emotive question, particularly for those who were involved in the events. Since the Dutch attacked the infant Indonesian Republic in 1945 as a Japanese creation, nationalists were initially at pains to show the world that they had no debts to Tokyo. Most Western scholars have been prepared to give the nationalists the benefit of the doubt, but it has not been so easy for the Japanese, some of whom felt wounded by the "ingratitude" of Indonesians.

This debate, like many others in modern Indonesian history, has focused on the dramatic events surrounding the proclamation of Indonesian independence on 17 August 1945. It is these events which have drawn the special attention of writers of memoirs, with firsthand accounts from Hatta, Adam Malik, Sukarno and Subardjo on the Indonesian side, and Nishijima and Miyoshi on the Japanese's.

Nishijima, the most prolific of the Japanese participants, explains that he began to write his version of the proclamation out of a sense of injury, when he learnt in 1951 that he could not obtain a visa to revisit his Indonesian friends because of Indonesian official sensitivity on this question.[1] In the several books he wrote or inspired, Nishijima insisted that it should not be forgotten that the independence proclamation was drafted in the house of his superior, Admiral Maeda, at a meeting in which both Maeda and Nishijima were seated at the principal conference table with Sukarno, Hatta and Subardjo. Miyoshi also represented the Japanese Army at the meeting, in the hope of implicating the Army in an effective *fait accompli*.[2] In a 1959 publication, a group of Japanese scholars renewed their complaint that these facts had been suppressed by

Indonesian writers, and pleaded that "a clarification of this would not soil their national history".[3] Hatta's subsequent memoir accepted only a part of the Japanese version.[4] On the occasion of Admiral Maeda's death in December 1977, the Japanese concerned were therefore understandably gratified to receive a telegram from Adam Malik, then Indonesian Vice President, but in 1945 a strenuous upholder of the view that independence should be proclaimed in complete defiance of the Japanese. 32 years after the event, Malik could generously acknowledge Maeda's "great help in the preparatory stage of our independence", and proclaim that Maeda's name "will be written in the annals of Indonesia with golden letters".[5]

The proclamation question has more to do with personal feelings and national pride than with historical causation. Here, as in the whole question of the Japanese period, it is important to remember that the important actors continued to be Indonesian. It is they who defined the eventual shape of independent Indonesia by responding to whatever political opportunities each period offered, whatever resonances each foreign model set up in their own tradition. The argument of this essay is that the Japanese occupation brought such profound change that it is not inappropriate to regard 1942 as the beginning of the whole revolutionary upheaval which gave birth to modern Indonesia. Nevertheless, these changes were in very few cases the result of deliberate Japanese planning, but rather of Indonesian responses to a radically altered environment.[6]

There are a number of reasons why 1942 marked a more permanent break with the past in Indonesia than in other parts of Southeast Asia. Some of them have to do with the fact that the Netherlands was not a major world power and could only have maintained its influence in Southeast Asia in conditions of great stability. A few embittered Dutch politicians complained after the war that Anglo-Saxons had deliberately manipulated the post-war crisis to ensure their interests prevailed in Indonesia at the expense of the Dutch. In reality, the dramatic events of the 1940s only telescoped a shift which was inevitable in the long run. The place of the Dutch language was a symptom of this shift. The Japanese officially discouraged English and French elsewhere in Southeast Asia, while in practice frequently made use of these languages for effective communication. By contrast, they had no use whatever for Dutch, and found Indonesian (or occasionally even English) much more practically useful. While the older, Dutch-educated generation of Indonesians naturally found it painful to have to forgo the public use of Dutch, they

Plate 7.1 Japanese troops coming ashore in Rembang, Java, 1942.

were themselves acutely aware that it was not internationally useful, and that there was an extra indignity in having been colonised by a second-class power.[7] Even if Japan lost the war, Holland could not win it.

The other remarkable feature of the Indonesian case was the harmonious start in Japanese-Indonesian relations by the almost universal Indonesian welcome to the invaders. The reasons usually given for this are the poor Dutch record in political (as opposed to social) emancipation, the exaggerated hopes of Japan dating back to the Russo-Japanese war, and the Joyoboyo prophecy in Java which strengthened popular belief that deliverance from oppression would come at the hands of another group of foreigners whose rule would be very short. If we compare the Indonesian response with the more ambivalent one in the Philippines, Burma, Malaya, or Vietnam, however, there are two other factors which assume larger proportions. First, the influence of "anti-fascist" preconceptions, whether of European democratic, Marxist, or Chinese derivation, was very low. Most of Indonesia's left-wing politicians remained impotent in exile. It is significant that the attempt of the most important

Marxist politician at liberty, Amir Sjarifuddin, to use Dutch money to start an anti-Japanese underground in Java, proved more of a handicap than a strength to him in his subsequent career as a nationalist leader. The other important factor was that the Japanese did not have to fight their way into Indonesia, with all the destruction and suffering that would have caused. After the fall of Singapore and the Battle of the Java Sea, the Dutch knew they were beaten and did not even attempt to defend the major cities. In some Muslim strongholds in the Outer Islands, such as Aceh (Sumatra), Gorontalo and Bone (both Sulawesi), Indonesians themselves acted to speed the Dutch departure, and could welcome the Japanese to already "liberated" areas. This relatively peaceful takeover encouraged a massive loss of Indonesian faith in Dutch competence, while placing few initial stains on the Japanese record.

The high hopes placed in the Japanese were quickly dashed with the banning of political activity and experience of military brutality; yet the effect of this harmonious start was not entirely lost. A number of battle-scarred Japanese soldiers were surprised and relieved to find themselves at last in a friendly environment, while the civilian "experts", accustomed to the idea that the Dutch had built a "model" colonial system, were puzzled at Indonesian enthusiasm to escape from it.[8] General Imamura Hitoshi, the conqueror of Java, was one who was very struck by his reception:

> Many natives gathered round us from far and near, the way country people in Japan run to the road when soldiers are marching during manoeuvres. The natives ... brought coconuts, bananas and papayas to the Japanese ... Many of the natives were cheerfully raising their hands with their thumbs up. Some Japanese officers took from their pockets the Japanese-Indonesian conversation dictionaries ... and began talking with the adults and children with the help of gestures. I wondered "Is this really a battlefield?" Spontaneously I said to Major-General Okazaki: "Chief of Staff, we have already won the battle ..."[9]

Throughout his 1942 term as commander in Java, Imamura was to insist that the warmth of this reception made the iron-handed approach applied in other areas, particularly Malaya, inappropriate for Java. To the argument of numerous high-powered emissaries from Tokyo and Singapore that "a forceful administration like that in Singapore is the way to make the coloured people obey us",[10] he replied that a milder policy based on pragmatism and economic incentives was the only way to restore production quickly without altogether alienating the population.

The so-called "soft" policy of Imamura was somewhat modified by his successors and was not replicated in most of the other islands. One of Imamura's most powerful critics in Tokyo, General Muto Akira, in fact became military commander in Sumatra in 1943. In Kalimantan, the Japanese committed some of the worst atrocities of the war, decimating the Indonesian political elite. Nevertheless, the model established by Imamura in Java was critical — first, because he won the open admiration of Sukarno and the cooperation of most other Indonesian politicians, who found it difficult to change course subsequently; second, because the very lack of political opportunity under the Japanese in the outer islands made it more certain that Java would be the model for the subsequent revolution.

Economic Change

The Japanese invasion of Southeast Asia was of course intended to secure the supply of strategic raw materials to Japan — in particular oil, rubber, tin, and other metals of Indonesia. The initial Japanese policy therefore was to continue and even accentuate the export orientation of the colonial economies and their dependence on industrial imports. The consequence of the war was the reverse of this. By the middle of 1943, the shortage of shipping was so acute that Tokyo ordered a reversal of the initial policy. All emphasis was now to be placed on the economic self-sufficiency of every region.[11] Food production was forcibly encouraged in every deficit area, and local authorities were directed to use every effort to produce cloth and other needed manufactures locally. During the last year of the war, there was virtually a total breakdown of Japanese shipping movements. Somehow the Japanese war machine was kept in remarkable combat readiness, but the civilian economy was brought to its knees.

As with all the colonial economies, the suspension of exports produced a massive dislocation. In the Indonesian case, the plantation economy was never able to recover from the blow. Beneficial as they would have been to independent Indonesia's balance of payments, the Dutch sugar, rubber, tobacco and tea estates were not tied to the interests of any important indigenous political force (as they were in the Philippines). Sugar cultivation had never been popular among the Javanese peasants who were obliged to devote much of their land and labour to it, while smallholders in Sumatra were only too anxious to turn the rich plantation land over to subsistence crops. This shift of resources away from agricultural estates proved the most enduring economic result of the war, precisely because it was politically popular — however damaging to the national budget.

The other contribution of the military administration to the Indonesian economy was still more negative, and still further at odds with Japanese official intentions. The wartime economy became increasingly a controlled economy as the war progressed. The movement of goods between residencies (*shu*), and even between the smaller districts now called *kabupaten* (*bunshu*), was made illegal without a government licence. Larger and larger percentages of the rice crop were requisitioned by the government at derisory prices, with scarce supplies of cloth, salt, and fertiliser distributed through the government hierarchy as an inducement to produce. All of this gave enormous economic power to officials, both Japanese and Indonesian, who had little experience in exercising it. A flourishing black market in consumer goods soon appeared, and fortunes could be made in "smuggling" goods from one district to another. During 1943–1944, the newspapers published numerous reports of the arrest of "smugglers" or of corrupt officials who had abetted them, though in the final year of the war, the situation appeared to be too far out of hand for such methods.[12] Some Indonesian informants suggest that it was Japanese lower officials and civilians who first instructed Indonesians in the art of discreet "inducements" for official favours, the filling out of invoices for lesser amounts than those received, and so forth. Certainly, there was unprecedented opportunity for enterprising dealers who were skilful in the ways of bending or breaking oppressive official regulations. Such skills have not lost their utility since.

If there were few successes in growing new crops, the controlled economy had a disastrous effect on the distribution of rice. Despite all Japanese efforts to open new lands and increase food production, the harvest dropped lower with each year, until even normally "surplus" areas were in a desperate situation. There seem to have been three main reasons for this. One was the shortage of manpower as a result of the heavy Japanese demands for forced labour on roads, airfields and defences. According to one estimate, only 60–65 per cent of *sawah* (wet-rice fields) in Sumatra were planted in 1945 for this reason.[13] Another reason was that farmers tended to hide their rice, to harvest and sell it to "smugglers" at night, or even to avoid cultivation altogether rather than to surrender it to the Japanese. In some areas where Indonesian officials appear to have declined to implement the draconian demands for requisitioned rice, farmers appear to have had enough to eat even though there was very little to be had in the market.[14] The third factor, which caused the greatest bitterness among Indonesians, was the determination of the Japanese to stockpile rice as a security against the time they might have to fight a defensive guerrilla war against Allied invasion of the Indonesian islands. The officer responsible for the stockpiling arrangements in Java conceded later that it was a source of much unnecessary bitterness, and that the officials concerned "misinterpreted this order and tried to accumulate excessive quantities of foodstuffs and munitions".[15]

The last year of the war was a time of unprecedented deprivation for most Indonesians. Many, especially in Java, were simply unable to obtain food and were seen, "waiting for death" along the road.[16] Cloth was out of reach to any but a favoured minority, and many were forced to dress in sacking and rags. Yet in the midst of this hardship, the Japanese were taking good care of the Indonesian political elite, whom they had very effectively drawn into government and propaganda functions. The *pamong-praja* administrative corps which had served the Dutch lived no less well under the Japanese, and had greater opportunities for making a profit from their office if they chose to do so. For the nationalist and Islamic leaders whom the Dutch had regarded as a nuisance, the change at Japanese hands was dramatic. They were given generous allowances, privileged access to cloth and other rations, and were provided with a captive audience for their propaganda. Even though many of them increasingly saw the activities they were engaged in as a *sandiwara* (theatre), they could not then withdraw from their exposed position as mediators between the Japanese and an embittered population. Already in 1943, people were reportedly saying, "Our leaders are now living the good life but we are as poor as ever".[17] By the end of the war, those who had claimed to be leaders of the masses felt themselves caught, together with the older elite, under the heavy yoke of privilege. As Ki Hadjar Dewantoro put it, "The reputation of the leaders is ruined in the eyes of the people".[18] Retribution came after the Japanese surrender, most of its victims being the *pamong-praja* through whom forced labour and rice deliveries had been imposed. There was no leadership to galvanise a peasant revolution in 1945, but the raw material was there to an extent which may be unique in Indonesian history.

Political Leadership

Before the war, the Indonesian nationalist movement had succeeded remarkably in extending the idea of an Indonesian national identity, through an active but low-circulation Indonesian press, to urban centres throughout the whole archipelago. It suffered, however, from two major handicaps. The first was the internal bickering among the small group of Dutch-educated political leaders, which caused frequent splits in old parties and the creation of new ones; the other was the absence of any substantial contact with the "masses" in whose name the politicians professed to act. Dutch surveillance of political activity was extraordinarily complete, and the authorities allowed politicians their freedom only so long as they seemed ineffective. Any radical party which began to obtain large-scale support in the countryside was quickly shackled with impossible restrictions, and its leaders were imprisoned or exiled.

The Japanese regime presented quite different opportunities: politicians lost even more of their freedom to say what they thought in print, to form parties of their choosing, and to associate with their comrades in other islands. In terms of the pre-war deficiencies of the nationalist movement, however, these losses were more than counterbalanced by the gains. Unity was virtually forced on politicians: if they wanted to be public figures at all, they had to join in the single propaganda body which was allowed in each area. If they did so, as the great majority did, they had the unaccustomed experience of addressing a mass audience, often with people trucked in from surrounding villages at government expense to add to the grandeur of a public occasion. The Japanese calendar was dotted with such festivities — the emperor's birthday, the anniversary of Pearl Harbour, the anniversary of the Japanese arrival in each area, the "acceptance" of each Japanese concession towards independence with appropriate speeches of gratitude, and the tours around his region by every leader who made a visit to Japan. The approved leadership of each area was built up through such means and in the controlled media.

Such exposure may not have brought the Indonesian masses to love their leaders; the earlier discussion suggests that would not be the right word. Still less did it make possible the building up of a loyal, efficient, and educated cadre structure — the lack of which has been a feature of Indonesian politics ever since. But it did at least make known to the masses who their leaders were. At each administrative level, the Japanese encouraged, or even forced, the emergence of a clearly acknowledged leadership among the more charismatic political or religious figures available. Previously antagonistic political party leaders were obliged to join unitary propaganda bodies; various shades of reformed or unreformed Islamic opinion were obliged to accept a part in an overarching Islamic body; Protestants and Catholics were represented in a unitary Christian body, which in turn in many areas was linked to an organisation for religious leadership in general. Although there were times when the leaders of these organisations felt themselves to be merely captive playthings of the Japanese, the period which followed the promise of independence in September 1944 saw them gradually emerging to positions where they could take over government without serious challenge from their colleagues.

It is difficult to categorise any of these *pemimpin*, whether at the "national" (meaning Java) or local levels, as quislings or puppets, in the sense of owing their position to their pro-Japanese attitudes rather than their capacity to arouse popular support. The overtly pro-Japanese figures were generally discarded within the first year, and the increasingly acute Japanese need to exhort the population to greater sacrifice led them to prefer figures who were really effective in this role. Sukarno was of course the outstanding beneficiary of this process. As he frequently said in defence of his cooperation with the Japanese, "I addressed 50,000 at one meeting, 100,000 at another. Sukarno's face, not just his name, penetrated the Archipelago. I have the Japanese to thank for that".[19] While less prepared than many nationalists to criticise the Japanese, Sukarno was adept at using his opportunities to arouse his mass audience to nationalist fervour. Many did hold him guilty for his share in Japanese oppression,[20] and he might well have been expected to fall rapidly from grace after the Japanese surrender. Yet even the symbol of non-cooperation with the Japanese, Sjahrir had to concede in October 1945 that Sukarno was indispensable as President. When, three years later, Sukarno's position was put to a public test by the communist denunciation of him as "Quisling, slave of Japan, romusha dealer and heiho propagandist", he appeared to emerge stronger than ever.[21] The point here may be that Sukarno's position rested not on specific actions he had taken or views he represented, but in having become pre-eminently *pemimpin kita* (our leader) in a situation of confrontation with outsiders.

Under the Japanese, Indonesia was divided into three parts, with very little Indonesian contact permitted between them. The Japanese 16th

Army guided Java along a relatively progressive path towards political emancipation; the 25th Army defended Sumatra against any leadership emanating from Java; while in the other islands, the Japanese Navy implemented a policy designed to retain permanent Japanese control. The leadership of Sukarno and Hatta strictly extended only to Java, therefore, although after April 1945, the Navy did allow these leaders also to visit Makasar, Bali, and Banjermasin. Since the overwhelming majority of national-level pre-war politicians were based in Java, however, their acceptance of Sukarno's and Hatta's pre-eminence was more than half the battle. In Sumatra and the Navy area, comparable *pemimpin* had emerged at the local residency level — Mohammad Sjafei in West Sumatra, Teuku Njak Arif in Aceh, Dr A.K. Gani in Palembang, Dr Ratulangie in Makasar, Pangeran Mohammad Noor in Banjermasin, and so forth. After the proclamation of Indonesian independence, these people were declared to be Residents or Governors of their five areas, and had as little difficulty as Sukarno and Hatta nationally in having their leadership accepted by their elite peers. The contrast with the pre-war factionalism is remarkable. In general, these leaders appear to have been accepted by the whole political elite because it was recognised that political leadership under the Japanese was a very dangerous and exposed game, and that those who had become proficient at it should continue to exercise responsibility, at least as long as the Japanese provided the principal potential threat to the Republic. By the time the Dutch had replaced the Japanese in this role, at the end of 1945, leadership had acquired its own momentum.

The Dutch had ruled the Indies as a centralised state, while resorting to sophisticated devices to prevent the unification of their opponents. The Japanese, by contrast, did divide Indonesia very effectively, yet the result was still further to strengthen the forces of political unity. Just because Java alone was allowed to develop an islandwide leadership, it was impossible for any other island to move in a radically different direction in 1945. In July and August 1945, when the 25th Army saw that it could not resist Tokyo pressure for independence any longer, it made belated plans for a separate Sumatran independence, but so bungled was its preparation that the effect was counterproductive.[22] Moreover, as I have remarked elsewhere,

> Almost every social and ethnic group in Sumatra was irked by the extreme isolation of the Japanese period. Only those with long memories

were particularly conscious of ethnic and regional suspicions at the war's end. The enthusiasm of youth for unity above all was heightened by the fact that they had never had the opportunity to enjoy it.[23]

Indonesian Identity

If colonial systems can be divided into crusading and exclusivist types, the Japanese emphatically represented the former — like the 16th-century Portuguese or the early Americans in the Philippines. Their most idealistic vanguard of this crusade, the young teachers sent to the south to open new schools and institutes, tended to believe that the Indonesians were essentially like the Japanese, but "spoiled and lacking in moral training as a result of insidious Dutch guidance".[24] As one headmaster told his carefully selected students, "You were not brought here to enjoy yourselves but to learn Japanese *seishin* (spirit), to learn discipline and hard work. I know how lazy the westerners are, and the laziness they have taught you for hundreds of years is going to be wiped out".[25] This onslaught on the colonial value system had some important results, as will be seen below. Far more important than any "Japanisation" of the Indonesian population, however, was the consolidation of a particular definition of Indonesian identity.

Language was an important part of this. Dutch was abolished and Indonesian made official in 1942, in a fashion more abrupt and complete than any independent Indonesian government could have brought about. Language commissions were established in Jakarta and in Medan to standardise the language, but more important was the practical experience of simply having to use it in areas where Dutch had previously held sway. Moreover, the freeing of Indonesian literature from its sense of cultural inferiority towards Dutch appeared to have a profoundly stimulating effect. A. Teeuw has made a strong case for regarding 1942 rather than 1945 as the real watershed, the birthdate of modern Indonesian literature.[26]

New Indonesian language textbooks were urgently required, and new historical myths to replace the overthrown mythology of Dutch imperialism. Here, the Japanese made little contribution from their own national mythology, and seemed content to encourage Indonesian nationalists in the anti-colonial emphasis which was natural to them. In the 20s and 30s, nationalist intellectuals had daringly attacked Dutch "heroes" and exalted anti-Dutch Indonesian "villains" in ephemeral undergraduate newspapers, but they now found their counter-myths proclaimed with all the force of the mass media and mass displays.

> In a lavish style they [the Japanese] encouraged the holding of mass rallies and simultaneous meetings. The statue of Jan Pieterszoon Coen which had been the symbol of Jakarta city and the symbol of colonial power was taken down with every form of ceremony which could mobilize national sentiment.[27]

In many areas, the Japanese consciously encouraged the rewriting of history in an anti-colonial sense, by establishing historical commissions and launching contests for historically-oriented works.[28] A film was made on the history of Sumatra by the Nippon Eiga Sha corporation, leading from the grandeur of the pre-colonial past and scenes from the Aceh war, to the climax of the Japanese landings in 1942.[29] The repertoire of the Aceh Seinendan's theatre group may be indicative of the type of mythology encouraged under the Japanese. One play, perhaps a necessary concession to the Japanese, crudely adapted the famous story of Momotaro. Momotaro, who represents Japan, is on his way to fight the devil of Western imperialism when he meets three suffering figures — Indonesia, the Philippines and China. They join him and defeat the enemy. Another play told the story of two Indonesian friends, one of whom was arrested by the Dutch for his nationalistic writings. Despite the torture he undergoes in prison, he tells his captors that they will never be able to build anything to rival the grandeur of Borobodur. The Dutch have reduced Indonesian literacy from the 40 per cent of Hindu times, he proudly claims, to the present four per cent. Meanwhile, his former friend has betrayed the cause by joining the Dutch police. Both die soon after the Japanese landings of 1942, one as a traitor, and the other as a hero. Two other works in the repertoire were set in the 1942 Acehnese revolt against the Dutch, and another during the 1926 "Bakongan revolt" in southwestern Aceh.[30]

The effect of all this raising of anti-colonial consciousness may have been to consolidate a new nationalist orthodoxy which has proved remarkably durable. The textbooks of national history written hurriedly by nationalists during the Japanese period have been reprinted many times since and adopted by the Republican school system. While Sanusi Pane's *Sejarah Indonesia* (1943)[31] is the most successful in this sense, it was replicated in numerous local and regional histories.[32] Moreover, it was in the last year of the occupation that Muhammad Yamin, later to be the cultural commissar of Sukarno's "Guided Democracy", developed his historical ideas as head of the propaganda department for Java.[33]

The central elements of the new orthodoxy of Pane, Yamin and their colleagues were a glorious pre-colonial past, followed by three and a half dark centuries of Dutch rule illuminated only by the sacrificial struggle of those from each region who fought the Dutch most stubbornly. Even in the large areas of the outer islands which had known less than 50 years of Dutch rule, this myth seemed irresistible, encouraged no doubt by the propaganda value of contrasting three and a half years of Japanese rule with three and a half centuries of Dutch. The pantheon of approved Indonesian heroes also grew better defined as streets were named and ceremonies held in their honour.[34] While the shape of this national past owed very little to the Japanese, its projection into an official orthodoxy for the new nation was greatly sped by wartime propaganda needs.

The same appears true of the implanting of the national flag and anthem as symbols of national identity for the whole population, not simply the urban nationalists who had taken them up before the war. Following Koiso's promise of "independence in the future", in September 1944, the flag and anthem became obligatory on every public occasion. As Dr Amir later observed, the Japanese-inspired propaganda "did more in one year for the idea of political unity and urge for independence than ten years of ordinary propaganda before the war".[35] In terms of these external symbols of national identity, the change between 1942 and 1945 was astonishing to outside observers. Indonesia was no longer an intellectual idea, but a vital factor in popular consciousness.

The development of an Indonesian style of political behaviour is far more difficult to trace. What can be stated is that the wartime environment created favourable conditions for one particular current of Indonesian political thought to find its way into the definition of this "Indonesian way".

Examining the 20 years which followed the Japanese occupation, Herbert Feith delineated three broad characteristics of Indonesian political thought — a "diffusely moral" quality, optimism, and what he called "a tendency to see society as undifferentiated". Even for the Islamic and Marxist parties, "there was little conception of segmental groups having legitimate interests. Nor was much concern expressed for the individual".[36]

Such a tendency could have been descried at least among Javanese intellectuals as soon as they came into collision with European democratic ideals. In the 1920s, the leading spokesman for a Javanese political model based on the natural leadership of a father within his family was Soetatmo Soeriokoesoemo, a member of the Paku Alam royal house and a great influence on the early development of the Taman Siswa educational movement. "Wise men should be at the head of the state," he insisted, "and should be chosen by the Wise, not by the people."[37] If such a current was always present, its political expression was not quite intellectually respectable among the modern-minded political activists of the nationalist movement in the 1930s.

While the Japanese appear to have contributed no political ideas of their own to the Indonesian political debate, they did create a climate in which it was good form to begin a speech with a ritual rejection of western individualism liberalism, which "invariably gave rise to imperialism and exploitation".[38] It would be impossible to evaluate the long-term effect of such a climate were it not that the documents which have become the central symbols of "the Indonesian way" in politics were drawn up at its height — notably the 1945 Constitution and the *Pancasila* idea. These were written and debated in the bodies appointed by the Japanese in the middle of 1945 to prepare for a Japanese-supervised "independence". While the Indonesian delegates were remarkably successful in excluding any direct Japanese influence, "western" ideas about individual rights and political pluralism undoubtedly played a smaller role in the discussions than they would have in pre-war or post-war conditions. Professor Supomo, the leading judicial official in Java under the Japanese and a great believer in a distinct Javanese model, took the lead in drafting the 1945 Constitution. As he explained the basis of this Constitution:

> The inner spirit and spiritual structure of the Indonesian people is characterized by the ideal of the unity of life, the unity kawulo-gusti, that is of the outer and the inner world, of the macrocosmos and the microcosmos, of the people and their leaders. All men as individuals, every group or grouping of men in a society ... is considered to have its own place and its own obligations [*dharma*] according to the law of nature, the whole being aimed at achieving spiritual and physical balance ... So it is clear that if we want to establish an Indonesian state in accordance with the characteristic features of Indonesian society, it must be based on an integralist state philosophy, on the idea of a

state which is united with all its people, which transcends all groups in every field.³⁹

In keeping with these ideas, the 1945 Constitution gave very strong powers to the President, to whom the cabinet was responsible, defined no specific rights for the individual except education and the freedom of religion, and stated that "the economy shall be organized as a common endeavour based upon the principle of the family system". In both the Constitution and Sukarno's Pancasila speech, the word *kerakyatan* (peopleness) tends to be preferred to *demokrasi*, and is defined in terms of a consensus principle — *musyawarah* and *mufakat*.

The relevant clause of the preamble to the Constitution is officially translated as "democracy which is guided by the inner wisdom in the unanimity arising out of deliberation among representatives".⁴⁰

In the reaction which followed the Japanese surrender, these documents were put aside for a time as both impractical and undemocratic, but in 1959 they again became the central elements of "the Indonesian way".

Military Mobilisation

The most striking contribution of the Japanese period, however, will probably be seen as the way it armed Indonesians for the revolution which followed. For those who had known the Javanese in particular as "the mildest people on earth", the transformation wrought by the war was astonishing. The mobilisation of the population for military purposes was the only major change which coincided with the deliberate intentions of the Japanese rulers, although it assumed a scale and direction which they could hardly have anticipated.

I have suggested the briefcase as a metaphor for the pre-war period because of the emphasis on technical and scientific superiority as the key to colonial power. Expertise was increasingly the justification for Dutchmen to remain in positions of authority. A good western education was the chief means the colonial system afforded to rise to a position of parity with the Dutch masters. The brightest stars of the Dutch East Indies were men like the Djajadiningrat brothers, Mohammad Hatta, and Dr Soetomo, who had absorbed the best that a Dutch education had to offer and thereby mastered what seemed to be the inner mysteries of Dutch control. It was of course precisely such people who could lead the nationalist movement, who could highlight Dutch failures to live up to Dutch ideas of democracy, efficiency and justice, and who could advance the credentials of Indonesians like themselves to do the job more thoroughly.

As indicated above, the Japanese military took the view that Dutch education had been disastrously elitist, academic and impractical. They put the heaviest emphasis in their own educational efforts on physical fitness, toughness, discipline, patriotism, and a spirit of sacrificial service to the group. Many Indonesians who went through Japanese schools and institutions testify to the startling change from the Dutch pattern, the closeness of the young Japanese teachers to their pupils, and the physical and mental toughness they gained from the process. By the end of the war, a very large proportion of Indonesian young men had had some exposure to Japanese methods of drilling and discipline, if not in the schools, then in one of the many youth and propaganda bodies which trained with wooden rifles or bamboo spears. As Adam Malik put it:

> ... through the controlled wartime economy and other measures such as forced labour and systematic drilling of all social strata, ... the impact of the four-year occupation upon our national mentality and spirit was very great. We could say that during those four years our whole nation underwent a fundamental spiritual revolution. In the course of four years of Japanese oppression the economic and social condition of Indonesia was progressively turned upside-down, dissolved, and destroyed ...[41]

No one was entirely immune from this process. Even sultans, rajas and political leaders were obliged to show a different sort of lead to their people than that to which they had been accustomed. Japanese-controlled media frequently displayed the startling sight of such worthies with their sleeves rolled up wielding a hoe before the cameras to open some new project. One Japanese agricultural training institute exhorted its graduates to work without a shirt on. The Japanese certainly failed to break the colonial white-collar mentality, but they cannot be accused of not trying.

If Leiden graduates were the wayward favourite sons of the pre-war regime, the Japanese military also spawned a favoured progeny in its own image. The new elite were the Indonesian officer corps of the PETA and Giyugun, bright young men who had undergone the same tough training as Japanese officers. They had drunk most deeply of Japanese *seishin*, the heroic spirit of the true patriot; they had learnt the style of sharp command, of violent action, so much at variance with the habits of both the traditional Javanese *priyayi* and the Leiden graduate; they had absorbed an impatience with bureaucratic methods and aristocratic niceties; they had earned not only the cropped hair and the Japanese-style uniform but eventually also the right to wear the new badge of status in wartime Indonesia — the sword of the *samurai*. They too found that Japanese practice did not match Japanese ideals, and reacted sharply when the Japanese failed to give them the equal treatment to which their rank entitled them. Experiencing the same mixture of outrage and admiration the Dutch had for their wayward sons, the Japanese military were now in turn faced with rebellion, by the PETA in Blitar and the Giyugun in East Sumatra and Aceh. The first real test of the *seishin* of these officers came after the surrender, when they demanded from their former patrons that Japanese arms be handed over to them.

When Indonesian independence was declared, most of this new elite were young men in their early 20s, in no position to challenge the older Dutch-educated nationalists for leadership. Four years later, however, they had tested their own claims to leadership in the violence of the revolution, while the old civilian leadership had frequently been found wanting in their eyes. Although they did not assume national leadership until 1966, they could never be ignored as an alternative source of authority in independent Indonesia.

Conclusion

This essay has attempted to show that the Japanese occupation had a major impact on the subsequent shape of Indonesia — whether for better or worse is not for me to judge. It armed Indonesians to resist successfully the reimposition of the pre-war regime, it witnessed the consolidation of Indonesian unity and identity, and it encouraged the emergence on the one hand of a new military elite, and on the other of a political leadership which was stronger on charisma and rhetoric than on political organisation and cadre formation.

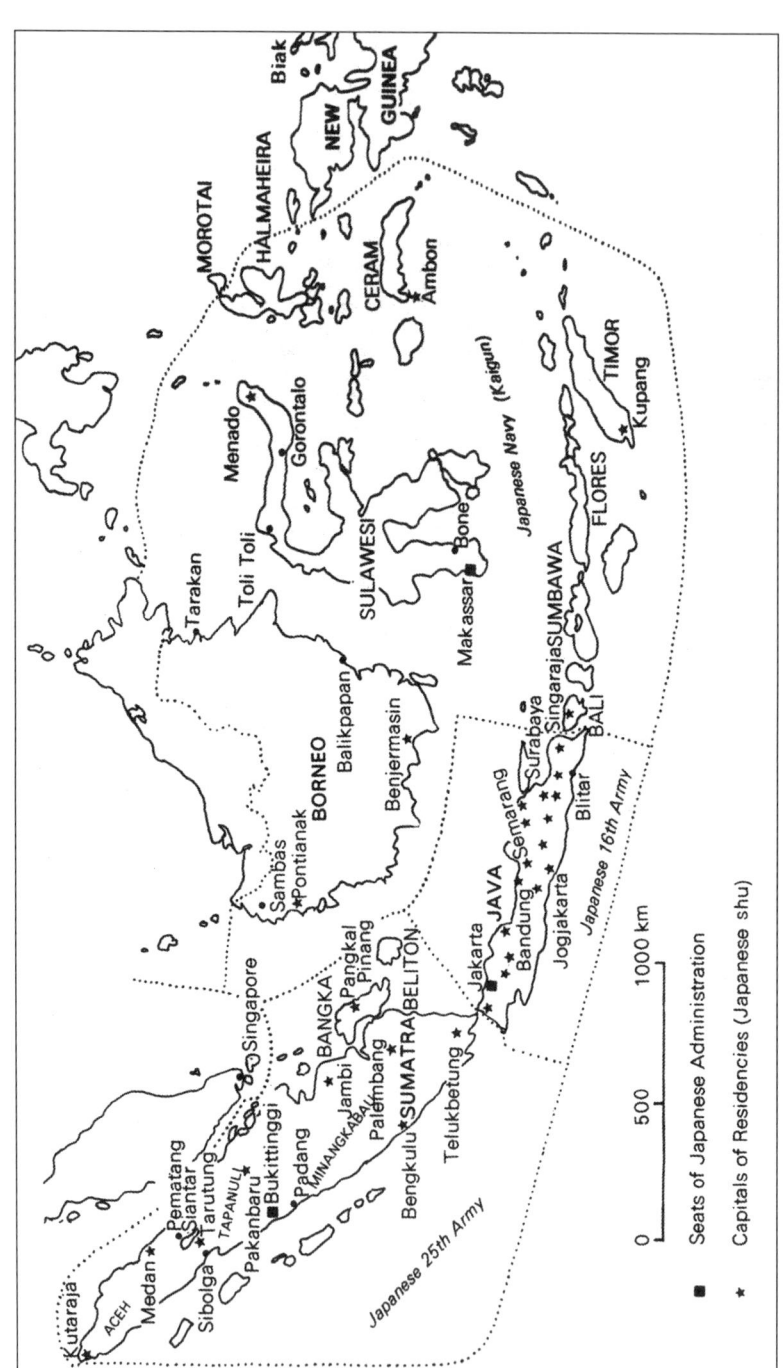

Map 7.1 Indonesia under the Japanese.

CHAPTER 8

The Revolution in Regional Perspective

It is frequently complained that an excessive focus on the national level has distorted our understanding of the Indonesian revolution, as of most things Indonesian.[1] Yet a brief survey of the academic research completed reveals that regional studies have been the dominant theme. As against the detailed studies of South Sulawesi by Harvey,[2] Aceh by Nazaruddin,[3] North Sumatra by Van Langenberg,[4] East Java by Anderson,[5] Surabaya by Frederick,[6] West Sumatra by Kahin,[7] East Sumatra and Aceh by myself,[8] Pekalongan by Lucas,[9] Surakarta by Soejatno,[10] Jakarta by Cribb,[11] and Ambon by Chauvel,[12] it is difficult to point to a single thesis which takes a thematic approach to the revolution in national terms. Anderson's *Java*[13] is the closest, though he obviously had a special affection for and knowledge of Surakarta. My own *Indonesian National Revolution*[14] was a by-product of the regional study on which I had originally embarked. Since then, the only national-level works of real research I can think of are biographies of figures such as Sukarno, Nasution, Tan Malaka and Amir Sjarifuddin, and a growing number of scholarly studies concerned more with the Dutch or Diplomatic story than the Indonesian one.[15]

In short, there seems no doubt when we look at the historiography of the revolution, particularly in the 1980s, that the major advance in understanding its nature has been in the form of regional studies — typically at the Residency/Province level. This provides a marked contrast with the historiography of the classic revolutions, notably the French and Russian, on which hundreds of scholarly volumes have been written without even asking the question whether Paris and Petrograd really represented the whole story. As recently as 1975, an embattled student of revolutionary Bordeaux complained that "historians of Revolutionary

France ... have concentrated their attention almost exclusively on national politics", so that the study of anything else had only just begun to seem respectable.[16] Western studies of the Russian revolution have been equally focused on the capital, though the difficulty of access to lower-level sources may make that more explicable.[17] Rather than rending our garments because we have not done enough local history, we should perhaps be asking why we have taken this direction so much sooner than our European colleagues.

I believe the answer to this question is that we are driven to the local level by our subject. The great European revolutions were (like most others) essentially urban phenomena, and they were made possible in large degree because the urban population was heavily concentrated in a single national centre of power. 30 per cent of France's urban population was in Paris in 1789[18] and a still higher proportion of Russia's in Petrograd in 1917.[19] Only 22 per cent of the Indonesian urban population was in Jakarta.[20] Moreover, Jakarta was seen as a particularly Dutch-dominated city, so that very little of the revolutionary action took place there. What we speak of as the "national" politics of the revolution constantly shifts its venue, from Jakarta to Surabaya, to Bandung, to Yogyakarta, to Surakarta, to Madiun, to Aceh and Makasar (and of course The Hague). During the "gerilya" period, the diffusion is almost complete, while the internal dynamics of the federal states cannot be ignored even by someone who is trying to tell the "national" story. Anti-colonial revolutions (notably those of the Western Hemisphere and Algeria, as well as Indonesia), have a readymade common enemy in the centralised colonial state. Anti-colonial revolutionaries of very different cultural, regional and class backgrounds had some basis for agreement about their goals, whereas there was none at all between Parisian *sans-culottes* and the peasants of the Vendée, or between Petrograd workers and Cossacks. To some extent, the same revolutionary story *can* be told in each region.

I will go further, and argue that the dichotomy between "national" and "regional" revolutions is a false one. There was but one revolution, which took place in many regions. That is not to discount the analytical distinction between *diplomasi* and *perjuangan*, between the contest to obtain independence from the Dutch and the internal processes which were transforming Indonesian society. It is the latter, however, which made this a revolution, and if we are to discuss it as revolution, we must look beyond "the executive committee of the nationalist elite", as

Smail[21] called the Republican central government. As the father figure of all regional studies, Smail should be quoted further. What he foresaw was a temporary segregation of local from national history until enough had been learnt "to write a full history of the revolution".[22] That stage has now passed, I suggest, and the most urgent priority facing us is to bring these local studies together so that we can better see what the full revolutionary dynamic was.

The first point that strikes me in this connection is the remarkable degree to which these studies do reinforce each other. Even though every author has been at pains to sketch in the historic legacy and particularity of his/her region in introductory chapters, and even perhaps to define the study as local history rather than revolutionary history,[23] the social forces at work seem surprisingly familiar from one place to another. It was not a case of "patriot (or red) armies" from the cities imposing a revolutionary position on the countryside, but rather of diverse regions independently undergoing a similar experience. One of the most striking lessons of the new research has been that even the regions we thought most at odds with the mainstream nationalist revolution in fact went through a very similar process. At one extreme, Ambon has been shown by Chauvel[24] to have produced a moderate nationalist majority at all elections during the revolution, with the conservative pro-Dutch rajas suffering the same collapse of status for much the same reasons as happened in Java and Sumatra. At the other extreme, successive studies[25] have revealed that revolutionary Aceh included the same set of Japanese-trained nationalist *pemuda*, veteran leftists, older Dutch-educated nationalists and *ulama* as other provinces, even if the last-named were to prove much stronger here than elsewhere. Audrey Kahin[26] has rightly noted that cities such as Medan, Makasar and Jakarta shared a similar revolutionary dynamic with each other, though less with their own respective rural hinterlands.

The issue of regionalism per se was remarkably subdued during the revolutionary period despite all Dutch efforts to cultivate it. The reason, as I have argued elsewhere, is largely that the Japanese had so isolated each region from contacts with others and with Java that contacts were renewed enthusiastically after the surrender. *Pemuda* in each region were especially inclined to believe that revolutionary purity lay elsewhere rather than with their own disappointingly compromising older leaders. Local rivalries and suspicions certainly became inflamed in many cases — Surakarta against Yogyakarta; Javanese against Sundanese; Malay against Batak; Toba against Karo; Aceh against Batak; everybody against local Ambonese and Chinese — but none of these could be interpreted as local patriotism against the "centre". Wherever the centre was, it was too weak and threatened itself to pose a convincing threat to any region. The only strong attack on Javanese "domination" of which I am aware was Dr Amir's after his defection from the Republic in April 1946, by which time he no longer represented anybody.

What then are the important common features of the Indonesian revolution as revealed in these new studies of a number of regions?

1. The 1930s

The assumption that the 1930s, especially after the crackdown of 1933, represented a quiet period in which there was little effective challenge to the colonial/aristocratic establishment, collapses once we look at the local level. The tensions which gave rise to the "social revolutions" of 1945–1946 were clearly evident in the late 1930s, even though the scholarly preoccupation with national political party-formation has tended to obscure this. The rise of an Acehnese Islamic movement, PUSA, and the journalistic onslaught on the aristocratic administrator class (*ulèëbalang*) in 1939–1941 was one dramatic demonstration of this pattern in Aceh. The Karo Batak demand for plantation land in East Sumatra, which led directly to the violent *aron* movement of 1942, was another. In West Sumatra and north coastal Java, it was the unauthorised school ordinance of 1933 which galvanised much of the *ulama*-led hostility to the aristocratic/bureaucratic elite which enforced this measure, as well as other unpopular measures such as the salt monopoly and the taking of blood samples.[27] In the Princely States of Jogja and Solo, two purely local organisations, Pakempulon Kawulo Surakarta and Pakempalan Kawulo Ngajogjakarta, mobilised tens of thousands of peasants, nominally in support of the rajas but leading quickly to the voicing of genuine peasant grievances against poll-tax, compulsory labour on the estates, and the impositions of unpopular *lurah*.[28]

Some of these local popular movements did intersect with urban nationalism. Gerindo made contact with the Karo farmers of East Sumatra during the disturbances there, while Parindra provided some of the leadership for the PKN of Yogyakarta. Other Islamic, local, or semi-criminal movements have remained outside the received view of the period for too long precisely because they found no common ground with the national political movement. Williams[29] has made the point that the elements which challenged the established order in Banten, the *ulama* and the semi-bandit *jawara*, "saw urban-based parties of the 1930s as a threat, unlike the PKI in the 1920s which had basically not sought to challenge their political roles". On the other hand, some of these communists and Islamic radicals associated with the 1926 revolts began to re-establish their contacts with Islamic and bandit "counter-elites" in the late 1930s after their return from Digul or from exile abroad. Anton Lucas' work[30] also obliges us to take more seriously those communists operating clandestinely in other areas of Java, often renewing contacts with potential leaders of protest in the countryside.

2. Effects of the Japanese

We now know a great deal more about the effects of the Japanese occupation, which was both more diverse and more uniform than was once assumed. More uniform in the sense that the economic autarchy and political isolation imposed by the Japanese on each Indonesian province, and especially on the three distinct zones of Java (16th Army), Sumatra (25th Army), and the eastern islands (Navy), did not prevent Indonesians in all these areas undergoing very similar pressures and opportunities. Everywhere, there was the same shock mixed with jubilation at the Dutch defeat, the same dangerous opportunities for larger roles by Islamic, nationalist and educated elites, the same mobilisation of youth, the same economic desire for retribution against those (typically village and local officials) held responsible for the terrible Japanese exactions. More diverse in that there appeared to be extraordinary Japanese individuals in every region who fished in troubled waters with the nationalists, the semi-criminal element, and even some of the communists, with or without approval from their superiors.

Such men in Aceh were Masubuchi Sahei and Aoki Eigoro, who in their respective ways did much to mobilise the anti-*ulèëbalang* elements and give them strategic positions which would be useful later. Similarly, Kuroiwa built a strong force in the Aceh *Tokobetsu Keisatsutai*, which later contributed much to the strength of Pesindo in Aceh. Inoue Tetsuro played an equally individualistic role in training and mobilising the rural youngsters who would form the radical *Barisan Harimau Liar* during the revolution in East Sumatra.[31] In Java, Shimizu Hitoshi worked with one circle of radical nationalists from his *Sendenbu* office, while the Navy group in Jakarta patronised another. Intelligence officers trained for work behind enemy lines were particularly inclined to seek out elements which could be counted on to sabotage any eventual Allied reoccupation. This was the thinking behind Yoshizumi Tomegoro's training and mobilisation of *jawara* roughnecks in Java,[32] as it was of the Nakano group of intelligence specialists in Sumatra. If these elements often went far beyond what appeared to be the line of their superiors, it was Japanese policy everywhere to train semi-military youth groups (in Java, the gamut of Keibodan, Seinendan, Barisan Pelopor, Hizbullah, Sabilillah, etc.) which could easily provide the basis for competing armed groups during the revolution.

3. The Pemuda

Local studies have given us more information about the *pemuda* phenomenon since it was identified clearly by Smail[33] and then romanticised by Anderson.[34] More, but still by no means enough to explain the social and ideological basis of the revolution. The most sustained attempt to analyze this phenomenon in a local context is that of Frederick,[35] yet it remains distinctly amorphous even so. Frederick sees the *pemuda* of Surabaya in 1945 as a broader group than in pre-war days, when the term had been virtually restricted to students and recent graduates of (Dutch-medium) high schools. During the height of the revolutionary process, *pemuda* became simply a synonym for revolutionary, as illustrated by the beautiful story of Anton Lucas' informant:[36]

> As we were passing the guard post an older man stood up and shouted "Merdeka!" I stopped to ask the person "who are you?" "I am *pemuda* Marto," he said, standing at attention. Marto was a well-known *lenggaong* (bandit) who used to enter people's houses by breaking down the wall with a crowbar in the Dutch time. I laughed, "You don't mean to tell me you're a *pemuda* with hair already growing out of your ears?" ... I asked him how old he was — he said *more than fifty!*

Japanese attempts to mobilise youth through the *Seinendan* (Youth Corps — with a maximum age of 24 or 25) and to a lesser extent *Keibodan* (auxiliary police) may have created linkages among young people which

Plate 8.1 Republican poster, 1945. A roadside poster urges Indonesians to boycott the returning Dutch. The Indonesian figures, left to right, are saying: "There's no room for Dutch COLONIALISTS"; "The Dutch won't get any [postal deliveries]"; "Even for 10 guilders a bunch, I won't sell!"

became important later, though *Seinendan* itself appears to have aroused much less enthusiasm than the more independent and amorphous groups under elite leadership which formed in the cities during the last few months of the occupation. Frederick argues that his "*arek* Surabaya" perceived the Seinendan as not greatly different from pre-war scout groups. Interestingly, the connection between *Seinendan* and Republican activity by youth appears more direct in Ambon than in Java.[37] The *Seinendan* does not look to be the key to a definition of *pemuda* identity in Surakarta either, whereas the Barisan Pelopor there did from December 1944 become a very important means by which elite nationalists mobilised potential fighters even among illiterate peasants.[38] During the revolution, the *pemuda* leadership at local levels is not difficult to locate among those who worked in Japanese propaganda organs (Domei, the newspapers, Sendenbu), most of whom had begun their political activity pre-war, and youngsters trained by the Japanese in PETA/Giyugun, the police or other semi-military bodies. Nobody has yet provided a social analysis, however, of their followers, the people who made the revolution in a physical sense — the street-fighter of Surabaya or Bandung, the *lasykar* around the Allied perimeter in Medan or Padang, or even the other ranks of the TKR/TNI.

4. Violence

The role of violence in the revolution is another question which the local studies have enabled us to ask, if not yet to answer. Smail[39] was once again the first of the academic historians to attempt to analyse the phenomenon, deeming the bloodiest phase of the *bersiap* period "a temporary pathological aberration".[40] The notion of aberration is also useful for official historiography, since it helps to preserve the symbolic purity of the "war of independence". When we look at other revolutions, however, it is clear that such phases are part of their dynamic, both in cowing potential opponents into support or passivity, and in giving rise to a popular revulsion which eventually stops or reverses the typical progress of revolutions to the left.[41] Indeed, Smail himself concedes[42] that this violence had important political consequences in promoting "the tendency towards the rule of force in society", the reliance on "bapakism", and the longing for peace and order. Later writers such as Frederick,[43] Lucas,[44] and Williams[45] have provided plenty of gruesome evidence in Java of the mob violence which killed thousands of Dutch, Eurasians, Chinese, Ambonese, and often Javanese identified by some bizarre "tanda NICA". In Sumatra, too, the larger cities had their *bersiap* period in which lesser numbers were killed, not to mention the much greater toll of the "social revolutions" and subsequent ethnic clashes. We are not yet far enough from these painful events for even a foreign researcher, still less an Indonesian one, to tackle the phenomenon directly and analytically. When this stage is reached, however, much data will have been preserved by the regional historians.

5. Social Revolutions

The "social revolution" within the national revolution is perhaps the most important aspect brought into the foreground by the local studies.

Its exclusion from earlier work was caused as much by uneasiness in handling this controversial subject as by the limitations of the "national" perspective. Naturally, Indonesians (of all political persuasions) have been most affected by this uneasiness,[46] while for outsiders, it could probably be said that there was an opposite response of fascination with the aspect of the revolution most in tune with the radical idealism of western campuses in the late 1960s. Ben Anderson[47] best reflected this fascination with "what might have been" in the revolution. Those who took up the challenge in ground-level research into the social revolutionary movements, on the other hand, have typically ended with a profound ambivalence about their mixture of idealism and brotherhood on the one hand, and grisly, counterproductive violence on the other. For those close to the events, a clinical academic analysis is apt to seem both cynical and callous. At this distance in time and space, however, I think we have an obligation to try to see the events as a necessary part of the revolutionary dynamic, for better or for worse.

It appears to me that the movements categorised as "social revolutions" in the regions have four different aspects which might usefully be kept distinct. First, we have the removal of hereditary rulers — best known because it was a permanent and spectacular change. In Surakarta, this was accomplished through a strong populist movement which nevertheless remained under the control of elite figures and was resolved without bloodshed through negotiation with the Republican Government.[48] In East Sumatra, it was a more profound and uncontrolled upheaval which involved much violence and ended by producing as much recrimination (personal, ethnic, and ideological) as popular sense of liberation. In Aceh, it began as something like a civil war against certain pro-Dutch *ulèëbalang* and ended as a popular removal of them all in the name of Islam, nationalism, justice, and (for some) "anti-feudal" progressivism. None of these actions were ever reversed, even when the presumed victims of the process returned to power (as notably during the NST in East Sumatra). On hindsight, they can be seen as overdue actions against figures who had lost their fundamental legitimacy and become an impediment to progress, even if the regions proved difficult to govern without them.

Second, there were the rural movements against village heads, local officials and authority figures, which affected most of the northern areas of Java acutely and other areas to some degree. In many regions (including Surakarta),[49] village heads who had become unpopular because of the way they had mediated the heavy Japanese demands for men and provisions were replaced in orderly elections by other figures not fundamentally different from themselves. In areas such as Banten, the "Tiga Daerah" of Pekalongan, and northern areas of Priangan, it was a *santri* element which typically replaced the established village heads. These changes were truly revolutionary, but their very radicalism stimulated a reaction from both within and without which destroyed them.

A similar change in West Sumatra in March–May 1946 proved more permanent because the Residency government succeeded in carrying through orderly elections at *nagari* level which transferred authority to respected Islamic leaders.[50] The West Sumatran revolution was perhaps the closest to the Acehnese in this respect, an unpopular *adat* hierarchy identified as Dutch-imposed being replaced by a popular Islamic leadership able to ensure grassroots support for the revolution — at least until interfered with from outside. Hereditary *adat* chiefs were also replaced by elected ones during the extension of the East Sumatran "social revolution" to Tapanuli in April–May 1946, though the new system there was often seen as imposed from outside and failed to generate much enthusiasm.[51]

The third element is the violence itself. For many Indonesians, this is the dominant image of "social revolution" — a time of anarchy, killing and looting in which murderers, bandits and pickpockets suddenly assumed great power and terror stalked the land. Violence appeared to take on a life of its own, the willingness to kill becoming for a time the key to leadership.[52] Yet even in this violence, which alarmed elite Indonesian observers and foreign scholars, there was a clear pattern — similar to that perceived by Guha in the peasant violence of 19th-century India or Lefebvre in that of revolutionary France. The Indonesian peasant too became involved in "social revolutions" no longer as the bandit feared by the elite, but as an angry rebel. He took arms "not to rob but to destroy the authority of his enemies by expropriating them".[53] Guha breaks down this destructive violence into four typical phenomena: wrecking, burning, eating and looting.[54] All of these could be found at the height of the "social revolutions" in northern Java and East Sumatra, with government offices, palaces and official houses often being burnt as well as ransacked. In one case in Simelungun, the "social revolutionaries" had a great feast around a fire made of the raja's possessions after his palace had been ransacked.

At least in the Indonesian case, two further elements, killing and humiliating, need to be added to the typology of this destructive violence.

The blood of the victims took on a sometimes talismanic quality, with the faint-hearted being ordered to lick bloodied swords, and the slogan "*Darah!*" especially prominent at the height of the "social revolutions".[55] A grisly killing and even mutilation was but the most extreme form of the total humiliation of elite figures which was often the purpose of revolutionaries. Lucas[56] has well described the *dombreng* phenomenon in the Tiga Daerah, where unpopular officials or even *pemuda* who strayed from the pure revolutionary path were paraded around the town naked or with faces blackened, the symbol of their crime slung around their necks.

Finally, the "social revolutions" were to some extent what their name implied — attempts to change the social order in a radically egalitarian direction. None of these attempts was a permanent success, largely because more conservative elements, shocked by the violence and galvanised by pressures from the national leadership, succeeded in undoing them.

The most radical attempts to introduce *sama rasa sama rata* (brotherhood and equality) were a result of temporary fusions of Marxist, Islamic and millenarian elements. This was the kind of mix in Kutil's movement within the Tiga Daerah as well as the Baso movement near Bukittinggi in the first four months of 1946. The latter has been briefly described by Audrey Kahin,[57] but deserves further analysis. Its millenarian attempt to realise heaven on earth through a brotherhood which held all things in common — land, food, allegedly even women — was especially alarming to the local government, and thus far, our only sources on the movement are hostile to it.[58]

In Banten, the Tiga Daerah, and East Sumatra, a primitive communism was attempted, particularly through the distribution of stockpiles of textiles or other goods. In the Tiga Daerah, each *kecamatan* was given a few rolls of cloth and some bags of rice in October, to distribute as they saw fit. In at least one case, it was popularly decided that *sama rasa sama rata* required that each person should receive an identical share of 13 centimetres of cloth, even though this was too small for any practical use.[59] In Banten, too, the revolutionary "Dewan Rakyat" played one of its major roles in distributing such captured stockpiles in an egalitarian manner, but lost much of its rationale once the stocks were exhausted in December.[60] More ambitious cooperatives were discussed in the Tiga Daerah,[61] and briefly put into practice in East Sumatra by the Ekonomi Rakyat Republik Indonesia (ERRI) at the height of the "social revolution". This body was given "full authority to organize the structure of the economy" throughout Sumatra in a decree of 7 March 1946. In practice, it managed to organise some groups of retailers in the Medan area into cooperatives, and to monopolise the supply of certain stockpiles of goods. These were used both as an economic weapon against the Allies and as a means to the egalitarian millenium of *sama rasa sama rata*. As part of the reaction against the whole "social revolution" in East Sumatra, however, this body was banned six weeks later and denounced as a corrupt "state within a state".[62]

The alliance between Islam and primitive communism never lasted for long, however. In Aceh, in Banten, and in a number of areas of northern Java, the "long-cherished goal" of the *ulama* was to replace westernised state officials in local leadership roles, and once this had been achieved, they had little desire to pursue *sama rasa sama rata* idealism.[63] While Dutch plantation land was broken up in Sumatra[64] and the claims of sugar estates on peasant land resisted in Java, it is striking that even the "social revolutions" of 1945–1946 neither attempted nor seriously discussed a major redistribution of rice-growing land. Some of the land of *ulèëbalang* families in Aceh was given to those considered to have been wrongfully deprived of it in the past, but beyond this, the *ulama* leadership did not seek to go. The communists raised this scheme only in September 1948, when as part of the crisis of Madiun, they supported peasant actions in many villages of Surakarta, Kedu, and Madiun to take over the official land (*bengkok* or *lungguh*) enjoyed by village heads and distribute it among poor peasants.[65] Although PKI activists had correctly identified these official plots as the major concentrations of land in rice-growing villages of central and east Java, the issue does not appear to have won them strong peasant support.

6. The Army

Even those concerned exclusively with "national" politics cannot now ignore the importance of the army, nor its roots in the revolutionary period. Yet once again, we cannot readily understand those roots except at local levels, since both the PETA and the earliest movements towards a Republican army were highly autonomous in each region. It is as a result of the labours of local historians that we now understand how overwhelmingly *priyayi* were the social origins of PETA officers in Java. The tendency to appoint Islamic figures as largely honorific *Daidancho*, noted by Benda and others, now appears as a largely irrelevant distraction from the aristocratic dominance at the operational level. Soejatno[66] has shown that the first eight *chudancho* (company commanders) in Surakarta comprised four nobles from the courts, three *priyayi*, and one member of the Legion Mangkunegoro. In the Pekalongan Residency, similarly, all but one of the PETA *chudancho* were of *priyayi* origins, typically the sons of officials.[67] This consistent pattern throughout Java resulted partly from the Japanese requirement that candidates for higher ranks should be high school graduates, though the initiative taken by well-placed local officials no doubt also played a role. The lower PETA ranks included a higher proportion of men from ordinary backgrounds, such as the future PKI-sympathiser Sutarto in Surakarta. In general, however, the PETA structure virtually ensured that the Indonesian revolutionary army in Java would have an officer corps heavily *priyayi* in composition.

The officer corps of the Sumatra Giyugun was more mixed. There was no Japanese requirement here for a completed secondary education, and more seems to have depended on the nomination of candidates by well-placed Indonesians, often from the *pergerakan*. In West Sumatra, Chatib Suleiman played the leading role in nominating potential officers, and the result was that three of the first four trainees were from prominent *ulama* families.[68] In Aceh, the majority of the first intake was from *ulèëbalang* families, but two were from the Islamic group around Said Abu Bakar.[69] In each region, the Giyugun trainees shared a strong *esprit de corps* which helped them form TKR divisions in the first four months of the revolution, though their differing social origins forced them onto different sides during some of the subsequent infighting. The leadership of the Republican Army persistently tried to advance the more secular-oriented officers, and succeeded in West Sumatra.[70] In Aceh, the minority Islamic element was the one which emerged on top after the "social revolution".

The TKR/TNI was a more effective weapon of the central government in Java partly as a result of the relatively homogeneous origins of its officers. There is no doubt of the critical role played by army units in suppressing the "social revolutions" of the northern Java coast. In the Tiga Daerah, the social revolutionaries saw the TKR as the weapon of the old *pangreh praja* class and attacked it accordingly. It was with some enthusiasm, therefore, that the army returned to suppress the "social revolution" in December 1945.[71] The more diverse origins of the young army officers in Sumatra made them both less able and less willing to act as an agent of the central government in defining how far the revolution should go. The Baso movement was extreme enough for the West Sumatran TKR to feel no qualms about suppressing it with particular vigour in April 1946, killing 113 of its adherents.[72] The movements which took place in northern Sumatra, on the other hand, had the effect of dividing the army or bypassing it as one competing group among others. The result in Aceh was to eliminate the original leadership of the army in favour of one much more responsive to local sentiments than to national demands. It was not until the late 1950s that the diverse Sumatran divisions of the TNI were effectively integrated into a centralised national army.

7. Regionalism and National Unity

Finally, we should repeat the apparent paradox that the focus on the local context has shown more clearly the extraordinary unifying power of the national revolution. In no region did the revolutionary dynamic lead into a distinct and separate path. Nowhere during the revolution itself did the forces of the centre collide with clearly regional or separatist forces (this phenomenon began with the Andi Aziz affair of April 1950). The powerful new forces evoked by the revolution were almost all of a centripetal kind.

In this, Indonesia was not alone. As a rule, revolutions have had a powerful centralising influence, however unconnected this may have been with their original aims. Revolutions create a sharp break with the separate pasts of each region; they destroy the legitimacy of proud local dynasties, and they create powerful new myths of shared sacrifice, new "imagined communities" to replace the discredited identities of the past. The Indonesian revolution is therefore not exceptional, but it is one of the most striking demonstrations of this general tendency. Indonesia before 1942 was less clearly or consciously a nation than most colonies. By 1950, it had certainly become one. Its subsequent development in the direction of an ever more integrated and centralised country has drawn heavily on the forces unleashed during the revolution.

Each regional study has shed further light on why this process was so powerful. Here we can only summarise some of the explanations which appear common to most.

1. In each region, the Dutch-supported aristocratic/bureaucratic hierarchy was severely weakened in legitimacy and effectiveness by the Japanese occupation.
2. The Japanese prevented any effective contact between Java and the Outer Islands such as might have provoked resentment in the latter. Each region felt itself to be on its own, yet looked for inspiration to what it believed to be the more advanced political climate in Java. There the nationalist elite could act *as if* for the whole nation (notably in the BPKI) without the problems of having to negotiate with outer islanders.
3. The "social revolutions" in rejecting the royal symbols of an older identity, also destroyed much of the force of that identity itself. As Soejatno[73] said of Surakarta, the revolution "brought profound and irreversible change to the area once considered the heartland of Javanese traditional aristocratic values".
4. Dutch strategy could not have been better designed to promote Indonesian unity. By attempting to "surround" the Republic with pro-Dutch states based on local sentiment, they not only destroyed the legitimacy of regionalism, but also weakened and distracted those forces within the Republic which might otherwise have proven difficult for the Republic to digest.
5. The disorder in Republican areas of Sumatra, notably East Sumatra, Tapanuli, and West Sumatra, made the intervention of central government authority both welcome and inevitable. Primordial sentiments were felt not primarily against the Javanese who were far away, but against the immediate ethnic rivals within the region.
6. Perhaps most important (though here in common with other revolutions), there was an enormously powerful common ideal at work, especially among youth — to make a new future that was free, dignified and prosperous. The very fragmentation of the revolutionary dynamic in dozens of autonomous processes, the reality of which was often painfully flawed, appeared to make this ideal shine ever brighter.

CHAPTER 9

Gestapu: A Hesitant Assessment, 1967

Even two years after the first upheaval [i.e. 1967],[1] it is still almost impossible for anyone to view with complete objectivity the trauma which shook Indonesia on and after the night of September 30, 1965. Among Indonesians, all are involved; there are few who have not felt their jobs, their property, or their lives threatened at some time either before or after *Gestapu*. In the outside world, on the other hand, reactions have mainly been governed by international alignments. The reversal of the foreign policy of Sukarno and Aidit has brought relief to the major targets of that policy — America, Britain, India and Malaysia — in particular and to a wider group interested in Asian stability and the authority of the United Nations. It has brought further annoyance to China.

To understand the coup itself and the bloodbath which followed, however, we must look not at the international power game, at the CIA- or Peking-inspired plots beloved of Djakarta wall-daubers, but at the tensions within Indonesian society itself. For if it was the greatest achievement of the Sukarno regime to have created a measure of horizontal national unity among peoples of diverse language and culture, it was among its greatest failures to have only accentuated the vertical divisions within each region, between rich and poor, landlord and labourer, *santri* and *abangan*.[2] Of course, this is to speak *with* the advantage of hindsight. Pressing that advantage further, we must consider the various factors combining to produce an explosively tense situation in Indonesia towards the end of 1965.

Economic Collapse

First, and underlying everything, there was the economic collapse. Extravagant spending on arms and diplomatic gestures, the burden of foreign debts, attacks against all the major foreign investors in turn, corruption and inexperience in nationalised concerns, and the severing of commercial ties with Malaysia all contributed to the Government's inability to pay its servants or maintain essential services. The value of the *rupiah* dropped with increasing speed (US$1 fetched Rp.5,000 on the Djakarta black market in January 1965; 10,000 in June; and 40,000 in September).

City-dwellers, who were worst affected, were accustomed to having their attention diverted from these ills by the increasingly violent attacks on foreign embassies and offices. In this exercise, Sukarno leaned heavily on the PKI for street demonstrations, and at the same time tried to tame it by making criticism of the government appear to be a betrayal of the nation in danger. But urbanites found it harder and harder to accept that the high price of rice was caused by *Nekolim*, Malaysia, and so forth. For a time, Sukarno kept PKI criticism of his economic mismanagement in check by including Communists in junior posts in his *Nasakom* cabinet. But by September 1965, the rising prices again provoked repeated Communist demonstrations in Djakarta streets. Usually, the government itself was not directly held responsible for their grievances, but "capitalist-bureaucrats, manipulators, and speculators". The PKI's Djakarta daily, *Harian Rakjat*, on 22 September, urged workers to "organise themselves and carry out quick and proper actions" against such elements. Such invitations to take the law into private hands were frequent during the few months before *Gestapu*, and were endorsed even by Subandrio in some statements. The economic collapse was making *Nasakom* cooperation more unworkable than it had ever been, but more importantly, it was rapidly undermining respect for government authority and the rule of law.

Land Reform

In rural areas, it was the land reform programme which began the spiral of increasing tension. In 1959, the Government had passed a Crop Division Law guaranteeing a 50-50 division of returns between tenant and landlord. The following year, a Land Reform Act imposed a maximum limit of five hectares (6.6 acres) of *sawah* for any one landowner. The excess was to be distributed among landless peasants who would repay the cost over a 15-year period (which, in Indonesian conditions of inflation, insured a minimal price). In fact, the government apparatus was too inefficient and the authority of the landholders too well-established in most areas to allow much effect to be given to the laws. During 1964, however, the BTI (*Barisan Tani Indonesia*, the PKI's peasant organisation) began a programme of *aksi sepihak* — unilateral action to enforce the land reform laws by seizing land from the wealthier farmers. Their degree of success in this depended on PKI strength and on the affiliation of the local military commander. The reaction of the central government was weak and uncertain. Although some pressure was put on the PKI to halt the *aksi sepihak*, there was no consistent attempt to prevent or disallow the forcible seizures. As far as landowners were concerned, the army was the only force to which they could appeal. A number of bloody clashes between the army and PKI activists on this issue were reported from Central Java during 1964 and 1965.

The crop division law also brought dislocation into the pattern of "shared poverty" which was the traditional mark of the Javanese village. It frequently occurred that the landlord, rather than content himself with the 50% to which he was entitled under the law, preferred to dismiss the tenant altogether and farm the land with daily-rated wage labour from another village. Thus, the group of uprooted landless labourers sympathetic to the BTI *aksi sepihak* programme was only increased.

The major effects of the BTI campaign appear to have been two. On the one hand, a disruption of the Javanese village pattern, in which, according to one sociologist "class distinctions play(ed) no effective role" in the early 1950s.[3] On the other hand, even more than in the cities, there was an obvious decline in government authority leading to a direct clash between BTI mobs and the army.

The Religious Reaction

The resistance of the wealthier peasants who were the target of the *aksi sepihak* naturally took on an ideological flavour. The strength of Islam in East and Central Java has always been among the wealthier peasants and small traders — the *santris*, many of whom had their status confirmed by the completion of the *haj*. Considerable areas of land were given as *waqf* to religious institutions rather than see them divided among the landless. Among students at Islamic schools in Java, most of whose fathers were the object of Communist hostility, a new mood was discernable to observers during 1964–1965. It eschewed the old political preoccupations of the rival Muslim parties (the traditionalist *Nahdatul Ulama* and modernist

Masjumi) in favour of a narrower concern with the defence and propagation of the faith, in which anti-communism was a large element.[4] For some months before *Gestapu*, observers noted the greater fervour of Muslim youth groups expressed in frequent drum marches through the street of provincial towns.

Throughout 1965, but especially during August and September, bloody clashes between Muslim groups (especially *ANSOR*, the *NU* youth organisation) and communists were constantly reported from East and Central Java. Though the land issue was probably at the root of the initial polarisation of opinion in these areas, the ideological antagonism developed its own momentum as these clashes spread. The PKI leadership was careful to avoid explicit attacks on Islam in its official pronouncements, but its strongest supporters were found among just those *abangan* (i.e., culturally more wedded to Javanese folk-religion than to Islam) Javanese among whom explicit anti-Muslim sentiment was not uncommon (see, for example, the *Permai* movement described in Geertz, *The Religion of Java*, pp. 112–8).

In the period immediately preceding 30 September, this tense ideological antagonism spread to the towns, where it focussed round the question of the HMI (the Masjumi-oriented Muslim students group). As it was among the most vociferous and effective opponents of the communists, the PKI began a campaign to have it banned on the grounds of being anti-NASAKOM. Sukarno had already shown his weakness in face of the PKI's ability to organise massive demonstrations when he had banned the anti-PKI *Body for the Promotion of Sukarnoism* in January 1965, after having initially given it his blessing. History seemed about to repeat itself, when Sukarno's declaration of 16 September that HMI should be allowed to function was followed by a series of noisy communist demonstrations aimed at forcing the President's hand. But the HMI, unlike the BPS, had a strong popular following, and reacted in kind. An indication of the tension over this issue came when Basiruan, a police commissioner and chairman of the Nationalist student group, urged the banning of HMI in a speech at the University of Indonesia. He was dragged away and beaten up by some HMI students (*Straits Times*, 27 September 1965).

Despite NASAKOM and the closeness of Sukarno and Subandrio to Peking in foreign policy, therefore, the PKI came into increasingly aggressive opposition to the status quo during 1965, partly as a result of the pressure from below over the economic crisis. The respect for law was rapidly collapsing, and the army emerging as the only hope for those who feared, but could not rival, the PKI's ability to organise popular demonstrations. Sukarno himself was not governing but trying to ride the storm, and the bureaucratic machine was paralysed by inflation, corruption, and the waywardness of the political leadership. The tension and distrust between the army leadership and the PKI was at such a level that a coup by one side was constantly feared by the other, and this atmosphere was sped into crisis by the failing health of the "Great Leader" and his dramatic collapse during a rally on the evening of 30 September.

The Guilt of Gestapu

This then is the background to the abortive coup and its horrific consequences. The immediate responsibility for the coup, however, has been the subject of the bitterest controversy. To the present Indonesian leadership, it is an article of faith that the PKI planned and executed the murder of the six generals, with or without direct orders from Peking. This view is overwhelmingly endorsed by currently expressed public opinion in Indonesia, and is held more tenaciously because this was and is the justification given for the ruthless and wholesale massacre of communists which followed. Many well-informed outsiders are sceptical, however — particularly those students of Communist tactics who felt that such a coup was out of character with PKI policy or capability at the time. They are inclined to give some weight to the statements of the PKI and Untung himself that it was an internal affair of the army, carried out by junior officers from Central Java dissatisfied with the army leadership (see especially Wertheim, *Pacific Affairs* XXXIX, 1–2; and in *De Groene Amsterdammer* 1, 8, and 15 October 1966; Lev, *Asian Survey* [February 1966]; the much publicised but unpublished views of some of the Indonesian experts at Cornell University; and to some extent, Vittachi's *The Fall of Sukarno*).

The exact degree of PKI responsibility for the murder of the generals will probably never be known — certainly not in the present atmosphere of recrimination. Future historians may not regard it as the central question at all. But from the welter of evidence and pseudo-evidence, three points already appear to stand out:

1. The PKI emphatically welcomed the coup (see especially the editorial in its *Harian Rakjat*, 2 October 1965), which expressed precisely its own fears about right-wing elements in and possibly outside the army; the PKI leadership and some members of its mass organisations were also a direct party to the killings at Halim airbase.
2. On the other hand, Untung himself, the commander of Sukarno's palace guard, had his own set of motives in kidnapping the generals, and though he may have been much influenced by the PKI, he did not believe himself to be an agent of it.
3. The position of the Head of State was extremely ambiguous, as he appeared to fear almost equally the threat to himself of either a "council of generals" or a PKI-dominated government. Since Sukarno had made empty all permanent constitutional structure except himself and his ideological formulations, *Gestapu* cannot meaningfully be portrayed as a treasonable blow against "the state" (in constitutional, as distinct from moral terms). Rather was it the first blow in a struggle for power, in which the embodiment of constitutional legality was an anxious bystander.

The Killings

Such niceties of distinction did not appear of much relevance in the tensely-divided country which received the news of the murders and the quick reassertion of military authority. The generals were proclaimed national heroes; their names and photographs appeared in every public place. Pictures of their mutilated bodies were repeatedly shown in the mass media, and their funeral became the occasion of mass hysteria against those responsible. The scream for vengeance was irresistible for those who had been for so long on the defensive against PKI demands. Already on 5 October, Muslim and Christian youth groups were in the Djakarta streets calling for a ban on the PKI, and on 8 October, they burnt down the Communist headquarters.

It was in Central and East Java and Bali that the PKI was strongest and the land issue most acute. It was also in Central and East Java that the only real fighting took place, with rebel troops, supported by PKI mass organisations, doing their share of the murdering until the leadership re-established control about mid-October.

From that time until the end of the year, the slaughter of communists was at its peak. Sukarno's figure for the tally of dead in these three months, after an official investigation, was 87,000. The army later gave a partial breakdown as follows:

Central Java	10,000
East Java	54,000
Bali	12,000
North Sumatra	2,000

All observers agree that these figures should be roughly doubled to give a more accurate picture. Moreover, the killings continued in spasms through 1966 and even 1967. The writer was told in Atjeh by some who claimed to be among the killers that 10,000 had died there in three days. A recent report suggested that the toll in North Sumatra, where most of the victims were immigrant Javanese workers on the plantations around Medan, was now nearer 100,000. Most estimates of the total losses are between 200,000 and 500,000.

Of course, only a minority of these were the victims of a systematic drive against the PKI by the army. Most of those killed were by no means "hardcore", and knew nothing of Communism, Aidit, Mao Tse-Tung or *Gestapu*. Most peasant members of the BTI, for example, had joined it because it expressed some of their grievances, or because they thought Sukarno was its president, or (as was reported in Atjeh), because they were told it meant Barisan Tani Islam. In the anarchy and bloodlust which swept Java, Bali, and parts of North Sumatra after it became clear that murders were going unpunished, a lot of old scores were also paid off which had even less to do with communism. Disputes over land were the most frequent causes of such vendettas in the rural areas, but many other issues were also "settled". In Bali, for example, one report told of the killing of 16 members of a Brahmanic family which had been the arch enemies of the ruling prince (the Dewa Agung) for generations.

The above account of prevailing tension in pre-*Gestapu* Indonesia is a preface to the grisly phenomenon of a nation running *amok*, but it clearly does not explain it. Nor can we lay the guilt exclusively at the feet of the army, or of Sukarno, or of the earlier activities of the PKI itself, though all bear a heavy responsibility. No doubt we must look further into the psychological makeup of the Javanese; the fatalism of many of the victims; the curious hypnosis which gave some of the killings the nature of ritual sacrifices (for example, the North Bali incident where the execution of some members of the PKI women's movement was carried out by a temple-dancer in a trance), the prophecies of Jeyabeya about "a time of madness" and so forth. The fact will remain to haunt us, that such things were possible in what was long thought to be the most tranquil corner of a peace-loving continent.

Gains and Losses

In attempting to weigh the total effect on Indonesia of *Gestapu* and its aftermath, there can be nothing to put in the balance against this holocaust, not only in terms of death and deprivation, but of the brutalising effect on the killers and on public opinion. Future conflicts in Indonesia will be more savage because of it, and future communist efforts in particular will follow more rigidly the Maoist dictum that power grows out of the barrel of a gun.

In other respects, there have been improvements, at least over the position in 1964–1965. Most importantly, there is a new note of realism in approaching the economic problems that lie at the root of much of Indonesia's political trouble. Where Sukarno urged his economists to throw their books into the sea, Suharto gives them pride of place among his civilian advisers. Conditions have not markedly improved, but at last in 1967, the inflation has begun to level off and rational plans are being made which give definite hope for the future.

There is also a more relaxed atmosphere among intellectuals — at least those who are now at liberty. Far from feeling crushed by the horror of the affair, most thoughtful Indonesians give the impression of relief that the bubble has burst at last, the tension has eased, and opinions can again be expressed without fear of an attack in the night (though this too is occasionally happening in some areas). The students' crusade against corruption in high places seems as much of a lost cause as ever, but it is a healthy sign that they have still not been forcibly silenced.

As against this, however, must be set the potential danger of the state's new commitment to organised religion. Indonesia's *pantjasila* philosophy has of course always enshrined belief in God, but for those, like the writer, who treasure this belief as a free act of the will, it is alarming to see the great religions caught up with the official bandwagon. Religious instruction has been made a compulsory subject in the universities (the student must choose between Islam and Christianity, with Hinduism as a third alternative for Balinese). Those of the Karo-Bataks, Dayaks, Torajas, etc., who are still animist, have been instructed by Government that they must *beragama* (adopt a religion) either as Muslims or Christians. This accounts in large measure for the numerically spectacular Christian gains recently, which have alarmed some Muslim commentators.[5] It is to be feared that in the long run, it is faith itself which will suffer most from its use as an arm of anti-communist state policy.

Finally, on the debit side must be put the renewed Chinese-phobia which threatens to create further misery and to upset the sensible plans at last being made for economic recovery. Any country in the financial condition of Indonesia will inevitably be prone to scapegoat-hunting. It was one of the few merits of Sukarno's foreign policy, however, that it spared the Chinese by directing hostility outwards.

The End of the Revolution

However they view the gains and losses of this traumatic period, it seems clear already that historians will regard October 1965 as a major turning point. It may be seen as an Indonesian thermidor, the end of the revolutionary process which began under middle-class leadership in 1945. Like so many of the classic (pre-Maoist) models before it, that revolution moved steadily further to the left as the "Great Leader" tried to ride the forces he had originally called forth without being thrown off by them. The end of the process was that there appeared to be no forces left in the field except the mob on the one hand, and the army on the other.

CHAPTER 10

"Asian Tradition" and Indonesian Politics: The One and the Many[1]

For a period in the 1990s, the dichotomy of East and West returned to the political and academic agenda. A century earlier, partly in response to a strong strain of European thought essentialising "Asia" or "the Orient" as inherently despotic or hierarchic, the first wave of Asianism had celebrated Okakura's famous aphorism that "Asia is One".[2] Then, its essence was a superior spirituality, aspiring to the universal rather than the particular. In the early 1990s, "Asian values" still included thrift and self-discipline, and was again justified as a response to western bullying. But the evidence of the merit of these common ideas now lay in the economic rather than the spiritual realm.

The New Order leadership of Indonesia was not a significant player in the international debates of the 1990s, though its development-oriented authoritarian political style was well suited as subject matter. The most articulate spokesmen in English were leaders of Malaysia and Singapore, for whom an "Asian" paradigm seemed attractive as a bond, or at least not an exclusion, for their Malay, Chinese and Indian populations. The "Singaporean cultural offensive" of the early 1990s,[3] and the Mahathir-Ishihara book of 1994,[4] sought to identify a set of "Asian" values representing a more hopeful path for the world than the decaying "West".

India was remarkably absent from this new "Asia", whereas it had been central to the first phase. Not only was it not (then) rich enough to be an attractive model, but its dizzying pluralism and robustly individualistic style of democracy sat uneasily with the values most of these writers wanted to uphold. Of the Southeast Asian politicians who saluted the new Asia, only Malaysia's Deputy Prime Minister Anwar Ibrahim included the Indian staples of an earlier generation — Tagore, Gandhi and Iqbal. He also distinguished himself (quietly) from Dr Mahathir by seeking "a global *convivencia*" rather than a line between "Asia" and "the West".[5]

This debate was a notable indicator of the globalising of the market in ideas as well as goods in the post-Cold War world. It was stimulated by the quest for a universal convention on human rights, stimulated particularly by the World Conference on the subject in Vienna in June 1993, preceded by a Bangkok meeting in March 1993 to seek a regional Asian consensus on the subject.

Indonesia was among the governments, along with China, Pakistan and Singapore, identified by the universalist camp as most hostile to a strong statement of universal human rights in Vienna. The spokesmen for these countries did not declare publicly that "Asia" had a contrary model, but they argued with considerable success for the cultural contextualisation of all rights, for the relative priority of social, economic and collective rights over civil and individual ones, and for limiting any potential for international monitoring or enforcement of human rights.[6] They were most comfortable speaking in negative terms about aspects of "the West" of which they did not approve — godlessness, family breakdowns, drug dependence, homosexual marriage, the US gun lobby, and so forth. The positive case for a common tradition of political culture is difficult to make in one civilisational tradition, and immensely demanding in "Asia".

While the Indonesian government played little part in the global debate in English on Asian values, its rhetoric for internal consumption under Suharto was a strong assertion of the inappropriateness of western democratic theory to Indonesia. It therefore represents an interesting contextualisation of what that debate was about.

The Organic "Family" State in Indonesian Rhetoric

From 1957 to 1998, Indonesia's political leadership made increasing use of a set of concepts which it traced to indigenous political tradition. Central to them was the notion of the state as a family, organically united in love, and governed by a father-head who best understands the needs of its members. As Reeve noted in the 1980s, "Apart from 'Pancasila' and 'the 1945 Constitution', there is no theme more frequently uttered by President Suharto and his Government than 'the family principle'".[7] Pancasila and the 1945 Constitution, both born at a period exceptionally favourable to the organicist "family state" (*kazoku kokka*) ideas promoted by the Japanese military then ruling Indonesia, have themselves been presented by the Suharto government as supporting the family principle (*kekeluargaan*). The political features held to grow out of these principles are the organic unity of state and society, harmony and consensus rather than open debate and majority decision, unitarism rather than federal or contractual relations, the primacy of group needs over individual needs, representation through "functional groups" rather than competitive parties, and rejection of the standard elements of liberal constitutionalism such as separation of powers and individual rights.

The revival in the mid-1980s of the concept of integralism as the animating principle for these ideas, and their systematic imposition in the indoctrination courses known in Indonesia as P4, gave rise to a scholarly backlash. Marsillam Simanjuntak and A. Buyung Nasution in Indonesia, and most fully David Bourchier in a 1996 Monash dissertation,[8] have traced the way in which these ideas have been adopted and implemented in a series of specific political manoeuvres since 1945. They trace their origins not to Indonesian or even Javanese tradition, but to the current of organicism in European political thought, now discredited in the West because of its association with fascism.

Rooted in German romanticism, these ideas became influential in Indonesia largely through the Leiden Law School. First Jacques Oppenheim (who headed the school from 1893), and then Cornelis van Vollenhoven, were the dominant figures in both the training of Indonesian lawyers until 1940, and in the proposing of constitutional arrangements for Indonesia (such as the colonial assembly, the *Volksraad*, and *adat* law courts) which reflected a view of the relations between state and society being more organic than that which prevailed in the Netherlands itself.[9] The insistence of this school that European social contract theories and a unified system of law for all Indonesia's inhabitants were inappropriate for the organic world of the Indonesian village looks today very much like paternalistic orientalism. It made a great impact on young Indonesian nationalists, however, both because van Vollenhoven was personally supportive of Indonesians and because he claimed to have discovered a coherent and distinctive pattern of law in the Indonesian Archipelago.

Van Vollenhoven's most influential student was Dr Raden Supomo, who in 1940 became the first Indonesian professor at the Jakarta Law School, and who in 1945 was the principal author of the Indonesian

Constitution. Supomo's ideas fitted well with those of the Japanese military occupation, and he became chief legal adviser to the Military Administration. As the acknowledged constitutional expert, he was influential in the debates of May–June 1945 about which state was to be given independence by the Japanese, and advised the assembled Indonesian delegates that:

> according to the integralist understanding of 'State' there will be no dualism between 'state and individual', there will be no dualism between State and civil society, there will be no need for basic rights or human rights for the individual against the State, because individuals are organic parts of the State.[10]

The constitution he drafted was, not surprisingly, based on a very strong, indirectly elected Presidency, and contained only a laconic reference to civil rights (apparently forced on him by Hatta and Yamin).[11]

These organicist ideas and their supporters were in retreat as soon as their Japanese protectors departed, and played a very marginal part in the heady and often violent multiparty democracy of 1946–1957. From 1957, however, following the inconclusive results of the first national elections in 1955, the coalition of extra-parliamentary forces opposing the multi-party parliamentary system — the army, sections of the bureaucracy, and President Sukarno — found them increasingly useful. The never-used 1945 Constitution was again promulgated by Sukarno in 1959, as he introduced what he called "Guided Democracy". This ideology owed something to Professor Supomo but even more to Ki Hadjar Dewantoro, Dutch-educated but even closer than Supomo to the Javanese aristocratic worldview. Ki Hadjar's model of political and social life was that of the family, who all "have the same rights but different tasks, have a unity of interests, a unity of strengths, and a unity of soul".[12] Leadership flowed naturally from wisdom and spiritual strength, and conflicts were overcome by cooperation and by recognition of wise leadership rather than by class struggle or majority vote. Under the New Order of President Suharto, the same ideas were constantly reiterated at the centre, even if just as frequently disputed by a healthy diversity of dissident voices. The organicist idea of representation through functional groups took a unique form in GOLKAR (Golongan Karya = functional groups), which from 1969 became the basis for managing elections through an army and bureaucracy whose vehicle this became. GOLKAR laid down in 1974 its two basic principles — "duties before rights", and "the general interest before the interests of persons or groups".[13]

In the 1960s, many western political scientists accepted that this authoritarian tendency was rooted in Indonesian, or more particularly Javanese, political "tradition". Harry Benda greeted Herb Feith's *Decline of Constitutional Democracy in Indonesia* with the protest that Indonesian politics was simply returning to its "procrustean bed".[14] Ann Ruth Willner[15] and Benedict Anderson sought the basis of modern integralist ideas of the state in pre-colonial Javanese traditions of thought. The case for continuity between pre-colonial and post-colonial thought was most influentially put by Anderson in his "Idea of Power in Javanese Culture":

> The good society is not strictly hierarchical, since a hierarchy presupposes a certain degree of autonomy at each of its levels. The movement of traditional Javanese thought implicitly denies this, seeking ideally a single, pervasive source of power and authority ...

Unity is always associated with power in this view, and the hostility of many nationalists to ideas of federalism or contractualism was caused not only by the Dutch promotion of these ideas in the 1940s (see Chapter 11), but by the sense that in Javanese tradition, "oneness is power and multiplicity is diffusion and weakness".[16]

As opposition grew within Indonesia to similar lineages for authoritarian ideas being constructed by New Order ideologues, foreign political scientists have become less inclined to articulate them. Among students of Indonesian history and literature, both within Indonesia and outside, there has never been much support for this notion of continuity between pre-colonial and post-colonial authoritarianisms. As Bourchier convincingly shows, it was originally lawyers with a strong foundation in German and Dutch organic-state romanticism who created the contemporary theoretical basis for the integral state, and the ideas have been revived since the 1980s by military and legal professionals and in some quarters of the bureaucracy.

Despite their scepticism about these authoritarian ideas, historians have only recently begun the positive work of developing an alternative picture of the exceptionally diverse and fragmented Indonesian political tradition. I want here to argue that throughout Southeast Asian history, concepts of a sublime, unifying state centre from which all power descends have always been associated with foreignness, while contractualism, plurality and diversity are the stuff of Southeast Asian social reality, against which the ideology of royal or state absolutism has had to fight a constant uphill battle.

Pluralism in the Archipelago

Attempts to peel the onion of culture down to an original, indigenous core are always dangerous, although frequently attempted. J.C. van Leur's dismissal of Indian, Islamic and early Dutch influences as "a thin, easily-flaking glaze on the massive body of indigenous civilisation" is no longer convincing, although Denys Lombard has recently brought more erudition and sophistication to a similar task.[17] Nevertheless, there are some helpful pointers from archaeology, anthropology, literature and the accounts of early travellers about the direction in which outside influences were leading. Minority populations, whom external influence is thought to have passed by, are still identified in out-of-the-way uplands of the Archipelago. The Bali Aga of Bali, the Buda population of the Tengger mountains in East Java, and the Baduy of West Java are examples of such pockets, whom Hefner characterises as being renowned "for their only modest internal differentiation and for their residents' aggressively egalitarian social and linguistic styles".[18] The interior of all the Indonesian islands except Java and Bali was dominated by essentially stateless peoples (Dayak, Toraja, Batak, Alfur, Atoni) who resisted the appeal of states until forced into the Netherlands Indian colonial state at the end of the 19th century. This resistance, despite familiarity with the monarchies of the ports for more than a thousand years, contrasts markedly with the history of Europe and China where the last of the marginal stateless peoples were incorporated into states 400 years ago. This suggests that the "traditional" idea in need of study is not that of divine kingship but the principles of social organisation which enabled Indonesians to develop sophisticated written cultures without states.

Even in the case of Java itself, on which the unitary theorising rests heavily, the archaeological and historical record does not support the idea of a single centre of cosmic power. Temple complexes and inscriptions are dispersed in hundreds of places throughout the island. Although there are modest ruins of a Majapahit court capital at Trowulan, Wisseman and others have pointed out that the real mystery of ancient Java, and of Sumatra, is how such apparently sophisticated Indian-influenced cultures developed without leaving the archaeological record of a central capital (such as Angkor or Pagan on the Mainland) (Wisseman 1977, 197–212). Even during the heyday of Majapahit when tribute missions to China were frequent around 1400, the Chinese perceived there to be two rival kingdoms which had coexisted over a long period in the Majapahit heartland itself, without even considering the diversities of Central and West Java.[19] Once more detailed European accounts of Java become available, they reveal a dozen kings or princes warring with one another throughout the pre-colonial period except 1620–1660. Ricklefs has effectively shown that the Javanese sources dealing with the period acknowledge this diversity, even though many of them felt that there "ought" to have been one king.[20] Nagtegal has recently gone further, showing that false Dutch expectations of a powerful king in Java were responsible for the VOC's blundering into the affairs of the interior, discovering only too late that the instructions of Mataram were obeyed by few power-holders on the ground.[21]

The Javanese culture area (Central and East Java) was extreme in 19th-century Indonesia in two ways — the importance of hierarchic principles of organisation, and the length of time with which it had been interacting with Europeans. In order to test whether the first of these phenomena is causally related to the latter, and what might have become of the Javanese states without Dutch intervention, it is useful to look not only at the Tengger and Baduy, but at Bali. There, a political and cultural system claiming descent from Majapahit held off European and Islamic influence until 1900. After a brief period of political unity at the same time as most other Indonesian societies were at the peak of what I call the age of commerce (i.e., the late 16th and early 17th centuries), Bali had returned to fragmentation by 1700. Although the nature of the Balinese state is complex and obscure, we know that the eight acknowledged Balinese states of the 18th and 19th centuries were themselves internally diverse, with two kings at their centre[22] multiple intermarrying lineages, and strong institutions such as the irrigation cooperatives (*subak*) and village (*bandjar*) over which the rulers had little control. As a puzzled Dutch official noted:

> Since my first arrival here, I have given myself the task of gaining a picture of the relationship between the rajas ... the way of their government, their power, etc. The more I learned about it, the more

I ... became entangled in a labyrinth of complex family relations and interests.[23]

Balinese culture was sophisticated and internally coherent — at least as much as stateless Batak or Minangkabau society were. What held it all together, however, was not an absolutist state of European type, nor even (although this is closer) a ritual performance of the type sketched by Geertz, but rather a web of complex family and personal relationships, often supernaturally sanctioned.[24] It is this robust pluralism, often co-existing with exalted Indic ideas of kingship, which merits our attention.

As we move to societies less influenced by Indic models, the principle of pluralism becomes even more marked, and even more puzzling in its tenacity. Maluku (the Spice Islands), now ably re-examined by Leonard Andaya, is a fascinating case because as the only source of the world's cloves and nutmeg until the late 18th century, it had even more constant attention from outsiders than Java or indeed anywhere else in Asia. If any area might have been expected to generate a strong state in order to deal with foreigners, it would have been Maluku. Yet despite all the attempts of firstly Muslims, then Portuguese and finally Dutch, to manipulate one state to dominate the others, the Malukans remained resolutely, almost fanatically, pluralist. The two strongest states, Ternate and Tidore, were on tiny volcanic islands only five kilometres apart, yet throughout their 500 years of warring with each other and intriguing with foreigners, one never absorbed the other. Beyond this primary duality which spread itself throughout Maluku, there was a four-way division representing the cardinal points which gave almost equal eminence to two other island kingdoms also within a day's sail of each other. The survival and interdependence of these states was seen to be crucial to Maluku's well-being, even while they warred mercilessly against each other. Their necessary relations with each other were spelt out in elaborate myths about the common origin of the two, four, or more kings. As Andaya points out,

> The Europeans were clearly puzzled by the relationship. Despite the sworn enmity between these two kingdoms, they continued to advise each other against any European activity which could threaten the other's well-being ... Even in the midst of war, intercourse between the people of the two kingdoms continued. The dualism of Ternate and Tidore within the tradition of the "four" kingdoms was viewed as essential for the survival of the group.[25]

This pattern was replicated throughout eastern Indonesia, where "speaking in pairs" has been identified as a central aspect of the way society is conceptualised.[26]

The major states generated in the eastern two-thirds of the Archipelago all had to incorporate the deep dualisms and pluralisms of their environment. Makasar, the most powerful, was built on a contractual dualism between the two states of Gowa and Tallo', which in turn were federations of seven or nine lineages, all with their clear rights within the united kingdom. The contractual basis on which all Bugis and Makasar states were built, reinforced by solemn oaths to maintain the system, created the same resistance to autocracy which Andaya chronicled in Maluku. The Dutch conqueror of Makasar, astonished at the series of extremely complex rights, contracts and obligations to which he became heir, noted that "The kings of Gowa and Tallo' cannot make one false step once outside their own gates".[27] The Bugis kingdoms, which flourished in the 18th and 19th centuries, had an even more developed sense of contractualism among the local communities who had formed a social contract of sorts to form the state. When enthroning the king, the head of each constituting lineage ritually expressed his autonomy: "I will conduct my own affairs, I will preserve my manners, I will maintain my custom, only if I need it will I appeal to your advice". In return, the ruler declared to the assembly: "I will not oppose myself to your will; I will not contradict your words; I will not prevent you from leaving Wajo' or returning to it".[28]

Sulu, the strongest pre-colonial concentration of power in what we today call the southern Philippines, was described by Thomas Forrest as a "mixed" government because the sultan was hereditary but was governed by a council of nobles in which he had two votes and each of the 15 *datos* had one. Also sitting in the Council were "two representatives of the people, called Manteries".[29] Forrest is unlikely to have fully grasped the extent of Sulu's pluralism, which baffled a succession of Spanish and American administrators. The first anthropologist to look seriously at Sulu society, Thomas Kiefer, declared two centuries later that all his preconceptions about a social structure based on groups of people had to be abandoned there. He believed that the Tausug thought not in terms of groups but in terms of the personal vertical relationship between two males. It was a kind of segmentary state in which the Sultan's powers were all exactly replicated in each of the hereditary *datus*.[30]

Sumatra presented a different challenge, and was constantly frustrating to European officials who expected to make deals with kings which would bind their subjects. Raffles, who usually claimed to be the most advanced of liberals, and who was dedicated to the ending of slavery and oppression, sought to act more ruthlessly in Sumatra:

> In Java I advocated the doctrine of the liberty of the subject, and the individual rights of man — here I am the advocate of despotism. The strong arm of power is necessary to bring men together, and to concentrate them in societies ... Sumatra is, in a great measure, peopled by innumerable petty tribes, subject to no general government ... At present the people are as wandering in their habits as the birds of the air, and until they are congregated and organised under something like authority, nothing can be done with them.[31]

In particular, the Pasemah of upland South Sumatra were reported by Dutch officials in the 19th century to be a people who consciously and consistently preferred their own customary freedoms to any kind of submission to the Palembang sultanate:

> The Pasemah is a Republic in the most democratic sense. The people rules itself; for that purpose great public meetings would be convened in which all important matters would be discussed and settled. Chiefs must carry out or get carried out all the resolutions of the gathering.

and:

> The untamed, freedom-loving masses in Pasumah are the tyrant of their own leaders; democracy prevails there to the point of anarchy.[32]

There were kings in Sumatra. In some cases, they enjoyed a moment of effective central power during the peak of the age of commerce. But when the foreign sources of that power were removed, the inherent pluralism, which seems so firm a part of Sumatran social structure, reappeared. In each coastal sultanate, there was pluralism at the centre, represented by the merchant-aristocrats (*orangkaya*) with a stake in commerce without whose support the sultans could do virtually nothing. There was another inherent dualism between the downstream (*hilir*) and upstream (*hulu*) arms of the state, the latter never having more than a very conditional reciprocity with the capital. The large number of substantial rivers ensured an almost equal number of small rulers of the river-mouth, who might sometimes send tribute to another ruler with greater charisma, but sometimes not. The two most numerous peoples of Sumatra, the highland Minangkabau and Batak, each developed a complex common culture in which the local community (Minangkabau *nagari*, Batak *huta*) appeared wholly autonomous despite their sophisticated interrelationships of commerce, kinship, literature, religion and warfare. The Minangkabau acknowledged the king of Pagaruyung as supernaturally powerful to an extent which Europeans found hard to comprehend. Even the distant Bataks believed that if his status was challenged, "their affairs would never prosper; that their *padi* would be blighted, and their buffaloes die", as Marsden put it. Yet the authority of the Pagaruyung kings was of quite a different character to that of the European Renaissance tradition. Lacking the economic or military resources to influence the behaviour of their subjects, their power rested on the charisma of their lineage and magical language. Like the Singamangarajas of the Bataks, they existed in a sphere which in no way curbed the complex autonomies of Sumatran society.[33]

The social reality of the pre-colonial Archipelago appears to have been characterised not by autocratic kings from whom all power descended, but by a complex web of contractual mutualities at the local level. The ideology of kingship did not so much contest this diversity as seek to disguise or absorb it into metaphors of oneness. One might almost say that the greater the contractual autonomies within society — as among the Minangkabau, Bugis, and Balinese — the more kings sought a magical domain in which they were master. The Minangkabau rulers claimed in their letters and seals to be equal heirs — on par with the kings of China and Constantinople — of the legacy of the world-conqueror Alexander the Great, to be the *khalif* (deputy) or shadow of God on earth (*zil'ullah f'il alam*), to possess all manner of miraculous inheritances of past empires, and to be able to strike dead miraculously any who doubted these claims. As Jane Drakard has convincingly shown, these grandiose words were effective in projecting Minangkabau power outwards throughout Sumatra and beyond, although they appeared in no way (except occasionally in war) to limit the autonomy of the Minangkabau *nagari*.

Perhaps this is not entirely dissimilar to the mystical habit, which is present everywhere but strongest in Java, of acknowledging plurality but seeking a deeper mystical level at which it blends into unity. The Indonesian motto, *Bhineka Tunggal Ika* (they are different, yet they are one), which was written as early as the 14th century to demonstrate the relation of Buddhism and Hinduism, beautifully expresses how the Javanese have sought to handle this problem. The many instances in modern politics in which very different leaders are said to be *dwitunggal* (two and yet one), like Sukarno and Hatta, or *manunggal* (different but one), like the five leaders of the PKI, show the continuing appeal of a formula which asserts unity within a lived reality of diversity.

External Models of the Strong State

If Indonesian social structure was particularly marked by relations of contract and reciprocity, how do we account for the rhetoric of cosmic uniqueness which is an undoubted feature of courtly texts and royal pronouncements? The foreign ideas seized upon by rulers and their court writers seeking to exalt the power of the centralised state above the Archipelago's troublesome diversity can be categorised in terms of four waves. These were the Indic, the Islamic, the colonial, and the high modern, each more intense and effective than the one before.

The Indic Tradition

The Indic tradition, as is well known, was brought to several kingdoms in Southeast Asia in the first millennium of the common era. It included a range of ideas about sacred kingship which have become important in the Archipelago, including enthronement and lustration rituals, identification of rulers with certain gods, and sacred architecture in the capital which sought to replicate Mount Meru. These ideas undoubtedly helped provide Southeast Asian kingdoms with the rhetorical means to exalt themselves above the confusing array of communities and chiefdoms which every part of Southeast Asia incorporated. Yet it seriously misrepresents the situation to take this rhetoric as implying that Majapahit and Sriwijaya were really structured in a centralised way when Chinese sources and the archaeological record clearly show the contrary. With hindsight, it appears that Cornell University's use of Heine-Geldern's *Conceptions of State and Kingship in Southeast Asia* to train specialists in contemporary Indonesia in the 1950s may have contributed to the one-sided picture of Javanese "tradition" advanced by a number of Cornell graduates (a phenomenon to which Merle Ricklefs has drawn attention).[34]

Islam

The importance of Islam in state-building is obvious enough in the growth of a number of 15th- and 16th-century port-states such as Pasai, Melaka, Demak, Banten and Ternate. But in some influential writing about Java, such as that by van Leur and Burger, Islam was regarded as an essentially "bourgeois" force like Dutch Calvinism, and opposed to the sacred and exalted role of the Hindu kings. In the implicit comparison with Europe, I believe the analogy between Javanese kingship and the Catholic Hapsburgs is even further from the mark than that between Islam and Calvinism. I have already devoted considerable attention elsewhere to show that, in reality, the most powerful centralised states of pre-colonial Indonesian history were the Islamic sultanates of the high "age of commerce". New trade wealth and firearms provided the opportunity for these concentrations to arise, but Islam provided the ideological legitimation to break with the contractual and intensely pluralist social pattern in the name of a higher goal.[35]

The Dutch Colonial State

The Dutch colonial state was much more powerful in newly bureaucratic ways. The *divide et impera* cliché is particularly misleading in the case of the Dutch East India Company, which routinely sought to find a "company's king" with whom it could establish monopoly contracts. The whole interest of the Company then became to extend the power of this king and to make him correspond to the illusion Dutch republicans carried to the east with them about how "eastern despots" ought to rule.[36] The interior kings of Pagaruyung (Sumatra) and Mataram (Java) were bolstered by the VOC in this way, partly as a lever against independent commercial ports which competed with the Dutch. Further east, the Dutch tried to reinvent Ternate and Bone as hierarchic kingdoms governing respectively Maluku and the Bugis area.

The colonial state of 1900–1942 was by far the most centralised model of state power Southeast Asia had ever experienced. Netherlands India was more centralised and absolutist than the Netherlands itself or any other European constitutional state of the period. Although colourful traditional monarchies retained some importance in the cultural and symbolic field, they were not in any way part of the decision-making steel structure of Netherlands India. This was provided by the omniscient Leiden-trained officials of the *Binnenlandse Bestuur* — a true meritocracy beholden wholly to the centre for their career advancement. It was the irrelevance of the traditional rulers to the real basis of power in Netherlands India, even more than their conservatism, which ensured that they would be swept away by the Indonesian revolution of 1945–1949.

High Modernism

The final onslaught on regional, cultural and individual particularity has come in the name of development, revolution, progress and modernity. Following the work of James Scott,[37] I will adopt his term "high modernism" for this "administrative ordering of nature and society", which is still with us, although perhaps in less virulent forms than those represented by Leninism and Maoism. If modernism was committed to the continual transformation and improvement of society by means of science and technology, then high modernism is the most radical form of such commitment. It represents a complete break with the past in the name of scientific transformation, and the reordering of society on the basis of simplified codes and categories which can be understood and implemented by a central bureaucracy. Within the state borders, there should be a unified administrative structure, a single system of landholding, accounting, education and measures.

Modernism was born in the progressive optimism of late 19th-century Europe, and institutionalised in the variety of Leninist and nationalist parties which adopted it as a project in the 20th century. As those parties took power, they often tried to implement programmes of reform as radical as those of Hitler and Stalin, which marked the high point of this trend in Europe. The attempt to obliterate the Chinese past by Mao, the Khmer past by Pol Pot, and the Korean past by Kim Il Sung, are tragic Asian outcomes of this imported ideology now on the wane. On the positive side, the confident commitment to social transformation from above represented since 1965 by the Singapore leadership — responsible for moving the majority of Singapore's population within a generation to new housing blocks of great efficiency but minimal connection with diverse neighbourhood pasts — is a striking demonstration of high modernism at work.

The Indonesian revolution of 1945–1950 was never in a position to impose high modernist solutions on this scale, even had it produced a single winner. It took place against a background of far greater political and cultural diversity than the above revolutions. Nevertheless, the new Indonesian Republic was also able to break many of the connections with its diverse pasts because of the revolutionary nature of its achievement of independence. The revolution provided the legitimacy for a unified bureaucratic structure, army, education system and syllabus, and symbolic rituals throughout the Archipelago; Suharto's New Order government only slowly and partially gave it the substance of transformative power. The rhetoric of unity, paternalism, hierarchy and obedience remained largely foreign-inspired, and at odds with the social structures inherited from a rich past.

Nevertheless, the refreshingly democratic climate since 1998 was made possible by the transformative unifying work of these ideas.

CHAPTER 11

Why not Federalism?

Indonesia and China are the only very large, multi-ethnic states to have rejected the federal model in favour of a unitary state. This chapter will investigate, for the Indonesian case, the hypothesis that the revolutionary path by which these and other countries arrived at modern nation-statedom is the most important factor in this choice. Comparisons will be drawn with Indonesia's federal neighbour Malaysia to explore the relative strengths and weaknesses of the federal and unitary models, particularly from a democratic perspective. And finally, the experiments with regional autonomy and asymmetric statehood in post-Suharto Indonesia will be examined with particular reference to Aceh.

States which achieved their current form through revolution have some advantages over those which evolved in the incremental manner of multiple compromises. They have powerful symbols, a clear identity, a centralised system of government and education, and an ideology that favours complete uniformity in the rights and duties of citizens. France has these advantages in comparison with the United Kingdom, but it also has some disadvantages, particularly from the viewpoint of regions or minorities that feel themselves profoundly different. In Asia too, the portentous comparison of post-revolutionary China with evolutionary, federal and democratic India is central to understanding the effects of modern political ideals on ancient and diverse cultures. The case of Indonesia is perhaps more manageable as a lesson in the strengths and dangers of rejecting federalism for political uniformity.

Colonial Heritage and the Path to Independence

The 1940s and early 1950s were a crucial watershed in the history of Asian states. This mid-century upheaval is usually portrayed in terms of war, revolution, independence or the end of colonialism. Looking back in a world-historical perspective, however, it needs more attention as the mother of all regime changes; as the birth-period of new states that have endured surprisingly effectively over the subsequent half-century. Some of those Asian states — India, Pakistan, Malaysia — were born as federations and have continued to be so. The remainder, including all those that asserted their independence through revolution, embraced a unitary model. In Asia, as elsewhere, revolution has proven to be hostile to federalism in the name of the sovereignty of the people.

Island Southeast Asia in the centuries preceding this watershed appeared most unlikely to be on a path leading towards strong, unitary states of this kind. Its highlands and smaller islands, where most of the pre-1800 population had been concentrated, never developed bureaucratic, law-giving states on a significant scale and were wary of the externally supported states in their midst. Even the highly complex polities of pre-colonial Java and Bali seemed to have "an alternative conception of what politics was about".[1] Much of the recent historical scholarship has been devoted to seeking to establish what it was "that looks like a bureaucracy, in early as well as contemporary times, but is not one, according to a Weberian definition".[2] Explanations have centred on the spiritual, charismatic nature of power, the system of complementarities between distinct parts of a plural system, and the environmental obstacles to centralised power.[3]

For the colonial powers in this region, it seemed clear that they were dealing with political traditions in which power was diffused into a great diversity of hierarchies, kinship networks and sacred centres. The English and Dutch sought to rule through a façade of very diverse rajas, sultans, *adathoofden*, *bupati* and chiefs, even while providing their own bureaucratic "steel frame" which, for the first time around 1900, acquainted Southeast Asians with the effective tools of a modern nation-state. Insofar as they thought of democratising or decolonising, feebly in the 1920s and 1930s but almost frenetically after 1945, they thought of complex federal structures as the only viable option. Most of the aristocratic elites who had a share in the colonial system agreed with them.[4]

The more radical nationalists of the 1930s and 1940s, however, perceived the underlying reality of centralised colonial power, and dismissed the indigenous inheritance of diversity as an anachronistic and "feudal" façade, its perpetuation being no more than a colonial trick to divide and rule. Moreover, they took seriously what they learnt in English and Dutch schools about the history and ideology of the modern nation-states who ruled them, with their ideals of the sovereignty of a free and equal people.

In terms of the massive regime change of the 1940s and 1950s, therefore, the major question would be which of these visions prevailed in the post-colonial successor states. Here, we have to distinguish two quite different paths, of which Malaysia and Indonesia might be held to be quintessential types — the evolutionary/pragmatic and the revolutionary. In evolutionary Malaysia, the communist-led revolutionaries were defeated and marginalised by an alliance of British Commonwealth forces and the conservative Malay establishment, and the latter fully accepted the symbolic compromises made by the colonial state towards pre-existing political institutions and communities. In Indonesia, the revolutionary nationalists were far more strongly placed, and rode a revolution uneasily to power, suppressing their communist extreme wing and thereby gaining the support of the US-led international community against the Dutch. The evolutionary Malaysian path led in the direction anticipated by the British, towards federalism with its constitutional sharing of powers, as well as an electoral democracy. The revolutionary Indonesian one abolished traditional monarchies and autonomies in its march towards a unitary state and the imagined equality of all citizens.

Were British Colonies More Likely to Achieve Independence as Federations?

There have been few examples of British colonies following the revolutionary path to independence since the early cases of the United States and Ireland. The classic Asian cases of anti-imperial revolution in our times — Philippines (the first, 1896), Indonesia (1945–1950), Vietnam (1945–1954), Laos (1954–1975), Cambodia (1954–1978), East Timor (1975) — have all been against continental European states which had their own more direct experience of the French revolution, Napoleon and the revolutionary upheavals of 1848 and 1870. Of British decolonisations in Asia, none have generally been classified as "revolutionary" by the historians, despite the degree of violence accompanying them in India, Burma and Malaya. A revolution *was* attempted by the Malayan Communist Party from 1948, and if it had succeeded, would probably have produced a unitary state with no serious place for the sultans. But since that revolution was crushed by military intervention from Britain, Australia and New Zealand, it had no opportunity to affect the shape or ideology of government, even for a brief period, as in the Philippines.

The correlation between federalism and a non-revolutionary, negotiated path to independence seems very clear in Asia, unless the post-revolutionary Soviet Union were to be accepted as a true federation. Without seriously entering this complex issue, I am here following most recent authorities in regarding it as authoritarian and unitary in practice even if federal in many of its formal constitutional arrangements. The centralising roles of an authoritarian party and a radically egalitarian ideology rendered meaningless the division of powers which should mark a true federation.[5]

The chief examples which obtained their independence in federal form (Malaysia, India, Pakistan and Australia) were all also under former British colonial control. Can we go so far as to say that there was a causal relation between colonial government by the British constitutional monarchy in the 20th century, evolutionary paths to independence, and forms of government that entrenched local, traditional autonomies behind a system of federalism? An adequate answer to that question would have to look carefully at the ambivalent case of Burma, treated elsewhere in this book. Considering Malaysia and Indonesia alone, there is much to be said for the hypothesis.

Since Malayan/Malaysian federalism arose in large part as a way to incorporate multiple monarchies within a single polity, we must consider also why monarchies survived in Malaya. One factor was the colonial one. British of the age of Victoria and subsequently appeared more likely to believe in monarchy as a natural system compatible with modernisation than did their Dutch colleagues, even though these also lived formally under the constitutional monarchy established in 1815 at the Congress of Vienna. Both sought to preserve and protect Malay rulers in Malaya and Sumatra respectively, but very differently. As Emerson remarked in the 1930s,

> The sovereignty of these [British Malayan] States has remained intact in the sense that they do not fall within the jurisdiction of the Imperial Parliament, that persons residing within their territories are subject only to the jurisdiction of the State within which they reside ... Several well-known cases in the British courts have testified to the fact that

the sovereigns of the Malay States are immune from suit save at their own pleasure.

In the Netherlands Indies the legal and administrative structure rests on quite a different basis since no protected states recognisable in international law have been left in existence. All the territories form a part of the Dutch colonial domain, and a common citizenship exists throughout.[6]

The sultans on the peninsula, all too weak politically or militarily to offer serious resistance to the British, were placed on exalted pedestals where their sovereignty and royal prerogatives were respected even though they had to follow the advice of the British Resident (as the British monarch had to follow that of the Prime Minister) in all matters except "Malay religion and culture". By contrast, the sultans of East Sumatra, very similar in their Malay origins to those of the Peninsula, were frequently refashioned, subdivided or interfered with in the interests of greater administrative efficiency. Having been reduced largely to expensive figureheads in the first decades of the 20th century, they were given new powers in decentralisation schemes of the 1930s which were patently motivated by a fear of Indonesian nationalist sentiment. Some monarchs of Bali and South Sulawesi were restored after 30 years of direct rule, and there was active discussion of bringing back the kings of Riau and Aceh, heirs to much more substantial pre-colonial sultanates.

Yet modern-minded Dutch officials, as well as Indonesian nationalists, regarded the extravagant rulers with dismay or even contempt. Their present maintenance by the Dutch as semi-foreign bodies in the colonial empire, irritatingly dividing powers and functions and yet, because of their special attributes, not fitting properly into the general decentralisation schemes, is to be explained less in terms of a concern for the spiritual and material ease of their people than in terms of Dutch dread of Indonesian communism and nationalism.[7]

Given the use of indirect rule as a means to curb and control the national movement, it was hardly surprising that even moderate members of that movement had little use for the rulers. The early stage of the national revolution of 1945–1949 generated a radical "social revolution", largely inspired by the Marxist left, which drove all the rulers of Republican-controlled Java and Sumatra from their thrones (with the notable exception of pro-Republican Yogyakarta). By contrast, the Malayan sultans survived this critical period because they "had been better prepared for a role as constitutional monarchs by the British Resident system; their prestige had not been sapped by such flamboyant excesses in the 1930s nor by such humiliation at the hands of the revolution [in 1945–1946]".[8]

It was the survival of the rulers, not democracy, which was the crucial initial ingredient of the unique Malayan (Malaysian) system of federalism, retaining nine monarchs within a single state. The advocates of more democratic outcomes in the 1940s were mostly on the other, anti-monarchic, side of the debate. But it can nevertheless be argued that Malaysian federalism has allowed a training-ground and safety valve for opposition which has served democracy relatively well.

Indonesia's Commitment to the Unitary State

The more radical section of the national movement, comprising the Marxist left and the nationalists around Sukarno and Hatta, had never had much interest in federalism. They were intellectually committed to the sovereignty of the people, and believed that independence could only come through a revolutionary kind of mass action to assert it. The much more numerous Muslim movement was also concerned for the solidarity of the *ummat* (Islamic community), not its division into ethnic units. Support for local autonomy in the 1930s came from ethnonationalist movements such as Pasundan and the South Sulawesi party of Nadjamoedding Daeng Malewa, and from traditional elites and *adat* (customary law) leaders less committed to independence in any form. The Japanese military administration in Java (1942–1945) encouraged Sukarno and Hatta as nationalist leaders, and downgraded further the status and autonomy of self-governing rulers, thereby weakening any voice in favour of federalism.

The principal Japanese contribution to the unitary idea, however, was paradoxically by accelerating preparations for independence in Java, while inhibiting any participation in that process from the other islands. Only Java-based delegates attended the principal opportunity to debate the shape of the future independent Indonesia, the Body for the Investigation of Indonesian Independence (Badan Penjelidik Kemerdekaan Indonesia, or BPKI) at the end of May 1945. Although a tenth of its 62 members had been born outside Java, there was no voice at that meeting for the concerns of the ethnic minorities. Not surprisingly, the body voted for a unitary republic. The Java-based nationalist Johannes Latuharhary, an Ambonese Christian, found only one supporter in the 19-man constitutional subcommittee for his plea for a federal state. Only six delegates in the full body favoured a monarchy rather than a Republic.[9] The revolutionary *ideal* of the unitary state appeared, in the hothouse atmosphere of the late Japanese occupation, untroubled by any practical diversities on the ground, since most of these same delegates believed their future unitary Indonesian state should include Malaya, British Borneo and Portuguese Timor, as well as Netherlands India.

Tokyo subsequently overruled the desire of the local military authorities in Sumatra, Borneo and the East to keep these areas separate from the more rapid independence preparations in Java. On the very day of the Japanese surrender, 14 August 1945, three delegates from Sumatra and five from Borneo and the East arrived in Jakarta for what was intended to be the next step in Japanese-sponsored "independence" for Indonesia. Suddenly, the theatre became reality. After independence was hastily proclaimed in a manner the Japanese could accept on 17 August, the Japanese-sponsored Committee for the Preparation of Indonesian Independence (PPKI) was called upon to authorise the constitution prepared earlier in Java, and lay the basis for a new state in a hurried three-day meeting.

The delegates from outside Java were uniformly concerned about the Java-centred state that was likely to result, but they had little effect on a format that had already been determined without them. The most articulate of them, Dr Mohammad Amir from Medan, pleaded "that the maximum decentralisation be allowed for the islands outside Java, that governments be set up there, and that the people there be given the right to manage their domestic affairs to the widest extent".[10] But far from allowing natural ethno-cultural units their own expression, the PPKI decided to establish only eight large provinces for the whole country — one each for Sumatra, Borneo and Sulawesi. Apart from the three in Java, each of the other five provinces was a mosaic of pluralism, with no dominant ethnicity or even religion.[11] But the governors appointed to these provinces had negligible power on the ground. The revolutionary dynamic marched to its own drum in each of the major regions in the period 1945–1947, and the Dutch occupation of the most lucrative areas thereafter gave even more responsibility to military units around the Dutch perimeter. The local Republican-appointed officials in Sumatra initially had to accept the self-governing rajas as a political reality, and began pragmatic negotiations about democratising them. It was the unplanned "social revolution" that swept these rulers away, killing some and humiliating all. Although there was ambivalence in the Republican leadership about these violent actions, the Republic accepted their consequences as meaning the end of monarchy in Sumatra.[12]

Aceh was the most critical test of the Republic's intentions for regional autonomy. It was a crucial bastion of Republican strength after the elimination during the "social revolution" of the 102 little "self-governments" on which the Dutch had relied. Until the victory of the Republic through the transfer of sovereignty at the end of 1949, therefore, the modernist *ulama* leadership which had led the "social revolution" was accepted as the local government with complete autonomy. The Dutch aggression in 1947 allowed Yogyakarta to appoint the most influential of these *ulama*, Daud Beureu'eh, as Military Governor of Aceh. This de facto provincial status was revoked in 1951, however, when the Republic felt strong enough to return to a uniform system of provinces and districts (*kabupaten*). Sumatra had in 1948 been acknowledged to be too big to govern as one province, but the three units it was broken into remained multi-ethnic amalgams, incapable of generating loyalty on an ethnic or historic basis. It was against this amalgamation into a North Sumatra Province that the revolutionary *ulama* (religious scholar) leadership of Aceh revolted in 1953.[13]

The Dutch embrace of a federal model for post-war Indonesia sealed the eventual doom of any such policy for republicans. The Dutch Lieutenant Governor-General, H.J. van Mook, first developed a strategy of surrounding and incorporating Republican Java by erecting large federal states in Sumatra, Borneo and the "Great East". These large units had already been established as part of an ineffective decentralisation programme in the 1930s. They replicated the large, multi-ethnic provinces of initial Republican design and proved equally impractical on the ground. Sumatra had to be conceded as also de facto Republican territory at the Linggajati Conference in November 1946. Nationalist sentiment and internal jealousies proved too strong even in Dutch-occupied Borneo to allow that state to come into being. Eventually, five weak federal states emerged in Borneo: two federations of rajas in the east, one "special region" in the the west, and two "neo-lands" still too inchoate to have much sense of identity. Only the Great East was assembled into a single large state, the Negara Indonesia Timur, at a conference in Bali in December 1946. A fragile new edifice of Cabinet, Parliament and civil service for this new state was quickly put together in its capital, Makasar. Internally, it rested on an extraordinary mosaic of local bodies. Some, representing pro-Dutch Christian areas like South Maluku (Ambon) and Minahasa, had indirectly elected representative councils; others were little more than confederations of traditional rulers, such as those of Bali and South Sulawesi.[14]

In a two-week campaign in July–August 1947, Dutch troops occupied the most economically important Republican-held areas, notably including plantation areas of East Sumatra and West Java, and the oil-rich Palembang area of South Sumatra. This made it possible for the Dutch to encourage two important new federal states, an ethnically complex Negara Sumatera Timur in East Sumatra, and a Sundanese-majority state in West Java which turned out to be markedly pro-Republican in orientation.[15]

The Netherlands eventually transferred sovereignty unconditionally, on 27 December 1949, to a federal republic, the Republik Indonesia Serikat (RIS), known in English as the Republic of the United States of Indonesia (RUSI). United Nations intervention had undercut the military advantage held by the Dutch, and led to an atmosphere of mutual recognition between the Republic, responsible for about half of Java and three-quarters of Sumatra (minus its three major conurbations) and the 15 states of federalist Indonesia erected under Dutch auspices.

The RIS emerged as a negotiated compromise, the kind of evolutionary independence that marked Malaysia eight years later. But in Indonesia, this compromise uneasily cloaked the revolutionary mindset of Republican "victory" over those who had been considered traitors to the revolution. As the Republican Chief of Staff described the military aspect of this compromise, "BFO [federalist] people who were previously traitors against the 17 August 1945 proclamation now have to be accepted as never having been traitors to the Republic and having similar positions and offices together with the Republicans; KNIL [colonial army] units, auxiliaries, federalists etc., the old enemies of the TNI [Republican army] have to be accepted as part of the new Indonesian National Army".[16]

In the event, federal Indonesia lasted only eight months. As Herb Feith put it, the fact that the compromises on which the transfer of sovereignty had been based were so quickly torn up "is barely relevant to a situation where revolutionary political reality was so rapidly outstripping legalities of every kind".[17] Beginning with the states in Java, where republican and unitary sentiment was always strongest, federal states dissolved themselves into the Republic under pressures of both long-term republican sympathisers in their midst and those eager to be on the winning side. The strongest federalist figures with some degree of military support, notably Sultan Abdul Hamid II in West Borneo and the Christian Ambonese leader Soumokil in the NIT, became compromised by association with abortive military coups designed to stop the incorporation of KNIL soldiers into a Republican-led national army. Abdul Hamid was arrested and the state he headed collapsed following the Westerling coup in January 1950. In April, Soumokil fled the NIT capital, where he had been Attorney-General, after the failure of the Captain Andi Azis coup against the landing of Republican troops. With the demise of his initial hope to preserve the autonomy or independence of the Negara Indonesia Timur, he inspired a declaration of independence of the Republic of the South Moluccas (RMS) on 25 April. This put up a strong resistance against the ten Indonesian battalions sent against it in November, and continued a guerrilla resistance in adjacent Ceram until 1962.[18]

The sense conveyed by the revolutionary winners that continuing support for federalism was a kind of treachery gained ground with each of these incidents. One Medan journalist rode the wave for dissolving the NST state by proclaiming that "as long as there are in Indonesia elements which defend Van Mook's colonial legacy ... as long as those elements are not swept out, political tensions will continue to exist like a thorn in a man's flesh".[19] Unitarism became a part of the victorious nationalist package, and hence something that was not negotiable. As viewed particularly in the key nationalist agencies, including the nationalist and communist parties and the army, people outside Java placing a high value on their ethnic identity "became tantamount to being pro-Dutch".[20]

The most prominent Sumatran in the shortlived federal government, Vice-President Hatta, conceded in 1953 that "a federal system is in fact suitable for such a far-flung archipelago and might be expected to strengthen the feeling of unity", but any such ideas had to be abandoned in face of the antipathy towards any schemes supported by the Dutch.[21] The victory of the revolutionary approach to state formation, in other words, equated unitarism with patriotism and federalism with treachery and foreign influence.

Demands for greater regional autonomy were quick to resurface in the 1950s, but they almost never used the label "federal" because of its negative associations. The regional rebellions of the 1950s, emerging as they did from the revolutionary winners, went to considerable lengths to suppress their ethnonationalism. The armed rebellion of Republican guerrillas in West Java under S.M. Kartosuwirjo declared its cause to be the Islamic State of Indonesia (Negara Islam Indonesia, NII) in 1949. In January 1952, another disgruntled group of Makasar-Bugis guerrillas in South Sulawesi, under Kahar Muzakar, declared for this organisation, even though its spirit was anything but national. Finally, the most explicitly regional of all the rebellions, that of the revolutionary-period Aceh leadership under Daud Beureu'eh in September 1953, began by declaring itself part of NII. It dressed its demands in theological terms, insisting that violence against the Dutch had only been justified by pursuit of an Islamic state. But its practical grievances were all about the loss of the total autonomy and control of local resources which they had enjoyed in the period 1946–1950.[22]

It was not long before the Acehnese heritage of separate statehood began to show beneath this cloak. From his position in New York, attached to the Indonesian mission to the UN, Hasan Tiro reacted to the rebellion by developing his desired format for a federal and Islamic Indonesia.[23] Similar ideas were taken up at the Batee Kureng Congress of groups supporting the rebellion on 23 September 1955. On the same date, Daud Beureu'eh declared Aceh to be no longer a "command" of NII but a federal state (*negara bagian*) with himself as its head of state (*wali negara*).

Following the rebellion and the heavy bloodshed involved in suppressing its passionate followers, the central government realised the fundamental mistake of having tried to amalgamate Aceh into a North Sumatra Province. As part of the negotiations to end the rebellion, provincial status was restored to Aceh on 1 January 1957. Many of the rebels, including the man appointed first Governor, Ali Hasjmy, were satisfied with this and other concessions, and made their peace with Jakarta. Daud Beureu'eh had meanwhile become convinced of the case for federalism, however, and he refused any arrangements that did not include it. Hasan Tiro returned to Aceh during a period of ceasefire and negotiations in 1959, and stiffened resistance to the idea of a mere province. He could then argue that many other rebel groups outside Java, who had joined the PRRI uprising in 1958, were coming around to the idea of a federal state.[24]

These rebel movements were however militarily defeated and politically divided by 1960. If anything, their flirtation with federalism confirmed the belief of the nationalist establishment that unitarism was a non-negotiable part of the post-revolutionary state. During the "Guided Democracy" period, when Sukarno's ideas became dominant and the free expression of dissenting views increasingly restricted, public discussion of federalism was impossible. Only some remaining guerrillas in the outer islands illegally promoted the idea.[25] Those of the rebels who survived into the Suharto era, however, increasingly opted for independence rather than a federal Indonesia.

Despite its hostility to federalism, post-revolutionary Indonesia during its liberal beginnings, when it did not in practice control its regions, offered them impressive-sounding legal autonomies. Laws passed in 1956 and 1957 allowed elected province and Kabupaten (district) assemblies to choose their local executives, as well as providing guaranteed proportions of state revenues for them. Neither law was ever effective. They were overtaken first by Sukarno's brand of revolutionary authoritarianism, and then by General Suharto's long period of bureaucratic authoritarianism (1966–1998). Suharto for the first time also had the military control needed to move the country towards an unusually centralised form of government. The law no. 5 of 1974 revoked the autonomy package of the 1950s, and replaced it with a system where governors were effectively chosen by the centre and received their budgets and guidelines from it.[26] Another law no. 5, in 1979, removed the ancient autonomies and electoral practices of villages all over Indonesia, replacing village heads and councils with a top-down and uniform bureaucracy across the whole country.

The fall of Suharto in May 1998 therefore released a great deal of pent-up frustration over these centralising trends. For the first time, federalism was openly debated in the press, the distinguished writer, architect and priest, Y.B. Mangunwijaya, making an effective case that it was the best and fairest means to keep Papua and Aceh in Indonesia.[27] Radical new autonomy laws were passed in 1999, providing elected local officials and a generous sharing of revenues.

The Aceh Concession

Attempts to reach agreement on autonomy for Aceh within the Indonesian framework began with the passing of an Aceh Autonomy Law by the

Indonesian Parliament in July 1999. This was widely rejected in Aceh as trying to give life to the totally ineffective and discredited "special region" (*Daerah Istimewa*) deal of 1959. A more consensual drafting effort under the Wahid government led to the NAD Law of July 2001, so called because it renamed the Province Nanggroe Aceh Darussalam (NAD), using the ambiguous Acehnese term *nanggroe* rather than either of the Indonesian terms — traditional *negeri* (town, principality or community) or modern *Negara* (sovereign state). Because it included a generous concession to Aceh of 70 per cent of the oil and gas revenues for eight years, and 50 per cent thereafter, it did gain support among many Acehnese politicians working in the Indonesian structures. It appeared to do little, however, to attract those who had been fighting a guerrilla war for independence since 1976, nor even the much larger element campaigning for self-determination through a referendum.[28]

In any case, none of this was effectively implemented before military rule was re-established in Aceh by President Megawati on 19 May 2003, making it once again the least autonomous of Indonesia's provinces. Between 45,000 and 60,000 army and policy units were concentrated in Aceh during the ensuing two years, substantially the largest force in Aceh's 130 years of intermittent military occupation.

On 26 December 2004, Aceh was hit by the most destructive tsunami and one of the worst earthquakes of modern times. Fortunately, President Yudhoyono (SBY) was by then better established with a popular mandate than any of his predecessors. He responded effectively to the devastation, allowing the military forces of the US, Australia, Singapore, Malaysia and other countries to move relief supplies in quickly. SBY had already shown a cautious interest in renewing negotiations with the GAM leadership in Sweden. In the aftermath of the massive international relief effort, he authorised ministerial-level negotiations and substantial concessions. Both sides appreciated the need for a new start to reconstruct Aceh in peace. This time, it was the Helsinki-based Crisis Management Initiative which brokered the peace deal, agreed in July and implemented immediately upon its signature on 15 August 2005.

In relation to the unitary bias of Indonesian state nationalism since 1945, the peace agreement was a remarkable reversal. It granted to Aceh "authority within all sectors of public affairs" except defence, foreign affairs, monetary and fiscal matters, justice and freedom of religion. National laws and international agreements "of special interest to Aceh" would only be agreed after consultation with the Aceh legislature. Aceh would have its own flag, crest and hymn, and a ceremonial head of state called a *wali nanggroe*, the term which GAM had applied to Hasan Tiro. Aceh could raise its own external loans and international investments, administer its ports and airports, and enjoy 70 per cent of the revenues from oil and gas "and other natural resources" in perpetuity. In return for GAM's acceptance of Aceh's place within Indonesia, its fighters would receive an allocation of land or a pension, and be permitted to play their part in the regional election of officials to be held in April 2006 (though in the end postponed). An exception would be made to the rule that only nationally organised political parties could contest elections in Indonesia, giving GAM the opportunity to create or support an Aceh-specific party for the first time.

There are many reasons to be sceptical about whether this federalism-by-another-name will succeed as a democratic solution to Aceh's problems, yet it is already a remarkable departure from Indonesia's unitarist, post-revolutionary traditions. Though the F-word is carefully avoided, the agreement would inaugurate the kind of "asymmetrical government" already long practised in the United Kingdom, and to a lesser extent, Canada, Spain and Malaysia. As Michael Keating has argued persuasively, when communities come together with different nationalist expectations and experiences, providing for differential claims on the state can be the strategy most compatible with justice and democracy.[29] Acehnese have a different memory of state and tradition of nationalism from most Indonesians. Aceh's relationship to Indonesian state nationalism is strong but distinctive. It may be that an anomalous or asymmetric status is the best way to keep Aceh within Indonesia voluntarily. If so, Indonesia will have discovered through a bitter and painful route a formula that Malaysia (not to mention the UK) adopted at the start.

Malaysia's Asymmetric Federalism

The British domain in the "Malay World" was always a patchwork of constitutionally very different pieces. Singapore, Melaka and Penang on the Peninsula formed one Crown Colony; Labuan off Borneo another. Four "protected" Malay monarchies on the Peninsula were federated under a common government in 1896, even though sovereignty was held to continue to reside with their sultans. Johor declined to join this federation despite its very long links to Singapore, and so did four more sultanates transferred from Siamese suzerainty in 1909. These five states remained "protected" but "unfederated". Sarawak, Brunei and North Borneo were also "protected" by Britain, though the first two were sovereign monarchies under English and Malay kings, respectively, and the third was governed by a chartered company.

Turning this into a country or countries was a challenge, to which federalism was the only evolutionary answer. Only if the revolutionary path taken by the Malayan Communist Party had prevailed could Malaya have emerged as a unitary republic. The British Labour post-war government sought to fold the sovereignty of nine sultans in the Peninsula into a Malayan Union, and to assume sovereignty over Sarawak (from the Brooke rajas) and North Borneo (from the Company). On the Peninsula, this was defeated by a Malay popular movement supported by many old Malaya hands in Britain. A Federation of Malaya replaced the Malayan Union in 1948, and became independent in 1957.

The nine sultans remained hereditary monarchs of their respective states in this federation, and with residual rights over religious affairs and land. The premiers had to dance carefully around the foibles of their still powerful sultans. The nine sultans took turns becoming head of state of the whole country for five-year terms as supreme king or *Yang di Pertuan Agong*.

The formation of Malaysia in 1963 brought more diversity into a still more asymmetric federation. Brunei's autocratic Sultan Omar Ali Saifuddin was strong enough to say "no", but Sarawak and Sabah (North Borneo) were bundled in by a Britain bent on decolonisation. Singapore under an elected Lee Kuan Yew government found this an ideal way to finesse the pro-China sentiment of a probable majority of its people. Each of the new states had different constitutional guarantees. Sarawak and Sabah were overrepresented in the federal Parliament, and Singapore underrepresented, since part of the rationale was to use the two Borneo territories to balance the Chinese population of Singapore. In return, Singapore enjoyed autonomies in financial and legal arrangements. Sparsely-settled Sarawak and Sabah, fearful of being swamped, obtained control over internal migration into their states. They were also reassured with guarantees that English would remain the official language and that Islam would not be the state religion as it always had been in the sultanates.

Malaysia's peculiar federalism therefore provides one kind of asymmetry, whereby citizens do not all have the same rights. The racial equation provided another. Where post-revolutionary Indonesia asserted the sovereignty and equality of the people, Malaya and Malaysia have constitutionally qualified their citizens by race, obliging the state to give certain unequal rights to Malays or *bumiputra*. Like the federal asymmetry, these features came about through the difficult pragmatic compromises needed to bring groups into the nation, not by revolutionary assertions of principle.

Malaysia and Indonesia: Comparing the Record

Malaysia and Indonesia are both truly new states, unable to draw on the state nationalism of a pre-colonial monarchy which had a claim to continuity with the post-colonial state as Burma, Vietnam, Korea and others did. The post-colonial states would have to be artificial constructs in both cases, within the artificial boundaries Britain, Holland and France had drawn between the Archipelago and the Peninsula, and across the Peninsula and Borneo. The two names, "Malaysia" and "Indonesia", are alternative scholarly inventions to describe broader identities of the "Malay world", or the world of Austronesian languages, taken over by politicians who had no satisfactory word for their imagined state.

But the path to that new identity divided them sharply. The revolutionary path gave the name "Indonesia" a supernatural aura demanding loyalty. The blood of revolutionary martyrs was held to sacralise the flag, the independence declaration, the constitution and the sacred sites and dates of dead heroes. The success of this revolutionary process, completed in 1950 with the destruction of the complex federal architecture of RIS, was almost magical. The steel of the Dutch colonial bureaucracy was inherited by the army, but now married to a new passionately held ideology of the sovereignty of the *Indonesian* people.

Malaysia, on the other hand, inherited a great variety of older political forms of monarchy and of authority within separated communities, only gradually establishing the higher authority of Kuala Lumpur among them. Sultans continued to have outrageous prerogatives and immunities from the law; political parties were based on what they considered immutable "race" rather than on programmes or ideologies. On the positive side of the revolutionary path, one might list many valuable coherences in which Indonesia rejoices, which Malaysia lacks to its cost:

1. An unquestioned national language.
2. A strong sense of identity as Indonesians, despite extraordinarily diverse histories.
3. Acceptance of the "one man, one vote" idea, with no special privileges in constitutional theory. Indonesian sultans have been trying to make some sort of comeback recently on a platform of *adat*, but it feels like a lost cause, as it would be in France or Russia.
4. Acceptance of the irrelevance of race, not mentioned in census data (until 2000), and thus the possibility of Chinese, Dayaks and Papuans being simply accepted as Indonesians.

On the negative side of the balance, the revolutionary assertion of these principles brought some clear political disadvantages.

1. The way heroic myths of revolutionary struggle take the place of history, denying all Indonesia's peoples, but especially the more marginal, their roots and their identity. By contrast, Malaysia's Dayaks, Kadazans, Chinese and Kelantanese know their distinct histories, even if the federal government does little to support that knowledge.
2. The huge gap between revolutionary expectations and Indonesia's diverse realities virtually required that the state fill the gap with force and the threat of force. People were expected to act as though Indonesia was united around these unifying ideals, and legitimate differences were often therefore equated with treason and suppressed by force. Even in times of democracy (1949–1957 and since 1998), it has been difficult for Indonesia to legitimate these differences, though progress is being made.
3. The unitary system, interpreted as meaning that there needed to be uniform administrative, educational and judicial systems throughout the country, drove particularists in Aceh, Papua and East Timor, and Islamists everywhere, into a cycle of rebellion and suppression. By contrast, Malaysia has become, through a succession of unsatisfactory but workable compromises, a striking example of what Keating (2001) calls "plurinational democracy" and "asymmetric government".
4. Basing the rights of endangered minorities such as Chinese and Christians on the myth of nationalist equality rather than legality and the right of redress has in practice not served them well. A pattern developed of affluent minorities having to buy protection and justice rather than relying on constitutional and legal means. In the process, the rule of law was further eroded.

The toll of political violence is one factor that can be measured, and Indonesia comes out on the wrong side of that equation. Both countries got off to a bad start in the violent aftermath of the Japanese occupation, but the British reoccupation of Malaya and the Borneo territories gave rise to far fewer casualties in both the short and long term than the failed attempt by the Dutch to do the same in Indonesia.

The tally of deaths in Malaysia would have to include the following:

1. 1945: a hundred or more killed in Malay-Chinese clashes immediately after the Japanese surrender.
2. 1948–1956: thousands of casualties of the Malayan Emergency, which pitted (predominately Chinese) guerrillas of the MCP against British, Australian and (predominately Malay) Malayan troops.
3. 1963–1967: some hundreds of casualties, chiefly in Sarawak, of the violent resistance to the formation of Malaysia, sustained first by Indonesia with the infiltration of military "volunteers", then by pro-communist Chinese in Sarawak and Indonesian Borneo.
4. 1969: around a hundred mostly Chinese casualties at the hands of Malay mobs, in the 13 May violence following the modest advances of left-wing (predominately Chinese) parties in the 1969 elections.

As against this, the Indonesian toll is unfortunately very heavy.[30]

- 1945: thousands of Chinese, Eurasian and Ambonese victims of the bersiap time in the early revolution.
- November 1945: tens of thousands killed in the "Battle of Surabaya" against British troops, after General Mallaby is killed trying to make peace.
- 1945–1946: thousands of victims of the "social revolutions" in Aceh, East Sumatra, West Sumatra, Pekalongan area, Solo.
- 1946: hundreds of victims of "3 July affair"; hundreds of Republican sympathisers killed by Lt. Westerling in South Sulawesi.
- 1947: Dutch aggression kills hundreds of Indonesian defenders; hundreds of Chinese, aristocrats and others killed in "scorched-earth" actions by Republicans in East Sumatra and elsewhere.
- 1948: Republican military units clash in Central Java, Tapanuli.
- 1948: thousands killed in violent suppression of PKI in so-called "Madiun rebellion".
- 1948–1949: second Dutch aggression followed by guerrilla activity, with low-level constant violence.

- 1949–1950: violence against Federal states in West Borneo, Bali, South Sulawesi.
- 1950–1951: Republik Maluku Selatan rebellion put down forcefully.
- 1948–1963: DI rebellion led by Kartosuwirjo in West Java, Kahar Muzakkar in South Sulawesi.
- 1953–1957: Aceh rebellion. Thousands killed in its violent suppression.
- 1958–1959: PRRI rebellion in West Sumatra, Tapanuli, South and North Sulawesi put down forcefully.
- 1964–1965: PKI-supported *aksi sepihak* [unilateral actions] against landowners in rural Central and East Java. Often violent land seizures.
- 1965–1966: up to a million killed in the aftermath of 1 October 1965 coup attempt, which was used to justify the violent destruction of PKI Indonesia-wide.
- 1975–: invasion of East Timor and subsequent fierce repression of resistance, causing tens of thousands of violent deaths. Technique developed in 1980s of arming pro-Indonesian militias to do much of the killing.
- 1976–1977: low-level guerrilla violence recommences in Aceh.
- 1982–1985: thousands of "mysterious killings" (*petrus*) of suspected gangsters by military-backed clandestine units.
- 1984: Tg Priuk affair, at least 27 Muslim victims of military repression (victims say hundreds).
- 1989: Lampung affair, perhaps 200 Muslim students killed by Brimob.
- 1959–1960, 1963, 1965–1967, 1973, 1980, 1982, 1994, 1996: sporadic violence against Chinese — usually few deaths but much physical damage and much harm to economy.
- 1989–1991: about 2000 victims of military crackdown on Aceh rebellion. East Timor technique of arming militias in image of revolutionary pemudas (young activists).
- 1996–1997, 1999: thousands killed in Dayak violence against immigrant Madurese in West Kalimantan.
- 1998: over 100 killed in anti-Chinese and other violence accompanying Suharto's fall.
- 1999–2002: about 5000 victims of Muslim-Christian violence in Ambon, spreading also to Poso in Sulawesi.
- 1999–2005: thousands killed in renewal of conflict in Aceh, notably in military crackdown of May 2003–August 2005[31]

It is possible to argue that federalism had something to do with Malaysia's better record here, while the unitary dream did have to be imposed by violence. Revolution itself is, however, a larger factor in the contrast. Once legality was breached by violence in the name of the "people", only a highly disciplined and usually undemocratic force could stop it running out of control. In the Indonesian case, this was the army, though in frequent contestation with the communist party before 1965. As Freek Columbijn has pointed out, state violence was often legitimated by the imagery of the violent foundation of the state in 1945–1949, with militia gangs using sharpened bamboo stakes and growing their hair long in evocation of the violent revolutionary youth gangs.[32]

In terms of economic performance, Malaysia has also fared much better than Indonesia since 1945. According to Angus Maddison's figures, in 1913, Indonesia's GNP per capita ($904) was a little more than Malaysia's ($899) though less than Singapore's ($1,279). Both countries boomed up to 1929, and staggered thereafter from the blows of the depression and the war. Malaysia, however, left Indonesia progressively further behind in the independent era. By 1965, Indonesia's per capita income ($990) was well below the levels of 1940, scarcely higher than it had been in 1913, and little more than a third of Malaysia's (without Singapore).[33]

If there is any link here with federalism, it can only be the indirect one of a more stable, open and democratic environment. The post-revolutionary violence and instability of Indonesia had a terrible effect on its economy. Not surprisingly, the other Asian states which made a revolutionary transition to independence, Vietnam, Laos, Cambodia, and (more ambivalently) Burma, were the only ones whose economy fared even worse than Indonesia's in this mid-century crisis period.

In conclusion, Indonesia's post-revolutionary drive towards uniformity increased the likelihood of violent outcomes to some regional, ethnic and even ideological tensions. An evolutionary federal path such as Malaysia's would have facilitated a less violent negotiation of the place of Aceh and East Timor, and perhaps also of Ambon, Papua and parts of Sulawesi and Sumatra, within Indonesia. While the possibility could not be ruled out that federal states would move towards secession, the examples of Sarawak and Sabah in Malaysia, and of many disgruntled states in the northeast, northwest and south of the Indian federation, suggest that federations do have effective means to prevent this outcome.

While greater democracy in Indonesia would have provided more space for federal ideas and campaigns, the reverse is less clear, that federalism would have encouraged democracy. One might say rather that some degree of democracy is a precondition for effective federalism, in that the legitimacy and leverage of constituent states can have no other basis than elected governments. Because post-revolutionary Indonesia provided a difficult climate for democracy to flourish, it was also an infertile field for federalism. Developments since 1998, however, should be watched closely for the interplay of democratic procedures and less symmetric political structures.

CHAPTER 12

Chinese and the State: The Jewish Analogy

Periods of rapid economic expansion and relatively weak government tend to widen the differences between individuals and social groups. Risk takers and innovators are rewarded more than most, sometimes by their ability to enter the yawning gap between the laws and values of an older era and the economic needs of the new one. Cultural minorities exist wherever international business is done, but their salience, and indeed their importance to the transformation taking place, become greater at such times. The European "miracle" known by such terms as the "capitalist transformation" or the "birth of the modern" is impossible to conceive of without the Jews, Hanseatic Germans, Lombards, and other entrepreneurial minorities who moved into innovative roles, first in trade, then in money management, and finally in manufacturing.

This crucial role in the modern transformation comes with high risks. Finding the pace of change unsettling to established values and lifestyles, some majority spokesmen fasten on foreigners and minorities the aspects of change they find most distressing. To the everyday resentment of people with wealth is added an element of moral indignation against the increasing commercialism of the age. That this takes place as states become absolutist, populist, and democratic, and as they encourage the sense of national or racial community necessary to give themselves coherence in this process, creates immense dangers for the very minorities who lie at the heart of the modernisation process.

This chapter was first written as part of a book examining these dilemmas in relation to the two most important entrepreneurial minorities of the modern transformation: "Jews" in Central Europe and "Chinese" in Southeast Asia. I will not tiresomely repeat the quotation marks upon future use, but they are necessary here to emphasise what assumptions are already made in bringing together even two minority ethnic labels. After a century of strident nationalism and racism, the labels "Jew" and "Chinese" have come to be widely accepted internally, even though, like most other ethnic terms, they originated with frequently hostile others. But it is difficult to establish any common criterion for members of either category, except that they have been seen as outsiders in the societies to which they migrated. By the nature of the migratory process, they lived and operated in different places and cultures, spoke a great variety of languages, and adhered to different religious traditions. Many made a successful passage into a different ethnic category; those who did not now carry one of the two labels, though always alongside others. Some were entrepreneurs or urban professionals, but most were salaried workers, peddlers, miners, or agriculturalists. Some were rich or educated, but most were poor and ignorant. It is not my assumption that "Jews" as a whole or "Chinese" as a whole can be usefully considered to have common characteristics, and still less that they should be compared with one another. The important comparison is in their creative and vulnerable role as "outsiders at the centre" in dynamic processes of change.

That the Jewish role in the transformation of Central Europe ended in the most traumatic way a half-century ago, whereas the Chinese role in Southeast Asia's transformation is currently at its most robust, made it clear, at the conference where these essays were first presented, that the comparison had greater urgency and intensity than it would have if we had generalised the issues to entrepreneurial minorities everywhere. We were prepared for the moral dilemmas that arose from this simple two-way comparison, and we believed scholars had an important responsibility to examine them fully. While attuned to the problems posed to sober analysis by the heritage of anti-Semitism and the guilts of Holocaust remembrance in European discourse, we were disconcerted to find that a derivative anti-Jewish rhetoric in Southeast Asia also presented problems. In some reformist Islamic circles in Malaysia and Indonesia, a demonisation of the concepts "Jew" (Yahudi) and "Zionist" has recently taken root that made that conference and book more important, despite the risk that in some quarters, it could be distorted rather than read. I will return to this dilemma at the end of these remarks.

Entrepreneurial Minorities

Specialised minorities have played a crucial role in the development of trade, money management, and capital accumulation in most of the Old World — with some interesting exceptions in eastern Asia. Kings and magnates needed such minorities, found them less threatening than their own subordinate populations, and encouraged them, rather than the upstart majority middle classes, to take on crucial brokering roles. Nevertheless, relations between the two groups could be poisoned by guilt, because the pariah minorities were not only religious or racial outsiders but were also engaged in protocapitalist activities (moneylending, petty trade, tax farming) denounced by the guardians of social morality. Much debate has centred on the two factors that kept the minority separate: its own desire to maintain its religious, racial, or ritual distinctiveness, and the majority's forcing economically distinctive roles upon it by denying access to preferred occupations.

Although numerous writers in both the East and West had noticed the phenomenon well before the modern era, comparative theories began to be developed by European (chiefly German) social scientists during the late 19th century. The Jews of Europe were naturally the central example for these writers, but even as early as Roscher (1875), analogies were made to the Chinese in Southeast Asia.[1] Most influential were the theories of Werner Sombart and Max Weber. Sombart made the case that capitalism flourished where Jews were given the greatest economic freedom, and he attributed Jewish economic success to the more positive attitudes towards wealth expressed in the Torah than in the Christian New Testament.[2] His views have been less quoted than Weber's, probably more because of his later sympathy for Nazism and anti-Semitism than because his argument on this point was any less cogent.

Weber sought to draw a sharp distinction between the "pariah capitalism" of the Jewish minority and the "rational capitalism" that developed from Puritan values into the dominant phenomenon of modern times:

> To the English Puritans, the Jews of their time were representatives of that type of capitalism which was involved in war, government contracts, state monopolies, speculative promotions, and construction and financial projects of princes, which they themselves condemned. In fact, the difference may, in general, with the necessary qualifications, be formulated: that Jewish capitalism was speculative pariah-capitalism, while the Puritan was bourgeois organisation of labour.[3]

In Weber's view, the capitalism of pariah minorities was incapable of becoming generalised or of stimulating modern rational capitalism because of the ritual distinctiveness of the pariah groups, who were segregated from the majority by their outcaste status and also by "taboos, hereditary religious obligations in the conduct of life, and the association of salvation hopes with their pariah status."[4] Although Weber's terminology has remained influential among modern theorists, including those dealing with Southeast Asia's Chinese,[5] the accumulating evidence for Chinese leadership in Southeast Asia's economic transformation makes his distinction untenable today in that case. And recent scholarship on the development of early modern European economies makes it difficult to sustain there as well.[6]

Other terms have therefore been coined to deal with this widespread and persistent phenomenon. Philip Curtin developed the notion, originally proposed by Abner Cohen, of a "trade diaspora" of merchant networks remaining distinct among the larger host population. He saw this as a long-term historical phenomenon, the need for which disappeared with the industrial era and domination by a single world trade culture.[7] In a looser sense, the term "diaspora" has undoubtedly become more popular of late, notably in the first worldwide "International Conference on the Chinese Diaspora" held in Berkeley, California, in November 1992. On that occasion, some Southeast Asian representatives objected to the term because of its origins in the Greek Bible, with its Jewish messianic implications that the diaspora would one day be regathered to the motherland.[8] It should be made clear that most of those using the term, including myself, do so with no such implications. Instead, I use it in Cohen's modern sense: "a nation of socially interdependent, but spatially dispersed communities".[9]

Some sociologists have argued for a more specific historical conjunction they label the "status gap" as the key to understanding why entrepreneurial minorities become necessary. Such minorities appear to fill "the discontinuity, the yawning social void which occurs when superior and subordinate portions of a society are not bridged by continuous, intermediate degrees of status."[10] In many societies, including feudal Europe, prerevolutionary Eastern Europe, and colonial Asia and Africa, the ruling group was so determined to maintain its distance from the subordinate majority population that a dysfunctional economic gap appeared that could be filled only by outsiders.

In what could be seen as a variation of the foregoing theme, Stanislav Andreski sought to explain the rise of anti-Semitism and other forms of hostility towards minorities by the emergence of small traders and urban artisans from the previously rural host population.[11] Andreski identifies this new competitiveness with the entrenched Jews as the source of anti-Semitism in Poland, as Wertheim and others have done for anti-Chinese movements in Southeast Asia.[12]

The most recently fashionable term in the North American sociological literature is "middleman minority". The term is rather too broad to be useful for my present purpose; it seeks to embrace not only the "status gap" type of historical society, but also, and pre-eminently, such an advanced economy as that of the United States, where successive waves of immigrants occupy particular niches in small business without thereby presenting political problems.[13]

Perhaps the central issue of this literature is whether the prominence of entrepreneurial minorities results from economic causes likely to occur in any society at some stage in its transition to capitalism, or whether it is rooted in particularly intractable cultural and political configurations. If the former, then the trauma such minorities undergo at the hands of nationalists can be seen as a temporary phenomenon that should ease if rational capitalism becomes generalised. If the latter, then racial hostility is likely to be an enduring feature of such societies, breaking out along particular fault lines whenever economic or political conditions deteriorate. As always, neither economics nor culture can explain everything. Cultural divides usually have origins at least partly economic, and they may in turn prolong and endanger the spread of market forces, locking some elites into a vicious circle in which they punish minorities with one hand while using them with the other.

Nationalism

Despite its enormous contribution to the making of the modern world, nationalism has until recently been poorly served in the literature. While self-evidently "natural" to its adherents, nationalism tended to be seen by scholars as a perverse false consciousness. "It claims to protect an old folk society while in fact it is helping to build up an anonymous mass society."[14] The political power of nationalisms, Benedict Anderson points out, contrasts with "their philosophical poverty and even incoherence".[15]

Only after the nationalist tide had receded in Western Europe, four decades after the world war it had produced, did the new comparative work of Anderson, Gellner, Anthony Smith, Eric Hobsbawm, and Liah Greenfeld produce a body of theory useful for both Europe and Asia.[16]

Nationalisms share the project of creating a link between a state and an artificial (or "imagined") community brought into being through modern communications. Immediately, one must distinguish between "liberation" movements seeking to create a national state and "official nationalisms", in Anderson's term, seeking to build mass support for an existing state or dynasty. Anderson has made a case for distinguishing racism as a separate phenomenon linked with the "official nationalism" sponsored by imperial states.[17] For most writers, however, and particularly for those researching Central and Eastern Europe, popular nationalisms arrange themselves along a kind of continuum between the incorporative, or civic, and the exclusive, or ethnic. Nationalism, says K.R. Minogue, "begins as Sleeping Beauty and ends as Frankenstein's monster".[18] The variety romantically associated with a presumed ethno-cultural identity, dubbed "biological nationalism" by Kohn, "ethnic nationalism" by Smith, and "blood nationalism" by Greenfeld[19] made its appearance in the wake of Darwinian theory in the second half of the 19th century and obtained a more strident character after 1880 with the development of germ theories of contagious disease and eugenic theories about improving the gene pool. It thus flourished during a particular period in European intellectual and social history (roughly 1880–1945) and had its greatest popularity east of the Rhine, where earlier civic nationalisms had not taken root.

In Southeast Asia, nationalisms are only now emerging from the enchanted honeymoon phase, during which they could not be subjected to rigorous analysis without seeming to give comfort to colonialism or its successors. They began life as the incorporative "liberation" type, directed primarily against foreign rule, with the Philippine movement against Spanish rule in the 1890s as the prototype. Only in the cases of Siam-Thailand (because it was never colonised) and Malay and Khmer nationalists (because they felt more endangered by Asian "immigrants" than by European "protectors") did the definition and defence of the race or people (Malay *bangsa*, Thai *chat*) often take precedence over the project of national sovereignty within colonial boundaries.[20] The civic variant of nationalism has been the dominant official ideology, particularly in Indonesia and the Philippines, where no single ethnic group dominates, but ethnic nationalism lives uneasily with it, seldom far from the surface where the Chinese are concerned. "Malaysian" nationalism is a fragile and very recent phenomenon (though proposed by Malaysian Prime Minister Mahathir to have become the norm by the year 2020), whereas Malay nationalism has been a vigorous reality since the 1920s.

Comparing Europe and Southeast Asia

The context in which Southeast Asia is being economically transformed is far removed from that of Central Europe in the period 1880–1945. The Central European transformation combined boom and bust economic development, populist electoral politics, the consequences of a terrible war and a vengeful peace in 1918, and the intellectual climate not only of nationalism and Marxism but also of social Darwinism and eugenics. None of these will necessarily be replicated in Southeast Asia in the coming decades, and certainly not in combination. The globalisation of economic and cultural life, in which eastern Asia has been a major player, makes any revival of economic nationalism extremely costly.

In cultural and religious terms, moreover, the Chinese experience is about as far from that of European Jewry as is possible within the spectrum of entrepreneurial minorities. The Jews were pre-eminently a homeless, vulnerable diaspora, maintaining some semblance of common identity only by ritual barriers against commensalism and intermarriage (imperfectly observed, of course), a heroic tradition of learning, and the hostility of their neighbours. Chinese emigrants were the superfluous, omnivorous, and relatively pragmatic errant sons (virtually no women left China until the late 19th century) of the greatest of empires, for whom, until the last century, the twin options of returning to China or assimilating into the majority population would have eliminated a common identity altogether were it not for periodic new waves of emigration.

Nevertheless, an explicit comparison of the situations of these largest and economically most important entrepreneurial minorities is overdue. It contributes to our understanding of the multiple paths that can be taken towards an advanced and expansive market economy and of the particular possibilities and limitations of vanguard minorities on those journeys. In this respect, the growing debate over the Chinese role in the flourishing economies of Southeast Asia can reinvigorate the stalled discussion of the Jewish role in European capitalism. Southeast Asia and Central Europe provide abundant case studies of the effects of different types of relationships between the nation-state and economically powerful but politically disadvantaged minorities. Finally, the disastrous outcome in Hitler's Third Reich needs to be approached in contexts broader than those of the fateful histories of Germany and the Jews. It may be that the moral weight of the *Shoah* (the "catastrophe") lies too heavily on those histories in isolation for fruitful analysis; comparison with less tragic outcomes can suggest some new ways forward.

In Asia, memories of these and other traumas of the 1940s are differently shaped. As Ian Buruma reminds us, "much of what attracted Japanese to Germany before the war — Prussian authoritarianism, romantic nationalism, pseudo-scientific racialism — had lingered in [post-war] Japan while becoming distinctly unfashionable in Germany."[21] Even less than Japanese politicians do Southeast Asian ones have a habit of public apology or self-criticism. Thanks to the colonial heritage, the sense of being historical victims rather than actors is even stronger in Southeast Asia than in Japan. When traumatic bouts of violence have occurred, as they did in Indonesia in 1965–1966 and 1997–2001, Malaysia in 1969, East Timor in 1975–1976, or Vietnam in 1978, the instinctive reaction has been not to probe and re-educate but to prescribe narrower limits to public discussion lest popular passions again get out of hand. As Ruth Benedict pointed out a long time ago, those who inhabit Protestant Christian "guilt cultures" should not expect the rest of the world to behave in the same way. Elsewhere (not only in Southeast Asia or Japan), shame is a stronger social sanction than guilt, and "confession appears only a way of courting trouble."[22]

The killing fields of Cambodia too have given rise to more public self-criticism in the United States than in Cambodia or its neighbours. Western scholars, increasingly dismayed by the persistence of ethnic nationalism in post-1978 Cambodia, have begun to interpret the killings under Pol Pot as a product, at least in part, of glorification of a certain kind of "Khmerness" at the expense of "alien" Vietnamese, Chinese, and bourgeois elements.[23] In Southeast Asia, however (as perhaps in Eastern Europe), neither these nor other events have yet served to disenchant ethnic nationalism of the romanticism and righteousness it acquired in the anti-colonial struggle.

For Southeast Asia's Chinese, the reluctance to draw comparisons from European history has to do with a long experience of hearing the comparison made only in negative terms. Throughout the period from 1600 to 1900, Europeans repeatedly labelled the Chinese "the Jews of the East" in terms that stressed commercial ability, greed, and subservience. Now that Europeans are less likely to continue these stereotypes, some of the Muslim fellow countrymen of Southeast Asian Chinese have begun to take up the same shop-worn anti-Semitic theories.

In the rest of this essay, I raise some comparative questions about three transitions through which the two minorities have passed, particularly in their relations to the economy and the state — the rise of key brokers for the expanding state; emancipation; and nationalism. There appear to be some instructive parallels in the types of problems that emerged as societies became more complex and commercialised and as new, imagined communities replaced older, experienced ones. Although Europe experienced the transitions discussed here earlier than Southeast Asia (and Germany and France earlier than the Slavic lands), there is nothing linear or necessary about these processes of change.

Sources of the Chinese and Jewish Diasporas

The stable and substantial Jewish community of Central and Eastern Europe originated in the late Middle Ages, from the 13th to the 15th centuries, when many long-established Jewish communities in Western Europe moved eastward to escape the heightened danger of persecution and pogrom in the aftermath of the Crusades. In 1264, the Polish king Boleslav granted an unusually liberal charter of self-government to Jews; so eager was he to encourage these productive settlers. The expulsion from Spain and Portugal in 1492, persecution, and the wars of religion in England, France, and Germany drove more Jews eastward. Jewish communal life flourished particularly in the enlarged kingdom of Poland-Lithuania in the century before the Cossack destruction of 1648. The Jewish population of Poland grew to about 150,000 in 1576 and 450,000 in 1648, by which time it represented between five and ten per cent of the Polish population and almost half the world's Jews.[24]

Southeast Asia has been the principal overseas destination of Chinese traders and migrants throughout the second millennium of the modern era. Until the Southern Song Dynasty (1127–1279), foreigners had carried most trade from the south to China. Thereafter, Chinese knowledge of the southern regions grew steadily. But private trade was banned, with varying effectiveness, before 1567, and as late as 1749, Chinese returning after making a fortune in the south could be imprisoned or executed for the crime of emigrating.[25] Substantial injections of Chinese population into Southeast Asia probably occurred by defection from massive imperial naval expeditions during two periods — under the Mongols in the 1290s, and in the reign of the Yungle (Ming) emperor in 1402–1424. These people appear to have assimilated locally, because of the difficulty of maintaining contact with China.[26] After Chinese trade from Fujian and Guangdong to the south was legalised and licensed in 1567, however, stable and distinct Chinese communities became a feature of Southeast Asia. In the mid-17th century, there were communities of 3,000 to 5,000 Chinese in the major port cities of Batavia and Banten in Java, Ayutthaya in Siam, and Hoi An in Vietnam. About twice that many lived in Manila, so the total Chinese population in Southeast Asia must have been at least 40,000.

The Chinese were only one commercial minority among many, including Gujaratis, Chettiars, Malays, Portuguese, and Japanese until the middle of the 17th century. Dutch and English dominance in the Indian Ocean then severely damaged the trade of all the rival networks. Subsequently, the Chinese remained dominant in East Asian trade, took over roles surrendered by the Japanese in the 1630s, and became indispensable buyers from and sellers to the large European companies. By 1700, the Chinese were unrivalled as the pre-eminent commercial minority everywhere in Southeast Asia. From this date at least, their position can usefully be compared with that of Jews in Central and Eastern Europe.

In the early centuries of immigration, both minorities were always welcome — the Jews first in Western and then in Eastern Europe, the Chinese in all the Southeast Asian states as well as in the European enclave cities of the region. Both were valued for their wealth, skills, and international contacts as well as for their disinclination to resort to arms. They virtually introduced urban life and manufacture to many areas that had known little of either. They made it possible for struggling dynasties or colonial port cities to aspire to become something more like states through a much broader revenue base and the commercial primacy of one city over others. If they grouped together, it was more for the convenience of trade and social life than because of legal restriction. In the Southeast

Asian case, Chinese intermarried with or even created ruling dynasties, notably in Ayutthaya (Siam), Brunei, Melaka, and Demak (Java), during this early and relatively open stage.

Commercial skills and disposition, along with international contacts, made it possible for the wealthiest migrants to dominate certain avenues of trade, while various crafts became the virtual preserve of poorer urban settlers. In the 17th century, a visitor remarked that "almost all trade is in their [Jewish] hands" in Poland;[27] similar comments were made about the Chinese in Cambodia, Patani, Jambi, and elsewhere in Southeast Asia.[28] They made their living through retailing, manufacture, or service functions, notably the keeping of inns (by Jews) and of drinking and gambling houses (by Chinese).[29] The ruling class in both cases (including both colonial and native rulers in Southeast Asia) found them indispensable as producers and providers of goods and as brokers with the majority agricultural population.

The gruesome slaughters that occasionally occurred in this situation were as much outbreaks of international or intertribal warfare as they were pogroms against minorities. Some of them could be seen as related to the mid-17th-century economic, political, and demographic crisis that affected Europe and eastern Asia in surprisingly parallel ways. The worst horrors in Central Europe were those the Cossacks visited on the Jews of Poland in the years following 1648. But Polish nobles and priests were equally the targets of these depredations, because it was Polish dominance that was under attack. Island Southeast Asia and China, like Poland, suffered from economic decline and a fragmentation of power (except in areas under Dutch control) in the mid-17th century. After the collapse of the Ming Dynasty in China (1644), the Zheng (Koxinga) resistance to its successor, based on sea power in Fujian, Taiwan, and the South China Sea, caused anxieties about the Chinese "threat" in the Philippines, Vietnam, and Cambodia because it seemed to foreshadow a Chinese naval expansion. But it was Europeans who were most inclined to respond to these anxieties by massacre and expulsion, notably the Spanish attacks on the Chinese in Manila in 1586, 1603 (the bloodiest, with almost 20,000 victims), 1639, 1662, and 1686. The Muslim sultanate of Aceh also banned Chinese in the 1630s, and again around 1700, during periods of religious zealotry.

The character of the interaction between Chinese and Southeast Asians was undoubtedly altered by the Europeans who established demographically insignificant but militarily impregnable footholds in Southeast Asia — in Melaka (Portuguese, 1511; Dutch, 1641), Manila (Spanish, 1571), Batavia or Jakarta (Dutch, 1619), Makasar (Dutch, 1669), and elsewhere. In these enclaves, and by example elsewhere, the Europeans provided an opportunity and even encouragement for the Chinese to remain distinct rather than assimilate into the indigenous majority.

Local-born Chinese willingly assimilated into a high-status ruling category whenever this was advantageous and possible, as it was in Thailand, Cambodia, and pre-Dutch Javanese and Malay societies. But where Europeans occupied the highest status category, they were as hostile as the Polish or Russian aristocracy to outsiders marrying their daughters (they were not so averse to taking local women as concubines themselves). For the Chinese, then, intermarriage with Southeast Asians was no longer a path to elite assimilation but instead created Creole communities distinct from the China-born, from indigenous people, and from Europeans. People in these communities typically began speaking dialects based on the local vernacular.[30] These *peranakan* (to use the Indonesian word) Chinese of the European enclaves thereby became distinctive diaspora communities with their own legal and cultural institutions, a position European Jewry had long enjoyed.

Becoming Brokers to the Expanding State

The stronger states that emerged in Europe in the 17th and 18th centuries, and in Southeast Asia in the 19th, developed a new revenue base in the cash economy that transformed society during these periods. Minorities such as the Jews and the overseas Chinese were the quickest to exploit the opportunities of the new commercialism because they were uninhibited by feudal tradition or landholding and because they had the necessary international contacts to move capital and goods across boundaries. Having initially little to lose and the world to gain, they tended to be the greatest risk takers, especially in trading across the battle lines and enmities that made life in both regions unstable. Their communities grew in wealth and mobility, but a few key figures flourished out of all proportion to others as tax farmers and purveyors to governments.

The rulers (or colonial regimes) that were growing in power at the expense of local lineages needed arms and supplies for their expanding armies and cash to pay for their public works and palaces. In Central

Europe, the court Jews (*hofjuden*) became indispensable financiers and purveyors to German and Austrian rulers, living dangerously by providing what the ruler needed, including cash through revenue monopolies and straight loans. The most spectacular was perhaps Samuel Oppenheimer of Heidelberg, originally contractor of the Palatinate Elector, to whom the Austrian Emperor Leopold I turned to supply the armies he needed to resist the onslaught of Louis XIV of France at the end of the 17th century. Oppenheimer was able to raise the money by turning to his fellow Jewish contractors at the courts of Mainz, Bamberg, and Hesse. Both ruler and contractor occupied lonely, vulnerable pinnacles of power, and there sometimes developed between them real affection on this account. Isolated and exceptional as they were, such figures could often provide protection and patronage for their fellow Jews still chiefly living in poverty in the ghettos, which in turn increased their ability to mobilise this useful underclass for their tax collection, commerce, and manufacturing purposes.[31]

The Jewish community as a whole lived an unstable life centred on the market towns of the Austrian Empire and Poland. Although Leopold I, later patron of Oppenheimer, had expelled all Jews from Vienna and Lower Austria in 1669–1671, by the middle of the following century, there were about 150,000 Jews in the Hapsburg Empire, mostly concentrated in what is today Czech and Hungarian territory. The largest group of Jews at that time was in Poland, however, where they numbered about 800,000, or ten per cent of the population, at the 1764 census, living chiefly around the Baltic ports.[32]

In Southeast Asia, the system of farming the collection of state revenues to prominent Chinese was at its height in the 19th century, but it had begun soon after the Dutch East India Company began to govern its enclave in Batavia in 1619. The Dutch appear to have introduced a system of farming taxes on gambling, alcohol, the slaughter of livestock, the weighing of goods, and so forth, because they were familiar with it in Europe, but it proved a particularly efficient means of drawing revenue from the Chinese commercial community without having to understand its inner workings.[33]

In the 18th century, the monopoly over opium imports became the main source of Dutch Company revenue, and in the 19th, the expanding colonial governments obtained much of their tax needs by farming the sale of opium to prominent Chinese entrepreneurs. The Singapore opium farm alone realised about 40 per cent of Singapore's revenue in the 1860s and nearly 50 per cent in the 1880s.³⁴ The Netherlands Indies government made greater use of land taxes and import duties (Singapore being a free port), but Chinese-run tax farms there represented more than a quarter of all revenue in the 1840s and over 20 per cent in the 1880s. The opium farm again provided the lion's share. In 1870, there were more Chinese engaged in tax-farming operations — about 7,000, or six per cent of adult male Chinese — than there were Dutchmen in government service in the Indies.³⁵ The Chinese tax farmer and his agents were the economic arms of government in rural areas. Buying a farm to operate tollgates and pawnshops, or to tax markets or the slaughter of cattle, enabled Chinese entrepreneurs to evade the many restrictions that the colonial government placed on their movements outside the cities. As a hostile Dutch report noted in 1897:

> The cattle slaughter farm gives the Chinese a means to move about in the villages without being controlled to any great extent. Persons authorized by the farmer are kept in almost all district and subdistrict towns to spy on behalf of their employer. They devote every moment to penetrating into the inner circles of the villages. The pass system is not applied to these people, a reason why the Chinese spend so much money on setting them up as part-employees. Where it would be necessary to engage three people, permission is asked for six.³⁶

The system of farming revenues to the Chinese appears to have been copied by Javanese rulers in the 1680s directly from Dutch practice, no doubt encouraged by the Chinese entrepreneurs who spread inland from the Dutch-governed coastal towns. By the late 18th century, the quasi-independent rulers of Java were primarily dependent on revenues from such farms to develop a state apparatus that could compete with the growing power of the Dutch.³⁷ Thai and Malay rulers also adopted the system in the 18th century, probably on Chinese urging, and by the second half of the 19th century, most of their revenues came from it. Incomplete Thai records show the revenue from Chinese-run revenue farms growing from three million to 13 million baht between 1871 and 1888, a period when King Chulalongkorn was desperately in need of resources to create a government capable of withstanding growing European pressures.³⁸ Through this system of revenue farming, a few Chinese became immensely powerful with both colonial and indigenous governments in the late

19th century: Thio Thiau Siat in Sumatra and Penang; Tan Seng Poh in Singapore; Loke Yew in Kuala Lumpur; Khaw Soo Cheang in South Thailand; and Oei Tiong Ham in Java. They used their strategic positions in charge of the opium and other farms to become the dominating figures in the Chinese economy of Southeast Asia.

The mid-18th century had been a watershed in relations between Chinese and Europeans in Southeast Asia, after which a distinction must be drawn between European-ruled and Asian-ruled areas. The alliance between Dutch and Chinese in Java was under increasing strain in the 1730s, as ever larger numbers of Chinese were attracted to Batavia after Beijing's restrictions on foreign trade were lifted. Dutch anxieties increased as regulations first to restrict and then to deport recent arrivals seemed impossible to enforce. When some criminal Chinese gangs began to attack Europeans outside the city in October 1740, a crackdown quickly degenerated into a wholesale massacre in which 10,000 people — most of the Chinese living in Batavia — were thought to have died. Other Chinese fled to join the enemies of the Dutch Company in Java, some becoming Muslims in the process.

It may be that this exceptional bloodbath was related to a structural shift in Dutch interests from trade to agricultural production in Java.[39] Such was more clearly the case in the Philippines, where a growing local-born middle class (Spanish, Chinese mestizo, and *indio*) resented the control of the domestic economy by China-born Chinese.[40] Non-Catholic Chinese were expelled from the Philippines in 1755 under a regulation repeated in 1766. Although the Chinese government's relationship with overseas Chinese is often seen as a major distinction from the Jewish predicament, since the Jews had no great imperial homeland, this was not so under the emperors, who were little interested in disasters befalling Chinese so unfilial as to have left the middle kingdom.

After these traumatic mid-18th-century events, the Chinese population of the Spanish and Dutch colonies was reduced to initially smaller but more stable Creole communities, secured against further pogroms at European hands by their essential loyalty to and symbiosis with the European order. The Chinese mestizos of the Philippines formed a flourishing Catholic middle class, representing 4.8 per cent (120,000) of the Philippine population by 1810 and 5.2 per cent (290,000) in 1890, by which time they were becoming integrated into a new Filipino elite. The Chinese *peranakan* of Java were a smaller Creole minority, representing between one and two per cent of Java's population (about 100,000 in 1810 and 250,000 in 1890). Like the *baba* of the British Straits Settlements (Singapore, Penang, and Melaka), the *peranakan* saw no attraction in assimilating into a subordinate indigenous community.[41] *Baba* and *peranakan* therefore remained as stable communities, retaining a form of Chinese religion (a shift from an older pattern in the Malay world of assimilation through Islamisation) but speaking a Malay-based Creole.[42] If *peranakan* speech (and *baba* Malay) was closer to standard Malay than Yiddish was to German, this was largely because of the important role these Chinese-descended urban Malay speakers played in the way modern Malay itself evolved. (An analogy might be the way Yiddish influenced the Viennese German dialect.)

By keeping a firm grip on the opium farms and other crucial bridges to the European administration, the Chinese tax farmers maintained control over the continuing influx of China-born Chinese into Netherlands India and Malaya throughout the 19th century. All three Sino-Southeast Asian communities were kept legally distinct by the colonial order in terms of residence, landowning, education, and dress. They largely governed their own affairs. Although they had lost much of their Chineseness, they were less likely to assimilate or integrate than they had been in the 17th century.

In Asian-ruled states, on the other hand, the second half of the 18th century witnessed a much increased influx of Chinese miners, planters, traders, and settlers, who often formed highly productive enclave economies. States such as Siam, Vietnam, Riau-Johor, Brunei, Sambas, and Sulu welcomed the new influx, which included some refugees from the European settlements, and profited greatly from them. In Siam, the Thonburi (1767–1782) and Bangkok dynasties that restored Siam's fortunes after the Burmese conquest were themselves half-Chinese and very dependent on other Chinese as traders in Bangkok, commercial cultivators in the southeast, and tin miners in the south. Autonomous Chinese polities were established at Hatien in the Vietnam-Cambodia borderland and in the goldfields of western Borneo. Except in Malaya-Singapore, where they were a far larger proportion of the population, the number of Chinese in the various populations of Southeast Asia in 1800 varied from the one to two per cent of Java to over ten per cent in Siam and Borneo.[43] The earliest global estimate, in the 1830s, was of "nearly a million" Chinese in Southeast Asia — more than two per cent of the total population.[44]

Relations with these autonomous communities were often tense, and conflicts were frequent over the proportion of the proceeds paid to the local elite. The Chinese as a group aroused resentment because of the influence they had over rulers and because of their direct authority as tax farmers. Peter Carey mentions the large number of attacks on Chinese tollgate keepers and traders in the Javanese princely states in the 1820s, as their demands on peasants for revenue increased. The rebel followers of Dipanegara put "whole Chinese communities ... to the sword" in 1825, just as the Tay-son rebels had done in the Saigon area of southern Vietnam in 1782.[45] Further massacres occurred in southeastern Siam in 1848, in Brunei in the early 1800s, and in the gold-mining area of upriver Kelantan (Malaya) in the 1830s.[46] These massacres were all authorised by rulers in response to some Chinese act of violence, usually provoked, in turn, by increased demand for taxes. Nevertheless, the killing went beyond the normal limits of Southeast Asian warfare. Thousands of Chinese were killed in each of these cases and often whole communities were wiped out.

In both Southeast Asia and Europe, the entrepreneurial minorities were crucial to the growth of a commercial economy on the one hand, and an absolutist state on the other. In both areas, the minority communities remained distinct from the majority populations in culture, religion, residence, and law, partly by choice and partly through the policies of governments that found their distinctiveness useful. A few of their number climbed dangerous pinnacles of power and wealth through their closeness to the ruling courts. Assimilation and intermarriages still occurred around the fringes of the minority community, though probably on a reduced scale as the communities became more settled and self-conscious.

Emancipation and Mass Education

A major transformation reshaped and modernised European Jewry between 1780 and 1848; the analogous period for Chinese in Southeast Asia was much shorter, between 1890 and 1920. The self-governing autonomy of the minority was lost in both cases, as was the privileged position of its leaders as brokers and financiers to the state. In exchange, more exciting opportunities were held out to members of the minority as citizens of a modern state entitled to take part in the upward march of Enlightenment ideas — education, progress, science, liberalism, and nationalism. The minority was able to play a disproportionately large role in the urban and educated middle class which the newly complex state required. The miserable poverty and insecurity of its poorer members were alleviated, even as the pinnacles of power of the few court brokers were toppled. Massacres and expulsions appeared to be things of the past. Yet the path out of the ghetto and into modern mass society was a potentially dangerous one as identities were redefined and questioned.

The process by which Jews, on a large scale, moved out of ghettos and into the mainstream of European cultural and commercial life was part of the broader development of investment capitalism, the rise of an urban, professional middle class, the spread of Enlightenment ideas, the growth of popular education, and the creation of the modern nation-state.

In economic and cultural terms, it was the Jews of the German cities who led the way, though they were relatively few in number. The most prominent Jewish success story was that of the Rothschilds, whose fortune began with Meyer Amschel Rothschild (1743–1812) in Frankfurt. Rothschild became immensely wealthy by taking judicious but ingenious care of the fortune of the ruler of Hesse-Cassel when that prince had to flee Napoleon. His Frankfurt bank became the epitome of successful Jewish international banking in the first half of the 19th century, and its influence spread throughout Europe. By contrast, Berlin was the centre where German-Jewish intellectuals such as Moses Mendelssohn (1729–1786) and Heinrich Heine (1797–1856) were able to make their biggest contribution to the German Enlightenment. The Jews of the Hapsburg Empire and the Slav lands — poorer, more numerous, and more autonomous in their *shtetls* — were nevertheless influenced in due course by this flowering of Enlightenment ideas in the German language.

The emancipation of the Jews of the Austrian Empire, whose numbers doubled in 1772 when the Hapsburgs annexed Polish Galicia, was begun by the reforming Emperor Joseph II (1780–1790). He gave Jews near equality before the law and decreed their right to attend schools and enter the professions. This impetus towards transforming Jewry into a religious minority of equal citizens was taken up by the French revolutionaries, who gave Jews full legal equality, and it was carried across Europe by Napoleon. Napoleon called together a "Sanhedrin" in Paris in 1807 which declared, in effect, that the Jews were not a separate people but a religious minority who were equal citizens of Napoleon's First Empire. Ideas of citizenship and equality before the law certainly had their setbacks in the years that followed, but they ultimately triumphed in Central Europe in the period from 1848 to 1871, and they were influential even in Russia, where, however, full legal equality was never achieved under Czarist rule.

Emancipation made possible a massive movement of Jews into the growing cities, the professions, and middle-class life in general. Vienna had counted only about 6,000 Jews before 1848, but the Jewish population rose even faster than that of the city as a whole, to 40,000 in 1869 and 175,000 (8 per cent of Vienna's two million) in 1910. Budapest counted 45,000 Jews in 1869 and 204,000 (23 per cent of the city's population) in 1910.[47] In the rapid modernisation of Central European society, Jews seized the new opportunities particularly rapidly. In Vienna, as in the Austrian Empire as a whole, Jews were about three times as likely as non-Jews to attend the *Gymnasien* (elite academic high schools) before the First World War. Over 60 per cent of those graduating from such schools in Vienna to become lawyers and doctors in that period were Jews, most of them from commercial family backgrounds.[48] Throughout Central Europe, urban middle-class Jews, largely excluded from positions in the bureaucracy, were playing a disproportionate, dynamic role in the key agencies of the intellectual and economic transformation of Europe — the universities, the press, commerce, the arts, and the new sciences.

In Southeast Asia, the equivalent of emancipation was the abolition of the revenue farms and the lifting of residence and travel restrictions on the Chinese. Beginning with the opium farm in Java in 1894, all the opium and pawnbroking farms of Southeast Asia were dismantled by 1910. The gambling farms under British and Dutch auspices followed in the next decade.[49] As a recent study put it, "revenue farming ... sowed the seeds of its own destruction. By funding the revenue needs of the weak state, it helped nurture a strong state, which eventually could establish the local control necessary to raise its own taxes."[50] Colonial states, and also Siam under Chulalongkorn and his European advisers, became more knowledgeable, powerful, and European in composition. They took over the application of these "vice taxes" themselves and raised vastly larger revenues from customs duties and individual and corporate taxes.

The new bureaucracies began to rule the Chinese directly, rather than through Chinese headmen (*Capitan China*), with specialist services such as the Protectorate of Chinese in Singapore (1877) and the Bureau of Chinese Affairs in Netherlands India. The British had begun during the 19th century to consider Chinese as citizens of their colonies, entitled to protection, and similar attitudes spread to the other colonies around the turn of the century. As they lost access to the hinterland through their revenue farms, the Chinese demanded the right to travel freely in Netherlands India, a right effectively granted to them between 1900 and 1910. Finally, all governments began to take an interest in modern education for their subjects, including local-born Chinese. As the most urban, commercial, and uprooted of Southeast Asia's communities, the Chinese responded vigorously to these opportunities.

Despite their relatively modest numbers, the Sino-Southeast Asian minorities played a role perhaps even more striking than that of European Jewry in the creation of the new national cultures that began to emerge at this time. The Chinese mestizos of the Philippines had been emancipated earlier through adoption of Catholicism, and in the late 19th century they seized the opportunity of Spanish education and manners. The national hero Jose Rizal, whose writings (in Spanish) remain the great classics of Philippine national literature, was but one of a brilliant *ilustrado* generation, descended from Chinese mestizos, who created both a Filipino identity and the political revolution of 1896 in its name. In the cities of Malaya and Netherlands India, the turn of the century marked what Claudine Salmon has called "the Sino-Malay moment", when the *peranakan* Chinese laid the basis for national literatures in Malay and Indonesian through Chinese-owned newspapers and publishing houses.[51] The Creole Malay patois began to give way to standard Malay and standard Chinese as well as English and Dutch, variously favoured by the new schools and printers. In Bangkok, it was Sino-Thais who pioneered the early publishing houses, newspapers, and film corporations.

Nationalism, Marxism and Race

The same forces and ideals that emancipated minorities thrust previously autonomous communities into direct competition with one another and gave rise to intellectual currents and mass movements that were ultimately the greatest dangers to minorities. Education, the printed word, a new rapidity of communication, and a gradual extension of suffrage, encouraged peoples from widely different local, ethnic, cultural, and social groups to identify with new imagined communities that conferred pride and status. The Romantic Movement celebrated rural landscapes and communities and empathised with "the people" — often imagined to embody the harmony and collective values urban intellectuals had lost. Socialism promised an egalitarian future in which workers would discover a new international solidarity in freeing themselves from capitalist exploitation. In the last quarter of the 19th century, social Darwinism encouraged the idea of history as a struggle for survival among peoples, whereby every group had to strengthen and mobilise itself internally. These currents all contended in 19th-century Europe. In Southeast Asia, they came first to the Philippine *ilustrados* in the late 19th century, but spread everywhere in the first two decades of the 20th.

Because they were relatively urban, uprooted, educated, and commercial, entrepreneurial minorities tended to feel all these currents earlier and more strongly than the majority communities. They contributed more than their share to the early stages of forging new socialist and nationalist identities in both regions. In their case, however, an additional possibility arose of imagining a new national community *as* minority diaspora, and of creating the common language, memory, school system, reform agenda, and eventually territory to give this possibility substance. It was those who acquired the best educations in the dominant European languages (German, Russian, French and English in Europe; Spanish, Dutch, French, and English in Southeast Asia) who felt these pressures for new community most strongly.

Whereas overseas Chinese nationalism somewhat preceded majority nationalisms in Indonesia, Malaysia, and Thailand, its Jewish equivalent was held back by the impracticality of having no territory to relate it to. Only in the 1880s and 1890s, after German, Italian, and Slavic nationalisms were well established, did Zionism emerge as a coherent option. The writer Eliezer Perlman (also known as Eliezer Ben Yehuda, one of the main architects of the revival and modernisation of the Hebrew language) in 1878 was one of the earliest to react to pan-Slav enthusiasm by asking the nationalist question, "Why should we be any less worthy than any other people? What about our nation, our language, our land?"[52] The rise of extreme and programmatic anti-Semitism in Germany, Austria, and France in the 1870s and 1880s, and the draconian measures taken against Jews in the Russian laws of May 1882, certainly encouraged the trend. When, in 1895, the Vienna columnist Theodore Herzl published his

Der Judenstaat (*The Jewish State*), even this most international of diasporas now had its nationalist programme, which would compete for half a century with various brands of socialism, liberalism, religious revival, and assimilation for the mind of European Jewry.

The enormous factor of China dominated the analogous phenomenon in Southeast Asia. To the great diversity of ancestral speech groups (Hokkien, Cantonese, Teochiu, and Hakka were the most numerous) was added the deeper division between the local-born and the China-born, whose numbers increased as contract labourers travelled south in unprecedented numbers after 1880. The first explicitly nationalist impetus came from China, in the form of visits by Sun Yat-sen and other nationalists in 1900. Support for their ideas, however, proved to be more widespread among the uprooted Chinese of Southeast Asia than in China itself. Modern schools began to be established using Mandarin, the "standard" speech of north China, rather than the dialects familiar to the migrants. In the first decade of the 20th century, there were strong moves to stress a "Chinese" identity, fostered by the changes in the colonies described earlier. Enthusiasm was stimulated by the Chinese Nationality Law of 1909, with its *jus sanguinis* claim over all overseas Chinese, and by the Chinese revolution of 1911.

The year 1910 has been identified as a watershed in the relationship between Thais and Chinese in Siam. Not only was there a change of ruler from Sinophile Chulalongkorn to Sinophobe Vajiravudh, but also a severe Chinese strike took place against the imposition of a uniform tax, bringing Bangkok to its knees.[53] The establishment of modern Chinese nationalist organisations in the Netherlands Indies and Malaya occurred at about the same time.[54] These organisations would remain a periodic problem for governments in Southeast Asia for the next three decades. Their attempts to organise boycotts of Japanese goods, most dramatically in 1928 and 1937, served more to underline how powerful a grip the Chinese had on many sectors of the economy than to deter Japanese aggression in China.

Diaspora nationalism gave rise to Chinese schools of modern type and to new collective organisations dedicated to reforms that would increase the status and strength of China as well as its overseas sons and daughters. Except in the Philippines, these organisations were led by prosperous, local-born Sino-Southeast Asians, but their formation was much influenced by the massive influx of Chinese contract labourers between 1880 and 1930. About 200,000 Chinese a year left southern China for Southeast Asia in the last decades of the 19th century, and nearer to 300,000 per year emigrated in the first decade of the 20th. Most returned after some years of harsh labour in tin mines or on estates, but enough remained to shift the demographic balance sharply in favour of the China-born in Malaya and to produce large Chinese-speaking populations everywhere. This shift added to nationalist pressures on the Sino-Southeast Asians to redefine their culture and loyalties in a more Chinese direction, especially in Malaya, where the *baba* gradually declined into insignificance.

The attractions of Marxism for entrepreneurial minorities merit particular attention. Somewhat simplistically taking Jews as a collectivity, Milton Friedman has recently drawn attention to the paradox that they "owe an enormous debt to free enterprise and competitive capitalism" and yet have been "consistently opposed to capitalism and have done much on an ideological level to undermine it."[55] On a practical level too, Jews were heavily overrepresented even in the Social Democratic Party (12 per cent of its Reichstag members in 1912) of Germany, where Jews were a tiny and affluent group.[56] In Russia, where Jews formed a real proletariat, socialism was still more attractive, and the Jewish Bund provided mass support for socialism. In Southeast Asia also, the Chinese minority has produced more ideologues of the left than of the free-market right and has given disproportionate support to communist parties.

Undoubtedly, Marxism's theoretical internationalism and its rejection of racial and cultural loyalties as false consciousness were welcome to minority intellectuals weary of attempting to reconcile conflicting and burdensome identities. So long as they were in the opposition, communist parties in Southeast Asia, like those in Europe, were consistent opponents of majority racism. Given the added factor of the strength of communism in China itself, it is not surprising to find that the Malayan Communist party was virtually a Chinese creation (1934), always struggling to find token Malays and Indians to broaden its Chinese image, that the Communist party of Thailand drew much support from ethnic Chinese, or that leading non-Chinese communists such as Ho Chi Minh and Tan Malaka spent many years in China and leant heavily on Chinese support. Although the smaller, relatively affluent Chinese minorities in Indonesia and the Philippines found Marxism less attractive, the Indonesian Communist party (PKI) was the only mainstream Indonesian party to give political leadership to *peranakan* Chinese such as Tan Ling Djie and Tjoo Tik Tjoen.[57]

The factor of China and Chinese communism had, of course, only an indirect analogy in Europe. Nevertheless, the perception of the anti-Semitic right in Europe after 1917 that Russia had fallen under the control of a "Judeo-Bolshevik" conspiracy created a fear about the giant, supposedly Jewish-dominated revolutionary power to the east somewhat similar to the worries that China engendered among anti-communists in Southeast Asia after 1949.

Although Comintern policy in the 1930s required that the communists of Malaya organise themselves in a national party that formally espoused independence for Malaya, its links with the Chinese Communist party were so close and its Chinese membership so overwhelming that the problems of identity were all on the side of non-Chinese who joined the party. And once communism triumphed in China, fear of China and suspicion of the overseas Chinese became more important sources of anti-communism than ideological commitment to private enterprise.

Colonial policies encouraged a division of function, a dual economy, between the "native" majority of peasants, under their own, often anti-commercial, aristocratic-bureaucratic hierarchy, and the commercial sector of Europeans, Chinese, and other minorities. In consequence, a majority bourgeoisie was slow to develop in Southeast Asia, as in Eastern Europe, and participation by majority groups in the modern economies that took shape in the 20th century was initially slight. Paradoxically, at first this limited the potential for anti-Chinese nationalism. In the 1920s and 1930s, anti-Chinese political rhetoric was most pronounced in the Philippines, partly because it was the only Southeast Asian country to experience mass-based democracy, but also because a relatively stronger Filipino bourgeoisie, most of it of mestizo Chinese descent, felt able to compete with the Chinese in commerce. The president of the Commonwealth of the Philippines, Manuel Quezon, could boast in 1941 (probably with exaggeration) that as a result of his curbs on Chinese business, Filipino control of retail trade had increased to 37 per cent from less than 20 per cent at the time the commonwealth was inaugurated in 1935.[58]

Nationalism in Southeast Asia was not necessarily directed against the entrepreneurial minorities. For the Western-educated intelligentsia, foreign, European rule was the enemy, and the Chinese were a problem primarily insofar as they supported that regime. For a time, Chinese and Southeast Asian nationalisms shared common goals of overthrowing Western domination and strengthening the Asian state. At the level of leaders and intellectuals, there was much cooperation between Chinese and indigenous nationalists.

On the other hand, the initial financial support for nationalist causes came from indigenous merchants such as the Muslim batik producers of Java and the Vietnamese silk producers of Cochin China, who were fighting unequal battles with stronger Chinese competitors. This explains the popularity during the period 1910–1925 of appeals to anti-Chinese sentiment, and the periodic attempts to boycott Chinese goods.

This undernourished bourgeoisie could not sustain effective national movements, but it did largely define the content of nationalism during that critical period. While many other foreign influences were accepted as part of the new national identities — Indian mythology, Buddhism, Islam, Christianity (in the Philippines), European dress, and "modernity" — Chinese influences were generally excluded from the package. Chinese cultural icons were being assertively mobilised at this time in the service of the competing overseas Chinese identity, and therefore Chineseness became one of the most important "others" against which the new national identities defined themselves.

As the nationalist movements of Vietnam and Indonesia broadened their bases, they found Marxist prophecies of the coming demise of both imperialism and capitalism more effective among the mass of the population than anti-Chinese economic nationalism. In the bigger colonies, therefore — Netherlands India, Burma, and Vietnam (or its three colonial constituents) — foreign rule always took precedence over anti-Chinese polemic as a focus of nationalist campaigns.

In independent Thailand, on the other hand, Chinese distinctiveness, economic success and, during the nationalist phase, perceived arrogance, were easier targets than Europeans for those wanting to mobilise opinion around the national idea. In the 1910s, it was the king himself who blazed this trail. The first Thai ruler to receive all his education in England, Rama VI (Vajiravudh) had picked up anti Semitic stereotypes in Europe and used them to attack the Chinese, following a pattern already well established by the European "Jews-of-the-East" school. In 1914, he pseudonymously published a series of articles in the Thai press that were later published as an influential pamphlet, *The Jews of the East*. He explained the factors behind anti-Semitism in Europe and attacked the

Chinese of Siam for characteristics he claimed to be the same as those of Jews: "racial loyalty", by which they regarded outsiders as mere barbarians, a double standard of morality towards themselves and others in business dealings, and a pursuit of money above all else.[59] More than anything else, he faulted Chinese entrepreneurs for being entrepreneurs:

> There are many reasons why the Chinese are able to make money more rapidly than other people, most of them no different from those that apply to the Jews ... According to Chinese thought, money is the beginning and end of all good. There is nothing greater. Chinese appear to be willing to do anything and everything for money ... Chinese are willing to endure every sort of privation for money ... No matter how small the wages, they are ready and glad to accept them, since they know how to sustain life on an incredibly small amount of food ... There is no kind of work that they will not do, provided that they are paid for it ... In matters of money the Chinese are entirely devoid of morals and mercy. They will cheat you with a smile of satisfaction at their own perspicacity.[60]

Mass politics in Thailand began, however, only with the 1932 revolution against absolute monarchy, which celebrated the race or nation (*chat*) rather than the monarch and sought greater control of the economy, largely at the expense of the Chinese. Local Chinese support for China in the Sino-Japanese War, and the government's for Japan, exacerbated the tensions. Anti-Chinese polemics and discriminatory measures reached their peak under the nationalist government of Pibun Songkhram in 1938–1945.[61]

In the Philippines too, Chinese control of the economy was the major nationalist issue during this period, for some of the same reasons. Because the United States overlords had already committed themselves to independence by 1946, colonialism itself was not the issue it was in Vietnam or Netherlands India. Malay and Khmer ethnic nationalists, by contrast, were in no hurry to remove the protective colonial umbrellas under which the two peoples had come to see themselves as endangered nations. More threatening to their newfound communities than colonialism was the prospect of being marginalised or absorbed by minorities more successful in both commerce and education — Chinese and Indians in Malaya, Chinese and Vietnamese in Cambodia.

The anti-colonial nationalisms of Southeast Asia show some similarities to Gellner's "Hapsburg" type, in which powerless and education-deprived groups share related cultures that, "with a good deal of effort and standardised and sustained propaganda, can be turned into a rival new high culture", leading to the establishment of a state that sustains the reborn culture.[62] More careful distinctions, however, are required. Benedict Anderson differentiates Thai nationalism from the anti-colonial nationalisms of the rest of Southeast Asia as a staged "official nationalism" like those of Japan, Austria, and Russia,[63] even though it appeared at the same time as similar anti-Chinese populisms in Vietnam and Indonesia. The more important distinction in the long run is between all the nationalisms of the Southeast Asian mainland, on the one hand, and the poly-ethnic new constructions of Indonesia and the Philippines, on the other.

Burmese, Thais, Khmers, Vietnamese, and Malays were all peoples of historically shifting boundaries, or no boundaries at all, who felt the call of nationalism to try to extend one particular construction of ethno-linguistic and historic identity to fill the larger fixed boundaries created by colonial rivalry. A variety of minorities, not only Chinese, had thereby to be included and given citizenship, but their relationship to the "definitive people", to use the former Malaysian Prime Minister Mahathir's phrase,[64] had considerable potential for violence if mismanaged — as it notably has been in Burma, Laos, and Cambodia. Even in Thailand, probably the most successful country in this process, the project "to make this cultural community coterminous with the autonomous and sovereign political unit ... requires constant tinkering and coercion."[65]

Indonesia and the Philippines, on the other hand, expressed themselves in nationalisms so manifestly new, without any single dominant language, that they had no alternative but to be nationalisms of citizenship. Although both nationalisms have so far been ambivalent or negative about including Chinese cultures among the ethnic diversity in which they rejoice, their inherent pluralism provides a framework within which it could be done. On the other side of the balance is the possibility in the particularly diverse Indonesian polity that the nationalism seen so far, for all its anti-colonial vigour and ingenious cultural syncretism, has not yet defused the possibility of more virulent and exclusivist nationalisms built around "definitive" ethno-linguistic groups — Acehnese, Toba-Batak, Javanese, Balinese, Timorese (Tetum), and so forth.

Although the ethnic nationalisms of the former Soviet and Yugoslav states are discouraging on this score, my belief is that the everyday openness and acceptance of diversity in countries such as Indonesia, the

Philippines, and India will prove a stronger safeguard against such dangers than the outward conformity of the Soviet or Chinese systems.

War and Crisis

The catastrophe that descended on Europe in 1933–1945 has become the moral allegory par excellence for all who are tempted to blame their misfortune or disadvantage on a particular ethnic group. Hatred of Jews was the most consistent political passion of Adolf Hitler, the Viennese painter who came to power in Germany in 1933. In consequence, six million Jews died from his systematic extermination campaign — most of them from the Central and Eastern European lands conquered by or allied with Germany after 1939. The number of Slavs who died at Hitler's hands was several times greater. The racial theories of Hitler and his followers became a licence for killing whoever was deemed inferior.

History offers innumerable examples of violence against entrepreneurial minorities, violence from which not only Jews and Chinese but also Indians, Armenians, Parsees, Germans, Lebanese, Palestinians, Greeks, Vietnamese, and many others have suffered. The Holocaust was different from all others both in scale and in having been carried out systematically over a period of several years by a democratically elected government that had made its racist policies clear from the beginning. In the modern world of mass politics, the dangers of racist political programmes could not again be taken lightly. This catastrophe was not inherent in a particular set of economic factors. The collapse of confidence in the liberal capitalist order caused by the Great Depression of 1929–1935, along with the particular problems Germany and Austria faced after a cruel peace was imposed on them in 1918, played its part in the scapegoating of Jews and the consequent rise of Nazism. Europe offered a diversity of relations between majority nationalists and entrepreneurial minorities even at a time of economic crisis and racial theorising. Although Berlin's conquest or bullying of various governments gives the last stage of the history of Central European Jewry an appearance of uniform horror, the governments concerned reacted to Nazi demands in a wide variety of ways, from eager collaboration to heroic resistance.

Is a repetition of this European nightmare possible? Even more than lessons consciously drawn from the Holocaust, the structural changes that have taken place during the long post-war boom have rendered any major conflict between a nationalist majority and an entrepreneurial minority unlikely in the democratic advanced economies. In those countries, racial theories remain largely discredited, even if they are sometimes privately expressed or even presented in tendentious pseudo-academic form. The public expression of racial hostility must be carefully camouflaged or it will lose more votes than it wins. In market economies where consumerism has become general and the majority have become educated employees of the service sector, distinctive entrepreneurial minorities are no longer as essential or as salient as they once were.

Moreover, the world economic system has changed profoundly since the 1930s, to the point where arguments stemming from the needs of the nation-state have to be balanced by the multinational needs of large corporations. After considering the arguments for the waning of nationalism, Ernest Gellner took the view that "the sharpness of nationalist conflict may be expected to diminish" but the congruence of political unit and culture will continue to apply.[66] Yet if one looks at the economic basis for nationalism that he erected in earlier chapters of the same book — "a mobile, literate, culturally standardized, interchangeable population" — it is clear that it now points towards internationalism.[67] Tariff barriers have been lowered until no one knows where an "American" or "Japanese" brand name has been produced. Capital, management, and increasingly even labour, are becoming mobile internationally, just as a century ago they became mobile nationally. Similarly, the "print capitalism" that Benedict Anderson described as defining potential nations begs for an analysis of the effect the replacement of newspapers by global electronic media networks has had on cultures, consciousnesses, and identities.[68] If explanations for the rise of homogeneous nation-states in the 19th century are adapted to contemporary economic conditions, they support hypotheses about still larger units of effective interchangeability.

Within each of the advanced economies, hostility towards the pioneers of capitalist activity weakens as a shared consumerist culture becomes generalised. Entrepreneurs are more likely to be upheld as models than deplored as greedy signs of disorder. In states such as Australia and Canada, multiculturalism is pursued as a national goal not only to civilise eating habits but also because cosmopolitan, multilingual citizens are particularly valuable in an increasingly integrated global economy.

The Second World War was a trauma of a different sort for Southeast Asia. The period of war and revolution that followed the Great

Depression might be seen in hindsight as a mid-century crisis of large proportions, from which the region began to emerge only in the 1970s. Mass migration from China largely ceased with the depression in 1930, and the Chinese minority everywhere gradually became a stable one in which the local-born formed an ever larger majority. A high birth rate nevertheless saw the numbers of those who self-identified as Chinese grow even faster than they had during the previous period of migration, from a total of about four million in 1930 to about ten million in 1960 and perhaps 24 million in 1990 — a growth not unlike that of European Jewry 50 years earlier. As a proportion of the total population, the Chinese ranged from about 40 per cent in Malaysia-Singapore down to merely one per cent in the Philippines and North Vietnam.[69] The end of colonial privilege created opportunities to replace European firms in the higher peaks of commerce and industry, which more than compensated for the controls that economic nationalism sought to place on Chinese minorities. The turbulence of the 1940s and 1950s ensured that most of those who did flourish in this era, however, were newcomers ready to take big risks rather than the established families of the colonial era.

Although patriotic passions were stirred in the 1930s and 1940s by the Sino-Japanese war and the eventual reconstitution of China under communist leadership, the subsequent Maoist period rendered the ancestral land unusually unattractive as a magnet or focus of loyalty. The idealistic youth who "returned" in the 1940s to build a fatherland they had never known, suffered miseries that became known in the diaspora. The minorities who could be manipulated by Beijing or Taipei became ever smaller, so that subsequent decades have seen a process of weaning the Southeast Asian Chinese away from the diaspora-nationalist push for identification with China. The antithesis between this process and Israel's effect on Jewish diasporas in the same period is striking. Whereas the core of the self-perceived Chinese community in each of the Southeast Asian countries in the early 20th century, except Java, was *totok* (first-generation), the only remaining *totok* are now elderly (though they include the most powerful entrepreneurs). By its considerable demographic growth in the same period and the education of two new generations in the national vernaculars, the Chinese diaspora has become more similar to pre-Holocaust European Jewry.

It would be difficult to say with confidence that the narrowing cultural gap between minority and majority which these changes entailed has reduced the threat of violence beneath the surface. Each major political upheaval has created new dangers for the resented minority. The Japanese occupation in 1941–1945 created sharp cleavages between Chinese, who had tended to be anti-Japanese since the Sino-Japanese war and who supported guerrilla resistance in Malaya and Borneo, and majority nationalists, for whom the Japanese brought some opportunities. The months immediately following the Japanese surrender in August 1945 witnessed an outbreak of racial violence almost everywhere as scores were settled by both sides and Chinese nationalists made provocative claims of victory. Revolutionary upheavals followed, particularly in Indonesia, where Chinese shops provided a safer and more profitable target than Dutch colonial institutions. The Chinese suffered disproportionately in all such political violence, even when they were not its primary target.

No more than in Europe is it easy to relate outbreaks of violence in Southeast Asia with particular economic or cultural conditions. In Thailand, where barriers to assimilation were lowest, there has indeed been little explicitly anti-Chinese violence since the 1950s. Yet at the other extreme, Malaysia, where the social and legal barriers between Chinese and Malay are highest, there has been only one major outbreak of violence since 1946, though this was the particularly traumatic riot and killings of May 1969. Indonesia has seen repeated outbreaks, in 1946 (Tanggerang in particular), 1959–1960, 1963 (Sukabumi), 1965–1967, 1973 (Bandung), 1980 (Makasar), 1982 (Surakarta), 1994 (Medan), and in many places in the peak of 1996–1999.[70]

The most systematic governmental attempt to destroy or expel an entrepreneurial minority occurred in Vietnam in 1978–1979, as relations between Beijing and Hanoi broke down. The million or more Hoa (ethnic Chinese) in the south were largely Vietnamese citizens but were pressured into becoming boat people by deprivation of their livelihood and the double prejudice against them as potential fifth columnists and as bourgeois. The smaller number of Hoa in the north previously had been allowed to retain Chinese citizenship, escape the draft, and act as intermediaries with the giant neighbour. Yet despite centuries of accommodation with the majority Vietnamese, this community was put under such pressure that almost all of its members had been forced to leave for China by April 1979. Subsequent census data showed only 5,000 Hoa in northern Vietnam, against 174,000 in the 1960 census.[71]

Though international hostility was the immediate cause of this crackdown, it also points to the paradoxical relationship between ruling communisms and nationalism. Marxist parties took strong theoretical stands against nationalism and racism as false consciousnesses, yet much of their appeal in Asia was, to parody Lenin, as "a higher stage of nationalism". For Western-educated intellectuals, Marxism was attractive because it could provide a rational, modern, non-racial explanation of why the currently poor and weak nations might hope to rise. To the broader population, communists appeared willing not simply to talk about overthrowing foreign control (Japanese in China, Western colonialism in Southeast Asia, "neocolonial" enterprise after the war), but to get on with it.

The weakness of a majority bourgeoisie in Indonesia, Vietnam, and Burma made a corporatist style of economic nationalism virtually irresistible there. The governments of these three countries in the 1950s and 1960s all had to deal with a political public that was passionately anti-colonial and believed that private capitalist activity was corrosive and anti-national and that the new states should intervene in the economy to deliver a good life for all. As in Eastern Europe, politically correct attitudes towards racial equality imposed from above did nothing to deal with the resentment of unequal (individual and group) success in the marketplace or, in the end, to educate citizens to handle questions of identity in a politically mature manner.

Contemporary Southeast Asia

The spectacularly successful opening of the Southeast Asian economies to foreign and domestic investment since 1970 (except for Burma and Indochina, which started on the same path some 20 years later) has improved living standards throughout the region. The 1970s brought Malaysia and Singapore a burst of phenomenal growth, averaging 7.6 per cent a year throughout the decade in real terms, so that national income more than doubled during this period. In these most advanced Southeast Asian economies, the economic gap between Chinese and others may be narrowing, though with the danger in Malaysia of making the Malay business elite more rather than less dependent on government discrimination in its favour.[72]

In Thailand and Indonesia, economic growth in the 1980s, also at rates higher than any experienced in Europe, increased the share going to risk-taking Chinese entrepreneurs to an extent well beyond what any minority group could have aspired to in the modern European cases.[73] Yet this danger was more than offset by an acceptance, to a degree unthinkable even in the 1960s, that money-making activity is legitimate and positive for the nation. Kasian Tejapira describes how fully Sino-Thai individuals and values have been incorporated into the newly dominant middle-class ethos of Thailand.[74] Although one cannot be as optimistic about Indonesia, even in face of the Medan riots of 1994, one internal commentator declared that "a multi-ethnic capitalist class is ... in active formation, economically and politically. Although this class remains far from anything near hegemony over Indonesian life, its very formation has helped soften old racial antagonisms".[75]

The negative side of this phenomenally rapid economic growth is the dissolution of established ties of kinship and locality, the challenge of competitive consumerism to cherished values, and the anomie of newly urban life. The increasing identification of young Malays and Indonesians with a scriptural and morally prescriptive definition of Islam is understandable in this context, particularly to anyone who has examined evangelical revivals in Europe and America. The new Islamic movements have provided both community and a moral anchor in the changing world. In Malaysia, Malay identity is always a further factor, and Islam has become more salient there as a boundary marker since the Malay language was imposed on the whole Malaysian education system in 1969–1970.[76]

For the young activists who drive these movements, scripturalist Islam helps resolve the dilemma of modernity. It provides a coherent morality that marks them off from both the old-world village syncretism of their parents and the godless consumerism and corruption they see around them in the cities. At an earlier stage, these negative aspects of modern commercialism could be comfortably associated with Chinese and Europeans. But as Muslims themselves join the new rich in ever-growing numbers, narrower explanations for these negative aspects have been imported from the Middle East and ultimately from the West.

In Malaysia and Indonesia today, the crudest racial formulations of the demonology of modernisation are directed against a "Jewish" minority known only as a theoretical construct. The secularism and the separation between church and state that these groups deplore in the modern West have made Christianity a less satisfactory target, particularly because Christian minorities in Malaysia and Indonesia are not easily demonised.

There are real personal and political costs in attacking them, whereas Jews seem a disembodied, costless target for group hatreds and ambivalence about the modernisation process.

The return of many students from periods of study in Egypt and Arabia, increased contacts with Middle Eastern governments, and the interest of young idealists in the Iranian revolution of 1979 have exposed Southeast Asians to explanations for Muslim weakness deriving from the Middle East, in which Israel and the "international Jewish lobby" play a large part.

In the 1980s in Malaysia and the 1990s in Indonesia, some of the explicitly anti-Semitic publications circulating in the Middle East began to appear in Malaysian and Indonesian editions. They ascribed all the evils of the modern world, particularly colonialism, communism, secular liberalism and commercialisation, to Jewish conspiracies along the lines of those sketched in the notorious Czarist forgery, "The Protocols of the Learned Elders of Zion".[77] The political configuration in Malaysia makes it difficult to condemn such excesses once they become associated with Islam, and Mahathir himself appeared to encourage them during the first six years of his prime ministership.[78]

In Indonesia, home of the world's largest Muslim community, Islamic ideas are much more diverse and more autonomous from the political needs of government, and cultural identities are less embattled and defensive than those of Malaysian Malays. The pleas of leaders such as Abdurrahman Wahid and Nurcholis Madjid to disentangle Islamic revitalisation from the political struggles of the past have led in the direction of tolerance and openness. Nevertheless, the current of Jewish-conspiracy theories has recently increased in virulence. Its most influential champion since 1991 has been *Media Dakwah*, a Jakarta Muslim monthly whose circulation has been rising along with its extremism and in 1994, stood at about 20,000. In attacking opponents such as Nurcholis Madjid, it regularly labels them agents of the Jews or of Zionism, whose only aim is to destroy Islam.

In August 1993, this campaign was extended to William Liddle, one of the world's leading analysts of Indonesian politics. In an analysis of contemporary Indonesian Islam, Liddle had given *Media Dakwah* a paradigmatic place within the current he called "scripturalist", as opposed to the "substantialist" stream of Nurcholis Madjid and Abdurrahman

Wahid, and he had deplored the anti-Semitic stereotypes into which the journal's defensive insularity was leading it.[79] The *Media Dakwah* response was to devote a whole issue to an attempt to discredit Liddle as part of the international Jewish conspiracy, arguing that all the evil and bloodshed that has befallen the world arose from the scheming of Jews.[80]

Anger over Israel's treatment of Palestinians only partially explains why such fantastic ideas have suddenly become popular and believable in Islamic Southeast Asia. Scapegoating and conspiracy theories are more credible as a familiar social system dissolves and the boundaries of the new remain unclear. Periods of rapid economic expansion followed by crisis encourage beliefs that the system is not working in "our" interests — as happened in Europe and the United States after 1873, during the First World War, and again, catastrophically, in the 1930s. Malaysia's sudden economic downturn in 1985–1987, after a period of dramatic growth, may well be an indication of such dangers. Moreover, the decline of Marxism has increased the desire for some coherent critique of Western hegemony that does not jettison modernity altogether.

One of the most extreme anti-Jewish diatribes (this one fortunately buried in a low-circulation university staff newsletter) emerged from the Malaysian debate in 1994 over whether to ban the film *Schindler's List*. Prominent Malay novelist Shahnon Ahmad argued that it was Hitler, not Schindler, who should be praised. The Jews whom the Nazis had regrettably failed to kill, in Shahnon's apocalyptic vision, were now responsible for leading the world to its destruction. The signs he perceived of this imminent collapse were precisely the ills of rapid economic growth — consumerism, commoditisation, the rule of money, and the abandonment of traditional values in the name of a spurious freedom.[81]

Alienation from the onward rush of commercialisation is familiar from European history and is inescapable in the much faster pace of Asian development. It is, on balance, remarkable (and a tribute to the smaller number of economic casualties suffered thus far in Southeast Asia's transition than in Europe's) that there has not been more scapegoating and that the Jewish target identified for demonisation is such an unreal and abstract one. Nevertheless, the experience of Europe strongly suggests that racist theory never stops with one target group. Whenever a large segment of society begins to find explanations acceptable that proceed from political arguments (whether about the role of Israel, the excessive consumption of the rich, or the extent of foreign influence) to the demonisation of whole racial groups, then the outlook for all minorities (and ultimately also majorities) becomes dark.

There are still crises of transition to be negotiated in Southeast Asia before minority status ceases to be a salient and resented feature of economic and political life. If the economies falter, domestic political conflicts again get out of hand, and desperate politicians look for scapegoats and saviours, the dangers of violence remain real. Yet this book ends with confidence that the region will learn from the salutary experience of the European transition and avoid its poisonous racial conflicts.

Notes

Chapter 1

1. The primary sources for this episode are the following Indonesian memoirs: Sidik Kertapati, *Sekitar Proklamasi 17 Agustus 1945*, 3rd ed. (Jakarta: Pembaruan, 1964), pp. 94–7; Adam Malik, *Riwajat dan Perdjuangan sekitar Proklamasi Kemerdekaan Indonesia 17 Agustus 1945*, rev. ed. (Jakarta: Widjaya, 1970), pp. 35–7; Sukarno and Cindy H. Adams, *Sukarno, An Autobiography as told to Cindy Adams* (Hong Kong: Gunung Agung, 1966), pp. 206–9; Mohammad Hatta, *Sekitar Proklamasi 17 Agustus 1945* (Jakarta: Tintamas, 1970), pp. 33–7. It is described in Anthony Reid, *The Indonesian National Revolution 1945–1950* (Hawthorn: Longman, 1974), p. 26, and Benedict Anderson, *Java in a Time of Revolution, Occupation and Resistance* (Ithaca, NY: Cornell, 1972), pp. 71–3.
2. Nagazumi Akira, *The Dawn of Indonesian Nationalism* (Tokyo: Institute of Developing Economies, 1972), pp. 27, 32.
3. Figures derived from *Statistical Pocketbook of Indonesia, 1941* (Batavia: Central Bureau of Statistics, 1947), p. 142.
4. J.S. Furnivall, *Netherlands India* (Cambridge: 1939), p. 401.
5. Onghokham, "The Residency of Madiun. Priyayi and Peasant in the Nineteenth Century" (PhD thesis, Yale University, 1976), p. 143.
6. C.J. Hasselman, *Algemeen Overzicht van de Uitkomsten van het Welvaart-Onderzoek Gehouden op Java en Madoera in 1904–1905* ('s-Gravenhage: Nijhoff, 1914), p. 115.
7. Dr Soetomo, quoted in Nagazumi, *Dawn*, p. 24.
8. F. Buchler, "Land Hunger and the Growing Power of Regional Elites in Cirebon Regency, 1903–1930", Paper presented to Second Asian Studies Association of Australia Conference, Sydney, 1978.
9. D.W. Fryer and J.C. Jackson, *Indonesia* (London: Ernest Benn, 1977), p. 153.
10. Derived from Furnivall, *Netherlands India*, p. 348, and Oki Akira "Social Change in the West Sumatran Village" (PhD thesis, Australian National University, 1977), p. 64.
11. *Statistical Pocketbook of Indonesia*, 1941, p. 96.

12. Richard Robison, *Indonesia: The Rise of Capital* (Sydney: Allen & Unwin, 1986); Matsuo Hiroshi, *The Development of the Javanese Cotton Industry* (Tokyo: Institute of Developing Economies, 1970), pp. 19–40.
13. These words, from the title of the collected letters of Raden Adjeng Kartini, are taken as a theme by Benedict Anderson in his perceptive essay on Dr Soetomo in *Perceptions of the Past in Southeast Asia*, eds. Anthony Reid and David Marr (Singapore: Heinemann Asia for the ASAA, 1980), pp. 219–48. On this theme, see also Anthony Reid, "'Heaven's Will and Man's Fault': The Rise of the West as a Southeast Asian Dilemma", Flinders Asian Studies Lecture 6 (Bedford Park: Flinders University, 1975).
14. R.Ng. Ranggawarsita, *Serat Kola Tida*, quoted in Anderson, *Perceptions*, p. 219.
15. Reid, *Indonesian National Revolution*, pp. 2–3.
16. Ki Hadjar Dewantara, "Onze Nationale Kleeding" (2 July 1914), in *Karja K.H. Dewantara* (Jogjakarta: Persatuan Taman Siswa, 1967), 2A: 267.
17. Ki Hadjar Dewantara, "Taal en Volk" (1917), in ibid., p. 106.
18. Dr Soetomo, *Kenang-kenangan*, quoted in Anderson, *Perceptions*, p. 243.
19. In interview with H.J. Kiewiet de Jonge, 20 October 1932, in *Het Onderwijsbeleid in Nederlands-Indie 1900–1940*, ed. S.L. van der Wal. *Een Bronnenpublikatie* (Groningen: J.B. Wolters, 1963), p. 537.
20. The best short survey of the rise of SI is in Bernhard Dahm, *History of Indonesia in the Twentieth Century* (London: Pall Mall Press, 1971), pp. 38–55.
21. Speech by Abdul Manap, 1920, quoted in Anthony Reid, *The Blood of the People: Revolution and the End of Traditional Rule in Northern Sumatra* (Kuala Lumpur: Oxford, 1979), p. 16.
22. *Rasa Doenia* (Yogyakarta), 1–8 March 1923.
23. Aliarcham, 1924, quoted in Ruth T. McVey, *The Rise of Indonesian Communism* (Ithaca, NY: Cornell University Press, 1965), p. 263.
24. Darsono, quoted in ibid., p. 298.
25. G.C. Allen and A.G. Donnithorne, *Western Enterprise in Indonesia and Malaya* (London: George Allen & Unwin, 1957), p. 288.
26. P.S. Gerbrandy, *Indonesia* (London: Hutchinson, 1950), p. 27.
27. Heather Sutherland, *The Making of a Bureaucratic Elite: The Colonial Transformation of the Javanese Priyayi* (Singapore: Heinemann [for the ASAA], 1979), p. 145.
28. Soetan Sjahrir, *Out of Exile*, trans. Charles Wolf (New York: John Day, 1949), p. 219.
29. *Continuity and Change in Southeast Asia: Collected Journal Articles of Harry J. Benda* (New Haven, CT: Yale University Southeast Asia Studies, 1972), p. 72. On this theme, see also Anthony Reid, "The Japanese Occupation and Rival Indonesian Elites: Northern Sumatra in 1942", *Journal of Asian Studies* 35 (1975): 49–61.

30. Sukarno, 9 March 1943, quoted in Benda, *Continuity and Change*, p. 71.
31. "Principles Governing the Administration of Occupied Southern Areas", 20 November 1941, in *Japanese Military Administration in Indonesia: Selected Documents*, eds. H.J. Benda, J.K. Irikura and K. Kishi (New Haven, CT: Yale University Southeast Asia Studies, 1965), p. 1.
32. The importance of this "Illegal PKI" is clear in Anton Lucas, *One Soul One Struggle: Region and Revolution in Indonesia* (Sydney: Allen & Unwin, 1991).
33. Sukarno and Adams, *Sukarno. An Autobiography*, p. 173.
34. Benda, Irikura and Kishi, eds., *Japanese Military Administration*, p. 7.
35. Imamura Hitoshi, "Imamura Hitoshi Taishù Kaisùroku", in *The Japanese Experience in Indonesia: Selected Memoirs of 1942–1945*, eds. Anthony Reid and Oki Akira (Athens: Ohio University Monographs in International Studies, Southeast Asia Series No 72, 1986), p. 72; *Sukarno. An Autobiography*, pp. 175–6, also describes this meeting, though Sukarno's admiration for Imamura is even more apparent at pp. 244–5.
36. Miyoshi Shunkichiro, in *Kokusai Mondai* (Tokyo) 73 (1966): 64–6, as translated in *The Japanese Experience in Indonesia: Selected Memoirs of 1942–1945*, eds. Anthony Reid and Oki Akira (Athens, OH: Ohio University Center for International Studies, 1986), pp. 122–4.
37. These figures, derived from Nasution, are in Dahm, *History*, p. 116.
38. The British counted 4,185 Indonesians killed up to 30 January 1946, but estimated that about another 13,000 must have died or been seriously wounded. British casualties throughout Indonesia were only 348 killed and 225 missing by May 1946, by which time the estimate of Indonesian dead had passed 20,000. Most of these losses were in the Surabaya fighting. Cables of 30 January and 28 May 1946, in Public Records Office, London, WO 203/5013 and 203/5015, respectively.
39. Soeyatno Kartodirdjo, "Social and Political Changes in Surakarta after 1945", *Review of Indonesian and Malayan Affairs (RIMA)* 8.1 (1974): 39.
40. Amir Sjarifuddin, 9 April 1946, cited in Reid, *Indonesian National Revolution*, p. 75.
41. Musso, 1948, quoted in Ruth McVey, *The Soviet View of the Indonesian Revolution* (Ithaca, NY: Cornell Modern Indonesia Project, 1957), p. 62.
42. Reid, *Indonesian National Revolution*, p. 154, quoting Iwa Kusuma Sumantri.
43. This process is best described in R. Robison, *Indonesia: The Rise of Capital*, partly summarised in R. Robison, "Toward a Class Analysis of the Indonesian Military Bureaucratic State", *Indonesia* 25 (1978): 18–23.
44. Karl Jackson and Lucien Pye, eds., *Political Power and Communications in Indonesia* (Berkeley, CA: University of California Press, 1978) especially two articles on "Bureaucratic Polity" by Karl Jackson; Ann Ruth Willner, "The Neo-traditional Accommodation to Political Independence: The Case

of Indonesia", in *Cases in Comparative Politics: Asia*, ed. L. Pye (Boston: Little, Brown, 1970); Harold Crouch, "Patrimonialism and Military Rule in Indonesia", *World Politics* 31 (1979): 571–84. For Weber's concept, see Max Weber, *Economy and Society. An Outline of Interpretive Sociology* (New York: Bedminster, 1968), pp. 231ff.; and for its modern application, S.N. Eisenstadt, *Traditional Patrimonialism and Modern Neo-Patrimonialism* (London: Sage Publications, 1973).

Chapter 2

1. An earlier version of the original chapter was given as a lecture in the Ecole des Hautes Etudes en Sciences Sociales, Paris. I am grateful for the valuable comments made by Robert Elson and Martin Klein on drafts of the chapter.
2. David Brion Davis, *The Problem of Slavery in Western Culture* (Ithaca, NY: Cornell University Press, 1966) and *Slavery and Human Progress* (New York: Oxford University Press, 1984); Robert William Fogel and Stanley L. Engerman, *Time on the Cross: The Economics of American Negro Slavery*, vol. 1 (Boston: Little, Brown, 1974); Orlando Patterson, *Slavery and Social Death* (Cambridge, Mass.: Harvard University Press, 1982). And see Chapter 5.
3. Michael Aung Thwin, "Athi, Kyun Taw, Hpaya-Kyun: Varieties of Commendation and Dependence in Pre-colonial Burma", in *Slavery, Bondage and Dependency in Southeast Asia*, ed. Anthony Reid (St Lucia: University of Queensland Press, 1983); Leonard Y. Andaya, "Man as Rare as Flowers" in *Glimpses of Indonesian History: The 1987 MacMillan Brown Lectures*, by Leonard Y. Andaya and Barbara Andaya (Auckland: Auckland University, 1988).
4. Herman J Nieboer, *Slavery as an Industrial System: Ethnological Researches*, 2nd ed. (The Hague: Nijhoff, 1910); Baron de Montesquieu, *The Spirit of the Laws*, trans. T. Nugent (New York: Hafner, 1949), p. 239; Simon de la Loubère, *Du Royaume de Siam* (Paris: Jean Baptiste Coignard, 1691) 1: 296–8; G.F. de Marini, *Delle Missione de Padri della Compagnia de Giesu nella Provincia di Giappone, particolarmente di quelle de Tumkino* (Rome: Nicolo Angelo Tinassi, 1663), p. 445.
5. Reid, *Slavery, Bondage and Dependency*.
6. Anthony Reid, *Southeast Asia in the Age of Commerce*, vol. 1, *The Lands Below the Winds* (New Haven, CT: Yale University Press, 1988), p. 130.
7. Ibn Muhammad Ibrahim, *The Ship of Sulaiman*, trans. J. O'Kane (London: Routledge and Kegan Paul, 1972 [orig. publ. 1688]).
8. In many areas of Indonesia, the phrase *makan gaji* (eat wages) still has the pejorative ring which *hireling* had for the English translators of the Bible.

9. R.E. Elson, "Sugar Factory Workers and the Emergence of 'Free Labour' in Nineteenth-Century Java", *Modern Asian Studies* 20, 1 (1986): 139–74.
10. P.-Y. Manguin, "Manpower and Labour Categories in Early Sixteenth-Century Malacca", in *Slavery, Bondage and Dependency*, ed. Anthony Reid (St Lucia: University of Queensland Press, 1983), p. 209.
11. Reid, *Slavery, Bondage and Dependency*, pp. 22–4.
12. Ibid., pp. 14, 18, 29.
13. Willard A. Hanna, *Indonesian Banda: Colonialism and its Aftermath in the Nutmeg Islands* (Philadelphia: Institute for the Study of Human Issues, 1978), p. 66.
14. Kirk Endicott, "The Effects of Slave Raiding on the Aborigines of the Malay Peninsula", in *Slavery, Bondage and Dependency*, ed. Anthony Reid (St Lucia: University of Queensland Press, 1983).
15. John Anderson, *Mission to the East Coast of Sumatra in 1823* (Kuala Lumpur: Oxford University Press, 1971 [orig. publ. 1826]), pp. 297, 315.
16. Leonard Blussé, "An Insane Administration and an Unsanitary Town: The Dutch East India Company and Batavia (1619–1799)", in *Colonial Cities*, eds. R. Ross and G.J. Telkampe (The Hague: Nijhoff. Bock, Carl, 1985 [orig. publ. 1881]); Heather Sutherland, "Slavery and the Slave Trade in South Sulawesi, 1660s–1800s", in *Slavery, Bondage and Dependency*, ed. Anthony Reid (St Lucia: University of Queensland Press, 1983).
17. H.G. Schulte Nordholt, "Macht, Mensen en Middelen: Patronen van Dynamiek in de Balische Politiek, 1700–1840" (PhD diss., Vrije Universiteit, Amsterdam, 1980).
18. Reid, *Slavery, Bondage and Dependency*, pp. 29–32.
19. Terence Bigalke, "Dynamics of the Torajan Slave Trade in South Sulawesi", in *Slavery, Bondage and Dependency*, ed. Anthony Reid (St Lucia: University of Queensland Press, 1983).
20. John Crawfurd, *History of the Indian Archipelago*, vol. 1 (Edinburgh: A. Constable, 1820).
21. F. de Haan, *Priangan* (Batavia: Kolff, 1910), 3: 208–9; Luc Nagtegaal, "Rijden op een Hollandse tijger: De noordkust van Java en de V.O.C., 1680–1743" (PhD diss., Rijksuniversiteit te Utrecht, 1988).
22. Reid, *Slavery, Bondage and Dependency*, p. 169.
23. M.R. Akin Rabibhadana, *The Organization of Thai Society in the Early Bangkok Period, 1782–1873* (Ithaca, NY: Southeast Asia Program, Cornell University, 1969), p. 110.
24. Victor Lieberman, *Burmese Administrative Cycles: Anarchy and Conquest, c.1580–1760* (Princeton, NJ: Princeton University Press, 1984), pp. 107–9, 163.

25. Sophia Raffles, *Memoir of the Life and Public Services of Sir Thomas Stamford Raffles* (London: James Duncan, 1835), 2: 175–85; Henry Lyman, *The Martyr of Sumatra: A Memoir of Henry Lyman* (New York: Robert Carter and Brothers, 1856), pp. 368–77; Carl Bock, *Head-hunters of Borneo* (Singapore: Oxford University Press, 1985 [orig. publ. 1882]), p. 260.
26. Munshi Abdullah, "The Hikayat Abdullah", trans. A.H. Hill, *Journal of the Malayan Branch of Royal Asiatic Society* 28, pt. 3 (1955 [orig. publ. 1849]): 161–2.
27. Lyman, *The Martyr of Sumatra*, p. 368.
28. Anderson, *Mission to the East Coast*, p. 298.
29. Alphonse van der Kraan, "Bali: Slavery and the Slave Trade", in *Slavery, Bondage and Dependency*, ed. Anthony Reid (St Lucia: University of Queensland Press, 1983), pp. 332–4; Lyman, *The Martyr of Sumatra*, p. 377.
30. Van der Kraan, "Bali Slavery", pp. 333–7.
31. Merle C. Ricklefs, *A History of Modern Indonesia* (London: Macmillan, 1981), pp. 115–6; G.F. Gonggrijp, *Schets ener Economische Geschiedenis van Indonesie*, 4th ed. (Haarlem: De Erven F. Bohn, 1957), pp. 90–1.
32. Gonggrijp, *Schets ener Economische Geschiedenis*, p. 98; see also Elson, "Sugar Factory Workers", pp. 39–40.
33. Clive Day, *The Policy and Administration of the Dutch in Java* (Kuala Lumpur: Oxford University Press, 1996 [orig. publ. 1904]).
34. Ricklefs, *A History*, p. 118.
35. J.S. Furnivall, *Netherlands India* (Cambridge: Cambridge University Press, 1967 [orig. publ. 1944]), pp. 184–5.
36. H.T. Damsté, "Hikajat Perang Sabi", *Bijdragen tot de Taal-, Land- en Volkenkunde van Nederlandsch-Indië* 84 (1928): 595.
37. L.S. Louwes, "Strafrecht", in *Encyclopedië van Nederlandsch-Indië*, 2nd ed. (The Hague: Martinus Nijhoff and E.J. Brill, 1921), p. 133.
38. *Koloniaal Verslag: Bijlage van het Verslag der Handelingen van de Tweede Kamer der Staten-Generaal* (The Hague: Ministerie van Kolonien, 1860–1900), 1860: App. A, p. 43.
39. Ibid., 1868, App. G, pp. 88–9.
40. Ibid., 1889, p. 67; 1900, p. 72.
41. Ibid., 1868, p. 193.
42. Ibid., 1900, pp. 72–3; G. Angoulvant, *Les Indes Néerlandais: Leur Rôle dans l'Économie Internationale* (Paris: Le Monde Nouveau, 1926) 1: 204–5.
43. Angoulvant, *Les Indes Néerlandais*, 1926, 2: 561.
44. *Koloniaal Verslag*, 1889, p. 67.
45. Ibid., 1899, p. 79.
46. Angoulvant, *Les Indes Néerlandais*, 1: 204.

47. James Rush, *Opium to Java: Revenue Farming and Chinese Enterprise in Colonial Indonesia, 1860–1910* (Ithaca, NY: Cornell University Press, 1990), p. 114.
48. Ibid., p. 113.
49. Mailrapporten, "From Batavia to Ministry of Colonies in The Hague" (The Hague: Algemeene Rijksarchief, 1872–1902): 1872/634; 1880/265; (henceforth Mailrapport).
50. Louwes, *Encyclopedië*, p. 147.
51. Elson, "Sugar Factory Workers".
52. Hugh Tinker, *A New System of Slavery: The Export of Indian Labour Overseas, 1830–1920* (London: Oxford University Press, 1974).
53. Anthony Reid, "Early Chinese Migration into North Sumatra", in *Studies in the Social History of China and South-east Asia*, eds. Jerome Ch'en and Nicholas Tarling (Cambridge: Cambridge University Press, 1970), p. 319.
54. The literature on this robust phase of plantation development is extensive, colourful, and often polemical. The liveliest account is the semi-autobiographical novel of Ladislao Szekely, *Tropic Fever* (Kuala Lumpur: Oxford University Press, 1979 [orig. publ. London, 1937]). Scholarly accounts are Breman, 1987; Pelzer, 1978; Stoler, 1985; and Reid, 1970.
55. Mailrapport 1875/338.
56. Ibid., 1877/11, Canne, 19 December 1876.
57. Ibid., 1878/23, 1879/626; Blokzeijl, 22 December 1877, and de Munniek, 22 September 1877.
58. Ibid., 1877/75, 1877/142, Laging Tobias, 15 December 1876, and 1 January 1877.
59. Ibid., 1877/423; Gijsberts, 4 April 1877.
60. Ibid., 1877/434; Blokzeijl, 8 June 1877.
61. Ibid., 1877/456; Versteege, 4 June 1877.
62. Ibid., 1897/438; de Kanter, 5 October 1896.
63. Ibid., 1902/236; Gryzen, 1 January 1902.

Chapter 3

1. Louis Lewin, *Phantastica: Narcotic and Stimulating Drugs, Their Use and Abuse* (London: Routledge and Kegan Paul, 1964), p. 231.
2. Rozy Munir, Budi Otomo and Bambang Sustrino, "Ketagihan Merokok pada Penduduk Desa", *Sinar Harapan*, 23 April 1982.
3. Antonio Galvão, *A Treatise on the Moluccas (c.1544). Probably the Preliminary Version of Antonio Galvao's Lost Historia das Molucas*, ed. H.Th.Th.M. Jacobs (Rome: Jesuit Historical Institute, 1970), p. 57.

4. N.M. Penzer, *Poison-Damsels and Other Essays in Folklore and Anthropology* (London: Chas. Sawyer, 1952), pp. 188–9.
5. Ibid., pp. 109–10.
6. Quoted in B. Terwiel, *The Tai of Assam and Ancient Tai Ritual* (Gaya: Centre for Southeast Asian Studies, 1980), 1: 112.
7. C. Hartwich, "Antwoord No. 19", in *Bidragen tot de Kennis van het Gebruik van Sirih in Nederlandsch-Oost-Indie* [*Contributions to the Knowledge of the Use of Betel in the Dutch East Indies*], *Bulletin van het Koloniaal Museum te Haarlem* 32 (1905): 49–50 (henceforth *BKMH*); Paul Wheatley, *The Golden Khersonese* (Kuala Lumpur: University of Malaya Press, 1961), pp. 52, 56, 78–9.
8. F. Hirth and W.W. Rockhill, eds., *Chau Ju-Kua: His Work on the Chinese and Arab Trade in the Twelfth and Thirteenth Centuries, Entitled Chu-fan-chi* (St Petersburg: 1911; Taipei: Ch'eng Wen, 1970), p. 155. Citations are to the 1911 edition.
9. Ma Huan, *Ying-yai Sheng-lan: 'The Overall Survey of the Ocean's Shores' (1433)*, trans. J.V.G. Mills (Cambridge: Hakluyt Society, 1970), pp. 92–3.
10. Boxer Codex, "The Manners, Customs, and Beliefs of the Philippine Inhabitants of Long Ago, Being Chapters of 'A Late 16th Century Manuscript'", eds. Carlos Quirino and Mauro Garcia, *The Philippine Journal of Science* 87, 4 (1958): 390.
11. Antonio Pigafetta, *First Voyage Round the World*, trans. J.A. Robertson (Manila: Filipiniana Book Guild, 1969), p. 32.
12. Galvão, *A Treatise on the Moluccas*, p. 57.
13. *De eerste schipvaart der Nederlanders naar Oost-Indië onder Cornelis de Houtman 1595–1597*, vol. I, eds. G.P. Rouffaer and J.W. Ijzerman (The Hague: Nijhoff for Linschoten-Vereniging, 1915), p. 115.
14. Galvão, *A Treatise on the Moluccas*, p. 115.
15. W.W. Skeat, *Malay Magic: Being an Introduction to the Folklore and Popular Religion of the Malay Peninsula* (London: 1900; New York: Dover Publications, 1967), pp. 398–402. Citations are to the 1900 edition; G.L. Forth, *Rindi: An Ethnographic Study of a Traditional Domain in Eastern Sumba* (The Hague: Nijhoff, 1981), p. 181; H. Scharer, *Ngaju Religion*, trans. R. Needham (The Hague: Nijhoff, 1905), pp. 68–9.
16. Pedro Chirino, *Relacion de las Islas Filipinas*, trans. B. Echevarria (Manila: Filipiniana Book Guild, 1969), p. 327.
17. For example, Boxer Codex, "The Manners, Customs, and Beliefs of the Philippine Inhabitants", p. 390; L.A.T.J.F. van Oyen, "Antwoord no. 16", *BKMH* 32 (1905): 126.
18. Forth, *Rindi: An Ethnographic Study*, p. 164; Greg Acciaioli, personal communication; field notes, South Sulawesi.

19. R.J. Wilkinson, *A Malay-English Dictionary* (London: MacMillan, 1959), p. 904.
20. Skeat, *Malay Magic*, pl. 14; R.H. Djajadiningrat, *Atjehsch-Nederlandsch Woordenboek* [*Acehnese-Dutch Dictionary*], 2 vols. (Batavia: Landsdrukkerij, 1934), pp. 490–1.
21. Snouck Hurgronje, *The Achehnese*, trans. A.W.S. O'Sullivan (Leiden: Brill, c.1906), 2: 369.
22. Forth, *Rindi: An Ethnographic Study*, p. 360; Liz Coville, personal communication.
23. S. Forman, "Descent Alliance and Exchange Ideology Among the Makassae of East Timor", in *The Flow of Life: Essays on Eastern Indonesia*, ed. J.J. Fox (Cambridge: Harvard University Press, 1980), pp. 162–3.
24. Sastro Winangoen, "Antwoord no. 4", *BKMH* 32 (1905): 134–41; field notes, South Sulawesi.
25. Penzer, *Poison-Damsels and Other Essays*, pp. 261–2.
26. Lenore Manderson, "Roasting, Smoking, and Dieting in Response to Birth: Malay Confinement in Cross-Cultural Perspective", *Social Science and Medicine* 15B (1981): 509–20.
27. James Low, *The British Settlement of Penang* (Singapore: Singapore Free Press, 1836), p. 72.
28. T.S. Raffles, *The History of Java*, 2 vols. (London: 1817; Kuala Lumpur: Oxford University Press, 1978), 1: 204. Citations are to the 1817 edition; also, Carl A. Trocki, *Prince of Pirates: The Temenggongs and the Development of Johor and Singapore, 1784–1885* (Singapore: Singapore University Press, 1979), p. 19.
29. Douglas Miles, *Cutlass and Crescent Moon* (Sydney: Centre for Asian Studies, Sydney University, 1976), p. 35; also, G. Stoll, "Sirih en Sirihkauwers" [Betel and Betel Chewers], *BKMH* 32 (1905): 16.
30. Penzer, *Poison-Damsels and Other Essays*, p. 291.
31. Ibid.; R.N. Chopra, S.L. Nayar and I.C. Chopra, *Glossary of Indian Medicinal Plants* (New Delhi: Council of Scientific and Industrial Research, 1956), p. 23; H. Jüptner, "Klinisch-experimentelle Beobachtungen über Intensives Betalkauen bei den Eingeborenen der Trobriand-Inseln (Neu-Guinea)" [Clinical-experimental Observations on Intensive Betel Chewing Among the Natives of the Trobriand Islands (New Guinea)], *Zeitschrift für Tropenmedizin und Parasitologie* [*Journal for Tropical Medicine and Parasitology*] 19, 2 (1968): 254–7; A.J. Porsius, E. Mutschler and P.A. van Swieten, "The Central Action of Various Arecaidine Esters (Arecoline Derivatives) on Blood Pressure and Heart Rate in the Cat", *Arzneim.-Forsch* 28, 8 (1978): 1373–6.
32. Lewin, *Phantastica: Narcotic and Stimulating Drugs*, p. 239; Penzer 1952: 291; William Emboden, *Narcotic Plants* (London: Studio Vista, 1979), p. 146; B.G. Burton-Bradley, "Papua and New Guinea Transcultural Psychiatry:

Some Implications of Betel Chewing", *Medical Journal of Australia* 2 (1966): 746.
33. Emboden, *Narcotic Plants*, p. 35.
34. G.A.R. Johnston, P. Korgsgaard-Larsen and A. Stephenson, "Betel Nut Constituents as Inhibitors of γ-Aminobutyric Acid Uptake", *Nature* 258 (1975): 627–8; D. Lodge, *et al.*, "Effects of the *Areca* Nut Constituents Arecadaine and Guvacine on the Action of GABA in the Cat Central Nervous System", *Brain Research* 136 (1977): 513–22; O. Nieschultz, "The Pharmacology of Betel Nuts" *Arzneim.-Forsch* 20 (1970): 218–9.
35. M.E. Stricherz and P. Pratt, "Betel Quid and Reaction Time", *Pharmacology Biochemistry and Behaviour* 4 (1976): 627–8.
36. C.C. Brown, trans., "Sejarah Melayu or 'Malay Annals'", *Journal of the Malayan Branch of the Royal Asiatic Society* 25 (1952): 78.
37. G.W.J. Drewes, ed., *Hikajat Potjut Muhamat: An Acehnese Epic* (The Hague: Nijhoff, 1979), pp. 223–5.
38. Tomé Pires, *The Suma Oriental*, trans. A. Cortesão (London: Hakluyt Society, 1944), p. 516.
39. James Bontius, *An Account of the Diseases, Natural History, and Medicines of the East Indies* (London: Donaldson, 1776), pp. 190–2.
40. N.M. Penzer, *Poison-Damsels and Other Essays in Folklore and Anthropology* (London: Chas. Sawyer, 1952), pp. 291–5.
41. R.G. Schamschula, B.L. Adkins, D.E. Barmes, G. Charlton, "Betel Chewing and Caries Experience in New Guinea", *Community Dentistry and Oral Epidemiology* 5, 6 (1977): 284–6.
42. I.J. Möller, J.J. Pindborg and I. Effendi, "The Relation between Betel Chewing and Dental Caries", *Scandinavian Journal of Dental Research* 85 (1977): 64–70.
43. Möller, Pindborg and Effendi, "The Relation between Betel Chewing and Dental Caries"; Ram S. Nanda and Krishna Kapoor, "Fluoride Content of Piper Betel and Its Constituents", *Indian Journal of Medical Research* 59 (1971): 1966–70.
44. R.G. Bachand, "Betel-chewing: Some Observations of the Habit among the Vietnamese", *Dental Student's Magazine*, April 1967.
45. Penzer, *Poison-Damsels and Other Essays*, pp. 197, 222, citing Linschoten and Garcia da Orta; F. de Haan, *Oud Batavia* (Batavia: G. Kolff, 1922), 2: 145.
46. Hirth and Rockhill, eds., *Chau Ju-Kua: His Work*, p. 214.
47. Lewin, *Phantastica: Narcotic and Stimulating Drugs*, pp. 240–1.
48. H.R. Rookmaker, "Antwoord no. 18", p. 20.
49. Edmund Scott, "An Exact Discourse of the East Indians", in *The Voyage of Sir Henry Middleton to the Moluccas, 1604–1606*, ed. W. Foster (London:

Hakluyt Society, 1943), p. 173; da Orta, quoted in Penzer, *Poison-Damsels and Other Essays*, p. 192.
50. Linschoten, quoted in Penzer, *Poison-Damsels and Other Essays*, p. 221; D. Schoute, *De geneeskunde in den Dienst der Oost-Indische Compagnie in Nederlandsch-Indie* (Amsterdam: de Bussy, 1929), pp. 107–8.
51. K.N. Arjungi, "Areca Nut: A Review", *Arzneim.-Forsch* 26 (1976): 955.
52. Ibid.
53. Pires, *The Suma Oriental*, p. 516.
54. Penzer, *Poison-Damsels and Other Essays*, pp. 223, 226, 298; R.N. Chopra, S.L. Nayar and I.C. Chopra, *Glossary of Indian Medicinal Plants* (New Delhi: Council of Scientific and Industrial Research, 1956), p. 23.
55. Hsia Liang Lin, "Betelnut as a Useful Taeniafuge", *Chinese Medical Journal* 50 (1937); W.C. Chung and B.C. Ko, "Treatment of Taenia Saginata Infection with Mixture of Areca Nuts and Pumpkin Seeds", *Chinese Journal of Microbiology* 9 (1976): 31–5; Chopra, Nayar and Chopra, *Glossary of Indian Medicinal Plants*, p. 23.
56. Sastro Winangoen, "Antwoord no. 4", p. 14; Chopra, Nayar and Chopra, *Glossary of Indian Medicinal Plants*, p. 194; field notes.
57. Rookmaker, "Antwoord no. 18", p. 37; Nguyen Duc Minh, "Medicinal Plants with Anti-Bacterial Properties", *Vietnamese Studies* 50 (n.d.): 52, 68.
58. A. de Beaulieu, "Mémoires du Voyage aux Indes Orientales du General Beaulieu, dressés par luy-mesme", in *Relations de Divers Voyages Curieux*, vol. 2, ed. Melchisedech Thévenot (Paris: Cramoisy, 1666), p. 102; John Crawfurd, *History of the Indian Archipelago*, 3 vols. (Edinburgh: Constable, 1820), pp. 1, 31.
59. Rookmaker, "Antwoord no. 18", pp. 37–8; Sastro Winangoen, "Antwoord no. 4", pp. 134–41; Chopra, Nayar and Chopra, *Glossary of Indian Medicinal Plants*, p. 194.
60. Nguyen Duc Minh, "Medicinal Plants", pp. 68–9.
61. For example, S.V. Kandarkar and S.M. Sirsat, "Changes in Vitamin A Conditioned Hamster Cheek Pouch Epithelium on Exposure to Commercial Shell Lime (Calcium Hydroxide) and Tobacco", *Journal of Oral Pathology* 6, 4 (1977): 19–202; D. Reed, "Current Status of Cancer Studies in the South Pacific", *National Cancer Institute Monograph* 47 (1977): 61–6; G.J. Kapadia, *et al.*, "Carcinogenicity of Some Folk Medicinal Herbs in Rats", *Journal of the National Cancer Institute* 60, 3 (1978): 683–6; K.J. Ranadive, S.V. Gothoskar, A.R. Rao, B.U. Tezabwalla and R.Y Ambaye, "Experimental Studies on Betel Nut and Tobacco Carcinogenicity", *International Journal of Cancer* 17, 4 (1976): 469–76.
62. E.H. Blair, and J.A. Robertson, eds., *The Philippine Islands, 1493–1898*, 55 vols. (Cleveland: Arthur H. Clark, 1903), 5: 116–7.

63. R. van Goens, *De Vijf Gezantschapsreizen van Rijklof van Goens naar het Hof van Mataram, 1648–1654* [The Five Missions of Rijklof van Goens to the Court of Mataram], ed. H.J. de Graaf ('s-Gravenhage: Nijhoff, 1956), p. 180.
64. John O'Kane, ed., *The Ship of Sulaiman* (London: Routledge and Kegan Paul, 1972), p. 179.
65. William Marsden, *A History of Sumatra* (London: Longman, 1811; Kuala Lumpur, 1966), p. 44.
66. M. de la Bissachère, *Etat Actuel du Tonkin, de la Cochinchine, et des Royaumes de Cambodge, Laos et Lac-Tho* (Paris: Galignani, 1812; Westmead, 1971), 1: 63–8.
67. M. Brugière, "Notices of the Religion, Manners, and Customs of the Siamese", *Chinese Repository* 8 (1844): 191.
68. Scott, "An Exact Discourse", p. 173.
69. M.C. Ricklefs, *Modern Javanese Historical Tradition: A Study of the Original Kartasura Chronicle and Related Materials* (London: School of Oriental and African Studies, 1978), p. 29.
70. Van Goens, *De Vijf Gezantschapsreizen*, p. 257.
71. Ibid., p. 235.
72. C.J. van Lookeren Campagne, "Tabak" [Tobacco], *Encyclopaedie van Nederlandsch-Indië*, The Hague, Brill, 4 (1905): 230–1; also, Raffles, *The History of Java*, 1:134.
73. J.S. Stavorinus, *Voyage to the East Indies*, trans. S.H. Wilcocke, 3 vols. (London: 1798; London: Dawsons of Pall Mall, 1969), 1: 245.
74. de Haan, *Oud Batavia*, 2: 135; van Lookeren Campagne, "Tabak", p. 222.
75. G.L. Apperson, *The Social History of Smoking* (London: Martin Secker, 1914), pp. 89–91.
76. van Lookeren Campagne, "Tabak", p. 231.
77. de Haan, *Oud Batavia*, 2: 25.
78. H. Yule and A.C. Burnell, *Hobson-Jobson: A Glossary of Colloquial Anglo Indian Words and* Phrases (London: 1903; New Delhi: 1979), pp. 126, 188.
79. Marsden, *A History of Sumatra*, p. 283; Teuku Iskandar, *Kamus Dewan* [*Dictionary of the Dewan*] (Kuala Lumpur: Dewan Bahasa dan Pustaka, 1970), p. 973.
80. Field notes; J.E.A. McNair, *Perak and the Malays* (London: 1878; Kuala Lumpur: Oxford University Press, 1972), p. 182.
81. Raffles, *The History of Java*, 1: 10.
82. James Rush, "Opium in Java: A Sinister Friend", *Journal of Asian Studies* 3 (1985): 549–60.
83. *De Eerste Schipvaart der Nederlanders naar Oost-Indië onder Cornelis de Houtman*, vol. 1, eds. G.P. Rouffaer and J.W. Ijzerman (The Hague: Nijhoff, 1915), pp. 112, 152.

84. Yule and Burnell, *Hobson-Jobson: A Glossary*, p. 363.
85. Marah Maradjo, *Tanaman Penyegar* [*Refreshing Plants*]: *Flora Indonesia Jilid 1* (Jakarta: Nusantara, 1977), p. 15.
86. Trocki, *Prince of Pirates*, pp. 19–20; Raja Ali Haji ibn Ahmad, *The Precious Gift: Tuhfat al-Nafis*, trans. Virginia Matheson and Barbara Andaya (Kuala Lumpur: Oxford University Press, 1982), pp. 90–1.
87. Crawfurd, *History of the Indian Archipelago*, 1: 406.
88. van Lookeren Campagne, "Tabak", pp. 222–3.
89. Marsden, *A History of Sumatra*, p. 283; Stavorinus, *Voyage to the East Indies*, 1: 245.
90. Crawfurd, *History of the Indian Archipelago*, 1: 105; cf. Raffles, *The History of Java*, 1: 101.
91. de Haan, *Oud Batavia*, 2: 145.
92. de Haan, *Oud Batavia*, 2: 135; Apperson, *The Social History of Smoking*, pp. 179–91.
93. G. Verschuur, quoted in van Oyen, "Antwoord no. 16", pp. 128–9.
94. A.J.A.F. Eerdmans, "Het Landschap Gowa", *Verhandeling van het Bataviaasch Genootschap* 50, 3 (1897): 57.
95. P.J. Veth, *Java, Geographisch, Ethnologisch, Historisch*, vol. 1 (Haarlem: E. F. Bohn, 1875), p. 547; van Oyen, "Antwoord no. 16", p. 128.
96. Rookmaker, "Antwoord no. 18", p. 29.
97. P. Creutzberg, ed., *Het Ekonomisch Beleid in Nederlandsch-Indie. Capita Selecta. Een Bronnenpublikatie* [*Economic Policy in Netherlands India. Selections. A Sourcebook*] (Groningen: Tjeenk Willink, 1975), pp. i, 265–72.
98. Parada Harahap, *Indonesia Sekarang* [*Indonesia Now*] (Jakarta: Bulan Bintang, 1952), pp. 144–5; W.A.I.M. Segers, "De Strootjes Industrie in Nederlandsch-Indie: Een Reddingsboei voor Een Bevolkings Economie in Nood" [The Native Cigarette Industry in Netherlands India: A Lifebuoy for a Popular Economy in Need] (MA thesis, University of Amsterdam, 1982), Bijl 2–6.
99. Segers, "De Strootjes Industrie in Nederlandsch-Indie", Bijl 57.
100. Spenser St John, *Life in the Forests of the Far East*, 2 vols. (London: 1862; Kuala Lumpur: Oxford University Press, 1974), 1: 50. Citations are to the 1862 edition.
101. Rosemary Firth, *Housekeeping Among Malay Peasants* (London: London School of Economics, 1943), p. 74.
102. Peter Metcalf, *A Borneo Journey into Death: Berawan Eschatology from Its Rituals* (Philadelphia: University of Pennsylvania Press, 1982), pp. 41–2.
103. <http://www.litbang.depkes.go.id/tobaccofree/media/FactSheet/FactEng/consumpprev_nov10.pdf>; World Health Organization, *The Tobacco Atlas* (2004), at <http://WHO.int/tobacco/en/atlas40>.

104. Patung, "Cigarette Production and Consumption", *Business and Economy*, 22 December 2006, at <http://www.indonesiamatters.com/1021/cigarette-production-consumption> [accessed 6 June 2010].
105. *Kretek* manufacturers revealed that 1,000 *kretek* cigarettes contain on average 1.2kg tobacco, 0.8kg dried clove flowers, 743g Vaniline crystals, 417g Coumarine crystals, and 330g Saccharine crystals (*Indonesia Raya*, 2 June 1970, Special Supplement).
106 S.S. Abeyasekere, "Slaves in Batavia: Insights from a Slave Register", in *Slavery, Bondage, and Dependency in Southeast Asia*, ed. Anthony Reid (St Lucia: University of Queensland Press, 1983), p. 308.
107. Rookmaker, "Antwoord no. 18", p. 30.
108. Van Niel, *Living Conditions of Plantation Workers in 1939–1940: Final Report of the Coolie Budget Commission* (Ithaca, NY: Cornell University Modern Indonesia Project, 1956), pp. 78, 92–3
109. SUSENAS, *Survei Sosial Ekonomi Nasional* [*National Socio-economic Survey*] (Jakarta: Biro Pusat Statistik, 1980), pp. 32–3, 116–7, 184–5.

Chapter 4

1. The first Growth Triangle in 1989 aspired to link Singapore with Malaysian Johor and Indonesian Riau (hence SIJORI), and had some success in making Indonesian Batam a workshop for Singapore firms. The second (IMT-GT), agreed in Langkawi 1993, sought to link North Sumatra and Aceh with Malaysia's Penang and Kedah and the five southernmost provinces of Thailand, but was dogged by the instability of these areas.
2. O.W. Wolters, *History, Culture and Region in Southeast Asian Perspectives* (Singapore: Institute of Southeast Asian Studies, 1982), p. 24.
3. A. Milner, *Kerajaan; Malay Political Culture on the Eve of Colonial Rule* (Tucson: University of Arizona Press, 1982), p. 27.
4. A. Cortesão, ed., *The Suma Oriental of Tomé Pires* (London: Hakluyt Society, 1944 [orig. publ. 1515]), p. 182.
5. L. Blussé, *Strange Company: Chinese Settlers, Mestizo Women and the Dutch in VOC Batavia* (Dordrecht/Providence: Foris, 1986), p. 123; Ng Chin Keong, "The Case of Ch'en I-lao; Maritime Trade and Overseas Chinese in Ch'ing Policies, 1717–1754", in *Emporia, Commodities and Entrepreneurs in Asian Maritime Trade, c.1400–1750*, eds. R. Ptak and D. Rothermund (Stuttgart: Franz Steiner, 1991), p. 381.
6. The Mongol invasion of Java in 1293 is briefly discussed in Anthony Reid, "Flows and Seepages in the Long-term Chinese Interaction with Southeast Asia", in *Sojourners and Settlers: Histories of Southeast Asia and the Chinese*, ed. Reid (Sydney: Allen & Unwin, 1996), pp. 17–20.

7. B. Watson Andaya, *To Live as Brothers: Southeast Sumatra in the Seventeenth and Eighteenth Centuries* (Honolulu: University of Hawai'i Press, 1993), p. 194.
8. A. Kumar, "Javanese Historiography in and of the 'Colonial Period': A Case Study", in *Perceptions of the Past in Southeast Asia*, eds. A.J.S. Reid and D. Marr (Singapore: Heinemann, 1979), p. 197 n.
9. E. Jacobs, "Van nood, deugd en handelspolitiek; Intra-Aziatische handel en scheepvaart van de VOC in the tweede helft van de achttiende eeuw; Een verkenning" (MA thesis, University of Leiden, 1985), pp. 9–10.
10. R. Laarhoven, "The Power of Cloth: The Textile Trade of the Dutch East India Company (VOC), 1600–1780" (PhD thesis, Australian National University, 1994), p. 296.
11. Blussé, *Strange Company*, p. 123; A.J.S. Reid, "The Unthreatening Alternative: Chinese Shipping in Southeast Asia, 1567–1842", *Review of Indonesian and Malaysian Affairs* 27 (1993): 13–32, 24–8.
12. J.L. van Zanden, "The Dutch Economy in the Very Long Run: Growth in Production, Energy Consumption and Capital in Holland (1500–1805) and the Netherlands", in *Explaining Economic Growth: Essays in Honour of Angus Maddison*, eds. A. Szirmai, B. van Ark and D. Pilat (Amsterdam: North-Holland, 1993), pp. 267–83.
13. Wong Lin Ken, "The Trade of Singapore, 1819–1869", *Journal of the Malaysian Branch of the Royal Asiatic Society* 33, 4 (1960): 301.
14. Ibid., pp. 219–30; cf. Altes W.L. Korthals, *General Trade Statistics, 1822–1940, Changing Economy in Indonesia*, vol. 12A (Amsterdam: Royal Tropical Institute, 1991), pp. 40–1.
15. A. van der Kraan, "Bali and Lombok in the World Economy, 1830–1850", *Review of Indonesian and Malaysian Affairs* 27 (1993): 97–9.
16. A.J.S. Reid, *The Contest for North Sumatra: Acheh, the Netherlands and Britain, 1858–1898* (Kuala Lumpur: Oxford University Press, 1969), p. 294.
17. This battle to privilege Dutch over cheaper British manufactured cloth is analyzed in Alfons van der Kraan, *Contest for the Java Cotton Trade, 1811–1840: An Episode in Anglo-Dutch Rivalry* (Centre for Southeast Asian Studies, Occasional Papers Series No. 32, University of Hull, 1998); and Anthony Reid, "Southeast Asian Consumption of British and Indian Cotton Cloth, 1600–1850", in *How India Clothed the World: The World of South Asian Textiles, 1500–1850*, eds. Om Prakash, Giorgio Riello, Tirthankar Roy and Kaoru Sugihara (The Hague: Brill, 2009), pp. 31–52.
18. Korthals Altes, *General Trade Statistics*, pp. 87–90, 100–3.
19. I. Nørlund, "The French Empire, the Colonial State in Vietnam and Economic Policy, 1885–1940", *Australian Economic History Review* 31 (1991): 83.
20. Reid, *The Contest for North Sumatra*, p. 38.

21. Ibid., p. 49.
22. H.J. Marks, *The First Contest for Singapore, 1819–1824* (The Hague: KITLV, 1959), pp. 252–62.
23. Reid, *The Contest for North Sumatra*, pp. 116, 129–39.
24. A.J.S. Reid, "Nineteenth-century Pan-Islam in Indonesia and Malaysia", *Journal of Asian Studies* 27 (1967): 271.
25. Reid, *The Contest for North Sumatra*, pp. 61–2.
26. Ibid., pp. 161–6.
27. Algemeen Rijks Archief (The Hague: Koloniën, Kab. I 14, 6154), Letter Van Eyk to Van Rees, 23 July 1884.
28. Reid, *The Contest for North Sumatra*, pp. 187–249.
29. Ibid., pp. 261, 268–9.
30. J.N.F.M. à Campo, "Steam Navigation and State Formation" in *The Late Colonial State in Indonesia: Political and Economic Foundations of the Netherlands Indies, 1880–1942*, ed. R. Cribb (Leiden: KITLV Press, 1994), pp. 11–30.
31. E. Gobee and C. Adriaanse, eds., *Ambtelijke adviezen van C. Snouck Hurgronje, 1889–1936* (The Hague: Nijhoff, 1957), pp. 115–6.
32. Campo, "Steam Navigation", p. 18.
33. Reid, *The Contest for North Sumatra*, pp. 275–9; J.M. Somer, *De Korte Verklaring* (Breda: Corona, 1934), pp. 248–88.
34. Campo, "Steam Navigation", p. 21.
35. A.J. Piekaar, *Atjeh en de oorlog met Japan* (The Hague: Van Hoeve, 1949), pp. 63–188; Anthony Reid, *The Blood of the People: Revolution and the End of Traditional Rule in Northern Sumatra* (Kuala Lumpur: Oxford University Press, 1979), pp. 84–93.
36. Twang Peck Yang, *The Chinese Business Elite in Indonesia and the Transition to Independence, 1940–1950* (Kuala Lumpur: Oxford University Press, 1998), pp. 70–116.
37. Michael van Langenberg, "National Revolution in North Sumatra, Sumatera Timur and Tapanuli, 1942–1950" (PhD thesis, University of Sydney, 1976), pp. 527–61.
38. Twang, *Chinese Business Elite*, pp. 140–1.
39. Ibid., pp. 203–12.
40. Ibid, pp. 127–42.
41. Van Langenberg, "National Revolution", p. 530.
42. Twang, *Chinese Business Elite*, pp. 240–1; Yong Mun Cheong, *The Indonesian Revolution and the Singapore Connection, 1945–1949* (Leiden: KITLV Press, 2003), p. 186.
43. Twang, *Chinese Business Elite*, pp. 238, 284–5.
44. Twang, *Chinese Business Elite*, p. 201.

45. *Colony of Singapore Annual Report* (Singapore: Government Printing Office, 1948), pp. 53–7.
46. Twang, *Chinese Business Elite*, pp. 184–5, 291–7.
47. "Curtains for the Singapore Connection" is the title of the final chapter, covering 1949, of Yong, *The Indonesian Revolution*, pp. 175–97.
48. *Statistical Pocketbook of Indonesia* (Jakarta: Biro Pusat Statistik, 1961), p. 109.
49. Republik Indonesia, *Statistik Perdagangan Luar Negeri: Expor* – Volumes for 1995, p. xli, and 2007, pp. xxx–xxxi.
50. Bill Guerin, "Indonesia-Singapore Gap more than Just Numbers", *Asia Times Online*, 27 June 2003, at <http://www.atimes.com>.
51. Erwiza Erman, "Rethinking Legal and Illegal Economy: A Case Study of Tin Mining in Bangka Island", *Southeast Asia: History and Culture* 37 (May 2008): 91–111.
52. Figures from Indexmundi.
53. Erwiza Erman, "Rethinking", p. 107.
54. Erwiza Erman, "Rethinking", pp. 91–2.

Chapter 5

1. I acknowledge with gratitude the contribution of the late Abdurrahman Surjomihardjo to the conception of this chapter, and to M.C. Ricklefs, Helen Creese, Amrih Widodo and A.C. Milner for their contributions.
2. From a manuscript in K'tut Tantri's private papers, as cited in Timothy Lindsey, *The Romance of K'tut Tantri and Indonesia* (Kuala Lumpur: Oxford University Press, 1977), pp. 232–3.
3. David Brion Davis, *Slavery and Human Progress* (New York: Oxford University Press, 1984), p. 111.
4. Perry Anderson, *Passages from Antiquity to Feudalism* (London: Verso, 1978), pp. 1–23; Moses I. Finley, "Slavery", in *International Encyclopedia of the Social Sciences* (New York: Crowell, Collier and Macmillan, 1968), p. 308.
5. E.S. Morgan, *American Slavery — American Freedom: The Ordeal of Colonial Virginia* (New York: Norton, 1975).
6. Orlando Patterson, *Freedom in the Making of Western Culture* (New York: Basic Books, 1991), pp. 9, 20, 41, 32.
7. Anthony Reid, ed., *Slavery, Bondage and Dependency in Southeast Asia* (Brisbane: University of Queensland Press, 1983), p. 21.
8. I use the modern Indonesian and Malaysian word "merdeka" without italics as the general term, leaving variants in various languages of the Archipelago in italics.

9. P.J. Zoetmulder, *Old Javanese-English Dictionary* (The Hague: Nijhoff, 1982), p. 1086. Th.G.Th. Pigeaud, *Java in the Fourteenth Century. A Study in Cultural History* (The Hague: Nijhoff, 1960–1963), vol. 3, p. 110; 4, p. 331.
10. K.R. Hall, "State and Statecraft in Early Sri Vijaya", in *Explorations in Early Southeast Asian History: The Origins of Southeast Asian Statecraft* (Ann Arbor: University of Michigan Center for South and Southeast Asian Studies, 1976), pp. 71, 99.
11. Denys Lombard, *Le 'Spraeck ende Woord-boek' de Frederick de Houtman: Première Méthode de Malais Parlé (fin du XVIe s.)* (Paris: EFEO, 1970), p. 215.
12. M.C. Ricklefs, *The Seen and Unseen Worlds in Java* (New South Wales: Allen & Unwin; Honolulu: University of Hawai'i Press, 1998). The 1847 *Javaansch-Nederduitsch Woordenboek* of Gericke and Roorda did not even derive *pardikan* from *Maharddhika*, but from *wartika* = proclamation. Later dictionaries always associated *pardikan* with *mardika*, and derived both from *Maharddhika*. I owe this information to Merle Ricklefs and Helen Creese.
13. The most *famous pardikan desa*, Tegalsari, was given this privileged status in 1742 in return for the spiritual assistance to the king of the holy mystic who lived there. Claude Guillot, "Le Rôle Historique des *Perdikan* ou Villages Francs: Le Cas de Tegalsari", *Archipel* 30 (1985): 137–62.
14. John Crawfurd, *History of the Indian Archipelago* (Edinburgh: Archibald Constable, 1820), 3: 43.
15. Benedict Anderson, "A Time of Darkness and a Time of Light: Transposition in Early Indonesian Nationalist Thought", in *Perceptions of the Past in Southeast Asia*, eds. Anthony Reid and David Marr (Singapore: Heinemann, 1979), p. 245.
16. Cited by C. Fasseur, "The French Scare: Taco Roorda and the Origins of Javanese Studies in the Netherlands", in *Looking in Odd Mirrors: The Java Sea*, eds. V.J.H. Houben, H.M.J. Maier and W. van der Molen (Leiden: Vakgroep Talen en Culturen van Zuidoost Azië en Oceanie, 1992), pp. 249–50.
17. James L. Watson, ed., *Asian and African Systems of Slavery* (Berkeley, CA: University of California Press, 1980), pp. 9–13; Reid, *Slavery, Bondage and Dependency*, pp. 156–81.
18. Liaw Yock Fang, *Undang-undang Melaka. The Laws of Melaka* (The Hague: Nijhoff for KITLV, 1976), pp. 74–6.
19. Ibid., p. 154.
20. *Adatrechtbundels* (The Hague: Nijhoff, 1910–1955), 17: 169–70.
21. *Adatrechtbundels*, 9: 277; B.F. Matthes, *Boegineesch-Hollandsch Woordenboek* ('s-Gravenhage: Nijhoff, 1874), p. 260.
22. Derek Freeman, *Some Reflections on the Nature of Iban Society* (Canberra: Department of Anthropology, Australian National University, 1981), pp. 43–9.

23. Reid, *Slavery, Bondage and Dependency*, pp. 166–9; Reid, *Southeast Asia in the Age of Commerce*, vol. 1, *The Lands below the Winds* (New Haven, CT: Yale University Press, 1988), pp. 132–6.
24. James C. Scott, "Freedom and Freehold: Space, People and State Simplification in Southeast Asia", in *Asian Freedoms: The Idea of Freedom in East and Southeast Asia*, eds. David Kelly and Anthony Reid (Cambridge: Cambridge University Press, 1998).
25. William Collins, "Besemah Concepts: A Study of the Culture of a People of South Sumatra" (PhD diss., University of California, Berkeley, 1979), pp. 90–3.
26. Rombouts, 1870, cited in ibid., pp. 93–4.
27. Gromberg, 1865, cited in ibid., p. 94.
28. Reid, *Age of Commerce*, 2: 251–66.
29. Leonard Andaya, *The Heritage of Arung Palakka: A History of South Sulawesi (Celebes) in the Seventeenth Century* (The Hague: Nijhoff for KITLV, 1981), pp. 11–5.
30. Speelman, Notitie II, p. 117, cited in Reid, "Kings, Kadis and Charisma in the Seventeenth Century Archipelago", in *The Making of an Islamic Political Discourse in Southeast Asia*, ed. Anthony Reid (Melbourne: Monash University Centre for SE Asian Studies, 1993).
31. J. Noorduyn, "Arung Singkang (1700–1765): How the Victory of Wadjo Began", *Indonesia* 13 (1972): 62; cf. Andaya, *Arung Palakka*, p. 111.
32. Andi Zainal Abidin, *Wajo' pada Abad XV–XVI. Suatu Penggalian Sejarah Terpendam Sulawesi Selatan dari Lontara* (Bandung: Penerbit Alumni, 1985), p. v.; cf. ibid, p. 115; Christian Pelras, "Hiérarchie et Pouvoir Traditionnel en Pays Wajo", *Archipel* 1 (1971): 174.
33. Zainal Abidin, *Wajo'*, p. 148.
34. Zainal Abidin, *Wajo'*, pp. 93–4, 122–4; J. Noorduyn, *Een achttiende-eeuwse kroniek van Wadjo': Buginese historiografie* (The Hague: Smits, 1955), p. 54; Pelras, "Hiérarchie", pp. 170–4.
35. Zainal Abidin, *Wajo'*, pp. 135–6; cf. Pelras, "Hiérarchie", p. 174.
36. Pelras, "Hiérarchie", p. 174.
37. R. Mundy, *Narrative of Events in Borneo and Celebes Down to the Occupation of Labuan: From the Journals of James Brooke, Esq. Rajah of Sarawak. Together with a Narrative of the Operations of H.M.S. Iris* (London: 1848), pp. 65–6.
38. Susan Abeyasekere, *Jakarta: A History* (Singapore: Oxford University Press, 1987), pp. 19–31; Leonard Blussé, *Strange Company: Chinese Settlers, Mestizo Women and the Dutch in VOC Batavia* (Dordrecht: Foris for KITLV, 1986), p. 165; Paramita Abdurrachman, "Portuguese Presence in Jakarta", Paper presented to the Sixth IAHA Conference, Yogyakarta, Indonesia, August 1974.

39. Reid, *Slavery, Bondage and Dependency*, pp. 29–30; Abeyasekere, *Jakarta*, pp. 19–65.
40. Reid, *Slavery, Bondage and Dependency*, pp. 30–1. The quotation is from John Anderson, 1826.
41. My translation from the romanised text in R.A. Datoek Besar and R. Roolvink, eds., *Hikajat Abdullah* (Jakarta: Djambatan, 1953), pp. 234–5. A full English translation is "The Hikayat Abdullah", trans. A.H. Hill, *Journal of the Malayan Branch of Royal Asiatic Society* 28, pt. 3 (1955 [orig. publ. 1849]): 161–3.
42. *Hikajat Abdullah*, pp. 294–5; cf. Hill translation, p. 195.
43. Anthony Milner, *The Invention of Politics in Colonial Malaya: Contesting Nationalism and the Expansion of the Public Sphere* (Cambridge: Cambridge University Press, 1994), pp. 31, 82.
44. William Marsden, *A Dictionary and Grammar of the Malayan Language* (1812, reprinted Singapore: Oxford University Press, 1984), pp. 451, 482.
45. John Crawfurd, *Grammar and Dictionary of the Malay Language*, vol. 2 (London: 1852), p. 113.
46. R.J. Wilkinson, *A Malay-English Dictionary (Romanised)* (London: Macmillan, 1959 [orig. publ. 1903]), p. 768.
47. Roorda van Eysinga, *Algemeen Nederduitsch-Maleisch Woordenboek* (Leiden: Gualph Kolff, 1853), pp. 1000–1. This pioneering dictionary was revised by Grashuis in 1878 without significant change to these terms, while Klinkert's more popular 20th-century dictionaries also borrowed heavily from their predecessors.
48. "*Merdaheka* Skr., also pronounced as *merdika*, a spiritual leader or priest, who is freed from corvée obligations; free from slavery or service obligations" [my translation of the entry in its entirety], H.C. Klinkert, *Nieuw Maleisch-Nederlandsch Woordenboek*, 5th ed. (Leiden: Brill, 1947), p. 975. The more subversive connotations of merdeka in the Straits Settlements than in Netherlands India in the 19th century, at least as suggested by these dictionaries, provides an interesting contrast to post-1957 Malaya/Malaysia, which was more successful than Indonesia in limiting the term to national independence.
49. Examples of the ideologies of these 19th-century struggles are Sartono Kartodirdjo, *The Peasants' Revolt of Banten in 1888. Its Conditions, Course and Sequel* (The Hague: Nijhoff for KITLV, 1966), especially pp. 341–3; Ibrahim Alfian, *Perang di Jalan Allah: Perang Aceh 1873–1912* (Jakarta: Pustaka Sinar Harapan, 1987), pp. 105–50; Peter Carey, *Babad Dipanegara: An Account of the Outbreak of the Java War (1825–30)* (Kuala Lumpur: MBRAS, 1981), especially pp. xxxix–xlvii.
50. Ruth T. McVey, *The Rise of Indonesian Communism* (Ithaca, NY: Cornell University Press, 1965), p. 176.
51. Takashi Shiraishi, *An Age in Motion: Popular Radicalism in Java, 1912–1926* (Ithaca, NY: Cornell University Press, 1990), p. 34.

52. A.K. Pringgodigdo, *Sedjarah Pergerakan Rakjat Indonesia*, 1949, 5th ed. (Jakarta: Pustaka Rakjat, 1964), p. 30.
53. Communist speaker in Sawah Lunto, West Sumatra, 1926, as translated by Ruth McVey, "The Enchantment of the Revolution: History and Action in an Indonesian Communist Text", in *Perceptions of the Past*, eds. Reid and Marr, p. 340.
54. "merasa merdika artinya merasa 'selamat' dan 'ayem'", *Hikayat Kadirun*, p. 92. I owe this reference to Semaun's novel to Amrih Widodo, to whom I am grateful for other insights into Javanese rural ideas.
55. Shiraishi, *Age in Motion*, p. 246; Benedict Anderson, *Language and Power: Exploring Political Cultures in Indonesia* (Ithaca, NY: Cornell University Press, 1990), pp. 235–7. These two authors attribute the 1924 novel *Rasa Merdika* to Soemantri, whereas earlier writers usually ascribed it to Mas Marco Kartodikromo, another SI/PKI journalist and politician; see A. Teeuw, *Modern Indonesian Literature* (The Hague: KITLV, 1967), p. 16.
56. Shiraishi, *Age in Motion*, p. 165.
57. Gati Semarang [pseud.], "Kemerdeka'an", in *Rasa-Doenia* (Jogjakarta, 1923).
58. Cited Shiraishi, *Age in Motion*, pp. 324–5.
59. Quoted in *Pedoman Rakyat* (2 May 1981).
60. Kenji Tsuchiya, *Democracy and Leadership: The Rise of the Taman Siswa Movement in Indonesia* (Honolulu: University of Hawai'i Press, 1987), especially pp. 55–63.
61. Quoted in Denys Lombard, *Le Carrefour Javanais: Essai d'Histoire Globale*, 3 vols. (Paris: EHESS, 1990), 3: 125, 185.
62. Benedict Anderson, *Java in a Time of Revolution, Occupation and Resistance, 1944–1946* (Ithaca, NY: Cornell University Press, 1972), p. 126.
63. Anton Lucas, *One Soul One Struggle: Region and Revolution in Indonesia* (Sydney: Allen & Unwin, 1991), p. 157.
64. Ibid., p. 158.

Chapter 6

1. This chapter is a revised version of two essays: "The Nationalist Quest for an Indonesian Past", in *Perceptions of the Past in Southeast Asia*, eds. Anthony Reid and David Marr (Singapore: Heinemann [Asia] for Asian Studies Association of Australia), pp. 281–98, and "Writing the History of Independent Indonesia", in *Nation-Building: Five Southeast Asian Histories*, ed. Wang Gungwu (Singapore: Institute of Southeast Asian Studies, 2005), pp. 69–89.
2. Review by Darmawidjaja in *Poedjangga Baroe* 6 (1938–1939): 99. Eijkman and Stapel, *Leerboek der Geschiedenis van Nederlandsch Oost-Indie*, was the standard text for senior secondary schools (AMS), in its ninth edition in 1939. An abbreviated version of it for lower secondary schools (MULO)

was in its 16th edition. Soedjatmoko et al., *An Introduction to Indonesian Historiography* (Ithaca, NY: Cornell University Press, 1965), p. 1a.
3. Abdul Hadi bin Hajj Hasan, *Sejarah Alam Melayu*, Penggal I (Singapore: Printed for the Dept. of Education by Malaysia Pub. House, 1925).
4. E.F.E. Douwes Dekker, *Ichtisar Riwajat Indonesia Koeno dan Permai, oentoek sekolah menengah* (Bandung: Pustaka Ksatria, [1942?]), pp. 5–6; John Echols, *Preliminary Checklist of Indonesian Imprints during the Japanese Period* (Ithaca, NY: Cornell Modern Indonesia Project, 1963), lists under the authorship of Siahaan what is presumably a reworking of the same book in 1944, with the title *Ichtisar Sedjarah Indonesia, untuk sekolah menengah*.
5. These debates are well discussed by Surya Ningrat [Ki Hadjar Dewantara], "Het Javaansch Nationalisme in de Indische Beweging", in *"Soembangsih": Gedenkboek Boedi-Oetomo 1902-20 mei-1918* (Amsterdam: Nederl. Indie Oud en Nieuw, 1918), especially pp. 30–2, 39–40.
6. Soeriokoesoemo, "Het Javaansche Vraagstuk", *Wederopbouw* 1 (1918): 6.
7. Soeriokoesoemo, "Gewijd aan mijn Kameraden in 'Insulinde'", *Wederopbouw* 1 (1918): 9. Abdurrachman Surjomihardjo kindly drew my attention to this source.
8. Soeriokoesoemo, "Kangdjeng Sultan Agoeng als Wijsgeer", *Wederopbouw* 2 (1919): 2–12. The same article appeared in *Nederlandsch Indie, Oud en Nieuw*.
9. Tjipto Mangoenkoesoemo, "Nationalisme Hindia dan hak hidupnja", late 1917, reproduced in M. Balfas, *Dr Tjipto Mangoenkoesoemo: Demokrat sedjati* (Jakarta: Djambatan, 1952), pp. 75–82. The original was presumably in Dutch.
10. Surya Ningrat, pp. 37–8.
11. Ibid., p. 43.
12. Ibid., *passim*, especially pp. 47–8.
13. Soeriokoesoemo, "Waarom Javaansch-en Geen Indisch-Nationalism?", *Wederopbouw* 1 (1918): 80–1. The same idea was repeated in an anonymous article "Cultuur", in ibid., p. 112, with specific reference to Jaka Suruh, the Pajajaran prince who in the *babad* tradition is credited with the foundation of Majapahit.
14. R. Koesoema Soedjana, "Aan mijn Javaansche broeders", *Wederopbouw* 1 (1918): 139–41.
15. For a description of the Bubat war in Javanese sources, see N.J. Krom, *Hindoe-Javaansche Geschiedenis* (The Hague: M. Nijhoff, 1931), pp. 402–4; and P.J. Zoetmulder, *Kalangwan: A Survey of Old-Javanese Literature* (The Hague: M. Nijhoff, 1974), pp. 423–6.
16. Dr M. Amir, "Sampai dimana 'Kemadjoen' kita?", *Poedjangga Baroe* 6 (1938–1939): 127.

17. Soeriokoesoemo, "Een beschouwing over de vormen der overheersching", *Wederopbouw* 2 (1919): 76–7.
18. Statutes of the JSB, *Jong-Sumatra* 1, i (1918): 5.
19. Inaugural speech of the first chairman, Tengku Mansoer, in *Jong-Sumatra* 1, i (1918): 3.
    The words quoted were cited again as the slogan of the memorial volume after five years of the JSB.
20. Statutes of the JSB, *Jong-Sumatra* 1, i (1918): 5.
21. Amir, "Datoek Katoemanggoengan", in *Jong-Sumatra* (Sept/Oct 1922).
22. Amir, "Lets over de Sumatranen als zeevarend volk", *Gedenknummer Jong Sumatranen Bond 1917–1922*, pp. 36–43.
23. Bahder Djohan, "De strijd der Padries", *Gedenknummer JSB*, pp. 58–65.
24. W. Fruin-Mees, *Geschiedenis van Java*, 2 vols. (Weltevreden: Commissie voor de Volkslectuur, 1919–1920).
25. W. Fruin-Mees, *Geschiedenis van Java*, Deel I: Het Hindoetijdperk, especially pp. 80–8. Compare maps at rear with the two maps in Muhammad Yamin, *Gadjah Mada: Pahlawan Persatuan Nusantara* (Jakarta: Balai Pustaka, 1953), pp. 100–1. An enthusiastic review of Fruin-Mees by Soemarsono is in *Wederopbouw* 3 (1920): 83–7. See also Supomo, "The Image of Majapahit in Later Javanese and Indonesian Writing", in *Perceptions of the Past in Southeast Asia*, eds. Anthony Reid and David Marr (Singapore: Heinemann, 1979), p. 181.
26. "Het rijk van Gadjah Mada", *Wederopbouw* 3 (1920): 5–6.
27. Ibid., p. 7.
28. Surya Ningrat, p. 45.
29. The fact that the earliest enthusiasts for the Sriwijaya empire wrote in French slowed their impact in Indonesia: G. Coedès "Le Royaume de Crivijaya", *BEFEO* 28, vi (1918); and G. Ferrand, *L'Empire Sumatranais de Crivijaya* (Paris: Imprimerie Nationale, 1922). It was primarily N.J. Krom who made the discoveries accessible to Indonesians, particularly in his popular *Hindoe-Javaansche Geschiedenis* ('s-Gravenhage: M. Nijhoff, 1931).
30. The nearest to the popular and general in this group are the two works of R.M. Noto Soeroto, *Het Sultanaat Jogjokarto* (Hadi Poestaka, 1920) (also serialised in *Nederlandsch-Indie Oud en Nieuw*, and in *Jong-Java*, 1921); and *De Ontwikkeling van het Volk van Java*, 1931.
31. Sukarno and Cindy H. Adams, *Sukarno: An Autobiography As Told to Cindy Adams* (Hong Kong: Gunung Agung, 1966), p. 71. This experience appears to have been distinct from, and earlier than Sukarno's period as a teacher in the *Nationale Middelbare School* headed by Sosro Kartono in Bandung, and reported on in 1927; S.L. van der Wal, ed., *Het Onderwijsbeleid in Nederlands-Indie 1900–1940: een bronnenpublikatie* (Groningen: J.B. Wolters, 1963), p. 425.

32. Sukarno, *Indonesia Menggugat. Pidato pembelaan Bung Karno dimuka hakim kolonial* (Jakarta: S.K. Seno, 1956), p. 118 (emphasis in original). For a modern discussion of "the Criwijaya myth and the Majapahit myth", see G.J. Resink, *Indonesia's History between the Myths* (The Hague: Van Hoeve, 1968), pp. 21–2.
33. R. Moh. Ali, *Pengantar Ilmu Sedjarah Indonesia* (Jakarta: Bhratara, 1963), pp. 114–5 (emphasis in original).
34. Hatta, "Kearah Indonesia Merdeka", 1932, and "Krisis dunia dan nasib Rakjat Indonesia", in *Kumpulan Karangan* (Jakarta: Penerbitan dan Balai Buku Indonesia, 1953), 1: 79, 130; Takdir Alisjahbana, "Menudju masjarakat dan kebudajaan baru", 1935, in *Polemik Kebudajaan*, ed. Achdiat K. Mihardja (Jakarta: Balai Pustaka, 1954), pp. 14–5.
35. "S. Dingley" [Iwa Kusuma Sumantri], *The Peasants' Movement in Indonesia* (Moscow: International Agrarian Institute, n.d. [1926?]), p. 11.
36. Sukarno, *Mentjapai Indonesia Merdeka*, 1933 (Jakarta: Tjita Agung, n.d.), p. 10.
37. An explicit elaboration of this theme is "Pergerakan kita" by "Indonesier" in *Soeloeh Indonesia* 1 (1926). Also Sukarno's 1945 introduction to Yamin, *Sedjarah Peperangan Dipanegara* (Jakarta: Jajasan Pembangunan, 1950), pp. 5–6.
38. Speech of Sarekat Islam propagandist Abdoelmanap in rural Aceh, 1920, cited in Reid, *'Heaven's Will and Man's Fault': The Rise of the West as a Southeast Asian Dilemma* (6th Flinders University Asian Studies Lecture, 1975), p. 35, where this theme is discussed at greater length. The same argument is emphasised in "Dari hal solidariteit, atau 'Satoe Boeat Semoea, Semoea Boeat Satoe'", in Sarekat Islam's *Oetoesan Hindia* (18 May 1914).
39. Nota Van der Plas, 7 December 1927, in *Het Onderwijsbeleid in Nederlands·Indie, 1900–1942. Een bronnenpublicatie*, ed. S.L. van der Wal (Groningen: Wolters, 1963), p. 438.
40. Radjiman speech of 27 June 1918, cited in Akira Nagazumi, *The Dawn of Indonesian Nationalism: The Early Years of Budi Utomo, 1908–1918* (Tokyo: Institute of Developing Economies, 1972), pp. 142–3.
41. Resink, especially pp. 15–25, 151–69.
42. "Kantteekeningen", by "Sumatraantje", *Jong-Sumatra* 9 (1926). See also Roeslan Abdulgani, *Penggunaan Ilmu Sedjarah* (Bandung: B.P. Prapantja, n.d. [1963]), pp. 19–20; and Yamin, cited by Deliar Noer, "Yamin and Hamka: Two Routes to an Indonesian Identity", in *Perceptions of the Past in Southeast Asia*.
43. Abdul Moeis, *Surapati* (Jakarta: Balai Pustaka, 1952 [orig. publ. Batavia, 1905]). Balfas, *Tjipto*, pp. 60–4, cites a 1913 speech of Tjipto in honour of Dipanagara, largely based on Van der Kerup's *BKI* analysis of him as a "Hamlet type".

44. Sukarno by 1945 called them *pahlawan tiga-sekawan*. See Yamin, *Sedjarah*, p. 5; ibid., p. 118.
45. Frantz Fanon, *The Wretched of the Earth* (Harmondsworth: Penguin, 1967), p. 54.
46. Successive editions of Tamar Djaya, *Pusaka Indonesia* (Bukittinggi: 1940), provide an indication of the changing pantheon. The earliest edition I have seen, the third (Bandung: Kolff, 1951) is still limited to Java and Sumatra. It includes three Acehnese anti-Dutch fighters and the standard representatives of Java (Dipanagara), Madura (Trunajaya), Minangkabau and Toba. A very personal inclusion of the author was the Mandailing hero Raja Gadombang, even though he allied with the Dutch against the Minangkabau Padris.
47. F.W. Stapel, *Geschiedenis van Nederlandsch Indie* (Amsterdam: Meulenhoff, 1930), pp. 306–19.
48. "Siapa Orang Besar dari Atjeh? — Teungku Tjhi' di Tiro atau T. Oemar", *Pandji Islam* (7 March 1940), and the articles there cited; also Amelz, "Teungku Tjihik di Tiro", *Penjedar* (Medan: 9 January 1941). Ismail Jakub's book, *Tengku Tjihik di Tiro (Muhammad Saman)* was first published in Sumatra in 1943, and a historical novel by Amelz about Tiro and Uma, *Korban Perdjoeangan*, was advertised in 1941. Despite this local preference for Tiro, it was the secular/aristocratic leaders, Teuku Uma and his militant widow Cut Nyak Dien who first became popular heroes at the national level, helped by the Dutch novelist Szekely-Lulofs. M.H. Szekely-Lulofs, *Tjoet nja Dien* (Amsterdam: 1948), Indonesian translation 1951; Hazil, *Teku Umar dan Tjut Nja Din: Sepasang Pahlawan Perang Atjeh* (Jakarta: Djambatan, 1951). Uma was among the first crop of national heroes officially declared by Sukarno when this system of secular canonisation was begun in 1959, Klaus Schreiner, *Politischer Heldenkult in Indonesien* (Hamburg: Dietrich Reimer, 1995).
49. "Maklumat 15 October 1945", in *Modal Revolusi 45* (Kutaraja: Komite Musjawarah Angkatan 45 Daerah Istimewa Atjeh, 1960), p. 61.
50. S. Supomo, "The Image of Majapahit in Later Javanese and Indonesian Writing," in *Perceptions of the Past in Southeast Asia*, eds. Anthony Reid and David Marr (Singapore: Heinemann, 1979), p. 183.
51. See, for example, *Djedjak Langkah Hadji A. Salim* (Jakarta: Tintamas, 1954), especially pp. 3–22; H.O.S. Tjokroaminoto, *Islam dan Sosialism* (written 1924, reprinted Jakarta: Lembaga Penggali dan Penghimpun Sedjarah Revolusi Indonesia, 1963), pp. 95–104; Taufik Abdullah, *Schools and Politics: The Kaum Muda Movement in West Sumatra (1927–33)* (Ithaca: Cornell Modern Indonesia Project, 1971), p. 60; James Siegel, *The Rope of God* (Berkeley, CA: 1969), pp. 115–30; Sjakieb Arsalan, *Mengapa Kaum Muslimin Mundur, dan mengapa Kaum selain Mereka Madju*, trans. Moenawar Chalil (Jakarta: Bulan Bintang, 1954) — a work prompted by a question from Indonesia in the 1920s asking the reason for Islamic decline.

52. For example, Tan Malaka, *Menudju Republik Indonesia* (1925) (Jakarta: Jajasan Masa, 1962), p. 21.
53. Tan Malaka, *Massa-Actie* (1926) as cited in R. Moh. Ali, *Pengantar Ilmu Sedjarah Indonesia*, p. 145.
54. Ibid., pp. 145–6; "S. Dingley" [Iwa Kusuma Sumantri], 1926, pp. 10–1. In a later period, Aidit's *Indonesian Society and the Indonesian Revolution* (Jakarta: Pembaruan, 1958), pp. 14–23, took dogmatism to more ingenious lengths, preceding this "feudal" period in Indonesia with a "slave society" before the Christian era.
55. Hatta, "Demokrasi Asli Indonesia dan Kedaulatan Rakjat" (1932) and "Collectivisme Tua dan Baru", 1933, in *Kumpulan Karangan*, I, pp. 81–4, 90–3. To the best of my knowledge, it is only in the work of the foreign Marxists, S.J. Rutgers and A. Huber, *Indonesie* (Amsterdam: Pegasus, 1937) that these opposing stereotypes were to some degree reconciled.
56. For example, Tan Malaka, *Menudju*, pp. 21–6. This was a point also much stressed by Sukarno in *Indonesia Menggugat*, pp. 33–67, 139–43, and "Swadeshi dan Massa-Aski di Indonesia", 1932, in *Dibawah Bendera Revolusi* (Jakarta: Panitya Penerbit Dibawah Bendera Revolusi, 1963), 1: 121–57.
57. Yamin, *Sedjarah* and *Gadjah Mada*.
58. *Atjeh Sinbun*, 12 April 1944. The contest was won by Surya (pseud. A. Miala), *Leburnja Keraton Atjeh*. The varied repertoire of the Atjeh *Gekidan* (drama group) is indicated in *Atjeh Sinbun* (4 April 1944) and *Sumatra Sinbun* (26 April 1943).
59. Sanusi Pane, *Sedjarah Indonesia* (Jakarta: Perpustakaan Perguruan Kem. P.P. dan K., 1965), pp. 186, 206, 265 n. 11.
60. R. Moh. Ali, *Pengantar Ilmu Sedjarah Indonesia*, p. 117.
61. Ibid., p. 107. Striking examples of these inhibitions were Ruslan Abdulgani, *Penggunaan Ilmu Sedjarah* (Bandung: n.d. [1963?]), and Yamin (see Deliar Noer, pp. 258–9).
62. Hasan Muhammad Tiro, *Perang Atjeh, 1873–1927 M* (stencilled, Jogjakarta: April 1948).
63. Klaus Schreiner, *Politischer Heldenkult*.
64. Nugroho Notosusanto, "Pengantar Umum", in Drs Ariwiadi, *Ichtisar Sedjarah Nasional Indonesia (awal-sekarang)* (Seri Text-book Sejarah ABRI, Jakarta: Pusat Sedjarah ABRI, 1971), p. vi.
65. Ibid., loc. cit.
66. Sartono Kartodirdjo, Marwati Djoened Poesponegoro, Nugroho Notosusanto, eds., *Sejarah Nasional Indonesia*, 6 vols. (Jakarta: Balai Pustaka, 1977). The conflict between Nugroho's desire to push through an "integral" view, and the misgivings of the non-military historians led by Professor Sartono, was long an open secret, now discussed by Rommel Curaming, "When Clio Meets the

Titans: Rethinking State-Historian Relations in Indonesia and the Philippines" (PhD diss., Australian National University, 2006, awaiting publication).
67. Jean Taylor, *Indonesia: Peoples and Histories* (New Haven, CT: Yale University Press, 2003), p. 362.
68. The fullest account of Nugroho's role is now in Katherine McGregor, *History in Uniform: Military Ideology and the Construction of Indonesia's Past* (Singapore: NUS Press, 2007).
69. Niels Mulder, *Indonesian Images: The Culture of the Public World* (Yogyakarta: Kanisius, 2000), pp. 36–44, 53–5, 72–83.
70. Hasan Muhammad Tiro, *Demokrasi untuk Indonesia* (n.p. [New York?]: Penerbit Seulawah Aceh, 1958). This is the only one of Tiro's works to have been properly printed, which may suggest the often rumoured CIA assistance at this stage of his career.
71. Whereas I have followed Indonesian usage since 1974, which changed the Dutch "tj" into "c" in words such as Aceh, Hasan Tiro consistently used an older English spelling "Acheh" in conscious rejection of both Dutch and Indonesian convention.
72. This is overstating the case. "Indonesia" or "islands of India" was first coined by European philologists in the mid-19th century, and became gradually more useful as a way to describe the languages and peoples of the Archipelago. The high point of colonial acceptance may have been at the end of the First World War, when the semi-official *Encyclopedia van Nederlandsch-Indië* used it as a linguistic category, and two men later to become influential officials — H.J. van Mook and J.A. Jonkman — both used the term in their theses. It was however the anti-Dutch nationalist movement which popularised and politicised the term in the following period, 1922–1945. Only after the Japanese occupation and the proclamation of the Indonesian Republic in August 1945 did the term enter official Dutch usage.
73. The Declaration is in *The Price of Freedom: The Unfinished Diary of Tengku Hasan di Tiro* (stenciled, n.p. [Stockholm?]: State of Acheh Sumatra, 1982), pp. 15–7.
74. David Bourchier, "The 1950s in New Order Ideology and Politics", in *Democracy in Indonesia: 1950s and 1990s*, eds. David Bourchier and John Legge (Melbourne: Monash University Centre for Southeast Asian Studies, 1994), p. 57.
75. Ariwiadi, *Ichtisar Sedjarah Nasional Indonesia*, p. 122.
76. Bourchier, "The 1950s", p. 57.
77. Ibid., p. 54.
78. Ibid., pp. 51–7.
79. While the six-volume set was edited by a team of Sartono Kartodirdjo, Marwati Djoened Poesponegoro and Nugroho Notosusanto, the final volume of *Sejarah*

Nasional Indonesia, covering the period since 1942, was edited by Nugroho, and apparently went to print without the blessing of Professor Sartono.
80. Adnan Buyung Nasution, *The Aspiration for Constitutional Government in Indonesia: A Socio-legal Study of the Indonesian Konstituante, 1956–1959* (Published PhD diss., Utrecht University, 1992).
81. Marsillam Simanjuntak, *Pandangan Negara Integralistik: Sumber, Unsur dan Riwayatnya dalam Persiapan UUD 1945* (Jakarta: Grafiti, 1994).
82. Benedict Anderson and Ruth McVey, *A Preliminary Analysis of the October 1, 1965, Coup in Indonesia* (Ithaca, NY: Cornell University Modern Indonesia Project, 1971 — first circulated 1966).
83. Robert Cribb, ed., *The Indonesian Killings, 1965–1966: Studies from, Java and Bali* (Melbourne: Monash University Centre for Southeast Asian Studies, 1990); Geoffrey Robinson, *The Dark Side of Paradise: Political Violence in Bali* (Ithaca, NY: Cornell University Press, 1995).
84. McGregor, "Claiming History".
85. Nugroho Notosusanto and Ismail Saleh, *The Coup Attempt of the '30th September Movement' in Indonesia* (Jakarta: Pembimbing Massa, 1968).
86. Taylor, *Indonesia*, p. 359.
87. Nico Thamiend, *Sejarah 2 untuk Kelas 2 SMU: Pendekatan Kurikulum Berbasis Kompetensi* (Jakarta: Yudhistira, 2003), pp. 20–49.
88. Ibid., p. v.
89. *Jakarta Post*, 6 October 2003.
90. *Jakarta Post*, 6 October 2003.
91. Ribka Tjiptaning Proletariyati, *Aku Bangga Jadi Anak PKI*, 2nd ed., with preface by Abdurrahman Wahid (Jakarta: Doea Lentera Agency, 2002).
92. *Kompas*, 22 August 2003.
93. Slamet Soetrisno, *Kontroversi dan Rekonstruksi Sejarah*, with preface by Suhartono Pranoto (Yogyakarta: Pressindo, 2003).
94. Rommel Curaming, "Towards Reinventing Indonesian Nationalist Historiography", *Kyoto Review of Southeast Asia* 3 (March 2003), on web.

Chapter 7

1. Nishijima Shigetada, *Shogen: Indoneshia Dokuritsu Kakumei — Aru Nihonjin Kakumeika No Hansei* (Tokyo: Shin Jinbutsu Orai-sha, 1975); see also Anthony Reid and Akira Oki, eds., *The Japanese Experience in Indonesia: Selected Memoirs of 1942–1945* (Athens, OH: Ohio University Monographs in International Studies, 1986), p. 251. Nishijima had previously written, in 1951, *Daisan no Shinso* [*The Third Truth*], an unpublished memoir reacting against the published recollections of Adam Malik and Hatta.

2. Nishijima, *Shogen*, pp. 210–21; Okuma Memorial Social Sciences Research Institute, Waseda University, *Indonesia ni Okeru Nihon Gunsei no Kenkyu* (Tokyo: 1959), as translated in *Japanese Military Administration in Indonesia* (Washington: US Department of Commerce, Joint Publications Research Service, 1963), pp. 501–5.
3. *Japanese Military Administration in Indonesia*, p. 505.
4. Mohammad Hatta, *Sekitar Proklamasi 17 Agustus 1945* (Jakarta: Tintamas, 1970), p. 58, states that Maeda withdrew upstairs while a five-man Indonesian committee drafted the proclamation, and that Miyoshi remained within earshot but said nothing.
5. Cable Adam Malik and Elkana Tobing to Iwasaki Hajime, 14 December 1977, in possession of Nishijima Shigetada.
6. I have argued this point with special reference to northern Sumatra in "The Japanese Occupation and Rival Indonesian Elites: Northern Sumatra in 1942", *Journal of Asian Studies* 35 (1975): 49–61, and in greater detail in *The Blood of the People: Revolution and the End of Traditional Rule in Northern Sumatra* (Kuala Lumpur: Oxford University Press, 1978), pp. 82–144.
7. The Japanese-controlled media lost no opportunity of driving this point home. The enemy powers were always listed as "Amerika, Inggeris dan belanda", the capital letter being studiously avoided for the Dutch.
8. Interviews Itagaki Yoichi and Miyamoto Shizuo.
9. Imamura Hitoshi, *Imamura Hitoshi Taisho Kaisoroku* (Tokyo: Jiyu Ajia-sha, 1960), 4: 106–7, as translated in Reid and Oki, *The Japanese Experience*, pp. 34–5.
10. Ibid., p. 148, as translated in Reid and Oki, *The Japanese Experience*, p. 54.
11. *Japanese Military Administration in Indonesia*, pp. 126–9 and 260ff.
12. For examples of smuggling, see *Sumatra Sinbun*, 27 July 2603 (1943); *Kita-Sumatora-Sinbun*, 9 September 2603; and the informative article, "Usaha memperbanjakkan makanan kita", in *Atjeh Sinbun*, 20 May 2604. A former Sumatran police officer, Abdullah Hussain, explained in his memoir, *Terjebak* (Kuala Lumpur: Pustaka Antara, 1965), pp. 276, 281–3, that smuggling was the chief police preoccupation during the occupation, followed by political reports and complaints about Japanese slapping people.
13. Pemerintah Poesat Soematera, *Boekoe Peringatan Satoe Tahoen N.R.I. di Soematera: 17-8-'45 – 17-8-'46* (Pematang Siantar: 1946), p. 39
14. *Japanese Military Administration in Indonesia*, p. 285.
15. Miyamoto Shizuo, *Jawa Shusen Shoriki* (Tokyo: Java Shusen Shoriki Kankoka, 1973), p. 40, translated in Reid and Oki, *The Japanese Experience*, p. 247.
16. Hamka, *Kenang-kenangan hidup*, 2nd ed. (Kuala Lumpur: Pustaka Antara, 1966), p. 231.

17. Mohammad Hatta, August 1943, as translated by William Frederick in *The Putera Reports: Problems in Indonesian-Japanese Wartime Cooperation* (Ithaca, NY: Modern Indonesia Project, 1971), p. 61.
18. Cited in Bernhard Dahm, *Sukarno and the Struggle for Indonesian Independence* (Ithaca, NY: Cornell University Press, 1969), p. 304. See also Hamka, *Kenang-kenangan*, pp. 230–4, 271; and Adam Malik, *Riwajat Proklamasi 17 Agustus 1945*, 4th ed. (Jakarta: Widjaya, 1962), p. 17.
19. Sukarno and Cindy H. Adams, *Sukarno, An Autobiography as Told to Cindy Adams* (Indianapolis: Bobbs-Merrill, 1965), p. 179.
20. Notably Abu Hanifah, *Tales of a Revolution* (Sydney: Angus & Robertson, 1972), especially pp. 125–7; and Hamka, *Kenang-kenangan*, pp. 231–4. Sukarno himself, in *An Autobiography*, pp. 183–94, makes clear that it was over his record during the Japanese occupation that he was most sensitive to criticism.
21. Anthony Reid, *The Indonesian National Revolution 1945–1950* (Clayton, Victoria: Longman Australia, 1974), pp. 73, 144.
22. Anthony Reid, "The Birth of the Republic in Sumatra", *Indonesia* 12 (1971): 22–30.
23. Ibid., p. 26.
24. Inoue Tetsuro, quoted in Reid, *The Blood of the People*, p. 129.
25. Abdullah Hussain, *Terjebak*, p. 206.
26. A. Teeuw, *Modern Indonesian Literature* (The Hague: M. Nijhoff, 1967), pp. 105–8.
27. Adam Malik, *Riwajat Proklamasi*, pp. 14–5.
28. See, for example, *Atjeh Sinbun*, 12 April 2604; and *Kita-Sumatora-Sinbun*, 17 September 2603.
29. *Atjeh Sinbun*, 3 April 2604.
30. *Atjeh Sinbun*, 4 April 2604; *Sumatra Sinbun*, 26, 27, and 29 July 2603; A.J. Piekaar, *Atjeh en de Oorlog met Japan* ('s-Gravenhage: Van Hoeve, 1949), pp. 210–1.
31. Sanusi Pane, *Sedjarah Indonesia*, 4 vols. (Jakarta: Balai Poestaka, 2603–5). The book was in its 7th edition in 1965.
32. L. Siahaan, *Ichtisar sedjarah Indonesia untuk Sekolah Menengah* (Bandung: Poestaka Ksatrian, 2604); Raden Prijono, *Sedikit tentang sedjarah Asia Tinoer Raja dan Sedjarah Tanah Djawa* (Jakarta: Balai Poestaka, 2605) — also published in Javanese and Sundanese; Ismail Jakub, *Tengku Tjhik di Tiro: Hidup dan Perdjuangannja* (Kutaradja: 2603, 3rd ed. Jakarta: Bulan Bintang, 1960); Ki Agoes Mas'oed, *Sedjarah Palembang, moelai sedari Seri Widjaya sampai kedatangan Balatentara Dai Nippon* (Palembang: "Sinar Matahari", 1942); and *Riwajat dan Perdjoangan pahlawan-pahlawan Indonesia sepintas*

lalu (Madiun: Panitya Pasar Malam Syuu Hookookai, 2605). This historiographical context of these writings is discussed above in the previous chapter.
33. Yamin's two important books of this period, both frequently reprinted, are *Sedjarah Peperangan Diponegoro. Pahlawan Kemerdekaan Indonesia* (Jakarta: Sinbun Kai, 2605), and *Gadjah Mada: Pahlawan Persatoean Noesantara* [2605?], 2nd ed. (Jakarta: Balai Poestaka, 1946).
34. Here and there, the Japanese appear to have attempted deliberately to build the image of a particular anti-Dutch *pahlawan* (hero). For example, the head of the Japanese administration in Sumatra celebrated the third anniversary of Pearl Harbour by visiting the grave of Singamangaradja XII, and honouring the widow and the son of this Batak hero. *Atjeh Sinbun*, 14 December 2604; *Kita-Sumatora Sinbun*, 11 November 2604.
35. Dr Amir's notes, 14 June 1946, Rijksinstituut voor Oorlogsdocumentatie I.C. 005964.
36. Herbert Feith, "Introduction", in *Indonesian Political Thinking 1945–1965*, eds. H. Feith and L. Castles (Ithaca, NY: Cornell University Press, 1970), pp. 18–9.
37. Extract from Soeriokoesoemo's *Sabdo Pandito Ratoe* (1920), translated in ibid., p. 187. A more syncretic "aristo-democratic" formula to blend Western and Javanese ideals was presented by R.M. Noto Soeroto, *Van Overheersching naar Zelfregeering* ('s-Gravenhage: Adi-Poestaka, 1931).
38. Professor Supomo's address, 31 May 1945, to the Body to Investigate Measures for the Preparation of Indonesian Independence (BPKI), as translated in Feith and Castles, p. 189.
39. Ibid., p. 190.
40. The 1945 Constitution, Sukarno's speech formulating the *Pancasila*, and various ancillary documents of 1945 are translated in *The Indonesian Revolution: Basic Documents and the Idea of Guided Democracy* (Jakarta: Department of Information, 2nd printing 1960). The "democracy" clause quoted from the preamble is on p. 58 and Sukarno's similar formulation on pp. 43–5.
41. Adam Malik, *Riwajat Proklamasi*, p. 9.

Chapter 8

1. See, for example, John Smail, *Bandung in the Early Revolution, 1945 1946. A Study in the Social History of the Indonesian Revolution* (Ithaca, NY: Modern Indonesian Project, Southeast Asia Program, Department of Asian Studies, Cornell University, 1964), p. vi; Anton Lucas, "The Bamboo Spear Pierces the Payung: The Revolution Against the Bureaucratic Elite in North Central Java in 1945" (PhD diss., Australian National University, 1981), p. v; and

1. Audrey Kahin, ed., *Regional Dynamics of the Indonesian Revolution: Unity from Diversity* (Honolulu: University of Hawai'i Press, 1985), pp. ix, 1.
2. Barbara Sillars Harvey, "Tradition, Islam and Rebellion: South Sulawesi, 1950–1965" (PhD diss., Cornell University, 1974).
3. Nazaruddin Sjamsuddin, *The Republican Revolt: A Study of the Acehnese Rebellion* (Singapore: Institute of Southeast Asian Studies, 1985).
4. Michael van Langenberg, "National Revolution in North Sumatra: Sumatera Timur and Tapanuli, 1942–1950" (PhD diss., Sydney University, 1976).
5. David Anderson, "Military Politics in East Java: A Study of the Origins and Development of the Armed Forces in East Java between 1945–1948" (PhD diss., University of London, 1976).
6. William Frederick, "Indonesian Urban Society in Transition: Surabaya 1926–1946" (PhD diss., University of Hawai'i, 1978), revised and published as *Visions and Heat: The Making of the Indonesian Revolution* (Athens, OH: Ohio University Press, 1989).
7. Audrey Kahin, "Struggle for Independence: West Sumatra in the Indonesian National Revolution 1945–1950" (PhD diss., Cornell University, 1979), revised and published as *Rebellion to Integration: West Sumatra and the Indonesian Polity, 1926–1998* (Amsterdam: Amsterdam University Press, 1999).
8. Anthony Reid, *The Blood of the People: Revolution and the End of Traditional Rule in Northern Sumatra* (Kuala Lumpur, New York: Oxford University Press, 1979).
9. Lucas, "The Bamboo Spear", published as *One Soul One Struggle: Region and Revolution in Indonesia* (Sydney: Allen & Unwin for ASAA, 1991).
10. Soejatno Kartodirdjo, "Revolution in Surakarta 1945–'50: A Case Study of City and Village in the Indonesian Revolution" (PhD diss., Australian National University, 1982).
11. Robert Cribb, "Jakarta in the Indonesian Revolution" (PhD diss., University of London, 1984), revised and published as *Gangsters and Revolutionaries: The Jakarta People's Militia and the Indonesian Revolution* (Sydney: Allen & Unwin, 1991).
12. Richard Chauvel, "Indonesia Merdeka/Ambon Merdeka? A Modern Social and Political History of the Ambonese Islands" (PhD diss., Sydney University, 1985), revised and published as *Nationalists, Soldiers and Separatists: The Ambonese Islands from Colonialism to Revolt, 1880–1950* (Leiden: KITLV Press, 1990).
13. Benedict R.O'G. Anderson, *Java in a Time of Revolution: Occupation and Resistance, 1944–1946* (Ithaca, NY: Cornell University Press, 1972).
14. Anthony Reid, *The Indonesian National Revolution 1945–1950* (Hawthorn: Longman, 1974).
15. Notably Pierre Heijboer, *De politionele acties: de strijd om 'Indië' 1945/1949* (Haarlem: Fibula-Van Dishoeck, 1979); J.C. Bijkerk, *De laatste landvoogd:*

Van Mook en het einde van de Nederlandse invloed in Indië (Alphen: A.W. Sijthoff, 1982); Yong Mun Cheong, H.J. van Hook and Indonesian Independence: A Study of His Role in Dutch-Indonesian Relations, 1945–1948 (The Hague: Martinus Nijhoff, 1982); and Jan Bank, De katholieken en de Indonesische revolutie (Baarn: Ambo, 1983).

16. Alan Forrest, Society and Politics in Revolutionary Bordeaux (London: Oxford University Press, 1975), p. 1.
17. G.J. Gill, Peasants and Government in the Russian Revolution (London: Macmillan, 1979), p. ix.
18. Charles Tilly, The Vendée (Cambridge: Harvard University Press, 1964), p. 23.
19. Gill, Peasants and Government.
20. 1930 census, taking cities of 50,000 as urban — the same definition as Tilly's. In reality, towns much smaller than this provided much of the leadership of the revolution.
21. Smail, Bandung in the Early Revolution, p. 157.
22. Ibid., p. vi.
23. Notably Frederick and Chauvel.
24. Not only in his "Indonesia Merdeka" but also in "Not a Revolution but a Counterrevolution", in Regional Dynamics of the Indonesian Revolution, ed. A. Kahin, pp. 237–64.
25. Nazaruddin, "The Course of the National Revolution in Aceh 1945–1949"; Reid, The Blood of the People; and Eric Morris, "Aceh: Social Revolution and Islamic Vision", in Regional Dynamics, ed. Kahin, pp. 83–110.
26. Kahin, ed., Regional Dynamics, p. 211.
27. Lucas, "The Bamboo Spear", pp. 32–4; Regional Dynamics, pp. 147–8.
28. Soejatno, "Revolution in Surakarta", pp. 21–5; William J. O'Malley, "Indonesia in the Great Depression: A Study of East Sumatra and Jogjakarta in the 1930s" (PhD thesis, Cornell University, 1977).
29. Michael Williams, "Banten: 'Rice Debts Will Be Repaid with Rice, Blood Debts with Blood'", in Regional Dynamics, p. 57.
30. Lucas, One Soul One Struggle, pp. 55–60, and Local Opposition and Underground Resistance to the Japanese in Java, 1942–1945 (Melbourne: Monash University Centre for Southeast Asian Studies, 1896).
31. Reid, The Blood of the People, pp. 116–7, 127–34.
32. Williams, "Banten", pp. 58–9; Cribb, "Jakarta", p. 117.
33. Smail, Bandung in the Early Revolution.
34. Anderson, Java in a Time of Revolution.
35. Frederick, "Indonesian Urban Society in Transition", pp. 509–54.
36. Lucas, One Soul One Struggle, p. 160.
37. Chauvel, "Ambon: Not a Revolution but a Counterrevolution", pp. 243–4.
38. Soejatno, "Revolution in Surakarta", pp. 47–59.
39. Smail, Bandung in the Early Revolution, pp. 104–28.

40. Ibid., p. 108.
41. In the endless historical debate about the Terror in the French Revolution, Barrington Moore — *Social Origins of Dictatorship and Democracy: Lord and Peasant in the Making of the Modern World* (London: Allen Lane, 1967), pp. 103–6 and *passim* — is one of those who make this point. Data on the violence was conveniently set out much earlier by Donald Greer in *The Incidence of Terror during the French Revolution* (Cambridge, Mass.: Harvard University Press, 1935).
42. Smail, *Bandung in the Early Revolution*, p. 109.
43. Frederick, "Indonesian Urban Society in Transition", pp. 659–91, 718–20.
44. Lucas, *One Soul One Struggle*, pp. 137–42.
45. Williams, "Banten", p. 64.
46. The *Sejarah Nasional Indonesia* (VI, 39n) for example has only a laconic footnote on the phenomenon.
47. Anderson, *Java in a Time of Revolution*, p. 409.
48. Soejatno, "Revolution in Surakarta", pp. 93–118; Anderson, *Java in a Time of Revolution*, pp. 347–69.
49. Soejatno, "Revolution in Surakarta", pp. 118–25.
50. Kahin, "Struggle for Independence", pp. 178–89, 371–3.
51. Lance Castles, "Internecine Conflict in Tapanuli", *Review of Indonesian and Malayan Affairs (RIMA)* 8, 1 (1974): 75–6; Van Langenberg, "National Revolution in North Sumatra", pp. 504–10.
52. Lucas, *One Soul One Struggle*, pp. 105, 253–4.
53. Ranajit Guha, *Elementary Aspect of Peasant Insurgency in Colonial India* (Delhi: Oxford University Press, 1983), p. 153.
54. Ibid., pp. 136–57.
55. Frederick, "Indonesian Urban Society in Transition", pp. 666–7; Lucas, *One Soul One Struggle*, pp. 157–8; Reid, *The Blood of the People*, p. 229.
56. Lucas, *One Soul One Struggle*, p. 155.
57. Kahin, "Struggle for Independence", pp. 142–7.
58. One such contemporary source was "Soeara Proletar", *Pembongkaran Tiga Rahsia Penting I* (Silungkang: Pustaka Sofjan Pondha, 1946), pp. 14–20, evidently a Marxist anxious to clear the name of the PKI ("which because it has an international character could not possibly intend to create chaos") from association with the Baso group he labels nihilists and "Pengkhianat [traitor] Komunis Indonesia". This source does reveal that the Baso movement created in each village a communal residence they called *Kebun Syorga* (heavenly garden), to which goods seized from the rich were brought — "in short any property of the populace which was substantial had to be divided, *disama ratakan*".
59. Lucas, Reid, *One Soul One Struggle*, p. 156.
60. Williams, "Banten", p. 67.

61. Lucas, *One Soul One Struggle*, p. 203.
62. Reid, *Blood of the People*.
63. Williams, "Banten", p. 68; cf. Reid, *Blood of the People*, pp. 210-1.
64. Michael van Langenberg, "East Sumatra: Accommodating an Indonesian Nation within a Sumatran Residency", in *Regional Dynamics*, p. 124.
65. Reid, "Marxist Attitudes to Social Revolution, 1946-1948", *RIMA* 8, 1 (1974): 53-6.
66. Soejatno, "Revolution in Surakarta", p. 55.
67. Lucas, *One Soul One Struggle*, p. 219.
68. Kahin, "Struggle for Independence", pp. 78-84.
69. Reid, *The Blood of the People*, p. 118.
70. Kahin, ed., *Regional Dynamics*, p. 260.
71. Lucas, *One Soul One Struggle*, pp. 218-35.
72. Kahin, "Struggle for Independence", p. 146.
73. Soejatno, "Revolution in Surakarta", p. 239.

Chapter 9

1. This paper was written in 1967, very soon after the events described, and has been left completely as it was to reflect the debates at that time.
2. The *santri* are those Javanese set apart from the community as a whole by their attachment to Islam. Their strength is found among the small traders grouped around the mosque in every market town, and to some extent also among the wealthier farmers; especially those who have earned the title *haji* by completing the pilgrimage to Mecca, a feat beyond the financial resources of all but a small minority. *Abangan* Javanese are the majority of peasants who usually consider themselves Muslims although the rhythm of their lives is governed almost entirely by pre-Islamic ritual practice.
3. Kattenburg, quoted Donald Hindley, *The Communist Party of Indonesia* (Berkeley, CA: University of California Press, 1964), p. 8.
4. Lance Castle, "Notes on the Islamic School at Gontor," *Indonesia* I (April 1966): 36-7, 43-4.
5. For example, "Indonesia — Christianity's New Target", *Muslim News International* 6, 1 (July 1967): 14.

Chapter 10

1. The original version of this article was presented as a Special Lecture at the 13th Conference of the International Association of Historians of Asia, at Sophia University, Tokyo, in September 1994, and published as "Political 'Tradition' in Indonesia: The One and the Many", *Asian Studies Review* 22, 1 (February 1998): 23-38.

2. The manifesto at the beginning of Okakuro Kakuzo's *The Ideals of the East* (1904) is conveniently reproduced in Theodore de Bary, ed., *Sources of East Asian Tradition* (New York: Columbia University Press, 2008), II: 549.
3. The term is that of Samuel P. Huntington, *The Clash of Civilizations and the Remaking of World Order* (New York: Simon & Schuster, 1996), p. 108. A representative writing of the Singapore group was Bilihari Kausikan, "Asia's Different Standard", *Foreign Policy* 92 (1993).
4. Mahathir Mohamad and Shintaro Ishihara, *The Voice of Asia: Two Leaders Discuss the Coming Century* (Tokyo: Kodansha, 1995 [orig. publ. in Japanese under the title *The Asia That Can Say No*, 1994]).
5. Anwar Ibrahim, *The Asian Renaissance* (Singapore: Times Books International, 1996), p. 45.
6. *Far Eastern Economic Review* (1993), pp. 16–7; Huntington, *Clash of Civilizations*, pp. 195–6.
7. David Reeve, *Golkar of Indonesia: An Alternative to the Party System* (Singapore: Oxford University Press, 1985), p. 359.
8. Adnan Buyung Nasution, "The Aspiration for Constitutional Government in Indonesia: A Socio-Legal Study of the Indonesian Konstituante 1956–1959" (PhD diss., Utrecht, 1992); Marsillam Simanjuntak, *Pandangan Negara Integralistik: Sumber, Unsur dan Riwayatnya dalam Persiapan UUD 1945* (Jakarta: Grafiti, 1994); David Bourchier, "Lineages of Organicist Political Thought in Indonesia" (PhD diss., Monash University 1996).
9. Bourchier, "Lineages of Organicist Political Thought", pp. 22–30.
10. Supomo speech to BPUPK on 31 May 1945, as translated in Bourchier, "Lineages of Organicist Political Thought", pp. 81–2.
11. Bourchier, "Lineages of Organicist Political Thought", pp. 88–97; Reeve, *Golkar of Indonesia*, pp. 65–75.
12. Cited in Reeve, ibid., p. 10.
13. Cited in ibid., p. 320.
14. Harry J. Benda, "Democracy in Indonesia", *Journal of Asian Studies* 23 (1964): 449–56.
15. Anne Ruth Willner, *The Neotraditional Accommodation to Political Independence: The Case of Indonesia* (Princeton, NJ: Center of International Studies, Woodrow Wilson School for Public and International Affairs, Princeton University, 1966).
16. Benedict Anderson, *Language and Power* (Ithaca, NY: Cornell University Press, 1990), p. 36.
17. J.C. van Leur, *Indonesian Trade and Society: Essays in Asian Social and Economic History* (The Hague: Nijhoff, 1955); Denys Lombard, *Le Carrefour Javanais: Essai d'Histoire Globale*, 3 vols. (Paris: EHESS, 1990).
18. Robert Hefner, "The Political Economy of Islamic Conversion in Modern East Java", in *Islam and the Political Economy of Meaning: Comparative Studies*

of *Muslim Discourse*, ed. William R. Roff (London: Croom Helm, 1987), p. 60.
19. Toru Aoyama, "A New Interpretation of the East-West Division of Majapahit in the Late Fourteenth Century", *Tonan Ajia: Rekisha to Bunka* [*Southeast Asia: History and Culture*] 21 (1992): 82–7.
20. Merle C. Ricklefs, "Unity and Disunity in Javanese Political and Religious Thought of the Eighteenth Century", in *Looking in Odd Mirrors: The Java Sea*, eds. V.J.H. Houben, H.M.J. Maier and W. van der Molen (Leiden: Vakgroep Talen en Culturen van Zuidoost-Azie en Oceanie, 1992), pp. 60–75.
21. Luc Nagtegal, *Riding the Dutch Tiger: The Dutch East Indies Company and the Northeast Coast of Java, 1680–1743* (Leiden: KITLV, 1996).
22. Clifford Geertz, *Negara* (Princeton, NJ: Princeton University Press, 1980), pp. 60–1.
23. Report of Schuurman, 1840, cited in Henk Schulte Nordholt, "Leadership and the Limits of Political Control. A Balinese 'Response' to Clifford Geertz", *Social Anthropology* 1, 3 (1993): 291.
24. Nordholt, "Leadership and the Limits of Political Control", pp. 305–6.
25. Leonard Andaya, *The World of Maluku: Eastern Indonesia in the Early Modern Period* (Honolulu: University of Hawai'i Press, 1993), p. 55.
26. James J. Fox, ed., *To Speak in Pairs: Essays on the Ritual Languages of Eastern Indonesia* (Cambridge: Cambridge University Press, 1988).
27. Cornelis Speelman, "Notitie" (1670), as translated in Anthony Reid, "Kings, Kadis and Charisma in the Seventeenth Century Archipelago", in *The Making of an Islamic Political Discourse in Southeast Asia*, ed. Anthony Reid (Clayton, Melbourne: Papers on Southeast Asia, Monash University Centre for SE Asian Studies, 1993), p. 87.
28. Cited in Christian Pelras, "Hiérarchie et Pouvoir Traditionnel en Pays Wajo", *Archipel* 1 (1971): 173–5.
29. Thomas Forrest, *A Voyage to New Guinea and the Moluccas, 1774–1776* (1780; repr. Singapore: Oxford University Press, 1980), p. 326.
30. Thomas Kiefer, *The Tausug: Violence and Law in a Philippine Moslem Society* (New York: Holt, Rhinehart & Winston, 1972), pp. 104–11.
31. Sophia Raffles, ed., *Memoir of the Life and Public Services of Sir Thomas Stamford Raffles* (London: James Duncan, 1835), pp. 141–2.
32. E.A. Rombouts 1870, and Gromberg 1865, cited in William Collins, "Besemah Concepts: A Study of the Culture of a People of South Sumatra" (PhD diss., University of California, 1979), pp. 93–4.
33. On this subject, see Jane Drakard, "A Kingdom of Words: Minangkabau Sovereignty in Sumatran History" (PhD diss., Australian National University, 1993).
34. Ricklefs, "Unity and Disunity", p. 61.

35. Reid, "Kings, Kadis and Charisma" and *Southeast Asia in the Age of Commerce c.1450–1680: Vol. 2, Expansion and Crisis* (New Haven, CT: Yale University Press, 1993), pp. 169–81, 251–66.
36. Nagtegal, *Riding the Dutch Tiger*, pp. 29–31.
37. James Scott, "Freedom and Freehold: Space, People and State Simplification in Southeast Asia", in *Asian Freedoms: The Idea of Freedom in East and Southeast Asia*, eds. David Kelly and Anthony Reid (Cambridge: Cambridge University Press, 1998).

Chapter 11

1. Clifford Geertz, *Negara: The Theatre State in Nineteenth-Century Bali* (Princeton, NJ: Princeton University Press, 1980), p. 135.
2. Tony Day, *Fluid Iron: State Formation in Southeast Asia* (Honolulu: University of Hawai'i Press, 2002), p. 288.
3. See, among others, Geertz, *Negara: The Theatre State*; Anthony Reid, "Political 'Tradition' in Indonesia: The One and the Many", *Asian Studies Review* 22, 1 (1998): 23–38; M.C. Ricklefs, "Unity and Disunity in Javanese Political and Religious Thought of the Eighteenth Century", in *Looking in Odd Mirrors: The Java Sea*, eds. V.J.H. Houben, H.M.J. Maier and W. van der Molen (Leiden University: Vakgroep Talen en Culturen van Zuidoost-Azië en Oceanië, 1992), pp. 60–75; Leonard Andaya, *The World of Maluku: Eastern Indonesia in the Early Modern Period* (Honolulu: University of Hawai'i Press, 1993); Jane Drakard, *A Kingdom of Words. Language and Power in Sumatra* (Shah Alam, Malaysia: Oxford University Press, 1999).
4. Rupert Emerson, *Malaysia: A Study in Direct and Indirect Rule* (New York: Macmillan, 1937); Anthony Reid, *The Indonesian National Revolution* (Melbourne: Longman, 1974).
5. Jeffrey Kahn, *Federalism, Democratisation and the Rule of Law in Russia* (New York: Oxford University Press, 2002), Chapter 3; Cameron Ross, *Federalism and Democratisation in Post-Communist Russia* (Mancester: Manchester University Press, 2003).
6. Emerson, *Malaysia: A Study*, p. 54.
7. Ibid., p. 464.
8. Anthony Reid, *The Blood of the People: Revolution and the End of Traditional Rule in Northern Sumatra* (Kuala Lumpur: Oxford University Press, 1979), p. 262.
9. Muhammad Yamin, ed., *Naskah Persiapan Undang-Undang Dasar 1945* (Jakarta: Jajasan Prapantja, 1959), 1: 259.
10. Ibid., pp. 410, 419.
11. Reid, *The Indonesian National Revolution*, pp. 19–29.

12. Reid, *The Blood of the People*; Omar Ariffin, *Bangsa Melayu: Aspects of Democracy and Community among the Malays* (Kuala Lumpur: Oxford University Press, 1993).
13. Nazaruddin Sjamsuddin, *The Republican Revolt: A Study of the Acehnese Rebellion* (Singapore: Institute of Southeast Asian Studies, 1985); M. Isa Sulaiman, *Sejarah Aceh: Sebuah Gugatan Terhadap Tradisi* (Jakarta: Pustaka Sinar Harapan, 1997); Anthony Reid, *Verandah of Violence: The Background to the Aceh Problem* (Singapore: NUS Press, 2006).
14. Reid, *The Blood of the People*, pp. 106–9; Richard Chauvel, *Nationalists, Soldiers and Separatists: The Ambonese Islands from Colonialism to Revolt* (Leiden: KITLV Press, 1990), pp. 233–57.
15. George McT. Kahin, *Nationalism and Revolution in Indonesia* (Ithaca, NY: Cornell University Press, 1950); Reid, *The Indonesian Revolution*, pp. 115–9.
16. General Nasution, as translated in Chauvel, *Nationalists, Soldiers and Separatists*, p. 324.
17. Herbert Feith, *The Decline of Constitutional Democracy in Indonesia* (Ithaca, NY: Cornell University Press, 1962), p. 71.
18. Chauvel, *Nationalists, Soldiers and Separatists*, pp. 347–92.
19. Mohamad Said, chairman of an "All East Sumatra People's Congress", lobbying to dissolve the NST, in his opening speech of 27 April 1950, as translated in Feith and Castles, *Indonesian Political Thinking, 1945–1965* (Ithaca, NY: Cornell University Press, 1970), p. 318.
20. Feith, *The Decline of Constitutional Democracy*, p. 74.
21. Mohammad Hatta, "Indonesia's Foreign Policy", *Foreign Affairs* 31 (April 1953): 441ff., quoted in Feith, *The Decline of Constitutional Democracy*, p. 72.
22. Feith, *The Decline of Constitutional Democracy*, pp. 54–5, 212–4; M. Isa Sulaiman, *Aceh Merdeka: Ideologi, Kepemimpinan dan Gerakan* (Jakarta: Pustaka al Kausar, 2000); M. Isa Sulaiman, "From Autonomy to Periphery: A Critical Evaluation of the Acehnese Nationalist Movement", in *Verandah of Violence*, ed. Anthony Reid (Singapore: Singapore University Press, 2006), pp. 121–48.
23. Hasan Muhammad Tiro, *Demokrasi Untuk Indonesia* (Atjeh, n.d. [1958?]), pp. 98, 103–4, 150–3.
24. Sulaiman, *Aceh Merdeka*, pp. 400–19; Sulaiman, "From Autonomy to Periphery", pp. 132–3.
25. In addition to note 23 in Hasan Tiro's book, see the Kahar Muzakar pamphlet of 1960, "Konsepsi Negara Demokrasi Indonesia", partly translated in Feith and Castles, *Indonesian Political Thinking*, pp. 330–5.
26. Michael Malley, "Regions: Centralization and Resistance", in *Indonesia Beyond Suharto*, ed. Donald K. Emmerson (New York: The Asia Society, 1999).

27. See Y.B. Mangunwijaya, *Menuju Republik Indonesia Serikat* (Jakarta: Gramedia, 1998); B. Simorangkir, ed., *Otonomi atau Federalisme: Dampaknya terhadap Pembangunan* (Jakarta: Sinar Harapan, 2000). A taste of this debate, Mangunwijaya for federalism and General Sudradjat against, is translated in Bourchier and Hadiz, *Indonesian Politics and Society: A Reader* (London: RoutledgeCurzon, 2003), pp. 269–72.
28. Michelle Miller, "What's Special about Special Autonomy in Aceh?", in *Verandah of Violence*, ed. Reid.
29. Keating, Michael, *Plurinational Democracy: Stateless Nations in a Post-Sovereignty Era* (Oxford: Oxford University Press, 2001), pp. viii, 102–33.
30. An extensive literature has grown around Indonesian political violence in the democratic climate since 1998, though curiously ignored in the earlier authoritarian one. See Benedict Anderson, ed., *Violence and the State in Suharto's Indonesia* (Ithaca, NY: Cornell University Centre for SE Asian Studies, 2001); Freek Columbijn and J. Thomas Lindblad, eds., *Roots of Violence in Indonesia: Contemporary Violence in Historical Perspective* (Leiden: KITLV Press, 2002); Ingrid Wessel and Georgia Wimhofer, eds., *Violence in Indonesia* (Hamburg: Abera, 2001); Charles Coppel, ed., *Violent Conflicts in Indonesia: Analysis, Representation, Resolution* (Richmond: Curzon, 2004).
31. Reid, *Verandah of Violence*, Chapters 11–15.
32. Freek Columbijn, "Explaining the Violent Solution in Indonesia", *The Brown Journal of World Affairs* IX, I (Spring 2002): 54–5.
33. Anne Booth, *The Indonesian Economy in the Nineteenth and Twentieth Centuries: A History of Missed Opportunities* (Basingstoke: Macmillan, 1998), pp. 53–67; Angus Maddison, *The World Economy: A Millennial Perspective* (Paris: Development Centre of OECD, 2001), pp. 215, 304.

Chapter 12

1. W. Roscher, "Die stellung der Juden in Mittelalter vom Standpunkt fur die allgemeine Handelspolitik", *Zeitschrift fur gesamte Staatswirtschaft* 31 (1875), quoted in Walter P. Zenner, *Minorities in the Middle: A Cross-Cultural Analysis* (Albany: State University of New York Press, 1991), p. 2.
2. Werner Sombart, *The Jews and Modern Capitalism* (Glencoe, Illinois: Free Press, 1951 [orig. publ. 1911]).
3. Max Weber, *The Protestant Ethic and the Spirit of Capitalism*, trans. Talcott Parsons (London: Unwin University Books, 1930), p. 271.
4. Max Weber, *The Sociology of Religion*, trans. E. Fischoff (London: Methuen, 1963), p. 109.

5. Joseph P. Jiang, "Towards a Theory of Pariah Entrepreneurship", in *Leadership and Authority: A Symposium*, ed. G. Wijeyawardene (Singapore: University of Malaya Press, 1968), pp. 147–62; Gary Hamilton, "Pariah Capitalism: A Paradox of Power and Dependence", *Ethnic Groups* 2 (Spring 1978): 1–15; Allen J. Chun, "Pariah Capitalism and the Overseas Chinese of Southeast Asia: Problems in the Definition of the Problem", *Ethnic and Racial Studies* 12, 2 (April 1989): 233–56.
6. For example, Jonathan Israel, *European Jewry in the Age of Mercantilism, 1550–1750* (Oxford: Oxford University Press, 1985).
7. Philip Curtin, *Cross-Cultural Trade in World History* (Cambridge: Cambridge University Press, 1984).
8. Although primarily a New Testament term (John 7:35; 1 Peter 1:1), the concept of the Diaspora harks back to Deuteronomy 28:25 — "The Lord shall cause thee to be smitten before thine enemies; thou shall... be removed into all the kingdoms of the earth."
9. Abner Cohen, "Cultural Strategies in the Organization of Trading Diasporas", in *The Development of Indigenous Trade and Markets in West Africa*, ed. Claude Meillassoux (London: Oxford University Press, 1971), cited in Curtin, *Cross-Cultural Trade*, p. 2n.
10. Irwin Rinder, "Strangers in the Land: Social Relations in the Status Gap", *Social Problems* 6 (1958–1959): 253–60.
11. Stanislav Andreski, "An Economic Interpretation of Anti-Semitism in Eastern Europe", *Jewish Journal of Sociology* 5, 2 (1963): 201–13.
12. W. Ph. Wertheim, *East-West Parallels: Sociological Approaches to Modern Asia* (The Hague: van Hoeve, 1964), pp. 76–80.
13. Edna Bonacich, "A Theory of Middlemen Minorities", *American Sociological Review* 38 (1973): 583–94, and "Middleman Minorities and Advanced Capitalism", *Ethnic Groups* 2 (1980): 311–20; Walter Zenner, "Middleman Minority Theories: A Critical Review", in *Sourcebook on the New Immigration*, eds. R.S. Bryce-Laporte, D.M. Mortimer, and S.R. Couch (New Brunswick, New Jersey: Transaction Books, 1980), pp. 413–25; Zenner, *Minorities in the Middle*.
14. Ernest Gellner, *Nations and Nationalism* (Oxford: Blackwell, 1983), p. 124.
15. Benedict Anderson, *Imagined Communities: Reflections on the Origin and Spread of Nationalism* (London: Verso, 1983), p. 14.
16. Anderson, *Imagined Communities*; Gellner, *Nations and Nationalism*; Anthony Smith, *The Ethnic Origins of Nations* (Oxford: Blackwell, 1986); Eric J. Hobsbawm, *Nations and Nationalism since 1780* (Cambridge: Cambridge University Press, 1990); Liah Greenfeld, *Nationalism: Five Roads to Modernity* (Cambridge, Mass.: Harvard University Press, 1992).
17. Anderson, *Imagined Communities*, pp. 129–40.

18. K.R. Minogue, *Nationalism* (London: Batsford, 1967), p. 7.
19. Hans Kohn, *Nationalism: Its Meaning and History* (Princeton, NJ: Van Nostrand, 1955); Smith, *The Ethnic Origins of Nations*; Greenfeld, *Nationalism*.
20. For Malay nationalism, see Tan Liok Ee, *The Rhetoric of Bangsa and Minzu: Community and Nation in Tension, the Malay Peninsula, 1900–1955* (Clayton, Victoria: Centre of Southeast Asian Studies, Monash University, 1988); and Ariffin Omar, *Bangsa Melayu: Malay Concepts of Democracy and Community 1945–1950* (Singapore: Oxford University Press, 1993). For Thailand, see Craig J. Reynolds, ed., *National Identity and Its Defenders: Thailand 1939–1989* (Clayton, Victoria: Centre of Southeast Asian Studies, Monash University, 1991); and Scot Barmé, *Luang Wichit Wathakan* (Singapore: Institute of Southeast Asian Studies, 1993).
21. Ian Buruma, *The Wages of Guilt: Memories of War in Germany and Japan* (New York: Farrar Straus Giroux, 1994), p. 8.
22. Ruth Benedict, *The Chrysanthemum and the Sword* (Boston: Houghton Mifflin, 1946), quoted in Buruma, *The Wages of Guilt*, p. 116.
23. Penny Edwards, "Cambodia's Melting Pot", in *The Woodstock Road Editorial* (Oxford: 1992); Ben Kiernan, *The Pol Pot Regime: Race, Power, and Genocide in Cambodia under the Khmer Rouge, 1975–79* (New Haven, CT: Yale University Press, 1996).
24. Hillel Levine, *Economic Origins of Anti-Semitism: Poland and Its Jews in the Early Modern Period* (New Haven, CT: Yale University Press, 1991), p. 32.
25. Ng Chin-keong, "The Case of Ch'en I-lao: Maritime Trade and Overseas Chinese in Ch'ing Policies, 1717–1754", in *Emporia, Commodities and Entrepreneurs in Asian Maritime Trade, c.1400–1750*, eds. R. Ptak and D. Rothermunde (Stuttgart: Franz Steiner, 1991), p. 395.
26. Anthony Reid, "Flows and Seepages in the Long-term Chinese Interaction with Southeast Asia", in *Sojourners and Settlers*, ed. Anthony Reid (Sydney: Allen & Unwin, 1996), pp. 17–33.
27. Levine, *Economic Origins of Anti-Semitism*, p. 33.
28. Anthony Reid, *Southeast Asia in the Age of Commerce* (New Haven, CT: Yale University Press, 1993), 2: 312–3.
29. Levine, *Economic Origins of Anti-Semitism*, p. 9; William Dampier, *Voyages and Discoveries*, ed. C. Wilkinson (London: Argonaut Press, 1931 [orig. publ. 1699]), pp. 94–5.
30. An excellent discussion of this phenomenon is that in G. William Skinner, "Creolized Chinese Societies in Southeast Asia", in *Sojourners and Settlers*, ed. Reid, pp. 51–93.
31. Howard M. Sachar, *The Course of Modern Jewish History*, rev. ed. (New York: Vintage Books, 1990), pp. 22–7. Levine, however, in *Economic Origins*

of Anti-Semitism, pp. 136–41, rejects a similar constructive role for the Jewish managers of feudal estates in Poland (the *arendar*) compared with that of the *hofjuden* in German-speaking Europe, largely because Poland's economy was in steady decline after 1648 and its religious atmosphere was growing increasingly intolerant.

32. William O. McCagg, *A History of Hapsburg Jews, 1670–1918* (Bloomington: Indiana University Press, 1989), p. 12; Levine, *Economic Origins of Anti-Semitism*, p. 32n.
33. John Butcher and Howard Dick, eds., *The Rise and Fall of Revenue Farming: Business Elites and the Emergence of the Modern State in Southeast Asia* (Basingstoke: Macmillan, 1993), pp. 73–7.
34. Ibid., pp. 198–204.
35. Ibid., pp. 198–204.
36. F. Fokkens, *Chinese Economic Activity in Netherlands India: Selected Translations from the Dutch*, trans., eds. M.R. Fernando and David Bulbeck (Singapore: Institute of Southeast Asian Studies/ECHOSEA, 1992), pp. 63–4.
37. Peter Carey, "Changing Javanese Perceptions of the Chinese Communities in Central Java, 1755–1825", *Indonesia* 37 (1984): 8–9, 24–5.
38. Butcher and Dick, *The Rise and Fall of Revenue Farming*, pp. 156–7.
39. This argument is forcefully made in A.R.T. Kemasang, "The 1740 Chinese Slaughters in Java: Officially Orchestrated Pogroms", *Kabar Seberang* 16 (December 1982): 65–91. Most other authorities see the massacre as having been more spontaneous.
40. Edgar Wickberg, *The Chinese in Philippine Life, 1850–1898* (New Haven, CT: Yale University Press, 1965), p. 22.
41. Ong-Tae-Hae (Wang Ta-hai), *The Chinaman Abroad: An Account of the Malayan Archipelago, Particularly of Java*, trans. W.H. Medhurst (London: John Snow, 1850 [orig. publ. 1791]), pp. 14–8; Claudine Salmon, "Ancestral Halls, Funeral Associations, and Attempts at Resinicization in Nineteenth Century Southeast Asia", in *Sojourners and Settlers*, ed. Reid, pp. 197–202.
42. Skinner, "Creolized Chinese Societies in Southeast Asia", pp. 59–61.
43. The rapidly increasing outflow from southern China in the 19th century was balanced by the high number of returnees, deaths without issue, and Chinese assimilated into Southeast Asian populations. In Java, for which figures are the least unsatisfactory, Ong-Tac-Hae (1791) and Raffles (1814) estimated that there were two per cent or more Chinese in the population, compared with only 1.39 per cent in the 1930 census (Carey, "Changing Javanese Perceptions", p. 14). In the Philippines, the group classified as "Chinese" has been well below one per cent in the 20th century, as compared with five per cent Chinese mestizo in the 19th, the descendants of whom are now considered Filipino.

44. T.J. Newbold, *Political and Statistical Account of the British Settlements in the Straits of Malacca* (1839; repr. Kuala Lumpur: Oxford University Press, 1971), p. 8.
45. Peter Carey, *Babad Dipanegara* (Kuala Lumpur: MBRAS, 1981), pp. xlii–iii; Alexander Woodside, *Vietnam and the Chinese Model: A Comparative Study of Nguyen and Ch'ing Civil Government in the First Half of the Nineteenth Century* (Cambridge, Mass.: Harvard University Press, 1971), pp. 3–4.
46. G. William Skinner, *Chinese Society in Thailand: An Analytical History* (Ithaca, NY: Cornell University Press, 1957), p. 144; Spenser St. John, *Life in the Forests of the Far East* (London: Smith, Elder & Co, 1863; Kuala Lumpur: Oxford University Press, 1974), 2: 312, 320–1; W.A. Graham, *Kelantan: A State of the Malay Peninsula* (Glasgow: Maclehose, 1908), p. 103.
47. McCagg, *A History of Hapsburg Jews*, pp. 145, 191; Steven Beller, *Vienna and the Jews 1867–1938* (Cambridge: Cambridge University Press, 1989), p. 44.
48. Seller, *Vienna and the Jews*, pp. 49–67.
49. Butcher and Dick, *The Rise and Fall of Revenue Farming*, pp. 35–6.
50. Ibid., p. 9.
51. Claudine Salmon, ed., *Le moment "Sino-Malais" de la Littérature Indonésienne* (Paris: Cahiers d'Archipel, 1992).
52. Cited in Sachar, *The Course of Modern Jewish History*, p. 306.
53. Skinner, *Chinese Society in Thailand*, pp. 155–63; Victor Purcell, *The Chinese in Southeast Asia*, 2nd ed. (London: Oxford University Press, 1965), pp. 118–9.
54. L.E. Williams, *Overseas Chinese Nationalism: The Genesis of the Pan-Chinese Movement in Indonesia, 1900–16* (Glencoe, Illinois: Free Press, 1960); Wang Gungwu, *Community and Nation: Essays on Southeast Asia and the Chinese* (Singapore: Heinemann, 1981), pp. 128–58.
55. Milton Friedman, "Capitalism and the Jews: Confronting a Paradox", *Encounter* 63, 1 (1984): 74.
56. Sachar, *The Course of Modern Jewish History*, p. 335.
57. Leo Suryadinata, *Pribumi Indonesians, the Chinese Minority and China*, 3rd ed. (Singapore: Heinemann, 1992), pp. 12–4, 36–8.
58. Purcell, *The Chinese in Southeast Asia*, p. 546.
59. The pamphlet is quoted in full in Kenneth P. Landon, *The Chinese in Thailand* (London: Oxford University Press, 1941), pp. 34–43.
60. Ibid., pp. 38–9.
61. A few months before Pibun came to power, his cultural commissar, Luang Wichit Wathakan, himself a *lookjin* (Sino-Thai) like many other leaders of anti-Chinese opinion, made a famous speech at Chulalongkorn University, where after referring to Hitler's actions against Jews, he declared that "it was

high time Siam considered dealing with their own Jews" — that is, Chinese. See Barmé, *Luang Wichit Wathakan*, pp. 133–6.
62. Gellner, *Nations and Nationalism*, p. 97.
63. Anderson, *Imagined Communities*, pp. 94–5.
64. Mahathir bin Mohammed, *The Malay Dilemma* (Singapore: Asia Pacific Press, 1970), pp. 122–30.
65. Reynolds, *National Identity and Its Defenders*, pp. 24–5.
66. Gellner, *Nations and Nationalism*, pp. 114–22.
67. Ibid., p. 46.
68. Anderson, *Imagined Communities*, pp. 66–97.
69. Mary Somers Heidhues, *Southeast Asia's Chinese Minorities* (Hawthorn: Longman Australia, 1974), p. 3; Purcell, *The Chinese in Southeast Asia*, pp. 169–75; "The Overseas Chinese", *The Economist*, 18 July 1992, p. 21.
70. For the earlier sequence, see J.A.C. Mackie, "Anti-Chinese Outbreaks in Indonesia", in *The Chinese in Indonesia*, ed. J.A.C. Mackie (London: Nelson, 1976), pp. 77–138; and the later Jemma Purdey, *Anti-Chinese Violence in Indonesia, 1996–1999* (Singapore: NUS Press, 2006).
71. *Vietnam Population Census 1989*, vol. 1 (Hanoi: Central Census Steering Committee, 1991). For the crisis of 1978–1979, see Michael Godley, "A Summer Cruise to Nowhere: China and the Vietnamese Chinese in Perspective", *Australian Journal of Chinese Affairs* 4 (1980): 35–59; Charles Benoit, "Vietnam's 'Boat People'" in *The Third Indochina Conflict*, ed. David W.P. Elliott (Boulder, Colorado: Westview Press, 1981), pp. 139–62.
72. Pang Eng Fong, "Race, Income Distribution and Development in Malaysia and Singapore", in *The Chinese in Southeast Asia*, eds. Linda Lim and Peter Gosling (Singapore: Maruzen, 1983), pp. 316–35; Harold Crouch, "Malaysia: Neither Authoritarian nor Democratic", in *Southeast Asia in the 1990s*, eds. Kevin Hewison, Richard Robison, and Garry Rodan (Sydney: Allen & Unwin, 1993), pp. 133–58.
73. Some gross estimates are found in *The Economist*, 18 July 1992, p. 21. In 1993, the Indonesian magazine *Info Bisnis* produced a list of the country's 300 richest taxpayers, 247 of whom were Chinese. The proportion is probably similar in Thailand, though the line between who is and is not "Chinese" is even less clear or meaningful there.
74. Kasian Tejapira, "Imagined Uncommunity: The *Lookjin* Middle Class and Thai Official Nationalism", in *Essential Outsiders: Chinese and Jews in the modern Transformation of Southeast Asia and Central Europe*, eds. Daniel Chirot and Anthony Reid (Seattle: University of Washington Press, 1997), pp. 75–98.
75. Ariel Heryanto, "A Class Act", *Far Eastern Economic Review*, 16 June 1994, p. 30.

76. Chandra Muzaffar, *Islamic Resurgence in Malaysia* (Petaling Jaya: Penerbit Fajar Bakti, 1987), especially pp. 13–29; K.S. Jomo and Shabery Cheek, "Malaysia's Islamic Movements", in *Fragmented Vision: Culture and Politics in Contemporary Malaysia*, eds. Francis Loh and Joel Kahn (Sydney: Allen & Unwin for ASAA, 1992), pp. 79–106.
77. The "Protocols" were first published in Malaysia in 1983, and in Indonesian translation in 1992. Other publications of this genre include two in English published by the "Thinker's Library" at Sungei Tua just outside Kuala Lumpur, both dated 1991: Shakil Ahmed Zia, *A History of Jewish Crimes* (first published in Karachi, 1969), and Misbahul Islam Faruqi, *Jewish Conspiracy and the Muslim World* (first published in Karachi, 1967). In Indonesia, Lukman Saksono translated from English both the "Protocols" and Gerald L.K. Smith's "Jewish-Zionist Capitalists", published in Henry Ford's private anti-Semitic newspaper, *The Dearborn Independent*, in the 1920s (Jakarta: Grafikatama, 1991). More of this type of literature published in 1991–1992 and more typically translated from Arabic intermediaries is reviewed by Margot Cohen in *Sources Age* (Melbourne), 26 March 1994.
78. This phase appeared to end after a couple of public brawls with the international press. The first was over a cancelled visit of the New York Philharmonic to Kuala Lumpur in 1984, which first revealed to the world Malaysia's policy of discouraging "works of Jewish origin". There was then a series of confrontations in 1986, culminating in the visit of the Israeli president to Singapore in November, against which Malaysian protests were vigorous.
79. Liddle's article was published in a rival journal as "Skripturalisme *Media Dakwah*: Satu Bentok Pemikiran dan Aksi Politik Islam Masa Orde Baru", *Ulumul Qur'an* (July 1993). The English version is "*Media Dakwah* Scripturalism: One Form of Islamic Political Thought and Action in New Order Indonesia", in *Towards a New Paradigm: Recent Developments in Indonesian Islamic Thought*, eds. Mark Woodward and James Rush (Tempe: Arizona State University Press, 1996).
80. *Media Dakwah*, Shafar 1414/August 1993.
81. Shahnon Ahmad, "Pola Pemikiran di Sebalik Halal-Haramnya *Schindler's List*", *Lidah* (Penang) 2 (1994): 9–12.

Glossary*

*Indonesian/Malay unless indicated as Ch = Chinese, D = Dutch, J = Javanese, Jp = Japanese

abangan	Geertz's term for the syncretic Javanese form of Islam
adat	custom, unwritten indigenous law
aksi sepihak	unilateral action
amok	a frenzied attack
arek Surabaya (J)	son of Surabaya
baba	local-born Chinese (especially in Malaya)
bengkok (J)	rice-fields allocated to Javanese village head, as salary
bersiap	literally prepare; the time of mobilisation for street action
BPKI	Badan penyelidik usaha-usaha Persiapan Kemerdekaan Indonesia (Body to investigate the preparation of Indonesian Independence), in 1945
bungkus	bundle, homemade cigarette wrapped in maize leaf
BTI	Barisan Tani Indonesia; Indonesian Peasant Front
bunshu (Jp)	Japanese-era term for districts, later *kabupaten*
bupati (J)	district head
Daidancho (Jp)	regimental commander, in PETA
diplomasi	diplomacy
dombreng	onomatopoeic term for ritual procession to humiliate enemies of the revolution

Glossary

GERINDO	Gerakan Rakyat Indonesia, Indonesian People's Movement
Giyugun (J)	volunteer soldier; Japanese-trained military force in Sumatra
Gestapu	*Gerakan September Tigapuluh*; 30 September Movement
GOLKAR	*Golongan Karyawan*, functional groups (state party under Suharto)
haj	pilgrimage to Mecca
HMI	Himpunan Mahasiswa Islam; Muslim Students' Union
kabupaten (J)	district, governed by *bupati*; modern Indonesian replacement of Dutch *afdeling*
kadi	Islamic judicial authority
kelobot (J)	*bungkus*, homemade cigarette
NISM	Nederlandsch-Indische Stoomvaart Maatschappij
KNIP	Komite Nasional Indonesia Pusat; Central Indonesian National Committee
KPM	Koninklijke Paketvaart Maatschappij (Dutch shipping line in Indies)
kretek	cigarette with clove addition
lasykar	member of a militia
Masjumi	Majlis Syuro Muslimin, Council of Muslims
mufakat	decision by consensus
musyawarah	discussion
nagari	supra-village community in Minangkabau
Nasakom	Sukarno's acronym for the unity of Nationalists (Nas), Muslims (A[gama]), and Communists (Kom)
NEKOLIM	Neo-colonialists and Imperialists
NICA	Netherlands Indies Civil Administration, the post-war Dutch administration demonised by many Republicans

NU	Nahdatul Ulama; organisation of traditionalist Ulama (as opposed to the modernism of Muhammadiah); also a political party 1952–1973
pancasila/pantjasila	five principles adopted as Indonesian state philosophy
Pangreh praja; pamong praja	Javanese aristocratic administrative corps under Dutch and Japanese
pemimpin	leader
peranakan	local-born, especially of Chinese
pergerakan	[national] movement
perjuangan	struggle
PETA	Pembela Tanah Air, Japanese-trained military in Java
pinang	areca, betelnut
PKI	Partai Komunis Indonesia; Indonesian Communist Party
PNI	Partai Nasionalis Indonesia
priyayi (J)	Javanese aristocracy
PUSA	Persatuan Ulama Seluruh Aceh, All-Aceh Ulama Association
rasa	feeling, sensation
rasa merdeka	taste of spirit of freedom
sama rasa sama rata	brotherhood and equality
santri	student in a religious school, adopted by Geertz for pious Muslims in Java
sawah	flooded rice field; paddy
Seinedan (Jp)	Youth Corps
seishin (Jp)	sacrificial spirit
Sendenbu (Jp)	Propaganda Office
Shu (Jp)	Japanese-era term for Dutch *Residentie*, and later Indonesian Province

SI	Sarekat Islam, Islamic Association
sirih	betel leaf
strootjes (D)	*bungkus*, homemade cigarette
tanda NICA	a [secret] sign of [loyalty to] NICA
Tiga Daerah	Three Regions, referring to Pemalang, Tegal and Pekalongan in north-central Java
totok (Ch)	foreign-born, newcomer (especially Chinese)
ulama	religious scholar
Ummat	Islamic community
VOC	Verenigde [Geoctroyeerde] Oost-Indische Compagnie
Volksraad (D)	People's Council; highest representative body of Netherlands India
waqf (Arabic)	religious endowment

Bibliography

Abdulgani, Roeslan. *Penggunaan Ilmu Sedjarah*. Bandung: B.P. Prapantja, n.d. [1963].
Abdullah, Munshi. "*The Hikayat Abdullah*", trans. A.H. Hill. *Journal of the Malayan Branch of Royal Asiatic Society* 28, 3 (1955 [orig. publ. 1849]): 1–354.
Abdullah, Taufik. *Schools and Politics: The Kaum Muda Movement in West Sumatra (1927–33)*. Ithaca, NY: Cornell Modern Indonesia Project, 1971.
Abdurrachman, Paramita. "Portuguese Presence in Jakarta". Paper presented to the Sixth IAHA Conference. Yogyakarta, Indonesia, August 1974.
Abeyasekere, S.S, "Slaves in Batavia: Insights from a Slave Register". In *Slavery, Bondage, and Dependency in Southeast Asia*, ed. Anthony Reid. St Lucia: University of Queensland Press, 1983, pp. 286–314.
Abeyasekere, Susan. *Jakarta: A History*. Singapore: Oxford University Press, 1987.
Abidin, Andi Zainal. *Wajo' pada Abad XV–XVI. Suatu Penggalian Sejarah Terpendam Sulawesi Selatan dari Lontara*. Bandung: Penerbit Alumni, 1985.
Adam Malik. *Riwajat Proklamasi 17 Agustus 1945*, 4th ed. Jakarta: Widjaya, 1962.
Adatrechtbundels, vol 17. The Hague: Nijhoff, 1910–1955.
Ahmad, Shahnon. "Pola Pemikiran di Sebalik Halal-Haramnya *Schindler's List*". *Lidah* (Penang) 2 (1994): 9–12.
Aidit, D.N. *Indonesian Society and the Indonesian Revolution*. Jakarta: Pembaruan, 1958.
Alfian, Ibrahim. *Perang di Jalan Allah: Perang Aceh 1873–1912*. Jakarta: Pustaka Sinar Harapan, 1987.
Ali Haji ibn Ahmad, Raja. *The Precious Gift: Tuhfat al-Nafis*, trans. Virginia Matheson and Barbara Andaya. Kuala Lumpur: Oxford University Press, 1982.
Ali, R. Moh. *Pengantar Ilmu Sedjarah Indonesia*. Jakarta: Bhratara, 1963.
Alisjahbana, Takdir. "Menudju masjarakat dan kebudajaan baru" (1935). In *Polemik Kebudajaan*, ed. Achdiat K. Mihardja. Jakarta: Balai Pustaka, 1954, pp. 12–20.
Allen, G.C. and A.G. Donnithorne. *Western Enterprise in Indonesia and Malaya*. London: George Allen & Unwin, 1957.

Amelz. "Teungku Tjihik di Tiro". *Penjedar* (Medan), 9 January 1941.
Amir. "Datoek Katoemanggoengan". In *Jong-Sumatra* (September/October 1922).
_____. "Lets over de Sumatranen als zeevarend volk". In *Gedenknummer Jong Sumatranen Bond 1917–1922*, pp. 36–43.
Amir, Dr M. "Sampai dimana 'Kemadjoen' kita?". *Poedjangga Baroe* 6 (1938–1939): 127.
Andaya, B. Watson. *To Live as Brothers: Southeast Sumatra in the Seventeenth and Eighteenth Centuries*. Honolulu: University of Hawai'i Press, 1993.
Andaya, Leonard Y. "Man as Rare as Flowers". In *Glimpses of Indonesian History: The 1987 MacMillan Brown Lectures*, eds. Leonard Y. Andaya and Barbara Andaya. Auckland: Auckland University, 1988.
Andaya, Leonard. *The Heritage of Arung Palakka: A History of South Sulawesi (Celebes) in the Seventeenth Century*. The Hague: Nijhoff for KITLV, 1981.
_____. *The World of Maluku: Eastern Indonesia in the Early Modern Period*. Honolulu: University of Hawai'i Press, 1993.
Anderson, Benedict R.O.'G. *Java in a Time of Revolution: Occupation and Resistance, 1944–1946*. Ithaca, NY: Cornell University Press, 1972.
Anderson, Benedict. "A Time of Darkness and a Time of Light: Transposition in Early Indonesian Nationalist Thought". In *Perceptions of the Past in Southeast Asia*, eds. Anthony Reid and David Marr. Singapore: Heinemann, 1979, pp. 219–48.
Anderson, Benedict, ed. *Violence and the State in Suharto's Indonesia*. Ithaca, NY: Cornell University Centre for SE Asian Studies, 2001.
Anderson, Benedict. *Imagined Communities: Reflections on the Origin and Spread of Nationalism*. London: Verso, 1983.
_____. *Language and Power: Exploring Political Cultures in Indonesia*. Ithaca, NY: Cornell University Press, 1990.
Anderson, David. "Military Politics in East Java: A Study of the Origins and Development of the Armed Forces in East Java Between 1945–1948". PhD diss., University of London, 1976.
Anderson, John. *Mission to the East Coast of Sumatra in 1823*. Kuala Lumpur: Oxford University Press, 1971 (orig. publ. 1926).
Anderson, Perry. *Passages from Antiquity to Feudalism*. London: Verso, 1978.
Andreski, Stanislav, "An Economic Interpretation of Anti-Semitism in Eastern Europe". *Jewish Journal of Sociology* 5, 2 (1963): 201–13.
Angoulvant, G. *Les Indes Néerlandais: Leur Rôle dans l'Économie Internationale*, vols. 1 and 2. Paris: Le Monde Nouveau, 1926.
Anwar Ibrahim. *The Asian Renaissance*. Singapore: Times Books International, 1996.
Aoyama, Toru. "A New Interpretation of the East-West Division of Majapahit in the Late Fourteenth Century". *Tonan Ajia: Rekisha to Bunka (Southeast Asia: History and Culture)* 21 (1992): 65–87.

Apperson, G.L. *The Social History of Smoking*. London: Martin Secker, 1914.
Arendt, Hannah. *Antisemitism*. San Diego: Harcourt, Brace, Hovanovich, 1968.
Ariffin, Omar. *Bangsa Melayu: Aspects of Democracy and Community among the Malays*. Kuala Lumpur: Oxford University Press, 1993.
Ariwiadi. *Ichtisar Sedjarah Nasional Indonesia (awal-sekarang) (Seri Text-book Sejarah ABRI)*. Jakarta: Pusat Sedjarah ABRI, 1971.
Arjungi, K.N. "Areca Nut: A Review". *Arzneim.-Forsch* 26 (1976): 951–6.
Arsalan, Sjakieb. *Mengapa Kaum Muslimin Mundur, dan mengapa Kaum selain Mereka Madju*, trans. Moenawar Chalil. Jakarta: Bulan Bintang, 1954.
Atjeh Sinbun (Koetaradja), 2602–5 (1942–5).
Aung Thwin, Michael. "Athi, Kyun Taw, Hpaya-Kyun: Varieties of Commendation and Dependence in Pre-colonial Burma". In *Slavery, Bondage and Dependency in Southeast Asia*, ed. Anthony Reid. St Lucia: University of Queensland Press, 1983.
Bachand, R.G. "Betel-chewing: Some Observations of the Habit among the Vietnamese". *Dental Student's Magazine* (April 1967).
Bahder Djohan. "De strijd der Padries". In *Gedenknummer JSB*, pp. 58–65.
Balfas, M. *Dr Tjipto Mangoenkoesoemo: Demokrat sedjati*. Jakarta: Djambatan, 1952.
Bank, Jan. *De katholieken en de Indonesische revolutie*. Baarn: Ambo, 1983.
Barmé, Scot. *Luang Wichit Wathakan*. Singapore: Institute of Southeast Asian Studies, 1993.
Beaulieu, A. de. "Mémoires du Voyage aux Indes Orientales du General Beaulieu, Dressés par Luy-mesme". In *Relations de Divers Voyages Curieux*, vol. 2, ed. Melchisedech Thévenot. Paris: Cramoisy, 1666.
Beller, Steven. *Vienna and the Jews 1867–1938*. Cambridge: Cambridge University Press, 1989.
Benda, H.J., J.K. Irikura and K. Kishi, eds. *Japanese Military Administration in Indonesia: Selected Documents*. New Haven, CT: Yale University Southeast Asia Studies, 1965, pp. 1–3.
Benda, Harry J. *Continuity and Change in Southeast Asia: Collected Journal Articles of Harry J. Benda*. New Haven, CT: Yale University Southeast Asia Studies, 1972.
————. "Democracy in Indonesia". *Journal of Asian Studies* 23 (1964): 449–56.
Benedict, Ruth. *The Chrysanthemum and the Sword*. Boston: Houghton Mifflin, 1946.
Besar, R.A. Datoek and R. Roolvink, eds. *Hikajat Abdullah*. Jakarta: Djambatan, 1953.
Bigalke, Terence. "Dynamics of the Torajan Slave Trade in South Sulawesi". In *Slavery, Bondage and Dependency in Southeast Asia*, ed. Anthony Reid. St Lucia: University of Queensland Press, 1983.

Bijkerk, J.C. *De laatste landvoogd: Van Mook en het einde van de Nederlandse invloed in Indië.* Alphen: A.W. Sijthoff, 1982.

Bissachère, M. de la. *Etat Actuel du Tonkin, de la Cochinchine, et des Royaumes de Cambodge, Laos et Lac-Tho.* Paris: Galignani, 1812. Reprint, Westmead, 1971.

Blair, E.H., and J.A. Robertson, eds. *The Philippine Islands, 1493–1898,* 55 vols. Cleveland: Arthur H. Clark, 1903.

Blussé, Leonard. "An Insane Administration and an Unsanitary Town: The Dutch East India Company and Batavia (1619–1799)". In *Colonial Cities,* eds. R. Ross and G.J. Telkampe. The Hague: Nijhoff. Bock, Carl, 1985 (orig. publ. 1881).

——. *Strange Company: Chinese Settlers, Mestizo Women and the Dutch in VOC Batavia.* Dordrecht: Foris for KITLV, 1986.

Bock, Carl. *Head-hunters of Borneo.* Singapore: Oxford University Press, 1885 (orig. publ. 1881).

Bonacich, Edna. "A Theory of Middlemen Minorities". *American Sociological Review* 38 (1973): 583–94.

——. "Middleman Minorities and Advanced Capitalism". *Ethnic Groups* 2 (1980): 311–20.

Bontius, James. *An Account of the Diseases, Natural History, and Medicines of the East Indies.* London: Donaldson, 1776.

Booth, Anne. *The Indonesian Economy in the Nineteenth and Twentieth Centuries: A History of Missed Opportunities.* Basingstoke: Macmillan, 1998.

Bourchier, David and Vedi Hadiz, eds. *Indonesian Politics and Society: A Reader.* London: RoutledgeCurzon, 2003.

Bourchier, David. "Lineages of Organicist Political Thought in Indonesia". PhD diss., Monash University, 1996.

Boxer Codex. "The Manners, Customs, and Beliefs of the Philippine Inhabitants of Long Ago, Being Chapters of 'A Late 16th Century Manuscript'", eds. Carlos Quirino and Mauro Garcia. *The Philippine Journal of Science* 87, 4 (1958): 325–448.

Brown, C.C., trans. "Sejarah Melayu or 'Malay Annals'". *Journal of the Malayan Branch of the Royal Asiatic Society* 25, parts 2 and 3 (1952).

Brugière, M. "Notices of the Religion, Manners, and Customs of the Siamese". *Chinese Repository* 8 (1844): 169–207.

Buchler, F. "Land Hunger and the Growing Power of Regional Elites in Cirebon Regency, 1903–1930". Paper presented to Second Asian Studies Association of Australia Conference, Sydney, 1978.

Burton-Bradley, B.G., "Papua and New Guinea Transcultural Psychiatry: Some Implications of Betel Chewing". *Medical Journal of Australia* 2 (1966): 744–6.

Buruma, Ian. *The Wages of Guilt: Memories of War in Germany and Japan*. New York: Farrar Straus Giroux, 1994.

Butcher, John and Howard Dick, eds. *The Rise and Fall of Revenue Farming: Business Elites and the Emergence of the Modern State in Southeast Asia*. Sydney: Macmillan, 1993.

Campo, J.N.F.M. "Steam Navigation and State Formation". In *The Late Colonial State in Indonesia: Political and Economic Foundations of the Netherlands Indies, 1880–1942*, ed. R. Cribb. Leiden: KITLV Press, 1994, pp. 11–30.

Carey, Peter. "Changing Javanese Perceptions of the Chinese Communities in Central Java, 1755–1825". *Indonesia* 37 (1984): 1–47.

──────. *Babad Dipanegara: An Account of the Outbreak of the Java War (1825–30)*. Kuala Lumpur: Malaysian Branch of the Royal Asiatic Society, 1981.

Castles, Lance, "Notes on the Islamic School at Gontur". *Indonesia* I (April 1966): 30–45.

──────. "Internecine Conflict in Tapanuli". *Review of Indonesian and Malayan Affairs* 8, 1 (1974): 73–80.

Charles Benoit. "Vietnam's 'Boat People'". In *The Third Indochina Conflict*, ed. David W.P. Elliott. Boulder, Colorado: Westview Press, 1981, pp. 139–62.

Chauvel, Richard. "Ambon: Not a Revolution but a Counterrevolution". In *Regional Dynamics of the Indonesian Revolution: Unity from Diversity*, ed. A. Kahin. Honolulu: University of Hawai'i Press, 1985, pp. 237–64.

──────. "Indonesia Merdeka/Ambon Merdeka? A Modern Social and Political History of the Ambonese Islands". PhD diss., University of Sydney, 1985.

──────. *Nationalists, Soldiers and Separatists: The Ambonese Islands from Colonialism to Revolt*. Leiden: KITLV Press, 1990.

Chirino, Pedro. *Relacion de las Islas Filipinas*, trans. B. Echevarria. Manila: Filipiniana Book Guild, 1969.

Chirot, Daniel and Anthony Reid, eds. *Essential Outsiders: Chinese and Jews in the Modern Transformation of Southeast Asia and Central Europe*. Seattle: University of Washington Press, 1997.

──────. "Conflicting Identities and the Dangers of Communalism". In *Essential Outsiders: Chinese and Jews in the Modern Transformation of Southeast Asia and Central Europe*. Seattle: University of Washington Press, 1997, pp. 3–32.

Chopra, R.N., S.L. Nayar, and I.C. Chopra. *Glossary of Indian Medicinal Plants*. New Delhi: Council of Scientific and Industrial Research, 1956.

Chun, Allen J. "Pariah Capitalism and the Overseas Chinese of Southeast Asia: Problems in the Definition of the Problem". *Ethnic and Racial Studies* 12, 2 (April 1989): 233–56.

Chung, W.C., and B.C. Ko. "Treatment of Taenia Saginata Infection with Mixture of Areca Nuts and Pumpkin Seeds". *Chinese Journal of Microbiology* 9 (1976): 31–5.

Coedès, G., "Le Royaume de Crivijaya". *BEFEO* 28, vi (1918).

Cohen, Abner. "Cultural Strategies in the Organization of Trading Diasporas". In *The Development of Indigenous Trade and Markets in West Africa*, ed. Claude Meillassoux. London: Oxford University Press, 1971, pp. 266–84.

Collins, William. "Besemah Concepts: A Study of the Culture of a People of South Sumatra". PhD diss., University of California, Berkeley, 1979.

──────. "Besemah Concepts: A Study of the Culture of a People of South Sumatra". PhD diss., University of California, Berkeley, 1979.

Colony of Singapore Annual Report. Singapore: Government Printing Office, 1948.

Columbijn, Freek and J. Thomas Lindblad, eds. *Roots of Violence in Indonesia: Contemporary Violence in Historical Perspective*. Leiden: KITLV Press, 2002.

Columbijn, Freek. "Explaining the Violent Solution in Indonesia". *The Brown Journal of World Affairs* 9, 1 (2002): 49–56.

Coppel, Charles, ed. *Violent Conflicts in Indonesia: Analysis, Representation, Resolution*. Richmond: Curzon, 2004.

Cortesão, A., ed. *The Suma Oriental of Tome Pires*. London: Hakluyt Society, 1944 (orig. publ. 1515).

Crawfurd, John. *Grammar and Dictionary of the Malay Language*, vol. 2. London: 1852.

──────. *History of the Indian Archipelago*, 3 vols. Edinburgh: Constable, 1820.

──────. *History of the Indian Archipelago*, vol. 1. Edinburgh: A. Constable, 1820.

──────. *History of the Indian Archipelago*, vol. 3. Edinburgh: Archibald Constable, 1820.

Creutzberg, P., ed. *Het Ekonomisch Beleid in Nederlandsch-Indie. Capita Selecta. Een Bronnenpublikatie (Economic Policy in Netherlands India. Selections: A Sourcebook)*, vol. 3. Groningen: Tjeenk Willink, 1975.

Cribb, Robert. "Jakarta in the Indonesian Revolution". PhD diss., University of London, 1984.

Crouch, Harold. "Malaysia: Neither Authoritarian nor Democratic". In *Southeast Asia in the 1990s*, eds. Kevin Hewison, Richard Robison, and Garry Rodan. Sydney: Allen & Unwin, 1993, pp. 133–58.

──────. "Patrimonialism and Military Rule in Indonesia". *World Politics* 31 (1979): 571–87.

Curaming, Rommel. "When Clio Meets the Titans: Rethinking State-Historian Relations in Indonesia and the Philippines". PhD diss., Australian National University, 2006.

Curtin, Philip. *Cross-Cultural Trade in World History*. Cambridge: Cambridge University Press, 1984.

Dahm, Bernhard. *History of Indonesia in the Twentieth Century*. London: Pall Mall Press, 1971.

⸻. *Sukarno and the Struggle for Indonesian Independence*. Ithaca, NY: Cornell University Press, 1969.

Dampier, William. *Voyages and Discoveries*, ed. C. Wilkinson. London: Argonaut Press, 1931 (orig. publ. 1699).

Damsté, H.T. "Hikajat Perang Sabi". *Bijdragen tot de Taal-, Land- en Volkenkunde van Nederlandsch-Indië* 84 (1928): 595.

Davis, David Brion. *Slavery and Human Progress*. New York: Oxford University Press, 1984.

⸻. *The Problem of Slavery in Western Culture*. Ithaca, NY: Cornell University Press, 1966.

Day, Clive. *The Policy and Administration of the Dutch in Java*. Kuala Lumpur: Oxford University Press, 1996 (orig. publ. 1904).

Day, Tony. *Fluid Iron: State Formation in Southeast Asia*. Honolulu: University of Hawai'i Press, 2002.

Dekker, E.F.E. Douwes. *Ichtisar Riwajat Indonesia Koeno dan Permai, oentoek Sekolah Menengah*. Bandung: Pustaka Ksatria, [1942?].

Dewantara, Ki Hadjar. *Karja K.H. Dewantara*, vol. 2A. Jogjakarta: Persatuan Taman Siswa, 1967.

Dingley, S. [Iwa Kusuma Sumantri]. *The Peasants' Movement in Indonesia*. Moscow: International Agrarian Institute, n.d. [1926?].

Djajadiningrat, R.H. *Atjehsch-Nederlandsch Woordenboek [Acehnese-Dutch Dictionary]*, 2 vols. Batavia: Landsdrukkerij, 1934.

Djaya, Tamar. *Pusaka Indonesia*. Bukittinggi: 1940; Bandung: Kolff, 1951.

Djedjak Langkah Hadji A. Salim. Jakarta: Tintamas, 1954.

Drakard, Jane. *A Kingdom of Words. Language and Power in Sumatra*. Shah Alam, Malaysia: Oxford University Press, 1999.

Drewes, G.W.J., ed. *Hikajat Potjut Muhamat: An Acehnese Epic*. The Hague: Nijhoff, 1979.

Echols, John. *Preliminary Checklist of Indonesian Imprints during the Japanese Period*. Ithaca, NY: Cornell Modern Indonesia Project, 1963.

Edwards, Penny. "Cambodia's Melting Pot". In *The Woodstock Road Editorial*. Oxford: 1992.

Eerdmans, A.J.A.F. "Het Landschap Gowa". *Verhandeling van het Bataviaasch Genootschap* 50, 3 (1897): 1–77.

Eerste Schipvaart. De eerste schipvaart der Nederlanders naar Oost-Indië onder Cornelis de Houtman 1595–1597, vol. I, eds. G.P. Rouffaer and J.W. Ijzerman (The Hague: Nijhoff for Linschoten-Vereniging, 1915).

Eisenstadt, S.N. *Traditional Patrimonialism and Modem Neo-Patrimonialism*. London: Sage Publications, 1973.

Elson, R.E. "Sugar Factory Workers and the Emergence of 'Free Labour' in Nineteenth-Century Java". *Modern Asian Studies* 20, 1 (1986): 139–74.

Emboden, William. *Narcotic Plants*. London: Studio Vista, 1979.

Emerson, Rupert. *Malaysia: A Study in Direct and Indirect Rule*. New York: Macmillan, 1937.

Endicott, Kirk. "The Effects of Slave Raiding on the Aborigines of the Malay Peninsula". In *Slavery, Bondage and Dependency in Southeast Asia*, ed. Anthony Reid. St Lucia: University of Queensland Press, 1983.

Erwiza Erman. "Rethinking Legal and Illegal Economy: A Case Study of Tin Mining in Bangka Island". *Southeast Asia: History and Culture* 37 (May 2008): 91–111.

Eysinga, Roorda van. *Algemeen Nederduitsch-Maleisch Woordenboek*. Leiden: Gualph Kolff, 1853.

Fanon, Frantz. *The Wretched of the Earth*. Harmondsworth: Penguin, 1967.

Fasseur, C. "The French Scare: Taco Roorda and the Origins of Javanese Studies in the Netherlands". In *Looking in Odd Mirrors: The Java Sea*, eds. V.J.H. Houben, H.M.J. Maier and W. van der Molen. Leiden: Vakgroep Talen en Culturen van Zuidoost Azië en Oceanie, 1992, pp. 241–57.

Feith, Herbert and Lance Castles, eds. *Indonesian Political Thinking 1945–1965*. Ithaca, NY: Cornell University Press, 1970.

Feith, Herbert. *The Decline of Constitutional Democracy in Indonesia*. Ithaca, NY: Cornell University Press, 1962.

Ferrand, G. *L'Empire Sumatranais de Crivijaya*. Paris: Imprimerie Nationale, 1922.

Finley, Moses I. "Slavery". In *International Encyclopedia of the Social Sciences*, ed. David Sills. New York: Crowell, Collier and Macmillan, 1968.

Firth, Rosemary. *Housekeeping among Malay Peasants*. London: London School of Economics, 1943.

Fogel, Robert William and Stanley L. Engerman. *Time on the Cross: The Economics of American Negro Slavery*, vol. 1. Boston: Little, Brown, 1974.

Fokkens, F. *Chinese Economic Activity in Netherlands India: Selected Translations from the Dutch*, trans., eds. M.R. Fernando and David Bulbeck. Singapore: Institute of Southeast Asian Studies/ECHOSEA, 1992.

Forman, S. "Descent Alliance and Exchange Ideology among the Makassae of East Timor". In *The Flow of Life: Essays on Eastern Indonesia*, ed. J.J. Fox. Cambridge: Harvard University Press, 1980, pp. 152–77.

Forrest, Alan. *Society and Politics in Revolutionary Bordeaux*. London: Oxford University Press, 1975.
Forrest, Thomas. *A Voyage to New Guinea and the Moluccas, 1774–1776*, 1780. Reprint, Singapore: Oxford University Press, 1980.
Forth, G.L. *Rindi: An Ethnographic Study of a Traditional Domain in Eastern Sumba*. The Hague: Nijhoff, 1981.
Fox, James J., ed. *To Speak in Pairs: Essays on the Ritual Languages of Eastern Indonesia*. Cambridge: Cambridge University Press, 1988.
Frederick, William. "Indonesian Urban Society in Transition: Surabaya 1926–1946". PhD diss., University of Hawai'i, 1978.
─────. *The Putera Reports: Problems in Indonesian-Japanese Wartime Cooperation*. Ithaca, NY: Modern Indonesia Project, 1971.
Freeman, Derek. *Some Reflections on the Nature of Iban Society*. Canberra: Department of Anthropology, Australian National University, 1981.
Friedman, Milton. "Capitalism and the Jews: Confronting a Paradox". *Encounter* 63, 1 (1984): 74–9.
Fruin-Mees, W. *Gescshiedenis van Java*, Deel I: Het Hindoetijdperk. Weltevreden, Commissie voor de Volkslectuur, 1919.
Fryer, D.W. and J.C. Jackson. *Indonesia*. London: Ernest Benn, 1977.
Furnivall, J.S. *Netherlands India*. Cambridge: Cambridge University Press, 1967 (orig. publ. 1944).
─────. *Netherlands India*. Cambridge: Cambridge: University Press, 1939.
G.F. Gonggrijp. *Schets ener Economische Geschiedenis van Indonesie*, 4th ed. Haarlem: De Erven F. Bohn, 1957.
Galvão, Antonio. *A Treatise on the Moluccas (c.1544). Probably the Preliminary Version of Antonio Galvao's Lost Historia das Molucas*, ed. H.Th.Th.M. Jacobs. Rome: Jesuit Historical Institute, 1970.
Geertz, Clifford. *The Religion of Java*. Princeton, NJ: Princeton University Press, 1980.
─────. *Negara: The Theatre State in Nineteenth-Century Bali*. Princeton, NJ: Princeton University Press, 1980.
Gellner, Ernest. *Nations and Nationalism*. Oxford: Blackwell, 1983.
Gerbrandy, P.S. *Indonesia*. London: Hutchinson, 1950.
Gill, G.J. *Peasants and Government in the Russian Revolution*. London: Macmillan, 1979.
Gobee, E. and C. Adriaanse, eds. *Ambtelijke adviezen van C. Snouck Hurgronje, 1889–1936*. The Hague: Nijhoff, 1957.
Godley, Michael. "A Summer Cruise to Nowhere: China and the Vietnamese Chinese in Perspective". *Australian Journal of Chinese Affairs* 4 (1980): 35–59.

Goens, R. van. *De Vijf Gezantschapsreizen van Rijklof van Goens naar het Hof van Mataram, 1648–1654 (The Five Missions of Rijklof van Goens to the Court of Mataram)*, ed. H.J. de Graaf. 's-Gravenhage: Nijhoff, 1956.
G.P. Rouffaer and J.W.Ijzerman, eds. *De eerste schipvaart der Nederlanders naar Oost-Indië onder Cornelis de Houtman 1595–1597*, vol. I. The Hague: Nijhoff for Linschoten-Vereniging, 1915.
Graham, W.A. *Kelantan: A State of the Malay Peninsula*. Glasgow: Maclehose, 1908.
Greenfeld, Liah. *Nationalism: Five Roads to Modernity*. Cambridge, Mass.: Harvard University Press, 1992.
Greer, Donald. *The Incidence of Terror during the French Revolution*. Cambridge, Mass.: Harvard University Press, 1935.
Guha, Ranajit. *Elementary Aspect of Peasant Insurgency in Colonial India*. Delhi: Oxford University Press, 1983.
Guillot, Claude. "Le Rôle Historique des *Perdikan* ou Villages Francs: Le Cas de Tegalsari". *Archipel* 30 (1985): 137–62.
Haan, F. de. *Oud Batavia*, vols. 1 and 2. Batavia: G. Kolff, 1922.
──────. *Priangan*, vol. 3. Batavia: Kolff, 1910.
Hajj Hasan, Abdul Hadi. *Sejarah Alam Melayu*, Penggal I. Singapore: Printed for the Dept. of Education by Malaysia Pub. House, 1925.
Hall, K.R. "State and Statecraft in Early Sri Vijaya". In *Explorations in Early Southeast Asian History: The Origins of Southeast Asian Statecraft*. Ann Arbor: University of Michigan Center for South and Southeast Asian Studies, 1976.
Hamilton, Gary. "Pariah Capitalism: A Paradox of Power and Dependence". *Ethnic Groups* 2 (Spring 1978): 1–15.
Hamka. *Kenang-kenangan hidup*, 2nd ed. Kuala Lumpur: Pustaka Antara, 1966.
Hanifah, Abu. *Tales of a Revolution*. Sydney: Angus & Robertson, 1972.
Hanna, Willard A. *Indonesian Banda: Colonialism and its Aftermath in the Nutmeg Islands*. Philadelphia: Institute for the Study of Human Issues, 1978.
Harahap, Parada. *Indonesia Sekarang (Indonesia Now)*. Jakarta: Bulan Bintang, 1952.
Hartwich, C. "Antwoord No. 19". In *Bidragen tot de Kennis van het Gebruik van Sirih in Nederlandsch-Oost-Indie (Contributions to the Knowledge of the Use of Betel in the Dutch East Indies)*. *Bulletin van het Koloniaal Museum te Haarlem* 32 (1905): 49–97.
Harvey, Barbara Sillars. "Tradition, Islam and Rebellion: South Sulawesi, 1950–1965". PhD diss., Cornell University, 1974.
Hasselman, C.J. *Algemeen Overzicht van de Uitkomsten van het Welvaart-Onderzoek Gehouden op Java en Madoera in 1904–1905*. 's-Gravenhage: Nijhoff, 1914.

Hatta, M. *Kumpulan Karangan*, vol. 1. Jakarta: Balai Buku Indonesia, 1953.
Hatta, Mohammad. *Sekitar Proklamasi 17 Agustus 1945*. Jakarta: Tintamas, 1970.
————. *Sekitar Proklamasi 17 Agustus 1945*. Jakarta: Tintamas, 1970.
Hazil. *Teku Umar dan Tjut Nja Din: Sepasang Pahlawan Perang Atjeh*. Jakarta: Djambatan, 1951.
Hefner, Robert. "The Political Economy of Islamic Conversion in Modern East Java". In *Islam and the Political Economy of Meaning: Comparative Studies of Muslim Discourse*, ed. William R. Roff. London: Croom Helm, 1987, pp. 57–78.
Heidhues, Mary Somers. *Southeast Asia's Chinese Minorities*. Hawthorn: Longman Australia, 1974.
Heijboer, Pierre. *De politionele acties: de strijd om 'Indië' 1945/1949*. Haarlem: Fibula-Van Dishoeck, 1979.
Heryanto, Ariel. "A Class Act". *Far Eastern Economic Review*, 16 June 1994, p. 30.
Hill, A.H., trans. "The Hikayat Abdullah". *Journal of the Malayan Branch of Royal Asiatic Society* 28, 3 (1955 [orig. publ. 1849]): 1–354.
Hindley, Donald. *The Communist Party of Indonesia*. Berkeley, CA: University of California Press, 1964.
Hiroshi, Matsuo. *The Development of the Javanese Cotton Industry*. Tokyo: Institute of Developing Economies, 1970.
Hirth, F. and W.W. Rockhill, eds. *Chau Ju-Kua: His Work on the Chinese and Arab Trade in the Twelfth and Thirteenth Centuries, Entitled Chu-fan-chi*. St Petersburg, 1911. Reprint, Ch'eng Wen, Taipei, 1970.
Hobsbawm, Eric J. *Nations and Nationalism since 1780*. Cambridge: Cambridge University Press, 1990.
Howard M. Sachar. *The Course of Modern Jewish History*, rev. ed. New York: Vintage Books, 1990, pp. 22–7.
Hsia Liang Lin, "Betelnut as a Useful Taeniafuge". *Chinese Medical Journal* 50 (1937).
Hull, Valerie J., "Women in Java's Rural Middle Class: Progress or Regress". In mimeograph. Yogyakarta: Universitas Gajah Mada Population Institute, 1976.
Huntington, Samuel P. *The Clash of Civilizations and the Remaking of World Order*. New York: Simon & Schuster, 1996.
Hurgronje, Snouck. *The Achehnese*, trans. A.W.S. O'Sullivan. Leiden: Brill, c.1906.
Hussain, Abdullah. *Terjebak*. Kuala Lumpur: Pustaka Antara, 1965.
Ibrahim, Ibn Muhammad. *The Ship of Sulaiman*, trans. J. O'Kane. London: Routledge and Kegan Paul, 1972 (orig. publ. 1688).

Imamura Hitoshi. *Imamura Hitoshi Taisho Kaisoroku*, vol. 4. Tokyo: Jiyu Ajiasha, partly translated in Reid and Oki, *The Japanese Experience*, pp. 31–77.

Indonesia. Departemen Penerangan. *The Indonesian Revolution: Basic Documents and the Idea of Guided Democracy*. Jakarta: Department of Information, 2nd printing 1960.

Iskandar, Teuku. *Kamus Dewan (Dictionary of the Dewan)*. Kuala Lumpur: Dewan Bahasa dan Pustaka, 1970.

Israel, Jonathan. *European Jewry in the Age of Mercantilism, 1550–1750*. Oxford: Oxford University Press, 1985.

Jackson, Karl and Lucien Pye, eds. *Political Power and Communications in Indonesia*. Berkeley, CA: University of California Press, 1978.

Jacobs, E. "Van nood, deugd en handelspolitiek; Intra-Aziatische handel en scheepvaart van de VOC in de tweede helft van de achttiende eeuw; Een verkenning". MA thesis, University of Leiden, 1985.

Jakub, Ismail. "Siapa Orang Besar dari Atjeh? — Teungku Tjhi' di Tiro atau T. Oemar". *Pandji Islam*, 7 March 1940.

──────. *Tengku Tjhik di Tiro: Hidup dan Perdjuangannja*. Kutaradja, 2605, 3rd ed. Jakarta: Bulan Bintang, 1960.

Jane Drakard, "A Kingdom of Words: Minangkabau Sovereignty in Sumatran History". PhD diss., Australian National University, 1993.

Jiang, Joseph P. "Towards a Theory of Pariah Entrepreneurship". In *Leadership and Authority: A Symposium*, ed. G. Wijeyawardene. Singapore: University of Malaya Press, 1968, pp. 147–62.

Johnston, G.A.R., P. Korgsgaard-Larsen and A. Stephenson. "Betel Nut Constituents as Inhibitors of γ-Aminobutyric Acid Uptake". *Nature* 258 (1975): 627–28.

Jomo, K.S. and Shabery Cheek. "Malaysia's Islamic Movements". In *Fragmented Vision: Culture and Politics in Contemporary Malaysia*, eds. Francis Loh and Joel Kahn. Sydney: Allen & Unwin for ASAA, 1992, pp. 79–106.

Jong-Sumatra. 1918.

Jüptner, H. "Klinisch-experimentelle Beobachtungen über Intensives Betalkauen bei den Eingeborenen der Trobriand-Inseln (Neu-Guinea)" [Clinical-experimental Observations on Intensive Betel Chewing Among the Natives of the Trobriand Islands (New Guinea)]. *Zeitschrift für Tropenmedizin und Parasitologie* 19, 2 (1968): 254–7.

Kahin, Audrey. "Struggle for Independence: West Sumatra in the Indonesian National Revolution 1945–1950". PhD diss., Cornell University, 1979.

Kahin, Audrey, ed. *Regional Dynamics of the Indonesian Revolution: Unity from Diversity*. Honolulu: University of Hawai'i Press, 1985.

Kahin, George McT. *Nationalism and Revolution in Indonesia*. Ithaca, NY: Cornell University Press, 1950.

Kahn, Jeffrey. *Federalism, Democratisation and the Rule of Law in Russia*. New York: Oxford University Press, 2002.
Kandarkar, S.V., and S.M. Sirsat. "Changes in Vitamin A Conditioned Hamster Cheek Pouch Epithelium on Exposure to Commercial Shell Lime (Calcium Hydroxide) and Tobacco". *Journal of Oral Pathology* 6, 4 (1977): 19–202.
Kapadia, G.J., E.B. Chung, B. Ghosh, Y.N. Shukla, S.P. Basak, J.F. Morton, and S.N. Pradhan. "Carcinogenicity of Some Folk Medicinal Herbs in Rats". *Journal of the National Cancer Institute* 60, 3 (1978): 683–6.
Kartodirdjo, Sartono. *The Peasants' Revolt of Banten in 1888. Its Conditions, Course and Sequel*. The Hague: Nijhoff for KITLV, 1966.
Kartodirdjo, Soejatno. "Revolution in Surakarta 1945–'50: A Case Study of City and Village in the Indonesian Revolution". PhD diss., Australian National University, 1982.
Kartodirdjo, Soeyatno. "Social and Political Changes in Surakarta after 1945". *Review of Indonesian and Malayan Affairs (RIMA)* 8, 1 (1974): 36–44.
Kausikan, Bilihari. "Asia's Different Standard". *Foreign Policy* 92 (1993): 24–41.
Keating, Michael. *Plurinational Democracy: Stateless Nations in a Post-Sovereignty Era*. Oxford: Oxford University Press, 2001.
Kemasang, A.R.T. "The 1740 Chinese Slaughters in Java: Officially Orchestrated Pogroms". *Kabar Seberang* 16 (December1982): 65–91.
Kertapati, Sidik. *Sekitar Proklamasi 17 Agustus 1945*, 3rd ed. Jakarta: Pembaruan, 1964.
Ki Agoes Mas'oed. *Sedjarah Palembang, moelai dari Seri Widjaya sampai kedatangan Balatentara Dai Nippon*. Palembang: "Sinar Matahari", 1942.
Kiefer, Thomas. *The Tausug: Violence and Law in a Philippine Moslem Society*. New York: Holt, Rhinehart & Winston, 1972.
Kiernan, Ben. *The Pol Pot Regime: Race, Power, and Genocide in Cambodia under the Khmer Rouge, 1975–79*. New Haven, CT: Yale University Press, 1996.
Kita-Sumatora-Sinbun (daily, Medan), 2603–5 (1943–1945).
Klinkert, H.C. *Nieuw Maleisch-Nederlandsch Woordenboek*, 5th ed. Leiden: Brill, 1947.
Kohn, Hans. *Nationalism: Its Meaning and History*. Princeton, NJ: Van Nostrand, 1955.
Koloniaal Verslag: Bijlage van het Verslag der Handelingen van de Tweede Kamer der Staten-Generaal. The Hague: Ministerie van Kolonien, 1860–1900.
Korthals, Altes W.L. *General Trade Statistics, 1822–1940, Changing Economy in Indonesia*, vol. 12A. Amsterdam: Royal Tropical Institute, 1991.
Kraan, A. van der. "Bali and Lombok in the World Economy, 1830–1850". *Review of Indonesian and Malaysian Affairs* 27 (1993): 91–105.

Kraan, Alphonse van der. "Bali: Slavery and the Slave Trade". In *Slavery, Bondage and Dependency in Southeast Asia*, ed. Anthony Reid. St Lucia: University of Queensland Press, 1983.

Krom, N.J. *Hindoe-Javaansche Geschiedenis*. 's-Gravenhage: M. Nijhoff, 1931.

Kumar, A. "Javanese Historiography in and of the 'Colonial Period': A Case Study". In *Perceptions of the Past in Southeast Asia*, eds. A. Reid and D. Marr. Singapore: Heinemann, 1979, pp. 187–206.

La Loubère, Simon de. *Du Royaume de Siam*, vol. 1. Paris: Jean Baptiste Coignard, 1691.

Laarhoven, R. "The Power of Cloth: The Textile Trade of the Dutch East India Company (VOC), 1600–1780". PhD thesis, Australian National University, 1994.

Landon, Kenneth P. *The Chinese in Thailand*. London: Oxford University Press, 1941.

Langenberg, Michael van. "East Sumatra: Accommodating an Indonesian Nation within a Sumatran Residency". In *Regional Dynamics of the Indonesian Revolution: Unity from Diversity*, ed. A. Kahin. Honolulu: University of Hawai'i Press, 1985, pp. 113–43.

──────. "National Revolution in North Sumatra: Sumatera Timur and Tapanuli, 1942–1950". Unpublished PhD diss., University of Sydney, 1976.

Leur, J.C. van. *Indonesian Trade and Society: Essays in Asian Social and Economic History*. The Hague: Nijhoff, 1955.

Lev, Daniel. "Indonesia 1965: The Year of the Coup". *Asian Survey* 6, 2 (February 1966).

Levine, Hillel. *Economic Origins of Anti-Semitism: Poland and Its Jews in the Early Modern Period*. New Haven, CT: Yale University Press, 1991.

Lewin, Louis. *Phantastica: Narcotic and Stimulating Drugs, Their Use and Abuse*. London: Routledge and Kegan Paul, 1964.

Liaw Yock Fang. *Undang-undang Melaka. The Laws of Melaka*. The Hague: Nijhoff for KITLV, 1976.

Liddle, William, "*Media Dakwah* Scripturalism: One Form of Islamic Political Thought and Action in New Order Indonesia". In *Towards a New Paradigm: Recent Developments in Indonesian Islamic Thought*, eds. Mark Woodward and James Rush. Tempe: Arizona State University Press, 1996.

Lieberman, Victor. *Burmese Administrative Cycles: Anarchy and Conquest, c.1580–1760*. Princeton, NJ: Princeton University Press, 1984.

Lindsey, Timothy. *The Romance of K'tut Tantri and Indonesia*. Kuala Lumpur: Oxford University Press, 1977.

Lodge, D., G.A.R. Johnston, D.R. Curtis, and S.J. Brand. "Effects of the *Areca* Nut Constituents Arecadaine and Guvacine on the Action of GABA in the Cat Central Nervous System". *Brain Research* 136 (1977): 513–22.

Lombard, Denys. Le 'Spraeck ende Woord-boek' de Frederick de Houtman: Première Méthode de Malais Parlé (fin du XVIe s.). Paris: EFEO, 1970.

―――――. Le Carrefour Javanais: Essai d'Histoire Globale, 3 vols. Paris: EHESS, 1990.

Lookeren Campagne, C.J. van. "Tabak" (Tobacco). In *Encyclopaedie van Nederlandsch-Indië (Encyclopedia of Netherlands India)*. 's-Graven-hage, Brill 4 (1905): 220–54.

Louwes, L.S. "Strafrecht". In *Encyclopedië van Nederlandsch-Indië*, 2nd ed. The Hague: Martinus Nijhoff and EJ Brill, 1921.

Low, James. *The British Settlement of Penang*. Singapore: Singapore Free Press, 1836.

Lucas, Anton. "The Bamboo Spear Pierces the Payung: The Revolution against the Bureaucratic Elite in North Central Java in 1945". Unpublished PhD diss., Australian National University, 1981.

―――――. *One Soul One Struggle: Region and Revolution in Indonesia*. Sydney: Allen & Unwin, 1991.

Lyman, Henry. *The Martyr of Sumatra: A Memoir of Henry Lyman*. New York: Robert Carter and Brothers, 1856, pp. 368–77.

Ma Huan. *Ying-yai Sheng-lan: 'The Overall Survey of the Ocean's Shores' (1433)*, trans. J.V.G. Mills. Cambridge: Hakluyt Society, 1970.

Mackie, J.A.C. "Anti-Chinese Outbreaks in Indonesia". In *The Chinese in Indonesia*, ed. J.A.C. Mackie. London: Nelson, 1976, pp. 77–138.

Maddison, Angus. *The World Economy: A Millennial Perspective*. Paris: Development Centre of OECD, 2001.

Mailrapporten, from Batavia to Ministry of Colonies in The Hague. The Hague: Algemeene Rijksarchief, 1872–1902.

Malaka, Tan. *Menudju Republik Indonesia (1925)*. Jakarta: Jajasan Masa, 1962.

Malik, Adam. *Riwajat dan Perdjuangan sekitar Proklamasi Kemerdekaan Indonesia 17 Agustus 1945*, rev. ed. Jakarta: Widjaya, 1970.

Malley, Michael. "Regions: Centralization and Resistance". In *Indonesia Beyond Suharto*, ed. Donald K. Emmerson. New York: The Asia Society, 1999, pp. 71–105.

Manderson, Lenore. "Roasting, Smoking, and Dieting in Response to Birth: Malay Confinement in Cross-Cultural Perspective". *Social Science and Medicine* 15B (1981): 509–20.

Manguin, P.-Y. "Manpower and Labour Categories in Early Sixteenth-Century Malacca". In *Slavery, Bondage and Dependency in Southeast Asia*, ed. Anthony Reid. St Lucia: University of Queensland Press, 1983.

Mangunwijaya, Y.B. *Menuju Republik Indonesia Serikat*. Jakarta: Gramedia, 1998.

Maradjo, Marah. *Tanaman Penyegar (Refreshing Plants): Flora Indonesia Jilid 1.* Jakarta: Nusantara, 1977.

Marini, G.F. de. *Delle Missione de Padri della Compagnia de Giesu nella Provincia di Giappone, particolarmente di quelle de Tumkino.* Rome: Nicolo Angelo Tinassi, 1663.

Marks, H.J. *The First Contest for Singapore, 1819–1824.* The Hague: KITLV, 1959.

Marsden, William. *A Dictionary and Grammar of the Malayan Language.* 1812. Reprint, Singapore: Oxford University Press, 1984.

──────. *A History of Sumatra.* London: Longman, 1811. Reprint, Kuala Lumpur: 1966.

Matthes, B.F. *Boegineesch-Hollandsch Woordenboek.* 's-Gravenhage: Nijhoff, 1874.

McCagg, William O. *A History of Hapsburg Jews, 1670–1918.* Bloomington: Indiana University Press, 1989.

McGregor, Katherine. *History in Uniform: Military Ideology and the Construction of Indonesia's Past.* Singapore: NUS Press, 2007.

McNair, J.E.A. *Perak and the Malays.* London: 1878. Reprint, Kuala Lumpur: Oxford University Press, 1972.

McVey, Ruth T. *The Rise of Indonesian Communism.* Ithaca, NY: Cornell University Press, 1965.

McVey, Ruth. "The Enchantment of the Revolution: History and Action in an Indonesian Communist Text". In *Perceptions of the Past*, eds. A. Reid and D. Marr. Singapore: Heinemann, 1979.

──────. *The Soviet View of the Indonesian Revolution.* Ithaca, NY: Cornell Modern Indonesia Project, 1957.

Metcalf, Peter. *A Borneo Journey into Death: Berawan Eschatology from Its Rituals.* Philadelphia: University of Pennsylvania Press, 1982.

Miles, Douglas. *Cutlass and Crescent Moon.* Sydney: Centre for Asian Studies, University of Sydney, 1976.

Miller, Michelle. "What's Special about Special Autonomy in Aceh?" In *Verandah of Violence*, ed. A. Reid. Singapore: NUS Press, 2006, pp. 292–314.

Milner, A. *Kerajaan: Malay Political Culture on the Eve of Colonial Rule.* Tucson: University of Arizona Press, 1982.

Milner, Anthony. *The Invention of Politics in Colonial Malaya: Contesting Nationalism and the Expansion of the Public Sphere.* Cambridge: Cambridge University Press, 1994.

Miyamoto Shizuo. *Jawa Shusen Shoriki.* Tokyo: Java Shusen Shoriki Kankoka, 1973. Partly translated in Reid and Oki, *The Japanese Experience*, pp. 217–50, 325–40.

Modal Revolusi 45. Kutaraja: Komite Musjawarah Angkatan 45 Daerah Istimewa Atjeh, 1960, p. 61.

Moeis, Abdul. *Surapati*. Jakarta: Balai Pustaka, 1952 (orig. publ. Batavia, 1905).

Mohamad, Mahathir and Shintaro Ishihara. *The Voice of Asia: Two Leaders Discuss the Coming Century*. Tokyo: Kodansha, 1995 (orig. publ. in Japanese under the title *The Asia That Can Say No*, 1994).

Mohammed, Mahathir. *The Malay Dilemma*. Singapore: Asia Pacific Press, 1970.

Möller, I.J., J.J. Pindborg, and I. Effendi. "The Relation between Betel Chewing and Dental Caries". *Scandinavian Journal of Dental Research* 85 (1977): 64–70.

Montesquieu, Baron de. *The Spirit of the Laws*, trans. T. Nugent. New York: Hafner, 1949.

Moore, Barrington. *Social Origins of Dictatorship and Democracy: Lord and Peasant in the Making of the Modern World*. London: Allen Lane, 1967.

Morgan, E.S. *American Slavery — American Freedom: The Ordeal of Colonial Virginia*. New York: Norton, 1975.

Morris, Eric. "Aceh: Social Revolution and Islamic Vision". In *Regional Dynamics of the Indonesian Revolution: Unity from Diversity*, ed. A. Kahin. Honolulu: University of Hawai'i Press, 1985, pp. 83–110.

Mundy, R. *Narrative of Events in Borneo and Celebes Down to the Occupation of Labuan: From the Journals of James Brooke, Esq. Rajah of Sarawak. Together with a Narrative of the Operations of H.M.S. Iris*. London, 1848.

Munir, Rozy, Budi Utomo, and Bambang Sutrisno. "Ketagihan Merokok pada Penduduk Desa". *Sinar Harapan*, 23 April 1982.

Muzaffar, Chandra. *Islamic Resurgence in Malaysia*. Petaling Jaya: Penerbit Fajar Bakti, 1987.

Nagazumi, Akira. *The Dawn of Indonesian Nationalism: The Early Years of Budi Utomo, 1908–1918*. Tokyo: Institute of Developing Economies, 1972.

Nagtegaal, Luc. "Rijden op een Hollandse tijger: De noordkust van Java en de V.O.C., 1680–1743". PhD diss., Rijksuniversiteit te Utrecht, 1988.

⸻. *Riding the Dutch Tiger: The Dutch East Indies Company and the Northeast Coast of Java, 1680–1743*. Leiden: KITLV, 1996.

Nanda, Ram S., and Krishna Kapoor. "Fluoride Content of Piper Betel and Its Constituents". *Indian Journal of Medical Research* 59 (1971): 1966–70.

Nasution, Adnan Buyung. "The Aspiration for Constitutional Government in Indonesia: A Socio-Legal Study of the Indonesian Konstituante 1956–1959". PhD diss., Utrecht, 1992.

Newbold, T.J. *Political and Statistical Account of the British Settlements in the Straits of Malacca, 1839*. Reprint, Kuala Lumpur: Oxford University Press, 1971.

Ng Chin Keong, "The Case of Ch'en I-lao: Maritime Trade and Overseas Chinese in Ch'ing Policies, 1717–1754". In *Emporia, Commodities and Entrepreneurs in Asian Maritime Trade, c.1400–1750*, eds. R. Ptak and D. Rothermund. Stuttgart: Franz Steiner, 1991, pp. 373–400.

Nguyen Duc Minh. "Medicinal Plants with Anti-Bacterial Properties". *Vietnamese Studies* 50 (n.d.): 51–76.

Nieboer, Herman J. *Slavery as an Industrial System: Ethnological Researches*, 2nd ed. The Hague: Nijhoff, 1910.

Nieschultz, O. "The Pharmacology of Betel Nuts". *Arzneim.-Forsch* 20 (1970): 218–29.

Nishijima, Shigetada. *Shogen: Indoneshia Dokuritsu Kakumei — Aru Nihonjin Kakumeika No Hansei*. Tokyo: Shin Jinbutsu Orai-sha, 1975. Partly translated in Reid and Oki, *The Japanese Experience*, pp. 251–75, 299–324.

Noer, Deliar. "Yamin and Hamka: Two Routes to an Indonesian Identity". In *Perceptions of the Past in Southeast Asia*. Singapore: Heinemann for ASAA, 1979, pp. 249–62.

Noorduyn, J. *Een Achttiende-eeuwse Kroniek van Wadjo': Buginese Historiografie*. The Hague: Smits, 1955.

_____. "Arung Singkang (1700–1765): How the Victory of Wadjo". *Indonesia* 13 (1972): 61–8.

Nordholt, H.G. Schulte. "Macht, Mensen en Middelen: Patronen van Dynamiek in de Balische Politiek, 1700–1840". PhD diss., Vrije Universiteit, Amsterdam, 1980.

Nordholt, Henk Schulte. "Leadership and the Limits of Political Control. A Balinese 'Response' to Clifford Geertz". *Social Anthropology* 1, 3 (1993): 291.

Nørlund, I. "The French Empire, the Colonial State in Vietnam and Economic Policy, 1885–1940". *Australian Economic History Review* 31 (1991): 72–89.

Noto Soeroto, R.M. *De Ontwikkeling van het Volk von Java*, 1931.

_____. *Het Sultanaat Jogjokarto*. Hadi Poestaka, 1920.

O'Kane, John, ed. *The Ship of Sulaiman*. London: Routledge and Kegan Paul, 1972.

O'Malley, William J. "Indonesia in the Great Depression: A Study of East Sumatra and Jogjakarta in the 1930s". PhD thesis, Cornell University, 1977.

Oki Akira, "Social Change in the West Sumatran Village". PhD thesis, Australian National University, 1977.

Okuma Memorial Social Sciences Research Institute, Waseda University. *Japanese Military Administration in Indonesia*. Washington: US Department of Commerce, Joint Publications Research Service, 1963.

Omar, Ariffin. *Bangsa Melayu: Malay Concepts of Democracy and Community 1945–1950*. Singapore: Oxford University Press, 1993.

Onghokham. "The Residency of Madiun. Priyayi and Peasant in the Nineteenth Century". PhD thesis, Yale University, 1976.

Ong-Tae-Hae (Wang Ta-hai). *The Chinaman Abroad: An Account of the Malayan Archipelago, Particularly of Java*, trans. W.H. Medhurst. London: John Snow, 1850 (orig. publ. 1791), pp. 14–8.

Oyen, L.A.T.J.F. van. "Antwoord no. 16". *BKMH* 32 (1905): 118–30.

Pane, Sanusi. *Sedjarah Indonesia*, 4 vols. Jakarta: Balai Poestaka, 2603–5 (1943–1945). Reissued as *Sedjarah Indonesia*. Jakarta: Perpustakaan Perguruan Kem. P.P. dan K., 1965.

Pang Eng Fong. "Race, Income Distribution and Development in Malaysia and Singapore". In *The Chinese in Southeast Asia*, eds. Linda Lim and Peter Gosling. Singapore: Maruzen, 1983, pp. 316–35.

Patterson, Orlando. *Freedom in the Making of Western Culture*. New York: Basic Books, 1991.

———. *Slavery and Social Death*. Cambridge, Mass.: Harvard University Press, 1982.

Pelras, Christian. "Hiérarchie et Pouvoir Traditionnel en Pays Wajo". *Archipel* 1 (1971): 161–91.

Pemerintah Poesat Soematera. *Boekoe Peringatan Satoe Tahoen N.R.I. di Soematera: 17-8-'45–17-8-'46*. Penatang Siantar, 1946.

Penders, Chr. L.M. *Indonesia: Selected Documents on Colonialism and Nationalism, 1830–1942*. St Lucia: University of Queensland Press, 1972.

Penzer, N.M. *Poison-Damsels and Other Essays in Folklore and Anthropology*. London: Chas. Sawyer, 1952.

Piekaar, A.J. *Atjeh en de oorlog met Japan*. The Hague: Van Hoeve, 1949.

Pigafetta, Antonio. *First Voyage Round the World*, trans. J.A. Robertson. Manila: Filipiniana Book Guild, 1969.

Pigeaud, Th.G.Th. *Java in the Fourteenth Century. A Study in Cultural History*. The Hague: Nijhoff, 1960–1963.

Pires, Tomé. *The Suma Oriental*, trans. A. Cortesão. London: Hakluyt Society, 1944.

Porsius, A.J., E. Mutschler, and P.A. van Swieten. "The Central Action of Various Arecaidine Esters (Arecoline Derivatives) on Blood Pressure and Heart Rate in the Cat". *Arzneim.-Forsch* 28, 8 (1978): 1373–6.

Prijono, Raden. *Sedikit tentang sedjarah Asia Tinger Raja dan Sedjarah Tanah Djawa*. Jakarta: Balai Poestaka, 2605.

Pringgodigdo, A.K. *Sedjarah Pergerakan Rakjat Indonesia*, 1949, 5th ed. Jakarta: Pustaka Rakjat, 1964.

Purcell, Victor. *The Chinese in Southeast Asia*, 2nd ed. London: Oxford University Press, 1965.

Rabibhadana, M.R. Akin. *The Organization of Thai Society in the Early Bangkok Period, 1782–1873*. Ithaca, NY: Southeast Asia Program, Cornell University, 1969.

Raffles, Sophia, ed. *Memoir of the Life and Public Services of Sir Thomas Stamford Raffles*. London: James Duncan, 1835.

Raffles, Sophia. *Memoir of the Life and Public Services of Sir Thomas Stamford Raffles*, vol 2. London: James Duncan, 1835.

Raffles, T.S. *The History of Java*, 2 vols. London, 1817. Reprint, Kuala Lumpur: Oxford University Press, 1978.

Ranadive, K.J., S.V. Gothoskar, A.R. Rao, B.U. Tezabwalla, and R.Y. Ambaye, "Experimental Studies on Betel Nut and Tobacco Carcinogenicity". *International Journal of Cancer* 17, 4 (1976): 469–76.

Reed, D. "Current Status of Cancer Studies in the South Pacific". *National Cancer Institute Monograph* 47 (1977): 61–6.

Reeve, David. *Golkar of Indonesia: An Alternative to the Party System*. Singapore: Oxford University Press, 1985.

Reid, A.J.S. "Nineteenth-century Pan-Islam in Indonesia and Malaysia". *Journal of Asian Studies* 27 (1967): 276–83.

——————. *The Contest for North Sumatra: Acheh, the Netherlands and Britain, 1858–1898*. Kuala Lumpur: Oxford University Press, 1969.

Reid, Anthony. "The Unthreatening Alternative: Chinese Shipping in Southeast Asia, 1567–1842". *Review of Indonesian and Malaysian Affairs* 27 (1993): 13–32.

——————. "Early Chinese Migration into North Sumatra". In *Studies in the Social History of China and South-east Asia*, eds. Jerome Ch'en and Nicholas Tarling. Cambridge: Cambridge University Press, 1970.

——————. "Flows and Seepages in the Long-term Chinese Interaction with Southeast Asia". In *Sojourners and Settlers*, ed. Anthony Reid. Sydney: Allen & Unwin, 1996, pp. 15–50.

——————. "Kings, Kadis and Charisma in the Seventeenth Century Archipelago". In *The Making of an Islamic Political Discourse in Southeast Asia*, ed. Anthony Reid. Clayton, Victoria: Papers on Southeast Asia, Monash University Centre for SE Asian Studies, 1993, pp. 83–107.

——————. "Marxist Attitudes to Social Revolution, 1946–1948". *Review of Indonesian and Malayan Affairs* 8, 1 (1974): 45–56.

——————. "Political 'Tradition' in Indonesia: The One and the Many". *Asian Studies Review* 22, 1 (1998): 23–38.

——————. "The Birth of the Republic in Sumatra". *Indonesia* 12 (1971): 21–46.

——————. "The Japanese Occupation and Rival Indonesian Elites: Northern Sumatra in 1942". *Journal of Asian Studies* 35 (1975): 49–61.

_____. 'Heaven's Will and Man's Fault': The Rise of the West as a Southeast Asian Dilemma. Flinders Asian Studies Lecture 6. Bedford Park: Flinders University, 1975.

_____. Southeast Asia in the Age of Commerce, 1450–1680, vol. 1, The Lands below the Winds; vol. 2, Expansion and Crisis. New Haven, CT: Yale University Press, 1988–1993.

_____. The Blood of the People: Revolution and the End of Traditional Rule in Northern Sumatra. Kuala Lumpur: Oxford, 1979.

_____. The Indonesian National Revolution. Melbourne: Longman, 1974.

_____. Verandah of Violence: The Background to the Aceh Problem. Singapore: NUS Press, 2006.

Reid, Anthony and David Marr, eds. Perceptions of the Past in Southeast Asia. Singapore: Heinemann Educational Books (Asia), for ASAA, 1979.

Reid, Anthony, ed. Slavery, Bondage and Dependency in Southeast Asia. St Lucia: University of Queensland Press, 1983.

Resink, G.J. Indonesia's History between the Myths. The Hague: Van Hoeve, 1968.

Reynolds, Craig J., ed. National Identity and Its Defenders: Thailand 1939–1989. Clayton, Victoria: Centre of Southeast Asian Studies, Monash University, 1991.

Ricklefs, M.C. "Unity and Disunity in Javanese Political and Religious Thought of the Eighteenth Century". In Looking in Odd Mirrors: The Java Sea, eds. V.J.H. Houben, H.M.J. Maier and W. van der Molen. Leiden University: Vakgroep Talen en Culturen van Zuidoost-Azië en Oceanië, 1992, pp. 60–75.

_____. Modern Javanese Historical Tradition: A Study of the Original Kartasura Chronicle and Related Materials. London: School of Oriental and African Studies, 1978.

_____. The Seen and Unseen Worlds in Java. New South Wales: Allen & Unwin; Honolulu: University of Hawai'i Press, 1998.

Ricklefs, Merle C. A History of Modern Indonesia. London: Macmillan, 1981.

Rinder, Irwin. "Strangers in the Land: Social Relations in the Status Gap". Social Problems 6 (1958–1959): 253–60.

Riwajat dan Perdjoangan pahlawan-pahlawan Indonesia sepintas lalu. Madiun: Panitya Pasar Malam Syuu Hookookai, 2605.

Robison, Richard. "Capitalism and the Bureaucratic State in Indonesia 1965–1975". PhD thesis, University of Sydney, 1977.

_____. "Toward a Class Analysis of the Indonesian Military Bureaucratic State". Indonesia 25 (1978): 17–39.

Rookmaker, H.R. "Antwoord no. 18". BKMH 32 (1905): 18–48.

Ross, Cameron. Federalism and Democratisation in Post-Communist Russia. Manchester: Manchester University Press, 2003.

Rush, James. "Opium in Java: A Sinister Friend". *Journal of Asian Studies* 3 (1985): 549–60.

―――――. *Opium to Java: Revenue Farming and Chinese Enterprise in Colonial Indonesia, 1860–1910*. Ithaca, NY: Cornell University Press, 1990.

Ruslan Abdulgani. *Penggunaan Ilmu Sedjarah*. Bandung: n.d. [1963?].

Rutgers, S.J. and A. Huber. *Indonesie*. Amsterdam: Pegasus, 1937.

Salmon, Claudine. "Ancestral Halls, Funeral Associations, and Attempts at Resinicization in Nineteenth Century Southeast Asia". In *Sojourners and Settlers*, ed. A. Reid. Sydney: Allen & Unwin, 1996, pp. 183–214.

Salmon, Claudine, ed. *Le Moment "Sino-Malais" de la Littérature Indonésienne*. Paris: Cahiers d'Archipel, 1992.

Sartono Kartodirdjo, Marwati Djoened Poesponegoro, Nugroho Notosusanto, eds. *Sejarah Nasional Indonesia*, 6 vols. Jakarta: Balai Pustaka, 1977.

Sastro Winangoen, "Antwoord no. 4". *BKMH* 32 (1905): 134–41.

Schärer, H. *Ngaju Religion*, trans. R. Needham. The Hague: Nijhoff, 1963.

Schoute, D. *De geneeskunde in den Dienst der Oost-Indische Compagnie in Nederlandsch-Indie*. Amsterdam: de Bussy, 1929.

Schreiner, Klaus. *Politischer Heldenkult in Indonesien*. Hamburg: Dietrich Reimer, 1995.

Scott, Edmund. "An Exact Discourse of the East Indians". In *The Voyage of Sir Henry Middleton to the Moluccas, 1604–1606*, ed. W. Foster. London: Hakluyt Society, 1943.

Scott, James C. "Freedom and Freehold: Space, People and State Simplification in Southeast Asia". In *Asian Freedoms: The Idea of Freedom in East and Southeast Asia*, eds. David Kelly and Anthony Reid. Cambridge: Cambridge University Press, 1998.

Scott, James. "Freedom and Freehold: Space, People and State Simplification in Southeast Asia". In *Asian Freedoms: The Idea of Freedom in East and Southeast Asia*, eds. David Kelly and Anthony Reid. Cambridge: Cambridge University Press, 1998.

Segers, W.A.I.M. "De Strootjes Industrie in Nederlandsch-Indie: Een Reddingsboei voor Een Bevolkings Economie in Nood" (The Native Cigarette Industry in Netherlands India: A Lifebuoy for a Popular Economy in Need). MA thesis, University of Amsterdam, 1982.

Shiraishi, Takashi. *An Age in Motion: Popular Radicalism in Java, 1912–1926*. Ithaca, NY: Cornell University Press, 1990.

Siahaan, L. *Ichtisar sedjarah Indonesia untuk Sekolah Menengah*. Bandung: Poestaka Ksatrian, 2604.

Siegel, James. *The Rope of God*. Berkeley, CA: University of California Press, 1969.

Simanjuntak, Marsillam. *Pandangan Negara Integralistik: Sumber, Unsur dan Riwayatnya dalam Persiapan UUD 1945*. Jakarta: Grafiti, 1994.

Simorangkir, B., ed. *Otonomi atau Federalisme: Dampaknya terhadap Pembangunan*. Jakarta: Sinar Harapan, 2000.

Sjahrir, Soetan. *Out of Exile*, trans. Charles Wolf. New York: John Day, 1949.

Sjamsuddin, Nazaruddin. "The Course of the National Revolution in Aceh, 1945-'49". Masters thesis, Monash University, 1974.

——. *The Republican Revolt: A Study of the Acehnese Rebellion*. Singapore: Institute of Southeast Asian Studies, 1985.

Skeat, W.W. *Malay Magic: Being an Introduction to the Folklore and Popular Religion of the Malay Peninsula*. London, 1900. Reprint, New York: Dover Publications, 1967.

Skinner, G. William. "Creolized Chinese Societies in Southeast Asia". In *Sojourners and Settlers*, ed. A. Reid. Sydney: Allen & Unwin, 1996, pp. 51-93.

——. *Chinese Society in Thailand: An Analytical History*. Ithaca, NY: Cornell University Press, 1957.

Smail, John. *Bandung in the Early Revolution, 1945-1946. A Study in the Social History of the Indonesian Revolution*. Ithaca, NY: Modern Indonesian Project, Southeast Asia Program, Department of Asian Studies, Cornell University, 1964.

Smith, Anthony. *The Ethnic Origins of Nations*. Oxford: Blackwell, 1986.

Soeara Proletar [pseud.]. *Pembongkaran Tiga Rahsia Penting I*. Silungkang: Pustaka Sofjan Pondha, 1946.

Soedjana, R. Koesoema. "Aan mijn Javaansche broeders". *Wederopbouw* 1 (1918): 139-41.

Soedjatmoko *et al*., eds. *An Introduction to Indonesian Historiography*. Ithaca, NY: Cornell University Press, 1965.

Soemarsono. "Review of Fruin-Mees". *Wederopbouw* 3 (1920): 83-7.

Soeriokoesoemo. "Een beschouwing over de vormen der overheersching". *Wederopbouw* 2 (1919).

——. "Gewijd aan mijn Kameraden in 'Insulinde'". *Wederopbouw* 1 (1918): 9.

——. "Het Javaansche Vraagstuk". *Wederopbouw* 1 (1918): 4-7.

——. "Kangdjeng Sultan Agoeng als Wijsgeer". *Wederopbouw* 2 (1919): 2-12.

——. "Waarom Javaansch- en Geen Indisch- Nationalism?" *Wederopbouw* 1 (1918): 80-1.

Soeroto, R.M. Noto. *Van Overheersching naar Zelfregeering*. 's-Gravenhage: Adi-Poestaka, 1931.

Sombart, Werner. *The Jews and Modern Capitalism*. Glencoe, Illinois: Free Press, 1951 (orig. publ. 1911).

Somer, J.M. *De Korte Verklaring*. Breda: Corona, 1934.
Speelman, Cornelis. "Notitie dienende voor eene Korte Tijd en tot nader last van de Hoge Regering op Batavia voor den Ondercoopman Jan van Oppijnen". Typescript copy held in KITLV, Leiden, 1670.
St John, Spenser. *Life in the Forests of the Far East*, 2 vols. London, 1862. Reprint, Kuala Lumpur: Oxford University Press, 1974.
Stapel, F.W. *Geschiedenis van NederlandschIndie*. Amsterdam: Meulenhoff, 1930.
Statistical Pocketbook of Indonesia, 1941. Batavia: Central Bureau of Statistics, 1947.
Statistical Pocketbook of Indonesia. Jakarta: Biro Pusat Statistik, 1961, p. 109.
Stavorinus, J.S. *Voyage to the East Indies*, 3 vols., trans. S.H. Wilcocke. London: 1798. Reprint, London: Dawsons of Pall Mall, 1969.
Stoll, G. "Sirih en Sirihkauwers" (Betel and Betel Chewers). *BKMH* 32 (1905): 11–7.
Stricherz, M.E. and P. Pratt. "Betel Quid and Reaction Time". *Pharmacology Biochemistry and Behaviour* 4 (1976): 627–8.
Sukarno and Cindy H. Adams. *Sukarno: An Autobiography as told to Cindy Adams*. Hong Kong: Gunung Agung, 1966.
Sukarno. "Swadeshi dan Massa-Aski di Indonesia" (1932). In *Dibawah Bendera Revolusi*, vol. 1. Jakarta: Panitya Penerbit Dibawah Bendera Revolusi, 1963.
―――. *Mentjapai Indonesia Merdeka* (1933). Jakarta: Tjita Agung, n.d.
―――. *Indonesia Menggugat. Pidato pembelaan Bung Karno dimuka hakim colonial*. Jakarta: S.K. Seno, 1956.
Sulaiman, M. Isa. "From Autonomy to Periphery: A Critical Evaluation of the Acehnese Nationalist Movement". In *Verandah of Violence*, ed. Anthony Reid. Singapore: NUS Press, 2006, pp. 121–48.
―――. *Aceh Merdeka: Ideologi, Kepemimpinan dan Gerakan*. Jakarta: Pustaka al Kausar, 2000.
―――. *Sejarah Aceh: Sebuah Gugatan Terhadap Tradisi*. Jakarta: Pustaka Sinar Harapan, 1997.
Sumatra Sinbun (Bukittinggi) 2603–5 (1943–1945).
Sumatraantje [pseud.]. "Kantteekeningen". *Jong-Sumatra* 9 (1926).
Supomo. "The Image of Majapahit in Later Javanese and Indonesian Writing". In *Perceptions of the Past*, eds. Reid and Marr.
Surya Ningrat (Ki Hadjar Dewantara). "Het Javaansch Nationalisme in de Indische Beweging". In *'Soembangsih': Gedenkboek Boedi-Oetomo 1902–20 mei-1918*. Amsterdam: Nederl. Indie Oud en Nieuw, 1918.
Suryadinata, Leo. 1992: 145–64.
―――. *Pribumi Indonesians, the Chinese Minority and China*, 3rd ed. Singapore: Heinemann, 1992.

SUSENAS. *Survei Sosial Ekonomi Nasional (National Socio-economic Survey)*. Jakarta: Biro Pusat Statistik, 1976, 1978, 1980.

Sutherland, Heather. "Slavery and the Slave Trade in South Sulawesi, 1660s–1800s". In *Slavery, Bondage and Dependency in Southeast Asia*, ed. Anthony Reid. St Lucia: University of Queensland Press, 1983.

———. *The Making of a Bureaucratic Elite: The Colonial Transformation of the Javanese Priyayi*. Singapore: Heinemann (for the ASAA), 1979.

Szekely, Ladislao. *Tropic Fever*. Kuala Lumpur: Oxford University Press, 1979 (orig. publ. London: 1937).

Szekely-Lulofs, M.H. *Tjoet nja Dien*. Amsterdam: 1948, Indonesian translation 1951.

Tan Liok Ee. *The Rhetoric of Bangsa and Minzu: Community and Nation in Tension, the Malay Peninsula, 1900–1955*. Clayton, Victoria: Centre of Southeast Asian Studies, Monash University, 1988.

Taylor, Jean. *Indonesia: Peoples and Histories*. New Haven, CT: Yale University Press, 2003.

Teeuw, A. *Modern Indonesian Literature*. The Hague: M. Nijhoff, 1967.

Terwiel, B. *The Tai of Assam and Ancient Tai Ritual*, vol. 1. Gaya: Centre for Southeast Asian Studies, 1980.

Tilly, Charles. *The Vendée*. Cambridge: Harvard University Press, 1964.

Tinker, Hugh. *A New System of Slavery: The Export of Indian Labour Overseas, 1830–1920*. London: Oxford University Press, 1974.

Tiro, Hasan Muhammad. *Demokrasi Untuk Indonesia*, Atjeh, n.d. [1958?].

———. *Perang Atjeh, 1873–1927 M* (stencilled). Jogjakarta: April 1948.

Tjipto Mangoenkoesoemo. "Nationalisme Hindia dan hak Hidupnja", late 1917, reproduced in M. Balfas, *Dr Tjipto Mangoenkoesoemo: Demokrat sedjati*. Jakarta: Djambatan, 1952, pp. 75–82.

Tjokroaminoto, H.O.S. *Islam dan Sosialism*, 1924. Reprint, Jakarta: Lembaga Penggali dan Penghimpun Sedjarah Revolusi Indonesia, 1963.

Trocki, Carl A. *Prince of Pirates: The Temenggongs and the Development of Johor and Singapore, 1784–1885*. Singapore: Singapore University Press, 1979.

Tsuchiya, Kenji. *Democracy and Leadership: The Rise of the Taman Siswa Movement in Indonesia*. Honolulu: University of Hawai'i Press, 1987.

Twang Peck Yang. "Indonesian Chinese Business Communities in Transformation, 1940–1950". PhD thesis, Australian National University, 1987, pp. 74–83.

———. *The Indonesian Business Elite in Indonesia and the Transition to Independence, 1940–1950*. Kuala Lumpur: Oxford University Press, 1998.

Veth, P.J. *Java, Geographisch, Ethnologisch, Historisch*, vol. 1. Haarlem: E.F. Bohn, 1875.

Vietnam Population Census 1989, vol. 1. Hanoi: Central Census Steering Committee, 1991.

Vittach, Tarzie. *The Fall of Sukarno*. London: Andre Deutsch, 1967.
Wal, S.L. van der, ed. *Het Onderwijsbeleid in Nederlands-Indie 1900–1940: een Bronnenpublikatie*. Groningen: J.B. Wolters, 1963.
Wang Gungwu. *Community and Nation: Essays on Southeast Asia and the Chinese*. Singapore: Heinemann, 1981.
Watson, James L., ed. *Asian and African Systems of Slavery*. Berkeley, CA: University of California Press, 1980.
Weber, Max. *Economy and Society. An Outline of Interpretive* Sociology. New York: Bedminster, 1968.
─────────. *The Protestant Ethic and the Spirit of Capitalism*, trans. Talcott Parsons. London: Unwin University Books, 1930.
─────────. *The Sociology of Religion*, trans. E. Fischoff. London: Methuen, 1963.
Wertheim, W. Ph. *East-West Parallels: Sociological Approaches to Modern Asia*. The Hague: van Hoeve, 1964.
Wertheim, W. "Indonesia Before and After the Untung Coup". *Pacific Affairs* 39 (Spring-Summer 1966): 115–27.
Wessel, Ingrid and Georgia Wimhofer, eds. *Violence in Indonesia*. Hamburg: Abera, 2001.
Wheatley, Paul. *The Golden Khersonese*. Kuala Lumpur: University of Malaya Press, 1961.
Wickberg, Edgar. *The Chinese in Philippine Life, 1850–1898*. New Haven, CT: Yale University Press, 1965.
Wilkinson, R.J. *A Malay-English Dictionary (Romanised)*. London: Macmillan, 1959 (orig. publ. 1903).
─────────. *A Malay-English Dictionary*. London: MacMillan, 1959.
Williams, L.E. *Overseas Chinese Nationalism: The Genesis of the Pan-Chinese Movement in Indonesia, 1900–16*. Glencoe, Illinois: Free Press, 1960.
Williams, Michael. "Banten: 'Rice Debts Will Be Repaid with Rice, Blood Debts with Blood'". In *Regional Dynamics of the Indonesian Revolution: Unity from Diversity*, ed. A. Kahin. Honolulu: University of Hawai'i Press, 1985, pp. 55–81.
Willner, Ann Ruth. "The Neo-Traditional Accommodation to Political Independence: The Case of Indonesia". In *Cases in Comparative Politics: Asia*, ed. L. Pye. Boston: Little, Brown, 1970.
─────────. *The Neo-Traditional Accommodation to Political Independence: The Case of Indonesia*. Princeton, NJ: Center of International Studies, Woodrow Wilson School for Public and International Affairs, Princeton University, 1966.
Wolters, O.W. *History, Culture and Region in Southeast Asian Perspectives*. Singapore: Institute of Southeast Asian Studies, 1982.

Wong Lin Ken. "The Trade of Singapore, 1819–1869". *Journal of the Malaysian Branch of the Royal Asiatic Society* 33, 4 (1960): 5–315.

Woodside, Alexander. *Vietnam and the Chinese Model: A Comparative Study of Nguyen and Ch'ing Civil Government in the First Half of the Nineteenth Century*. Cambridge, Mass.: Harvard University Press, 1971.

World Health Organization. *Controlling the Smoking Epidemic: Report of the WHO Expert Committee on Smoking Control*. N.p.: World Health Organization, 1977.

Yamin, M. *Sedjarah Peperangan Dipanegara*. Jakarta: Jajasan Pembangunan, 1950.

Yamin, Muhammad, ed. *Naskah persiapan Undang-Undang Dasar 1945*, 3 vols. Jakarta: Jajasan Prapantja, 1959.

Yamin, Muhammad. *Gadjah Mada: Pahlawan Persatuan Nusantara*. Jakarta: Balai Pustaka, 1953 (first published 1945).

Yamin. *Sedjarah Peperangan Diponegoro. Pahlawan Kemerdekaan Indonesia*. Jakarta: Sinbun Kai, 2605

Yong Mun Cheong. *H.J. van Mook and Indonesian Independence: A Study of His Role in Dutch-Indonesian Relations, 1945–1948*. The Hague: Martinus Nijhoff, 1982.

_____. *The Indonesian Revolution and the Singapore Connection, 1945–1949*. Leiden: KITLV Press, 2003.

Yule, H., and A.C. Burnell. *Hobson-Jobson: A Glossary of Colloquial Anglo Indian Words and* Phrases. London, 1903. Reprint, New Delhi, 1979.

Zanden, J.L. van. "The Dutch Economy in the Very Long Run: Growth in Production, Energy Consumption and Capital in Holland (1500–1805) and the Netherlands". In *Explaining Economic Growth: Essays in Honour of Angus Maddison*, eds. A. Szirmai, B. van Ark and D. Pilat. Amsterdam: North-Holland, 1993, pp. 267–83.

Zenner, Walter P. *Minorities in the Middle: A Cross-Cultural Analysis*. Albany: State University of New York Press, 1991.

Zenner, Walter. "Middleman Minority Theories: A Critical Review". In *Sourcebook on the New Immigration*, eds. R.S. Bryce-Laporte, D.M. Mortimer and S.R. Couch. New Brunswick, New Jersey: Transaction Books, 1980, pp. 413–25.

Zoetmulder, P.J. *Kalangwan: A Survey of Old-Javanese Literature*. The Hague: M. Nijhoff, 1974.

_____. *Old Javanese-English Dictionary*. The Hague: Nijhoff, 1982.

Index

1824 Anglo-Dutch treaty, 88, 91, 96
1871 Sumatra Treaty, 89, 92
1945 Constitution, 28–9, 34, 142, 144–5, 150, 164–5, 194, 223
1965 coup attempt, 141–2, 145–6, 149–50, 184, 188–9, 226

Aceh (Atjeh), 4, 7–8, 10, 15–6, 47–8, 50, 52–3, 55, 57, 86, 88, 90–101, 107–8,154, 160, 167, 169–73, 180–2, 190, 208, 212, 215, 218–21, 224–5, 227, 239
  Autonomy Law, 219
  historiography, 135–8, 142–3, 147
  rebellion of 1953, 33, 143, 215, 226
  resistance (1873–1912), 140
  social revolution (1945–1946), 32–3, 177, 180
  War, 96, 135–6, 140, 162
Aidit, D.N., 1–2, 184, 190
Alisjahbana, Takdir, 133–4, 137
Allies, 1, 27, 30, 34–5, 37, 180
Allied forces, 30–1, 34, 100, 157, 174, 176
Amir, Dr. M., 129, 163, 172, 214
Amir Sjarifuddin, 22, 24, 32, 34–6, 39–41, 154, 169
anti-Semitism, 231, 233, 237, 252–3
areca nut, 63–7, 69–70, 73, 75
ASEAN, 85, 104

Badan Penjelik Kemerdekaan Indonesia (BPKI), 183, 213, 295
Bahder Djohan, 129
Banten, 50, 65, 72, 74, 86, 108, 132, 173, 178–80, 205, 238
Barisan Tani Indonesia (BTI), 186, 190
Batavia, 45, 49–50, 53, 58–9, 61, 73, 75–6, 84, 86–90, 93, 95, 114, 125, 130, 238, 240–1, 243
betel
  -chewing, 63–70–3, 75–7, 79, 81, 83
  leaves, 63–7, 69–71, 73–7, 79, 81–3
bondage, 47–9, 51, 61–2
Budi Utomo, 4, 13, 15, 19, 21, 124–5, 127

capitalism, 5, 7, 17–8, 43, 137, 231–3, 236, 246, 251, 253, 257
cash-cropping, 8, 10–1
Central National Committee (KNIP), 34, 40
Chau Ju-kua, 64, 70
Chinese diaspora, 147, 229–30, 232–3, 235, 237–45, 247–55, 258-60
  in Indonesia, 236, 240–5, 251–3, 255, 259, 261
  in Philippines, 243, 248, 250–2
  in Thailand, 242, 253–4, 260–1
  anti-Chinese violence, 236, 239, 243, 245, 259

Christianity, 22, 51, 191, 253, 261
cigarette-smoking, 63, 68, 76–7, 79, 80–1, 83
Cold War, 36, 145–6, 194
Colijn, Hendrik, 7, 21
colonial
    authorities, 12, 60, 117
    boundary/boundaries, 124, 131, 234
    cities, 13, 52
    empire, 143, 212
    government, 54, 56, 59, 119–20, 211, 241–2
    policy, 5, 20–1, 252
    power, 43, 54, 143, 162, 165, 209
    regime, 22, 136, 240
    society, 76–7
    state, 52, 116, 170, 198, 205, 209–10, 247
    system, 8, 21, 154, 161, 165
    wars, 7, 92, 135
colonialism, 2, 4–5, 77, 84, 88, 98, 140, 143, 148, 209, 234, 254, 260, 262
Comintern, 17, 252
Committee for the Preparation of Indonesian Independence (PPKI), 19, 214
communism, 17–8, 33, 118, 145, 179–80, 190, 212, 251–2, 260, 262, *see also* Partai Kommunis Indonesia
convict labour, 56–8
corvée (forced labour), 8, 51, 54–6, 60, 61, 109, 116, 284
cosmopolitanism, 13, 44, 107, 257
Crawfurd, John, 51, 72, 115–6
cultuurstelsel (Cultivation System), 54–5, 89

democracy, 104, 106, 110, 114, 118, 145, 165–6, 193, 210, 213, 221, 224, 227–8
diplomasi, 30–2, 34–5, 42, 170
Diponegoro/Dipo Negoro/Dipanagara/Dipanegara, 54, 134–5, 245
Douwes Dekker, E.F.E., 124, 130, 132
Dutch colonial army (KNIL), 39, 216–7
Dutch East Indies, 22, 51, 95, 114, 143, 160, 165, 205, *see also* Netherlands Indies *and* Netherlands India
Dutch East India Company, 49, 53–4, 56–7, 87, 135, 241, 243, *see also* VOC

Ekonomi Rakyat Republik Indonesia (ERRI), 179
Enlightenment, 113, 115, 246
Ethical Policy, 5, 11, 117

Federal Indonesian Republic (RIS), *see* Republik Indonesia Serikat (RIS)
federalism, 36–8, 144, 197, 208–11, 213, 217–9, 221–3, 226–8
First World War, 6, 78, 89, 124, 129, 134–5, 247, 263
freedom
    as ideal, 14, 105–6, 110–3, 116–22, 133, 165, 202, 263, *see also merdeka*
    from slavery, 59–60, 106–9, 114–6

Gajah Mada, 127, 130–1
GERINDO, 21–2, 24, 172

Index

GOLKAR, 196
Great Depression, 9–10, 78, 256–7
Guided Democracy, 43, 102, 135, 139, 142, 163, 196, 219

Hague, The, 58, 89, 93–4, 124, 170
Hasan Muhammad Tiro, 140, 143, 218, 221
Hatta, Mohammad, 1–2, 19–20, 24, 26, 29, 32, 35–6, 101, 133, 137, 144, 151–2, 160, 165, 196, 204, 213, 217
herendienst, see corvée
Hikayat Perang Sabil, 55
human rights, 105, 111, 147, 193–4, 196

imperialism, 4, 17, 19, 137–8, 161–2, 164
independence, 1–2, 15, 18, 21, 23, 25, 27–30, 35, 37, 41, 43, 62, 79, 91, 100, 102, 112, 120, 140, 163, 167, 170, 176, 209–11, 213–4, 219, 227
  declaration of (August 17), 121–2, 160, 223
Indian Ocean, 86–7, 238
Indische Partij, 15
Indies Socialist Party, 17, 117
Indonesian Communist Party, see Partai Komunis Indonesia (PKI)
Indonesian Nationalist Party, see PNI
Indonesian revolution, 41, 121, 139, 169, 172, 182, 206–7
Islam, 4, 43, 51, 91, 118, 128, 133, 177, 186–7, 191, 205, 222, 253, 261–2
ilustrados, 248–9

Japanese
  25th Army, 25, 99, 160, 173
  invasion, 98, 155
  occupation, 15, 22, 27–8, 99, 101, 120, 138, 152, 163, 167, 173, 175, 183, 196, 214, 225
Java War, 54
Jewish diaspora, 229–32, 235–41, 245–7, 249–51, 256
  in Indonesia, 230, 262–3
Jong Java, 128–9, 131
Jong Sumatranen Bond (JSB), 128–9
Jonge, B.C. de, 20–1

Keibodan (Vigilance Corps), 27, 174
KNIL, see Dutch colonial army
KNIP, see Central National Committee
Koninklijke Paketvaart Maatschappij (KPM), 95–7, 100, 102
KPM, see Koninklijke Paketvaart Maatschappij
kretek, 75, 78–81, 83, 278

Land Reform Act, 185–6
lime, 63–5, 68–70, 73, 82
Linggajati Agreement, 37, 215

Madiun, 38, 146, 170
  communist revolt, 36, 180, 225
Mahathir, 193–4, 235, 255, 262
Majapahit, 86, 125, 127, 130–4, 137–9, 198–9, 204
Makasar, 4, 8, 50, 52, 76, 86, 108–9, 111–2, 140, 160, 170–1, 201, 216, 240, 259

Malacca/Melaka, 48, 50, 86, 114, 205, 221, 239–40, 244
  Straits, 84, 98–101, 103
Malay
  Archipelago, 88
  nationalism, 234–5, 254–5
  World, 86, 88, 221, 223, 244
Malaya, 25, 49, 67, 73–4, 84, 95, 98–102, 123, 129, 153–4, 210–1, 214, 222–3, 225, 244–5, 248, 250–2, 254, 259
Malaysia 222–7, 234–5, 259, 260–3, *see also* Malaya
  compared with Indonesia, 153, 211–3, 223–8
Malayan Communist Party, 210, 222, 251
Maluku/Moluccas, 29, 65, 73–4, 142, 200
Marxism, 17–8, 235, 248, 251, 260, 263
MASJUMI, 15, 35, 43, 187
Mataram, 72, 132, 135, 199, 205
Mecca, 9, 92, 95, 128
merdeka, 105–8, 110, 112, 114–22
Minangkabau, 5, 8, 19, 59, 107, 128–9, 137–8, 140, 200, 203
modernisation, 13–4, 77, 211, 229, 247, 261–2
  high modernism, 206–7
Muhammadiah, 14–5, 17, 39
Munshi Abdullah bin Abdul Kadir, 115–6, 123

Nahdatul Ulama, 14, 186
Napoleonic wars, 87–8
Nasution, A.H., 39, 141, 169
national history, 123–4, 132, 138–9, 141, 146, 148, 150, 152, 162, 171

nationalism, 2, 19, 41, 118, 120, 123, 126, 128, 132,172, 177, 212, 221, 223, 230, 233–7, 246, 249–50, 252–5, 257, 260
  cultural, 124
  economic, 102, 235, 258, 260
  ethnic, 42, 234–6, 253, 255
  Indisch, 124–9
  Indonesian, 2, 4, 21, 99, 123, 220–1
  Javanese, 125–9, 131
  official, 234, 255
  secular, 15, 18
Nederlandsch-Indische Stoomvaart Maatschappij (NISM), 94–6
Netherlands India, 12, 20, 53–4, 56, 61, 92, 97, 205–6, 214, 244, 248, 253–4, *see also* Netherlands Indies
Netherlands Indies, 8, 10–1, 17, 20–1, 26, 72, 84, 88–9, 96, 134, 139, 212, 242, 250, *see also* Netherlands India
  government, 58
New Order government, 122, 142, 144–5, 148, 150, 193, 196–7, 207
NISM, *see* Nederlandsch-Indische Stoomvaart Maatschappij
NIT, *see* State of East Indonesia
Nugroho Notosusanto, 141–2, 144, 146–8, 290–2

Ombilin mines, 56–7
opium, 69, 74, 79, 88, 95, 97, 101, 247
  farms, 241–4,
Outer Islands, 5, 7–9, 11, 16, 25, 28–9, 37, 43, 59, 89, 97–8, 154, 163, 183

Pacific War, 23, *see also* Second World War
Padri movement, 77, 129, 135, 289
Palembang, 4, 9, 74, 86–7, 100–2, 108, 110, 160, 202, 216
Panca Darma, 14
Panca Sila/Pancasila, 14, 142, 146, 148, 164–5, 191, 194
Pangreh Praja, 21–5, 28–30, 32–3
PARINDRA, 19, 21, 25, 172
Partai Komunis Indonesia (PKI), 17–9, 22, 24, 33–4, 36, 42–3, 117, 141, 145–6, 149, 173, 181, 185–90, 204, 225–6, 251
Partai Nasional Indonesia (PNI), 19–20, 35, 131–2
PARTINDO, 20
perjuangan, 30, 32, 35, 42, 170
Pekalongan Residency, 26, 33–4
pemuda (youth), 27, 33, 122, 171, 174–6, 179
sumpah pemuda (1928), 131
Perhimpunan Indonesia, 19, 120
perjuangan (struggle), 30, 32, 35, 40, 42, 170
PESINDO, 36
PETA, 27, 39–40, 166–7, 180–1
-*Giyugun*, 27, 30, 176
Philippines, 64–5, 72–3, 155, 161, 235, 243, 248, 254
compared with Indonesia, 153, 210–1, 254
Pigafetta, Antonio, 65
Pires, Tomé, 69–70, 85
PKI, *see* Partai Komunis Indonesia
pluralism, 164, 193, 198, 200–2, 214, 255
PNI, *see* Partai Nasional Indonesia
PPKI, *see* Committee for the Preparation of Indonesian Independence (PPKI)

priyayi, 4–6, 16, 23, 27, 167, 180–1
"new priyayi", 10
PUTERA, 25

Raffles, Stamford, 115, 202
regional autonomy, 103–4, 208, 215, 217
regionalism, 171, 182–3
Republic, 28–30, 32, 34–8, 40, 43, 84, 100–1, 110, 121, 142, 144, 151, 160, 172, 183, 207, 214–5, 216–7
Republican Army, 30, 33, 39, *see also* TNI
Republik Indonesia Serikat (RIS), 19, 216, 223
revolution, 27–8, 34–8, 41–2, 121–2, 136, 148, 155, 165–7, 169–72, 174–8, 181–3, 192, 206–11, 212–3, 216, 225, 227, 257, *see also* Indonesian revolution
anti-colonial, 43, 170
Chinese revolution of 1911, 250
French, 121, 169, 210, 246, 298
Iranian revolution of 1979, 262
Russian, 118, 169–70
social, 26, 32–4, 122, 172, 176–81, 183, 212, 215, 225
RIS, *see* Federal Indonesian Republic
Russo-Japanese war, 153

Samin movement, 117
Samin Taib, 98
Sanusi Pane, 123, 138–9, 162–3
Sarekat Islam (SI), 15–9, 98, 118–9, 133
Sarekat Rakyat, 118
Second World War, 79, 143, 234, 257, *see also* Pacific War

Seinendan (Youth Corps), 27, 162, 174–5
Sejarah Melayu, 68
Sino-Japanese war, 254, 258–9
Singapore, 53, 84–5, 87–8, 91–2, 103–4, 114–5, 154, 193–4, 206, 241–2, 260
  fall of (1942), 22, 154
  trade with Indonesia, 26, 52, 84, 88–9, 95–104
slavery, 45–61, 96, 105–12, 114–5, 122, 137, 202, 284
Snouck Hurgronje, C., 8, 95–7
social revolution, *see* revolution
South China Sea, 86–7, 239
Sriwijaya, 64, 84, 86, 131–2, 137, 139, 204
State of East Indonesia (NIT), 37–8, 217
Straits of Malacca, *see* Malacca Straits
Straits Settlements, 53, 90–4, 244
Sudirman, 39–40
Suharto/Soeharto, 25, 103, 105, 122, 144–50, 191, 194–6, 207–8, 219
  regime, 141–2
Sukarno/Soekarno, 1–2, 19–26, 28–9, 32, 34–6, 38–40, 43–4, 84, 102, 120–1, 131, 133–4, 140, 142, 144–6, 148, 150–1, 155, 159–60, 163, 165, 169, 184–5, 187–92, 196, 204, 213, 219
Sultan Agung, 125, 132, 135, 139
Sulu (southern Philippines), 201
Surabaya, 22, 24, 169–70, 174–5,
  battle of (1945), 31–2, 225, 267
Surakarta, 2, 11, 16, 32–3, 118–9, 134, 169, 170–1, 175, 177, 180–1, 183, 259
Sutan Sjahrir, 19–20, 24, 34–5, 39–40, 100, 159

Taman Siswa school system, 13–4, 21, 120, 164
Tan Malaka, 35, 38, 118–20, 137, 141, 149, 169, 251
Telaga Batu inscription, 107
Ternate, 4, 60, 64–5, 200, 205, *see also* Maluku/Moluccas
Teuku Imam, 93, 95
Thailand, 241–3, 250, 253–5, 259–61
Tidore, 60, 200, *see also* Maluku/Moluccas
Tjipto Mangoenkoesoemo, 13, 124–6, 134, 288
TKR, 176, 181–2
TNI, 176, 181–2, 216, *see also* Republican Army
tobacco, 58–9, 68–9, 71–9, 81–3, 90, 155, 278

Undang-undang Melaka, 110
unitary
  leadership, 24
  model, 208–9
  Republic, 28, 38, 213, 222
  state, 131, 208–11, 213–4
  system, 224
United Nations, 38, 42, 184, 216
unity, 4, 16, 19, 41, 44, 99, 127–9, 133–4, 139, 158, 160, 164, 195–7, 203–4, 207, 217
  cultural, 125
  historical, 124
  Indonesian, 130–2, 167, 183
  national, 2, 125, 141, 182, 184
  natural, 84
  political, 139, 160, 163, 199

Vietnam, 64, 70–1, 238, 244–5, 255, 258–9

compared with Indonesia, 227, 253–4
violence, 31–3, 58, 142, 167, 176–9, 186, 210, 225–7, 245, *see also* Chinese
  state, 146–7, 150, 226–7
  1965 killings, 145–6, 150, 188–91
VOC, 86–9, 134, 199, 205, *see also* Dutch East India Company
Volksraad, 18–9, 21, 134, 195

Weber, Max, 43
Westernisation, 22
women, 53, 65, 67, 81, 111, 117, 140, 179, 235, 240
World War II, *see* Second World War

Yamin, Muhammad, 129–30, 138, 148, 163, 196
Yogyakarta/Jogjakarta, 2, 13–4, 37–8, 40, 78, 148, 170–2, 212, 215